THE SHARK
WATCHER'S HANDBOOK

THE SHARK
WATCHER'S HANDBOOK

A guide to sharks and where to see them

MARK CARWARDINE
& KEN WATTERSON

BBC

For Roz Kidman Cox – a kind and valued friend for more years than we care to admit.

Mark Carwardine

This book is for Dot, Claire and Vicki, with all my love.

Ken Watterson

Published by BBC Worldwide Ltd, 80 Wood Lane, London, W12 OTT

First published 2002
© Mark Carwardine and Ken Watterson 2002
The moral right of the authors has been asserted.

ISBN 0 563 53794 9

PICTURE CREDITS
Ardea page 25; BBC Natural History Picture Library 52, 90/91; Mark Carwardine 11, 15, 46, 53, 64, 78, 84; Matthew D Harris 76; Seapics.com 2, 8, 12/13, 20, 22, 26, 28, 33, 34, 38, 41, 43, 48, 50, 55, 56, 59, 62, 67, 69, 71, 73, 82/83, 88; Mo Yung Productions 19, 49, 86.

Commissioning Editors: Rosamund Kidman Cox and Emma Shackleton
Project Editor: Rebecca Kincaid
Copy Editor: Mandy Greenfield
Art Director: Linda Blakemore
Book Designer: Philip Lewis
Picture Researcher: Kirsten Sowry
Cartographer: Olive Pearson
Illustrator: Ian Coleman
Production Controller: Christopher Tinker

Printed and bound in France by Imprimerie Pollina s.a.
Colour separations by Kestrel Digital Colour, Chelmsford

Contents

Acknowledgements

This book would have been impossible to research and write without the generosity, advice and enthusiasm of a great many people. We would like to thank everyone who has been involved.

For the past two years we have been corresponding with more than 2000 dive operators in about 50 different countries around the world, who very kindly completed our long and detailed questionnaires, answered our many e-mail and telephone enquiries and then checked the final text for each shark-dive site.

We are particularly indebted to many of the world's top shark experts, who willingly shared their knowledge and helped us with sound advice. We would especially like to thank Pascal Kobah, Andy Cobb, George Burgess, Peter Rowlands, Jeff Rotman, John Gunn, Sean van Sommeran, John Stevens, Merry Camhi, Vic Peddemors, Jeremy Stafford-Deitsch, Susie Watts, Sarah Fowler, Arthur Myrberg, Harold 'Wes' Pratt, Shoubu Yamada, Charles Anderson and Marcelo R. de Carvalho. We benefited enormously from the help of four diligent and enthusiastic researchers: Christine Bathgate, Caroline Williams, Lisa Browning and Caitlyn Toropova. Simon Roberts also very kindly assisted with research and we are most grateful to John Ruthven and other members of the BBC's *The Blue Planet* team for feedback on shark sites in many parts of the world.

We are grateful for the chance to have worked with our skilful editor, Mandy Greenfield, whose patience and professionalism have been an inspiration. Rebecca Kincaid and Emma Shackleton, at BBC Books, provided just the right kind of encouragement and understanding.

Finally, Roz Kidman Cox is the person who made this book possible. Her enthusiasm, encouragement, understanding, guidance and friendship have been incredible. It has been a great pleasure working with her, as always.

None of these people is in any way responsible for any errors of fact or emphasis that remain.

Note from the authors

Future editions

We would welcome comments on *The Shark-watcher's Handbook* and would be most grateful for any information on shark sites that may be useful for future editions. We have set up a special e-mail address for this purpose: sharkwatcher@btinternet.com

Before travelling

Before booking a shark dive it is important to check the level of experience that is required. Some of the dives in this book are not suitable for novices – they are challenging and potentially dangerous, perhaps taking place in deep water or strong currents and in the company of large numbers of sharks. Even if you have already booked such a dive, you must be the judge of your own skills: if you have any doubts, just sit it out and wait for the next suitable dive.

Disclaimer

The authors and publisher have made every effort to ensure that the information in this book is as accurate and up-to-date as possible at the time of going to press, but we cannot be held responsible for any injury or inconvenience caused when using it. Sharks are potentially dangerous and unpredictable animals, and anyone getting in the water with them does so entirely at their own risk.

Foreword

I well remember the first time I had the opportunity to observe sharks in their natural habitat. It was at Walker's Cay in the Bahamas. Gliding back and forth a few metres out from the shore were half a dozen of the ominous, dark shapes that a group of fellow shark enthusiasts and I had travelled halfway around the world to swim with: bull sharks!

Our divemaster threw a fish scrap into the water, the catalyst for an awesome display of speed, efficiency and power. End of fish scrap! As I approached the water, someone started humming the tune from *Jaws*. Despite knowing the facts, my subconscious came to the fore in a rising tide of anxiety. I thought of my family and friends – was I really going to get into the water and snorkel with these sharks?

Having stopped at the water's edge to take a deep, soul-searching breath, I gingerly entered the sea. As the first bull shark glided past a few metres in front of my mask, I felt as alive and alert as I am ever likely to be! Within a few minutes, however, my fear receded and was replaced by awe and curiosity. The effortless elegance of these robust, highly evolved animals was simply majestic. Repeat dives enforced a growing sense of the colossal and barbaric injustice being inflicted on sharks today. Perpetuated by many in the media, misinformation and ignorance have led to these super-predators becoming a scapegoat for collective human terror.

The Shark-watcher's Handbook is addressed to those who want to see these splendid creatures as they are and who want to form their own opinions. Lucidly written and designed, and packed with everything a diver needs to know – from species identification and safety tips to prime shark locations and conservation issues – it will be an invaluable source of information and inspiration. With input and advice from more than 2000 shark-dive operators and help from many of the world's top shark experts, Mark Carwardine and Ken Watterson have produced an authoritative and comprehensive book that will become a standard work of reference for shark divers everywhere. And the authors do not shirk controversial issues: for example, feeding wild sharks, a subject on which the Shark Trust is frequently consulted and on which it has therefore published guidelines.

Wherever and however you choose to witness sharks in their own environment, I hope you will increasingly come to recognize the privilege of being in their presence. Sharks are an integral part of the marine inheritance that all scuba divers are obliged to secure for future generations. May this book lead you to many wonderful shark experiences and to your active support for their continued existence in our seas, rivers and oceans.

Clive James, *Shark Trust Executive Director*

1 Shark Diving

Diving with sharks is one of the world's great wildlife experiences and quickly becomes an all-consuming lifelong passion. The lure of observing such extraordinary creatures in their natural environment, combined with the inescapable adrenalin rush, means that one close encounter is never enough. You simply have to dive again . . . and again, and again. An overwhelming sense of awe begins to eclipse the initial fear as you realize that spending time with wild sharks is a very special privilege.

Only a generation ago, anyone diving with sharks was considered mad, reckless or outrageously adventurous. But in the late 1960s and early 1970s, a few pioneering dive operators, particularly in the Maldives and the Bahamas, began to take recreational divers on organized shark encounters. Slowly but surely, others began to follow suit. The shark-diving scene suddenly exploded about 20 years later, and this once-unlikely industry has been growing exponentially ever since.

Hundreds of thousands of people around the world are not only choosing to jump into seas full of sharks, but are also planning it months in advance and, very often, digging deep into their pockets for the experience. Shark diving has become an everyday occurrence, and at any given moment you can be sure that someone, somewhere, will be enjoying a face-to-face encounter with a shark.

With nearly 300 recognized shark-dive sites around the world, there have never been more opportunities for encountering sharks than there are today.

In California, off the coast of San Diego, divers intent on watching blue sharks descend 3–4 m/10–13 ft to a cage suspended in the open ocean, with the seabed more than 1.6 km/1 mile away in the hidden depths. Cages are also used in the North and South Neptune Islands, South Australia, for dramatic close encounters with great whites that gather in the area to hunt sea lions and fur seals.

In the cold waters around the Isle of Man, in the Irish Sea, snorkellers participate in a research project studying harmless basking sharks while, on the other side of the world, a spotter aircraft helps snorkellers at Ningaloo Reef, in Western Australia, to locate and swim with gargantuan whale sharks. Divers in Rangiroa Atoll, in French Polynesia, are swept along in a strong current in the company of grey reef sharks and whitetip reef sharks. And one of the most challenging shark dives takes place at Cocos Island, a long day-and-night sail off

Daily shark feeds in the Bahamas attract huge numbers of divers from all over the world.

the coast of Costa Rica, where divers descend to a depth of up to 40 m/ 130 ft to look up at hundreds of schooling scalloped hammerheads.

At the other extreme, in some parts of the world you can see wild sharks without even getting your feet wet. Diners at Pier 1 Restaurant in Freeport, Grand Bahama, watch wild lemon sharks competing for scraps from their dinner tables; and in Canada, there have even been trips to observe sixgill sharks 200 m/650 ft below the surface from inside a deep-sea submersible.

Chumming and baiting

While sharks can be seen in almost any ocean in the world, finding them – let alone getting close to them – is another matter. There are a few places, such as Protea Banks in South Africa and the Marshall Islands in Micronesia, where a normal dive is likely to result in heart-stopping encounters with sharks – whether you like it or not. Elsewhere in the world shark sightings are surprisingly few and far between. Even if you do happen to bump into one of the ocean's apex predators, it is likely to be rather shy, and you will be lucky to get more than a fleeting glimpse at a frustrating distance.

This is why many operators use a type of bait, called chum, to attract the sharks artificially. Mammal blood is sometimes preferred, but chum normally consists of fish such as herring or mackerel, which are ground up into a liquid mash and released gradually into the water to form a slick on the surface. The chum may be kept in a perforated container underwater or dripped into the sea via a hosepipe or through a hole in the boat's hull, and can attract sharks from a long distance away.

Once the sharks have arrived, it is possible to keep them interested with the help of yet more bait – but this time, something they can really get their teeth into. The bait may simply be hidden under a coral head or placed in a sealed container, which is then opened by a pull-cord. Or it may literally be handed piece-by-piece to individual sharks by a professional feeder. Perhaps the most innovative variation is seen at Walker's Cay, in the Bahamas. Huge numbers of sharks of several different species are attracted to a regular feeding site with the help of a large quantity of fish bait mixed with water. This 'chumsicle' (named after a giant fishy ice lolly or 'popsicle') is frozen around a metal bar, which is both anchored to the seabed and suspended from a float, ensuring that it hangs in mid-water. Divers are free to swim around it – and the sharks. Bait is also used at Dangerous Reef, in South Australia, but there the sharks are great whites, and the divers are in cages.

Not all sharks can be coaxed in with bait – and not all shark dives

Setting a chum trail to attract great white sharks at Dyer Island, in South Africa.

involve chumming or feeding – but in many cases, without it, divers may not have the chance to see and photograph sharks close up. The lure of the bait is the guarantee of success. It is, however, very controversial.

Is shark diving acceptable ecotourism or unacceptable and dangerous exploitation?

There are some very strong views about certain aspects of shark diving and, in particular, little agreement about chumming and baiting. This is a complex issue and there are no simple answers: until we know more about sharks and the impact of different shark-diving techniques, much of the debate will rely on conjecture.

A major turning point came on 1 January 2002, when Florida became the first state in the US to prohibit divers from feeding sharks. Although the vast majority of shark dives do not involve chum or bait, the decision has provoked strong reactions from both the

OVERLEAF
Every shark diver's dream is to see scalloped hammerheads; this large school was photographed in the Galápagos Islands.

environmental movement and the diving industry. The World Wildlife Fund, Defenders of Wildlife and others immediately hailed the ban as a major victory for wildlife and divers. The Florida-based non-profit Marine Safety Group said that 'divers all over the state will once again be able to enjoy the natural beauty of the undersea world without being continually mugged by aggressive fish seeking handouts.' But commercial dive groups, including the Professional Association of Diving Instructors (PADI), Rodale's *Scuba Diving* magazine and *Skin Diver* magazine, were very unhappy about the decision. A recent Rodale's editorial said that the ban 'provides a classic example of the triumph of fear over reason'.

The potential risks and benefits of chumming and baiting are very different from country to country, location to location, species to species and even from season to season. But there are some general points to consider. Supporters of the ban argue that shark feeds: dim the natural fear sharks have for humans (and vice versa); attract a larger number of potentially dangerous sharks into an area; encourage sharks to associate people with food; and encourage the sharks to grow dependent on 'free lunches' (which will change their distribution and hunting patterns). They also argue that sharks should be viewed in their natural state and should not be trained to become 'circus sideshows'. Critics of the ban argue that: there is no evidence that commercial shark feeding has increased the risk of attacks on humans (pointing out that the nearest attack to any shark-feeding operation in Florida was 160 km/100 miles away); only a handful of Florida-based dive operators have been involved in shark feeding; the two shark species being fed (nurse and Caribbean reef) have not been implicated in any of the recent attacks; and fishing boats have been chucking huge quantities of fish offal overboard every day since time immemorial, with no measurable effect on the incidence of shark attack (so the relatively small amounts of bait being thrown into the sea during shark dives will have little or no impact). They claim that the decision was made in order to 'satisfy political and public pressure to respond to the hysteria generated by the media over a below-average summer of shark bites in Florida and around the world'.

The Marine Safety Group is optimistic that other US states will soon follow suit with bans of their own, but commercial dive interests have vowed to fight the ban in Florida's courts.

One possible compromise is to create guidelines for shark feeding. These already exist in some parts of the world and might include: a requirement to locate feeding sites away from living reefs and to use a zonation system to separate them from areas used by other water users; a limit to the number of feeding sites and the frequency of feeds; compulsory diver education programmes; and so on.

There are four main considerations in developing a responsible and environmentally friendly shark-diving industry: the safety of the participants; the safety of swimmers, surfers and other water users in the area; the impact on the sharks; and the risk of ecological disruption.

The safety of the participants on a shark dive is paramount. It is essential for operators to put safety first, which means training divers in shark-friendly behaviour and warning them about the inherent risks. Then it is up to the divers themselves to make an informed decision about whether or not to participate in the dive. Unfortunately, it is not that simple because some operators are far less responsible than others. The worst are both inexperienced and reckless, and may take extraordinary risks to make extra money or put on a show of bravado. There have already been a number of serious accidents: most recently, a woman on an organized shark dive in South Africa had to have 37 stitches in her hand after being bitten by a sand tiger shark. A serious accident could also undermine worldwide efforts to protect sharks by reinforcing the *Jaws* image. But to put this risk into perspective, even without proper regulation the number of 'incidents' during shark dives is minuscule. There are no precise figures, but the order of magnitude is likely to be well within the acceptable limits of most popular adventure sports.

The safety of other water users near shark-dive sites, especially

A battle-scarred great white watches closely as a diver tentatively enters a cage to observe sharks underwater.

where the creatures are being attracted with chum and then fed, is far more controversial. The shark-feeding ban in Florida is particularly noteworthy, because the state has long been a hotspot for shark attacks. The year 2000 was fairly typical when, according to the International Shark Attack File, there were 79 confirmed cases of unprovoked shark attack around the world – and no fewer than 34 of them occurred in Florida. Many possible reasons have been proposed, ranging from the sheer number of people in the sea to the fact that Florida is home to many potentially dangerous sharks. But exactly the same could be said of the Bahamas, where there are many more long-established shark feeds taking place every day, and yet there were only four attacks during the same year. Even there, when a diver was bitten on the head at a feeding site on a non-feeding day, some people automatically pointed the finger of blame at the local dive operators. Similarly, in South Africa, a recent spate of six attacks on surfers and divers within a five-week period prompted accusations that the cage-diving industry was responsible, but only one of these attacks occurred within 150 km/93 miles of a cage-diving site; other environmental factors, such as the proximity of sardine schools, were more likely to blame.

Another concern is that all these human admirers will love the sharks to death. We have a responsibility to cause as little disturbance as possible: proper respect and etiquette are the most important tools of the trade. Yet, in some places, there is little doubt that the sharks have not been receiving the respect they deserve. Until remedial action was taken, one of the worst examples was in South Africa, where operators taking divers to see great white sharks around Dyer Island were literally fighting over limited anchorage space and using bait-filled nets to catch the sharks and haul them alongside their boats to give their clients a better view. The scramble by dive operators for a piece of the action (and the cowboy mentality of some) ultimately led the South African government to impose urgently needed codes of conduct. Other governments have followed suit with similar efforts to control the new industry. These may be voluntary or legally binding and include, for example, a limit on the number of boats licensed to operate shark dives and a minimum amount of equipment that must be carried on board (such as a working radio and trauma kit), as well as regulations concerning staff experience and qualifications and the kind of bait and baiting techniques permitted to attract the sharks.

The risk of ecological disruption is perhaps the most difficult concern to quantify. Critics argue that the large concentrations of sharks at established feeding sites are unnatural and that the sharks may stop feeding on their natural prey if the alternative is an easy meal provided by dive operators. It has also been argued that these two concerns (too many predatory sharks *and* less predation) cancel one another out. In truth, the impact of shark feeding on the local ecology is largely unknown. Another ecological concern is easier to quantify and solve: while many operators use the fish remains discarded by commercial and sports fishermen for their bait, others actively hunt local fishes (even juvenile sharks in at least one dive site) and undoubtedly this may ultimately harm local populations.

Shark diving has some interesting parallels with whale watching. The whale-watch industry was growing exponentially before most people had even considered the possibility of diving with sharks. At first, it went largely unregulated. But, to protect the whales, and the whale watchers, many countries introduced guidelines to bring the industry under control. As our experience and knowledge of whale watching continue to increase, these guidelines are being improved and adapted accordingly. Many whale experts would prefer not to have such a colossal whale-watching industry, but accept it as essential in order to achieve and maintain a high level of public support for whale conservation and research. We are still going through a similar process of enlightenment with sharks and, now that the shark-diving industry is showing a comparable exponential growth rate, it is beginning to face similar challenges. The trick will be to learn from the mistakes of the whale-watching industry and get it right sooner rather than later.

It is also important to remember that shark diving can directly benefit the sharks: it provides a much better alternative to hunting (making the sharks worth more alive than dead) and ensures that more people are better informed.

A dead shark is worth relatively little for its fins but, now that shark diving has become a multimillion-dollar business, a living shark can be worth a fortune. According to one study, a single reef shark is worth US$100,000 every year to local businesses. Better still, it provides a source of income for life – not just for the short-term – and benefits many different people. When divers visit an area to see the local sharks, they patronize hotels, guesthouses, restaurants, cafés, shops, buses, taxis, and many other businesses, as well as the dive operators. This financial value also gives people a vested interest in protecting sharks. In the Bahamas, for example, when rogue fishermen wiped out the sharks associated with a feeding operation, there was such an outcry that the government banned longlining for sharks once and for all.

Shark diving can also help to dispel some of the myths about sharks and to change attitudes towards these much-maligned creatures. The sharks themselves make terrific ambassadors for marine conservation, lighting an internal fire that makes people determined to do something positive to help – but it is up to the dive operators to ensure that their captive audiences are well-informed. There is still a long way to go in this respect, and the opportunity to dive with sharks does not necessarily result in an improved understanding and respect for them, but there are already a great many trips that show respect for sharks and provide accurate information about their natural history and conservation. They drum up public support for their cause, by swelling the ranks of shark devotees, and ensure that part of the income from shark diving helps to fund urgently needed research and conservation work. There is no doubt that sharks need as much help and support as they can possibly get and, in a unique way, professional, responsible shark diving has the potential to help enormously.

Ultimately, there are two fundamental challenges: to improve the overall quality of shark-diving tours and to do more research. When we understand how to arrange our meetings with sharks better, we will be in a stronger position to ensure that there are more good operators than bad ones.

Planning a shark dive

Careful planning is essential to ensure that your dive is safe, environmentally friendly, successful and memorable.

While it is not essential to join an organized shark dive, at a known hotspot, it certainly helps. It is safer to dive with sharks in the company of experts, and the probability of seeing a particular species is much higher.

First of all, decide which species you would most like to see. Many sharks are not only restricted to certain parts of the world, but may also congregate there for only a few months of the year, and so proper timing is crucial. One of the best places to see whale sharks, for example, is Ningaloo Reef in Western Australia – but you have to go there from mid-April to the end of May to have a good chance of a close encounter.

Next, think about live-aboard dive boats versus shore-based diving. Sometimes, where the best diving is in a remote location, there will be no alternative: to see silvertips in Papua New Guinea, for instance, you normally have to join a live-aboard dive boat for at least a week. At many shark hotspots, however, there is a choice between staying in a hotel onshore or joining a 7- to 14-day trip on a live-aboard dive boat. Staying onshore may suit non-diving partners and children better, enables you to include other activities in your holiday and makes a shorter, less expensive stay possible. It is also a good alternative if you just want to test the water with your first shark dive – in the Bahamas, for example, a half-day trip at any time of the year can

virtually guarantee sightings of Caribbean reef sharks. But live-aboards are probably better if your main aim is to pack in as much diving at as many different dive sites as possible.

The golden rule is to choose your dive operator with great care. The quality and performance of shark dives vary enormously, and your choice of operator can make or break the holiday. Be wary if one deal is much cheaper than another and ask friends for recommendations, read dive magazines and check websites for further information.

If you plan to attend a shark feed, make sure that a few basic rules are enforced. The bait should be readily accessible to the sharks and should not be presented in such a way that it could harm them. Live fish should never be speared in front of the sharks because they may become agitated, and spearfishing is, of course, illegal on many reefs. Divers should position themselves at least 3 m/10 ft away from the bait and must not be down-current, because sharks are more likely to sample anything (including divers) inside the scent trail. Never, under any circumstances, try to handfeed the sharks yourself – it is a skill that requires detailed knowledge and a steep learning curve and should be left to the professionals.

There are many advantages in shark diving as part of an organized group, rather than doing it alone. Apart from the fact that it is more fun to be in the company of like-minded people, it has the benefit of

Timing is often crucial when planning a shark dive – visit Western Australia at the wrong time of year for whale sharks and you are unlikely to be rewarded with a close encounter like this.

an experienced tour leader with local knowledge and the ability to smooth out occasional difficulties during the trip. It can also be considerably cheaper overall.

Before you leave home, ensure that your equipment is complete and in perfect working order. If you do not dive regularly it is a good idea to have a practice beforehand, or at least do a check-out dive with the dive master as soon as you arrive. This will enable you to check all your gear and will refresh your basic diving skills. Too many divers wait until they are inside a shark cage or on the seafloor, surrounded by sharks, before realizing that their masks are leaking or their weight belts are too light. All dive operators require proof of certification, and so take your dive card with you, and on advanced dives you may be required to

A professional feeder hands bait to a Caribbean reef shark in the Bahamas.

show your dive log to demonstrate that you are adequately experienced.

Finally, insurance is another important consideration. You may not be covered by your normal insurance if you dive with sharks. A good source of advice is the American-based diving insurance and accident -management service, the Divers Alert Network (DAN), which has an inexpensive annual membership fee. In the USA and Canada contact dan@diversalertnetwork.org; in Europe contact mail@daneurope.org; and in South-East Asia and the Pacific contact danseap@danseap.org

When you have chosen your preferred shark species and dive site, selected a suitable operator, checked your equipment and had a practice dive . . . finally, you are ready to meet the sharks face to face. There are a few simple guidelines to follow underwater, which will help to make the dive safe and more enjoyable.

The dive master will brief you on the sharks you are about to encounter and will explain how to act during the dive. Follow the instructions carefully, especially if you are joining an organized feed. The sharks are used to a certain routine and, if the pattern changes, they may become confused. Never dive alone with sharks and never be fooled by operators who pretend that sharks are no more dangerous than playful puppies – the most experienced shark divers always retain a healthy respect for every species. It is largely a matter of common sense. Cage dives are perhaps the safest way to encounter sharks, although they have their own inherent risks. Some cages are not shark-proof but merely provide a tactile and visual barrier between the sharks and the divers, and they often have gaps for photography that are large enough to permit small sharks to enter – and small sharks really do enter more often than you might imagine. Some cage dives also involve swimming, unprotected, through open water to get into and out of the cage.

In many cases the sharks will be as frightened of you as you are of them. Try to avoid intimidating them – stay still or move very slowly – and slow your breathing to minimize the noise from your exhaust bubbles. If you feel it is safe to get closer, swim on a converging course rather than in a direct line. When the sharks feel confident, they may approach you instead. They are naturally inquisitive, so if this happens do not automatically assume that you are in trouble . . . and try not to panic. After all, a real-life close encounter with one of the most beauti-ful, awe-inspiring and mysterious creatures on earth is why you jumped into the sea in the first place – and it is certainly something you will never forget.

2 How Dangerous are Sharks?

Statistically, even if you spend a great deal of time in the sea, the likelihood of being attacked by a shark is very small indeed. But, the fear and anxiety fuelled by the movie industry and the popular press have made the risk of attack a real concern for many divers and non-divers alike.

It did not really become a significant fear in the public mind until the twentieth century. A more cosmopolitan news-gathering system and a greater demand for shocking and titillating stories was partly to blame: a headline reading 'Shark Attacks Man' sells newspapers and does little to curtail our fear of sharks. Another contributory factor was the growing amount of time that people spent by the sea – and, perhaps inevitably, they took a personal interest in what might be lurking in the hidden depths. But at least some of the blame must rest with the book *Jaws*, published in 1974, and with the high-profile movies that followed. Many shark conservationists believe these were largely responsible for the anti-shark hysteria that has gripped the western world ever since. Even the book's author, Peter Benchley, publicly laments the impact of his book on our attitude towards sharks.

In those days, many experts were just as unenlightened. Until surprisingly recently, dive magazines and books used to suggest that the only sensible thing to do if a shark appeared was to leave the water. The mere hint of sharks at a dive resort was enough to threaten the livelihoods of the local operators. Now we know better. That is not to say that shark experts have become cavalier. There is a huge difference between being afraid of sharks and being cautiously respectful of them. After all, no one in their right mind would go on safari and waltz around with a pride of lions; yet, in theory, that is precisely the risk many divers are taking underwater with some species of sharks. They are supreme predators and need to be treated with respect.

The bottom line is this: sharks possess such acute senses, are such powerful predators and have such a wide distribution that few people would emerge from the sea unharmed if they really were out to get us. But they are not out to get us. Sharks can be dangerous and are a *potential* hazard that should be considered by anyone working or playing in the sea, but the vast majority of them are not intent on hurting people at all.

Great white sharks are reputed to be responsible for more than a quarter of all attacks on people, but often investigate divers closely without harming them.

The International Shark Attack File

The primary source of information on shark attack is the International Shark Attack File (ISAF), which is a detailed compilation of all known shark attacks around the world from 1580 to the present day. Established in 1958, following a conference involving scientists from 34 nations concerned about the lack of reliable information on shark attacks, the file is administered by the American Elasmobranch Society (see page 87) and the Florida Museum of Natural History (www.flmnh.ufl.edu).

More than 3300 individual investigations are currently housed in the ISAF, of which 2154 have been confirmed as unprovoked shark attacks. Approximately 26 per cent (554 attacks) of these proved fatal. Information on each attack is screened and computerized, but the database also includes a permanent archive of all associated material, from original notes and press clippings to video tapes and medical or autopsy reports.

How many people are attacked?

Worldwide there are probably 70–100 shark attacks every year, resulting in about 5–15 deaths. The figures are a little vague because not all shark attacks are reported. Indeed, even these days, some are intentionally kept quiet for fear of adverse publicity.

Historically, the death rate was much higher than it is today. This has nothing to do with the number or severity of attacks, but reflects the advent of readily available emergency services and a dramatic improvement in the quality of medical treatment. Ironically, though, while the death rate has been decreasing, the number of people attacked by sharks actually increased during the twentieth century. Overall there were more attacks (536) during the 1990s than during any previous decade on record. Again, this does not reflect a change in the *per capita* rate of attack. There are simply many more people in the sea these days – swimming, snorkelling, diving, surfing and spearfishing – so more attacks are to be expected. In addition, the scientific network and techniques used to discover and investigate shark attacks have improved enormously in recent years.

The ISAF investigated 90 alleged incidents of shark attack worldwide in 2000 and concluded that 79 of them involved genuine unprovoked attacks. This figure was higher than for previous years (58 in 1999, 54 in 1998 and 60 in 1997) and, indeed, was the highest since shark attack statistics were first recorded by the ISAF in 1958. It included 10 fatalities. Shark-inflicted damage to people who were already dead (normally drowned), provoked incidents (usually involving divers or fishermen handling sharks), and interactions between sharks and divers in public aquariums or research tanks are not considered to be attacks and are not included in these statistics. The remaining 11 incidents included four attacks on boats, four 'provoked' attacks, two dismissed as 'doubtful' and one with insufficient information.

Why do sharks attack?

Sharks have been known to attack people for many different reasons and, on occasion, for no apparent reason.

A few large sharks will eat people given the chance, although no species actually favours the taste of human flesh. Most do not even seem to *like* the way we taste. The problem is that they do not have hands to test things with, so they have to use their mouths instead, but since their limits are very different from our own, even a single exploratory bite can prove fatal. Such attacks are normally unprovoked, although if the victim is distressed or injured (for example, after an aircraft or ship disaster) sharks may be stimulated to attack. Some researchers studying great white sharks believe that they bite unfamiliar objects to test them as a potential food source, and, if they have a low fat content – as do humans or surfboards – they are

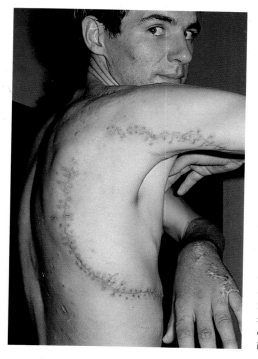

Rodney Fox shows the scars from an attack by a great white shark, while competing in the South Australian spearfishing championship in 1963.

rejected. Even the most overweight person would be insufficiently fat to satisfy a hungry great white, which may be why most people are bitten once and then spat out. It would take a great white several days to digest a human and, meanwhile, it could be feeding much more productively on a calorie-rich seal or tuna. Other researchers believe that great whites make an initial strike, then release their prey and retreat a safe distance away until it has bled to death. Recent research in South Africa does not support this bite-and-wait theory, although it has been observed in California and might be a local adaptation for tackling large and powerful elephant seals.

Even if a shark has no intention of eating you, or tasting you, it may still bite in self-defence. Many animals will bite if they feel threatened – and sharks are no exception. Species that are normally docile can, quite understandably, react aggressively if they feel harassed. Nurse sharks, for instance, are generally considered harmless: they feed mainly at night, on bottom-dwelling invertebrates, and spend most of the day asleep. But some divers cannot resist the urge to grab their dorsal fins for a free ride, or to pull their tails when they find them sticking out of a cave or from underneath a ledge. The result is fairly predictable – the shark takes a defensive bite and rapidly swims away. To be fair to the sharks, we should change the terminology for such injuries from 'shark attacks' to 'shark defences'.

A videographer at Burma Banks, in Thailand, takes a break from filming to stroke a tawny nurse shark.

The risk of attack may also be increased by luring the sharks with

food. This is particularly true if they are denied access to the food once they have arrived on the scene. Some experts consider spearfishing, for example, to be the underwater equivalent of drink-driving: in other words, it is asking for trouble. It results in low-frequency, erratic vibrations (because they are not killed outright) of distressed fish, which are highly attractive to sharks and can result in a confrontation.

Another possible reason for attack is personal space. A diver inadvertently wandering into a shark's space may receive an aggressive social warning, typically resulting in a slash wound similar to those found on the sharks themselves. There are numerous instances where sharks have apparently attempted to force divers away from 'their' area (which could be a radius of 10 m/33 ft or more around the sharks, but varies from species to species and from individual to individual).

The ISAF identifies three distinct kinds of unprovoked shark attacks: 'hit-and-run', 'bump-and-bite' and 'sneak' attacks.

Hit-and-run attacks are by far the most common. The victims are normally swimmers or surfers in the surf zone, seldom see their attacker and get bitten only once. Most of the bites are on the leg, typically below the knee, and are rarely life threatening. These attacks are probably cases of mistaken identity. The shark attacks once, then realizes its error and swims away. Imagine the scenario: a hunting shark in poor water visibility and in a harsh environment with breaking surf; add a person splashing about, perhaps with shiny jewellery, a brightly coloured swimsuit or wetsuit and uneven tanning (especially white soles of the feet). What is surprising is that, under these conditions, sharks do not misidentify human limbs for their normal prey more often.

Bump-and-bite attacks are less common, but more dangerous. The victims are normally swimmers or divers in deeper water and, typically, the sharks circle and then bump them prior to the actual attack. When they do bump, their abrasive skin causes wounds that spill blood into the water, and it is this that can trigger a shark's instinct to feed. Sneak attacks are equally dangerous, but normally occur without warning. In both cases, the sharks will often attack repeatedly and multiple injuries are the norm. Most fatalities occur as a result of these two forms of attack. Bump-and-bite and sneak attacks are unlikely to be cases of mistaken identity, since the sharks are likely to be actively feeding or defending their personal space.

Where do sharks attack?

The 536 unprovoked shark attacks recorded worldwide during the 1990s were centred on surprisingly few locations: Florida (186), South Africa (65), Australia (53), Brazil (50), Hawaii (33), California (30), New Zealand (17) and the rest of the world (102).

In 2000, 69.6 per cent (55) of all attacks occurred in North American waters and, as usual, most of these (34) occurred in Florida. There are several possible reasons why Florida has a relatively high incidence of shark attack: it has 2054 km/1277 miles of coastline, it is home to many potentially dangerous species of sharks, and there are huge numbers of people (both residents and tourists) in the water at any one time.

Nearly a third of the attacks during 2000 were on surfers. It is probably no coincidence that most shark-attack hotspots around the world are also major surf centres. There has been a phenomenal increase in the popularity of surfing since the early 1950s, and surfers spend much longer in the sea than swimmers and venture farther offshore. Traditional theory suggests a large shark can easily mistake a surfer on a surfboard for its natural prey, because the silhouette looks remarkably like an elephant seal or sea lion when viewed from below, although some experts doubt this as a plausible explanation; a smaller shark might mistake the soles of the feet and palms of the hands, which tend to be much lighter than the rest of the surfer's wetsuit or skin, for the flashing white of fish. New Smyrna Beach in Florida is a particular hotspot; some 10–15 surfers are bitten here in an average year and there were no fewer than six attacks over a single weekend in August 2001.

Shark attacks on divers

Divers have been attacked by sharks any time from the moment they entered the water to more than an hour after entry. In the vast majority of cases, a single shark in the size range 1.5–2.4m/5–8 ft was deemed responsible. Great whites accounted for 42.6 per cent of attacks, tiger sharks for 10.3 per cent and a further 26 species for the remainder. As the available information improves, however, bull sharks are also likely to be found responsible for a significant number of attacks.

Attacks on divers are, however, extremely rare. Most sharks are unfamiliar with human divers and their instincts warn them to treat anything unfamiliar with caution. We can only be thankful that the larger, open-water sharks have no idea how vulnerable human divers actually are underwater.

In the past 20 years, just over 5 per cent of all the world's unprovoked shark attacks have been on scuba-divers and approximately 14 per cent on snorkellers. A diver underwater usually attracts less interest from a shark than a snorkeller or swimmer on the surface. Indeed, many people who have happily been diving with sharks for years do not feel comfortable swimming on the surface, especially in deep water, without a mask, snorkel and fins. It is imperative to know if sharks are present

Seen from below, a surfer on a surfboard creates a silhouette that some experts believe could be mistaken for an elephant seal or sea lion – the natural prey of large sharks.

and what they are doing. If they do appear, it may not be necessary to leave the water, but at least you can make an informed decision.

Whether diving or snorkelling, spearfishing undoubtedly increases the chance of a shark encounter. According to ISAF statistics, nearly two-thirds of victims were spearfishing or carrying fish. Spearfishing on an outgoing tide is probably more dangerous than on an incoming tide, because there are more sharks offshore and they tend to be larger, more dangerous species. But whatever the tide, trailing fish juices and swimming erratically is a sure way of attracting hungry sharks.

Divers participating in organized shark dives are not immune to attack, although, in these instances, human error of judgement is usually a contributory factor. Even during cage dives, people have been bitten on their hands when they have placed them outside the cage to take photographs or to try to touch passing sharks. In recent years, more than a dozen injuries have occurred during organized shark feeds, although most of the victims were host dive masters.

The message is clear: do not be lulled into a false sense of security by the sheer scale of shark diving or by the ill-considered activities promoted by some operators. The risk of being attacked is very small indeed, but it is undoubtedly increased by foolish or careless behaviour.

Dangerous sharks

By their very nature, no sharks are actually friendly. Most of them are, however, surprisingly placid in the company of divers, and the two largest, the whale shark and the basking shark, have a positively mellow disposition.

In the majority of shark attacks it is difficult to identify the species responsible. In particular, very little is known about those involved in hit-and-run attacks, because they are seldom seen. Even with more prolonged bump-and-bite and sneak attacks, few victims are able to make a positive identification (quite understandably) and their wounds rarely provide sufficient clues to enable experts to do it for them. Nevertheless, the ISAF has been able to implicate no fewer than 42 shark species in a total of 980 attacks over the past 420 years.

According to these statistics, three species accounted for more than half of all attacks: the great white shark (348), the tiger shark (116) and the bull shark (82). This is not particularly surprising, since they are all large, widely distributed sharks and are capable of tackling sizeable prey. The great hammerhead, scalloped hammerhead, shortfin mako, oceanic whitetip, Galápagos and Caribbean reef sharks, among others, have all been implicated in bump-and-bite and sneak attacks as well.

The list of attackers also includes some rather unlikely species, such as the cookiecutter shark, spiny dogfish and Greenland shark, although in these particular cases just one incident was attributed to each species. The youngest shark to bite a human was an unborn sand tiger pup, which bit a marine biologist while he was examining the uterus of its dead mother. Every shark should therefore be treated with respect.

Reducing the risk

There are two golden rules for reducing the risk of shark attack: never underestimate the shark and never overestimate your own abilities or knowledge as a diver. Remember that nearly all dangers arise from inexperience or misjudgement of a situation.

Inevitably, the more time you spend with sharks, the better you become at identifying different species – which in turn helps to make a preliminary assessment of the potential threat – and the better you become at understanding their unspoken language. It is also helpful to be aware of the kind of human behaviour that makes sharks forget their manners.

But predicting and interpreting shark behaviour are not as simple as they may sound, because all sharks behave differently, and like humans, they can have bad days and act out of character. So, faced with a fast-swimming shark rushing straight towards you, there may be no way of telling whether it is going to attack or veer off at the last moment. As Jacques Cousteau once commented, the only predictable thing about sharks is that they are unpredictable.

There are, however, certain warning signs that make it possible to predict a potential attack or, at least, recognize an unhappy shark. These are more marked in some species than in others, but include swimming fast or jerkily, swimming in a tight figure of eight, tight circling, contorting the body into a distinctive S-shape, arching the back, pushing the pectoral fins downwards, lifting the snout, swinging the head from side to side and jaw-gaping. These ritualized displays work, in some species, as warnings (and may precede a direct attack), so it is essential that divers recognize them.

It is also useful to consider what might attract a shark in the first place. This is not a precise science, of course, but there are some interesting factors for recreational scuba-divers to bear in mind:

- Colour: some sharks may be able to tell one colour from another and many can distinguish light colours from dark. There is some evidence to suggest that bright colours such as yellow, white and silver may attract them and, rightly or wrongly, 'yum-yum yellow' has a particularly bad reputation. It is not unusual for sharks to bite at light-coloured fins (perhaps because they look like separate small fish), at the glint of light on face masks and camera lenses or at shiny jewellery (which may resemble fish scales). Uneven tanning may have a similar effect. According to ISAF statistics, 60 per cent of divers and snorkellers attacked were wearing highly contrasting colours, very bright colours or shiny items such as jewellery. Although such statistics are difficult to evaluate without analysing the popularity of different colours and jewellery among divers, some experts do prefer to wear dull-coloured clothing and equipment.

- Sound: unusual or irregular sounds definitely attract sharks, often from a long distance away. They will investigate the impact of an aircraft plunging into the sea or even that of a person diving in from a boat. Irregular movements, such as those made by a swimmer in trouble or merely splashing about for fun, are also an attractant.

- Blood: traces of blood may attract some species of shark. So do vomit, urine and other bodily fluids.

- Loners: sharks are more likely to attack a solitary individual or some- one apart from other members of the group.

- Time of day: some sharks are believed to be crepuscular in their feeding habits, and so the risk of an attack may increase substan- tially if you dive early in the morning or late in the afternoon – and, of course, they can see you while you probably cannot see them. The same sharks that are timid and unapproachable during the day may be more inquisitive at dusk and dawn. At these times, it is not advisable to dive with larger, open-water species, such as oceanic whitetips.

- Location: swimming in murky water increases the risk of shark attack, because it is more difficult for the sharks to distinguish between your limbs (which might appear to be separate animals) and their natural prey.

- Marine mammals: many shark species accompany or hunt seals, dolphins and other marine mammals. Anyone tempted to swim with them should be alert to the very real possibility that they may be accompanied by sharks. These sharks can be aggressive, perhaps because human intruders are seen as an easy meal or unwanted competition. Certainly never swim with marine mammals without wearing a mask, snorkel and fins, which ensure that you swim smoothly without too much splashing and enable you to see if sharks are present. It is also advisable to wear a wetsuit, which provides some protection if the sharks bump you.

A diver's behaviour may also be relevant. When in the company of sharks: breathe deeply and slowly and avoid rapid or exaggerated

movements; keep at least 5 m/16½ ft and preferably 10 m/33 ft from the sharks; do not descend towards them from above; do not make them feel cornered or trapped; do not swim towards them at an angle of less than 45 degrees; avoid using your hands to maintain buoyancy; do not attempt to chase, touch or ride them; and avoid unsatisfactory conditions for shark diving (such as low visibility or unusual activities such as, in South Africa, the sardine migration). Above all, relax and enjoy the encounter.

With sufficient care and experience it is possible to dive with potentially dangerous pelagic sharks, such as this oceanic whitetip off the coast of Hawaii.

If a shark begins to show too much interest or appears to be unhappy, the best response is to stay together and move away slowly. If the shark persists, it may be possible (as a last resort) to push it away with a gloved hand, camera or stick. Some experts recommend a hard hit on the snout to deter it from approaching too closely, but unless the shark is actually attacking, this can be provocative and it may produce an immediate aggressive response. Other experts prefer to avoid an attack by being the aggressor and swimming hard and fast towards the shark but, again, in some cases, this could actually provoke an attack.

Finally, professional shark divers always ensure that they have a rapid means of exit – into a boat or onto dry land – and never get embarrassed about leaving the water if they sense an uncomfortable situation developing.

Shark repellents and protection

Many potential shark repellents have been tested over the years. There was a rush to find a suitable one during the Second World War, when the US Navy and Royal Navy wanted to reassure terrified servicemen and their relatives concerned about downed planes and shipwrecks in 'shark-infested waters', and the determination to find a repellent has not really slowed in the years since.

Poison gases, copper acetate, sea-marker dyes, human sweat and many other weird and wonderful substances have been tried, with dubious effect, and people have tested some bizarre theories, such as dressing a diver in black-and-white to imitate a sea snake (an idea that was dropped when it was realized that some sharks eat sea snakes). Most experts are cynical about the promise of any of these repellents, and the best help most of them can provide is mental relief and a false sense of security.

A rather different approach has been taken by shark researchers in South Africa, who have ignored the role of smell in shark predation in favour of the role of minute electrical fields. They have developed the battery-powered Shark Protective Oceanic Device (or Shark POD).

A close encounter with a great white shark – the diver is wearing a Shark Protective Oceanic Device, or Shark POD, and is effectively enclosed within a weak electrical field.

It effectively encloses a human diver within a weak electrical field, with a range of about 4–5 m/13–16½ ft, which interferes with a shark's natural electrical receptors, known as the ampullae of Lorenzini. This disruption is believed to be irritating to the shark and may force it to move away. Humans, and most other forms of marine life without sensitive electroreceptors, are not affected by the electric field.

The main component of the POD is strapped to the dive cylinder and this is linked by wire to a small plate attached to the diver's fin; there is a switch to turn it on before entering the water, and a warning light reveals that the unit is working. A few experts are still cautious about the POD's effectiveness, but it has been rigorously tested over a period of five years by Australian underwater photographers and shark experts Ron and Valerie Taylor and by the South African Natal Sharks Board. They have found that the electrical field is sufficient to keep sharks a safe distance away, and even when 4.6-m/15-ft great whites hit the edge of the field they reacted immediately and retreated. After two weeks of testing the POD while free-diving with great whites off the coast of South Africa, Valerie Taylor commented that they 'felt invincible . . . there were a dozen or more sharks around . . . and they all kept their distance'. The Taylors had similar success with many other species, including bull sharks and tiger sharks. The only time the POD failed to work was during experiments when it was switched off temporarily to allow the sharks to feed – switching it back on again did not encourage them to release their meal.

Variations of the POD are being developed for shark-proof surfboards, bodyboards, sailboards, canoes and life jackets. Its potential for commercial divers and even surfers (to avoid the need for destructive shark nets around surf beaches) is widely recognized. However, there is some concern about the risk of long-term impact on the sharks and it has already been banned at several shark-dive sites (including Aliwal Shoal, South Africa).

Stainless steel and aluminium cages were originally developed in the 1960s to allow photographers to work safely around great white sharks. These days they are employed by photographers, researchers and tour operators to observe a number of large shark species in safety. In Australia, abalone divers have developed transportable shark cages to protect them while they are on the move.

Some professional shark divers wear protective steel-mesh suits and gloves. Developed in the early 1980s, these fit over a wetsuit and prevent a shark's teeth from penetrating the diver's skin. An average-sized, single-mesh suit weighs approximately 9 kg/20 lb and contains around 400,000 electronically welded rings, but there are several variations on this basic design: double mesh for the tremendous tearing power of tiger sharks; heavier steel made into smaller rings for makos and other narrow-toothed sharks; and even specially constructed Kevlar plates to distribute the pressure of bites by larger sharks.

Chainmail suits are highly effective and allow divers to swim freely among small- to medium-sized sharks (a large shark can crush an arm or leg in its mouth or even pull it right out of its socket), but are expensive. Nevertheless, they have become standard equipment for divers filming sharks in feeding situations, those who feed sharks for shark watchers, and some shark scientists.

Poles with explosive heads and a hypodermic gas device called a 'shark dart' have been used to kill or seriously injure sharks that threaten divers, but these are cruel and unnecessary, except in extraordinary circumstances. As with other deterrents, they encourage a false sense of security – which is more likely to result in an aggressive encounter – and enable panicked divers to kill mostly harmless sharks.

At the end of the day, nothing beats the right frame of mind. Divers should always go on shark dives with humility and understanding – not with a macho them-against-us attitude.

Learning from an 'inevitable' attack

When a diver was attacked by sharks on 23 July 1996, many experts concluded that the attack had been virtually inevitable. As Jeremy Stafford-Deitsch observes in his excellent book *Red Sea Sharks*, 'the attack culminated after several high-risk details came together.' It serves as an important warning to other divers.

The attack took place about 1 km/ 1/2 mile off Marsa Bareika, Sharm El Sheikh, in the Red Sea. It was late in the afternoon when the diver and two friends went swimming in deep water with a small pod of five bottlenose dolphins. Soon after his friends had clambered back into the boat, leaving him alone in the water, the diver was attacked by at least two sharks. Experts concluded that they were probably tiger sharks. The largest bite was 46 cm/18 in in diameter, suggesting that one of the attackers was at least 4 m/13 ft long. Three of the dolphins surrounded the diver and may have saved his life by beating their flukes and fins on the surface of the water to keep the sharks at bay until he could be rescued. He received four major bites but, thanks to the prompt application of tourniquets on the boat, emergency treatment in Sharm El Sheikh and rapid evacuation to the Egyptian military hospital at El Tur, he survived.

With the wisdom of hindsight, this diver was probably courting disaster. He entered the water late in the afternoon, which is precisely when many sharks are hunting, and in deep water, where larger and more dangerous sharks are more common. He swam with a group of dolphins, which are often accompanied by sharks seeking the same food or intent on hunting them. By splashing about on the surface he would have given off vibrations that any sharks nearby would have mistaken for an injured animal – and the dolphins would have added to the cacophony by swimming excitedly around him. Without a mask, he would not have seen sharks in the area or been aware of any exploratory passes in time to get out of the water. Finally, he stayed in the water after his friends had returned to the boat – yet sharks typically target a solitary individual or someone away from the main group. It really does appear to have been an accident waiting to happen.

Interestingly, a tiger shark at least 4 m/13 ft in length could easily have bitten right through the diver; so although the resulting wounds were terrible and life-threatening, there is every chance that the sharks were merely taking tentative, exploratory nips.

Shark attacks in perspective

While statistics offer little comfort to the unfortunate few who *are* attacked by sharks, they do put the risk of shark attack into perspective. Here are a few revealing comparisons:

- There is a far greater chance of winning a national lottery than of being attacked by a shark.

- According to figures published by the New York City Health Department, for every person around the world bitten by a shark, 25 people are actually bitten by New Yorkers.

- A study on one Australian beach, which teems with sharks, revealed that only one out of every 30 million bathers is attacked by a shark.

- A great many more people are injured or killed on land while driving to and from the beach than by sharks in the water.

- Many more people die in skiing accidents in the Alps every year than are attacked by sharks worldwide.

- More than six times as many people are struck by lightning every year in Florida (one of the world's shark-attack hotspots) than are attacked by sharks.

Perhaps the most shocking statistic of all – and this really puts things into perspective – is that, in an average year, for every person killed by a shark, we in turn kill many *millions* of sharks. Now that really is frightening.

3 Shark Photography

Shark photography is challenging, frustrating, enormously satisfying and heart-poundingly good fun. Shooting in mid-water is particularly difficult and intense, as the sharks can come at you from any direction – straight up from the invisible depths, down from the surface, from behind or in front, or from either side. But the satisfaction of obtaining a dramatic close-up of a fierce-looking sand tiger shark, a wide-angle image of a diver next to a gigantic whale shark or a silhouetted blue shark swimming through a spectacular sunburst makes it more than worthwhile.

With recent advances in technology and more opportunities than ever before for close encounters with sharks, photography of these beautiful creatures is now within reach of almost anyone with enough determination and patience.

There are many aspects to successful shark photography, but to begin with, five golden rules will help enormously:

- Be a competent diver. It is essential to be comfortable in the water in order to concentrate on your photography instead of your diving technique, and good buoyancy control is vital for remaining motionless and manoeuvring into position without damaging the marine environment, kicking up a sandstorm or frightening the sharks. Diving with camera equipment makes otherwise simple tasks, such as mask-clearing or monitoring gauges, a little more complicated, and without mastery of such fundamental skills it is not practical, or even safe, to attempt underwater photography.

- Be competent with your camera equipment and understand the basics of photography (shutter speeds, apertures, exposure, depth of field, etc.) to avoid wasting time and missed opportunities when you are underwater with the sharks. It is not difficult – if you can handle dive tables, you can certainly cope with f-stops – and yet there is no doubt that if manufacturers made waterproof instruction booklets, many people would spend their shark dives sitting on the seabed reading about which buttons to press and when to press them.

- Stay calm – shark photography can get pretty lively and hair-raising underwater, and it is easy to get swept along in all the excitement and shoot your pictures prematurely or make simple errors that can

Photographing sharks in mid-water is particularly challenging; this photographer is shooting a blue shark off California.

ruin your shots. Avoid any sudden movements, which may frighten the sharks, and breathe very slowly and evenly.

■ Get close . . . and then get even closer. This was a phrase first coined by the renowned underwater photographer Norbert Wu a few years ago, and it is advice that will instantly improve your photography; the less water you shoot through, the better your pictures will be – colours will look snappier and the sharks will appear sharper.

■ Understand the sharks and their behaviour. The better your knowledge of the subject, the better your photographs are likely to be, and the safer the dive.

Most professional shark photographers plan their pictures well in advance. They tend to target a particular species, and even a specific image, then go to the right place at the right depth at the right time of year. They work out what equipment they might need – depending on whether they want a portrait, a shark with a diver, a silhouette or several sharks together. In shark photography, when the action is often so fast and furious that there is barely enough time to think, careful planning can make all the difference.

Perhaps the best piece of advice is to practise. There is no substitute for taking as many pictures as possible and learning from your mistakes. It is likely to be a steep learning curve, with disappointing results in the early days, but the end result will be worth the wait.

Cameras

There are basically four kinds of underwater camera system: disposable single-use cameras, compact cameras, dedicated rangefinder cameras and waterproof housings for land cameras. There are already digital alternatives for some of these systems, and as digital cameras improve in quality (and drop in price) there are likely to be more in the near future.

Inexpensive single-use underwater cameras are perfect for holiday snapshots, and no technical knowledge of photography is required, but the quality is not brilliant and they can only be used in shallow water. Better quality can be obtained with compact underwater cameras, made by Aquatica, Ikelite, SeaLife, Sea & Sea, Minolta, Canon, and others. These are easy to use and the more expensive models come with a range of accessories and can be taken to depths of up to 50 m/164 ft.

More serious photographers should consider a dedicated underwater camera system with interchangeable lenses, variable focus,

exposure control and a facility for underwater strobe lighting. Many professionals choose the Nikonos V, which is the industry standard and probably the most widely used underwater camera in the world (although Nikon has recently announced that production will cease in the near future). It is flexible and versatile, robust in construction and all the controls can be operated easily underwater. The optics are excellent and many of the underwater pictures published in books and magazines have been taken with this camera. A less expensive alternative is the Motor Marine II-EX, produced by Sea & Sea, which is also very versatile but not quite as sophisticated as the Nikonos. Both can be taken to a depth of about 50 m/164 ft. Their main drawback is that they are non-reflex cameras, which means that you look through a separate viewfinder instead of through the lens. There is a waterproof reflex camera, the Nikonos R5, which is used by many professional underwater photographers, but it is no longer being manufactured.

Advanced and professional photographers frequently use water-proof camera housings, made of moulded plastic, metal or aluminium, for a 35 mm SLR (single lens reflex) land camera. Basically, the housing keeps your land camera safe and dry underwater while giving you access to all the controls. This system has several advantages: you can see the image through the lens and therefore have much more accurate control over focusing and composition (what you see is what you get); it can accommodate a wide variety of lenses, including macros, wide-angles and zooms; and it provides greater flexibility in terms of

Not for the faint-hearted: photographing a great white off the coast of South Australia.

auto-focus, auto-exposure and motor-drive film transport for action shots of fast-moving subjects. But there are also some disadvantages: underwater housings are bigger and heavier; they are slightly more complicated and need more setting up than amphibious cameras; and they are more expensive. Housings are made by Subal, Ikelite, Nexus, Aqua Vision, Sea & Sea and others. An alternative worth considering is the Ewa Marine flexible housing, a vinyl bag that allows you to shoot through an optical-grade glass port, which is less convenient and less rugged but considerably cheaper.

Your final choice of equipment must depend on your reasons for photographing sharks, your budget and your personal preference. But it might be a good idea, if you are just starting in shark photography, to keep it simple. Begin with a basic system and you will have fewer variables to worry about.

Lenses

Whether you are shooting a close-up, an entire shark or a school of sharks, it is important to fill the frame. There are exceptions, of course, but when it comes to shark photography size does matter: too much 'empty' space around the main subject tends to weaken the image.

Wildlife photography on land normally requires a telephoto lens to take frame-filling shots, but the opposite is true underwater, where most shark photographers tend to use wide-angle lenses. Bearing in mind the importance of getting as close as possible when taking pictures in water (see 'Get close . . . and then get even closer', p.47), the best shark pictures are normally taken from no more than a metre or two away. A wide-angle lens is necessary because a telephoto would probably not focus down to such a short distance; even if it did, it would reproduce only a small part of the shark. A wide-angle lens also adds drama and impact to a frame-filling picture, because the shark appears to be 'right there'.

Do not assume that the wider the lens, the better. It is not always easy to get close enough to sharks to fill the frame and, even if they do approach closely, they tend to veer away before there is a chance to take the perfect shot (the veering away angle is not as strong as the angle of approach). The final choice of lens depends on the desired result, as well as the approachability and size of the shark, but a shark photographer's lens arsenal might include a 15 mm or 20 mm to capture the whole creature and lenses of 28 mm, 35 mm or even 60 mm for portrait shots of the face or details of the body.

It takes practice to use a wide-angle lens for shark photography, because it is surprising how close you need to be. In all the excitement of diving with sharks, they tend to look much closer in the viewfinder

This action-packed, frame-filling shot of grey reef sharks in Bikini Atoll, Micronesia, demonstrates the value of getting in close with a wide-angle lens.

than they really are and, to make matters worse, many people make the mistake of only 'seeing' the centre of the frame without realizing how much space there is around the outside. Think big and the results will be that much better.

Film

There are two fundamental decisions to make concerning film: what sensitivity to use and whether to take prints or slides.

Take prints if you just want to put the pictures in an album or send them to family and friends. Print film is cheaper and much easier to use because it has a greater tolerance for exposure errors. With print film you can get the exposure completely wrong and still get a reasonable picture. A badly exposed slide film is virtually useless, but most professionals take slides because they can be projected to larger audiences and are essential if you want to get pictures published (although this is changing as negatives can now be scanned just as easily as slides).

Wherever sharks are encountered near the surface and light levels are reasonably good, any slide or print film with a medium-sensitivity rating of ISO 50 to 100 is suitable for much of the time. In deeper water, or in dull weather, the same film can be used if extra light is provided by a strobe (underwater flash). Films with sensitivity ratings of ISO 200 are useful for freezing action, because they allow the use of faster shutter speeds, and ISO 400 films are good for beginners because they allow faster shutter speeds *and* good depth of field. The problem with the faster films, though, is that they are more grainy and the colours are rarely as good as those of their slower counterparts. Most professionals use a variety of films, with different speeds, depending on such variables as light, visibility, depth and subject.

The make of film is largely a matter of personal choice. Most professionals use Kodak or Fuji and tend to favour ones with high colour saturation, such as Kodak's E100VS (VS means 'very saturated') or Fuji's ISO 50 Velvia or ISO 100 Provia F.

Exposure

The exposure can make or break an image, and so it is critically important to expose accurately – especially with slide film, which offers little room for error. Because many sharks are dark above and light below, the camera's light meter can easily be fooled into overexposing the upperside and underexposing the underside. Therefore it is important to learn how to compensate by overriding the camera's automatic exposure functions and setting them manually.

If the situation allows, it is worth bracketing your exposures by a third or half a stop either side of the 'correct' exposure. But this is not as straightforward as in topside photography, simply because it is impossible to change film underwater, and so there is less room for manoeuvre. You basically have a maximum of one roll of film per dive. Checking to see how many exposures you have left is a very important – and constant – part of underwater photography and is a good way of making sure that every frame really counts. The trick in shark photography is to pick your shots carefully and then to save a couple of frames for your return to the surface, when (thanks to Murphy's Law) the best photo opportunities occur surprisingly often.

Artificial flash

The deeper you dive, the more colours disappear from the spectrum. Water filters them out selectively: red first (at a depth of about 5 m/16½ ft), then orange, yellow, green and finally, at about 20 m/65 ft, blue.

One way to restore their original hues is to use the artificial light of an underwater flashgun, or strobe (filters can also be used to restore colour, but they reduce the amount of light getting onto the film and their use can be quite involved). Even near the surface, a punch of light from a strobe can go a long way towards 'pulling' a shark out of a background of blue water and making an otherwise ordinary picture really sparkle. It adds contrast, colour and highlights to the subject.

One strobe is normally sufficient, but some photographers use two – one on each side of the camera. This is not to increase the intensity of light, but to 'fill in' (reduce the harsh shadows caused by the main flash) or to increase the area illuminated for a wide-angle lens. The catch, of course, is that a second strobe adds extra weight, is more hassle during a dive and is yet another piece of equipment to worry about. Underwater photography with strobe lighting takes patience to master with one unit, let alone two, and it is a good idea to bracket exposures when the lighting is a little difficult. This means shooting identical, or at least similar, frames with some exposed with the strobe at full power, some at one-half power and some at one-quarter power to ensure that at least one picture is correctly exposed. The trick is not to overpower the subject with too much flash; instead, the lighting should be a subtle flash fill, with just enough light to add colour and highlights while retaining the available light background of the picture. Otherwise, the scene will appear unnatural.

Finally, it is not unknown for sharks to bump or bite underwater strobes – perhaps because they are attracted by the electrical fields or the high pitch of the rapid recycle. If a shark does take an excessive amount of interest in your strobe, turn it off for a while.

Backscatter

'Backscatter' is the enemy of beginners and professional shark photographers alike. It is caused by the light from a strobe reflecting off all the particles in the water and back into the camera lens. The problem is particularly bad with wide-angle lenses and the result is a ruined picture looking, at worst, like an underwater snowstorm.

Some common sources of backscatter in shark photography are particles of chum and bait used to attract sharks at organized feeds, plankton, the small bubbles that are constantly created by the movement of shark cages, and sand kicked up by fellow divers. But even seemingly crystal-clear water has enough suspended matter to cause a problem.

There are several ways to reduce or even eliminate backscatter: place or hold the strobe away from the camera (which causes the light to bounce off all the particles at an angle and not directly into the lens); use a smaller lens aperture to limit the amount of backscatter registered on the film; and get as close as possible to the shark to reduce the amount of water you are shooting through. Whenever possible, it is also wise to position yourself against or across the current, so that any bubbles or particles disturbed by your movements will be carried away from where you are shooting.

Backscatter – caused by incorrect use of a strobe – has ruined this otherwise good picture of a Caribbean reef shark in the Bahamas.

Get close ... and then get even closer

This is a tip that will instantly improve your photography: the closer you get to a shark before you release the shutter, the sharper the image and the better the colour. Get close . . . and then get even closer. It is the cardinal rule of underwater photography.

There are four reasons why the quality of the picture is inversely proportional to the amount of water between the lens and the shark. First, no matter how clear the water may seem, light is scattered by ever-present particles, and so to get a really sharp image, the camera must be as close as possible to the subject. Second, these particles cause backscatter, and so the fewer of them between you and the shark the better. Third, because underwater flash is needed to restore colour at depths greater than a few metres, you need to be close for the flash to have sufficient impact. Finally, when light goes underwater the rays are bent or refracted, which effectively narrows the angle of view of a camera lens. This is important when using a lens behind a flat port: a 35 mm lens underwater, then, has roughly the same angle of view as a 50 mm lens above the surface – so you need to get that much closer to fill the frame.

Composition

There are several easy ways to improve the composition of a shark photograph to give a feeling of balance and harmony.

Do not automatically frame the shark's head dead centre in the frame. It is less appealing to the eye if half the picture is blank or, worse, if half the shark is missing. Instead, use a tried-and-tested system called the 'rule of thirds', in which you imagine the picture divided into thirds by horizontal and vertical lines and then place the main action or focal point at one of the places where the imaginary lines meet.

Think about the background, not just the sharks. Sharks are designed by nature to blend into their surroundings, and so one of the greatest challenges in shark photography is to make them 'pop' or stand out. A punch of light from a strobe can help, but it is also important to avoid cluttered or dark backgrounds. Try to avoid a distracting line across the picture where the seabed meets the sea, and do not shoot against a nearby reef (which makes it almost impossible to distinguish the teeth, eyes and other features that need to be prominent in the final image). One solution is to shoot at a slightly upward angle of 15–40 degrees, which ensures a clear blue background; this also adds drama, by drawing attention to the teeth and mouth and making the shark look more imposing. Selecting the right angle can make all the difference between a dramatic photograph and a mediocre snapshot.

One advantage of photographing sharks in open water, such as this shortfin mako off the coast of California, is that there are no distracting backgrounds.

If you can, shoot the shark when it is swimming towards you. The front view is often the most exciting one and provides an opportunity to photograph the head, mouth, eyes and even pectoral and dorsal fins – which are the most interesting components. Side views are also good, providing an overall view of the shape and markings of the body. Photographs from immediately above are particularly difficult to capture and rarely work in mid-water photography, because the shark's camouflage makes it almost disappear against the darkness of the depths (you end up with a black blob on a dark-blue background); the only exception is a shark swimming over a white sandy bottom, which provides the necessary contrast.

Finally, try to be creative. Sometimes it is good to ignore all the advice and rules and shoot by instinct instead. If the shark is some distance above you, for example, try shooting vertically against the bright surface to produce a powerful silhouette; or, if it is really close, try homing in on a detail, such as its eye or tail. These experimental shots may not always work, but they could produce something really different.

Safety

Shark photography is all-engrossing and, as such, can be dangerous. It is easy to get so absorbed in taking pictures that you become unaware of what is happening around you. The risks are that you miss the warning signs of an unhappy shark or, while you are composing a picture of one shark, you miss others approaching from behind.

Whatever the circumstances, it is wise not to photograph sharks alone. When photographing with a group of divers, the temptation is to move away from the crowd, because this gives you a better chance of isolating a single, slower-moving creature and helps to keep bubbles, fins and elbows out of your shots. But it also makes you more vulnerable. The solution is always to dive with a buddy. Having a vigilant companion to watch over your shoulder keeps you safe and leaves you free to concentrate on the photography. Even when photographing from a shark cage, it is useful to have a safety diver: you may find it necessary to extend your camera and arms through the bars to obtain a good shot and, although you can see the shark you are photographing, you might not see another one approaching from the side or below.

It is very important to be a confident diver before jumping in with lots of camera gear. If something goes wrong during a tense shooting situation, your experience and instinctive reactions may make all the difference. And remember to listen carefully to divemasters – their local knowledge can be invaluable.

Photographing sharks from inside a cage may sound relatively easy, but it poses its own unique challenges.

4 The World of Sharks

Sharks come in all shapes, sizes and colours. They range from tiny lantern and spined pygmy sharks, which are small enough to fit in a human hand, to gargantuan whale sharks, which are larger than many of their namesakes in the mammalian world. There are typical 'movie' sharks, ray-like and eel-like sharks, and there is even one with an elongated, flattened snout in the shape of a paddle. Some are brightly coloured, others perfectly camouflaged or rather drab; they may be blue, white, grey, tan, brown, black, green, orange or purple, and spotted or striped.

Found in all the seas and oceans of the world, and even thousands of kilometres up some rivers, sharks live everywhere from the freezing cold waters of the poles to the warm waters of the tropics. They can be found swimming at the surface or down in the coldest, darkest ocean depths several kilometres below. Some live in the pounding surf close to shore, while many prefer the open ocean and swim perpetually in mid-water, and others choose to lie on the seabed.

Their lifestyles are just as varied. Some sharks actively pursue swift and agile prey; others lie in wait, ready to ambush much slower-moving prey. A few of the larger species survive by straining microscopic plankton from the seawater, while some of their close relatives bite off enormous chunks of flesh from large fish and dead whales.

Origins and ancestors

Sharks have been common inhabitants of our seas and oceans for some 400 million years – since long before dinosaurs roamed the earth.

But the ancestors of modern sharks are difficult to study. Shark palaeontologists have relatively few fossil records to examine, because their cartilaginous skeletons usually disintegrate soon after the sharks have died. The discovery of perfect impressions of sharks in outcrops of Cleveland shale (a type of soft rock from the Devonian Period) from Ohio south to Arkansas, in the USA, helped enormously – some of them are so detailed that it has even been possible to identify the contents of their stomachs. For the most part, however, the evolutionary history of sharks has to be pieced together mainly from fossilized teeth, with small scales and calcified vertebrae adding

A diver is dwarfed by this whale shark, the largest fish in the sea, which was found swimming off the coast of Thailand.

Basking sharks have tiny, hooked teeth but use their giant gill rakers to filter planktonic crustaceans and fish eggs out of the water.

a few extra clues. It is like working on an enormously complicated jigsaw puzzle, with most of the pieces missing.

Sharks produce prodigious numbers of teeth, and they fossilize readily, so fossil teeth are very common. They have been found everywhere from beaches to mountain tops, and from the Antarctic to the deepest part of the ocean. For some extinct species they provide the only record of their existence; in fact, quite a few species are known only from a single tooth.

Studying prehistoric sharks through their teeth can be both challenging and frustrating, for several reasons. First, fossilized teeth provide relatively few clues about the rest of the shark. It is possible to infer something about their original owners, by their size and shape, but this requires a lot of informed guesswork. If the teeth are long and pointed, for example; they might have been used for grabbing soft-bodied, elusive prey, which would suggest a shark that was probably a fast, aggressive swimmer. If they are much flatter and more peg-like, their owner was probably a bottom-feeder specializing in hard-bodied but slow-moving prey. Shark palaeontologists have to be careful about drawing too many firm conclusions, though, because some sharks have different teeth in different parts of the jaw, and these may vary between males and females.

The study of fossilized shark teeth was further complicated by the recent discovery that some baby sharks shed and replace their teeth while still inside the womb. These baby teeth can be quite different in shape from those of the adults, and the fear is that some fossilized embryonic teeth may have been mistakenly identified as belonging to different species altogether. The embryonic teeth of a great white shark, for instance, look almost identical to the adult teeth of a sand tiger shark – and they are in completely different families.

It is also possible that the earliest sharks did not have teeth at all. Tiny scales, which certainly came from sharks of one kind or another, have been found in deposits more than 450 million years old. They represent the earliest sharks known, but no teeth of a similar age have ever been found from this early period. The oldest fossil shark teeth found so far are estimated to be around 400 million years old, and so there is a mysterious gap of 50 million years.

Not surprisingly, most experts believe that the vast majority of pre-historic sharks have probably escaped our attention altogether. We have no clues that they ever existed, but it is surprising how much information has been accumulated by painstaking work over many years.

The oldest shark fossil consisting of more than teeth and scales has been called *Antarctilamna* and is believed to be about 380 million years old. As its name suggests, it was first discovered in Antarctica. The first modern-looking sharks probably appeared nearly 200 million years later. They had streamlined bodies, five pairs of external gill slits, two well-developed dorsal fins, pectoral and pelvic fins and a powerful vertical tail. Most of the shark families in existence today are believed to have evolved within the past 150 million years. The sixgill and sevengill sharks were among the earliest to appear in the fossil record and, at the other extreme, some hammerhead species are known only from the past five million years.

One of the most intriguing of all the ancient sharks is the mega-tooth, or megalodon (*Carcharodon megalodon*). This was the largest

The fossil tooth of an extinct megatooth, or megalodon, is many times larger than the tooth of a modern great white shark.

shark ever to have lived and one of the largest predators ever to stalk the planet. It is a close relative of the great white shark, which looks tiny in comparison, and was a monster predator at the top of the food chain from about 20 million years ago. Estimated to have grown to a length of at least 15 m/50 ft, to have weighed 25–50 tonnes/tons and to have had a mouth gape of about 2 m/6½ ft, it was many times larger than *Tyrannosaurus rex*. Its scientific name means 'the shark with big teeth', and, indeed, its arrow-shaped teeth are up to 18 cm/ 7 in high – three times higher than those of modern great white sharks. Megalodon inexplicably disappeared around two million years ago.

Classification of sharks

There are three major kinds of fishes in the world: jawless fishes, bony fishes and cartilaginous fishes.

Jawless fishes make up the smallest group (although they are no longer classified separately), with fewer than 50 living species of lampreys and hagfish. They have skeletons made of cartilage but, as their name suggests, no jaws.

With more than 24,000 living species – accounting for about 95 per cent of all the world's fishes – bony fishes form the largest group. They belong to the class Osteichthyes, their skeletons are made of bone and they include many familiar species, such as tuna, swordfish, mackerel and herring.

Cartilaginous fishes are the sharks, rays and chimaeras. They belong to the class Chondrichthyes, which accounts for less than 5 per cent of all the world's fishes. The precise number of species is a matter of considerable debate and, including some that have yet to be named, more than 1100 are known to science. Their skeletons are made of cartilage (a tough, flexible material that is also found in human joints, such as knees and elbows) and they are quite different from bony fishes in their structure, physiology and biology.

Chimaeras are primitive, deep-water fishes rarely encountered by divers. Also known as ratfish, elephantfish or ghost sharks, they have rabbit-like noses, long spines on their dorsal fins, a smooth skin without scales and long, tapered tails. They form a separate sub-class known as the Holocephali.

The sharks and rays are grouped together in the subclass Elasmobranchii (they are often referred to as elasmobranchs). Rays are basically flat-bodied sharks, with their gill slits on the underside, and have two large pectoral fins attached to the head; most swim by flapping or undulating the pectorals. Sharks tend to be cylinder-shaped, with their gill slits on the sides, and have two relatively small pectoral fins attached to the body; they swim by moving the head from side to side, sending 'waves' down to the tail to make it oscillate. They also 'swing' the tail itself. But there are exceptions, and some members of the two groups can easily be confused. Angel sharks have flattened, ray-like bodies, for example, while certain rays, such as guitarfishes and sawfishes, swim with the help of lateral movements of their tails like sharks.

There are eight main groups, or orders, of sharks:

ORDER HETERODONTIFORMES
One family (Heterodontidae). Port Jackson, bullhead and horn sharks. Bottom-dwelling; large squarish head with crests over eyes; short pig-like snout; five gill slits each side; two large dorsal fins with spines; pectoral fins used for walking on seabed; anal fin present.

ORDER ORECTOLOBIFORMES
Eight families (Parascylliidae, Brachaeluridae, Orectolobidae, Hemi-scylliidae, Pseudoginglymostomatidae, Stegostomatidae, Ginglymosto-matidae, Rhincodontidae). Zebra, leopard, nurse, whale, and others. Predominantly bottom-dwelling (except whale shark); squarish or flattened head; five gill slits each side; mouth well in front of eyes; barbels (fleshy, whisker-like structures probably used to feel around in the sediment for prey) on inside edges of nostrils; two dorsal fins without spines; anal fin present.

The bull shark is just one of more than 1100 species of sharks and rays known to science; this individual was recently tagged and released by scientists working in the Bahamas.

ORDER LAMNIFORMES
Eight families (Carchariidae, Odontaspididae, Mitsukurinidae, Pseudo-carcharidae, Megachasmidae, Alopiidae, Cetorhinidae, Lamnidae). Collectively known as 'mackerel sharks'. Sand tiger, megamouth, thresher, basking, great white, shortfin mako, and others. Long snout; five gill slits each side; mouth stretches behind eyes; no nictitating eyelids; two dorsal fins without spines; anal fin present.

ORDER CARCHARHINIFORMES
Eight families (Scyliorhinidae, Proscylliidae, Pseudotriakidae, Lepto-chariidae, Triakidae, Hemigaleidae, Sphyrnidae, Carcharhinidae). Collectively known as 'ground sharks'. Members of Carcharhinidae known as 'requiem sharks'. Hammerheads, bronze whaler, leopard, reef, tiger, blacktip, silvertip, spinner, silky, bull, Galápagos, blue, lemon, and others. Long mouth stretches behind eyes; five gill slits each side; nictitating eyelids present; two dorsal fins without spines; anal fin present.

ORDER HEXANCHIFORMES
Two families (Chlamydoselachidae, Hexanchidae). Sixgill, sevengill and frilled sharks. Members of Hexanchidae known as 'cow sharks'. Six or seven gill slits each side; one dorsal fin; anal fin present.

ORDER SQUALIFORMES
Seven families (Echinorhinidae, Squalidae, Centrophoridae, Etmop-teridae, Somniosidae, Oxynotidae, Dalatiidae). Dogfish, Greenland and cookiecutter sharks, and others. Roughly cylindrical body; short snout; five gill slits each side; nictitating eyelids present; two dorsal fins, often with spines; no anal fin.

ORDER PRISTIOPHORIFORMES
One family (Pristiophoridae). Saw sharks. More closely related to rays than any other sharks. Slightly flattened body; elongated, saw-like snout; five or six gill slits each side; long barbels protrude from snout; mouth on underside; two large dorsal fins without spines; no anal fin.

ORDER SQUATINIFORMES
One family (Squatinidae). Angel sharks and monkfish. Bottom-dwelling; flattened, ray-like body; mouth at front; five gill slits each side; two small dorsal fins without spines; pectoral fins not joined to head; caudal fin small with larger lower lobe; no anal fin.

The lemon shark is one of many familiar species, including the tiger, silvertip and blue, belonging to the order Carcharhiniformes.

The perfect body

Sharks may have a long ancestry and still retain many ancient anatomical features, but they are also superbly adapted to life in the sea and, in many ways, are 'technologically advanced'.

Their cartilaginous skeletons are their most defining characteristic (more precisely, it is the specific pattern in which they are calcified). Cartilage is an elastic connective tissue, which is more flexible than bone, yet still provides protection and support for the internal body organs. Where necessary, some shark bones that regularly experience severe physical stress, such as vertebrae, jaws and parts of the skull, are specially strengthened by deposits of calcium compounds.

But the main advantage of cartilage is its light weight. Whereas bone is twice as dense as water, cartilage is only slightly more dense. This is a major factor in enabling sharks to maintain a degree of neutral buoyancy – the ability to 'hover' in the water without sinking or floating up to the surface. Bony fishes have heavier bones, but to compensate they have a gas-filled swim bladder that can be inflated or deflated according to their depth to keep them perfectly positioned in the water without having to swim. There is, however, a price to pay for this facility. Adding or removing the gas in a swim bladder is quite a slow process, and if a fish rises to the surface too quickly, the volume of air in the bladder expands with the decreasing pressure and it is likely to burst.

Sharks do not have a swim bladder and this enables them to move up and down the water column very quickly without any risk. They still need help in maintaining neutral buoyancy, but use their enormous oil-filled livers instead. A shark's liver can account for as much as 25 per cent of its total body weight and, since the oil is less dense than water, it dramatically reduces the overall weight of the shark underwater.

Even with cartilage and an enormous liver, most sharks are still heavier than water (some deep-water sharks have enough liver oil to achieve perfect neutral buoyancy, but they are the exception). If most sharks were ever to stop swimming, they would slowly sink into the abyss. So they make the swimming easier, and help to counteract their negative buoyancy, by having pectoral fins and tails that are shaped like aeroplane wings and provide a natural upward lift. In hammerheads and some other species, their heads also create lift.

An interesting exception is the sand tiger shark, which may be on the first rung of the evolutionary ladder towards developing its own bony-fish-like swim bladder. It goes to the surface to swallow air, then holds it inside its stomach. This enables it to remain motionless in the water without expending energy on swimming and without sinking.

Shark fins are also rather different. They are not the thin, flexible

fins supported by spines that are found in many bony fishes, but are thick and stiffened by cartilaginous rods and internal fibres of collagen. The unpaired dorsal and anal fins are designed to prevent the shark from yawing or deviating from its straight-line course (rather like the keel of a sailing boat), while the paired pectoral and pelvic fins help to provide natural lift and are used for steering. The tail, or caudal, fin produces forward thrust.

The connoisseur's shark: the silky shark has a perfect, stream-lined body.

Shark skin feels smooth if it is stroked from front to back, but is so rough when stroked from back to front that it can scrape human skin raw. Some small fish actually rub themselves against it to remove their own external parasites.

The skin is covered in tiny placoid scales, each of which is a tooth-like dermal denticle. The denticles are rather like normal teeth, in miniature, and normally face backwards. They help to improve hydro-dynamic efficiency by breaking up the interface between skin and water, thus reducing turbulence when the shark is swimming. They are so effective that engineers are now attempting to replicate dermal denticles to reduce turbulence in aircraft, submarines and racing yachts. But they also form an impressive armour to protect the shark against injury. The skin on the upperside of a whale shark is so impen-etrable that harpoons and rifle bullets fired at close range have been known to bounce off its back. The denticles, which are uniquely shaped on different parts of the body, do not grow, but as the shark increases in size more of them appear to fill in the 'gaps', and old ones are quickly replaced by new ones.

Sharks 'breathe' by inhaling water through the mouth and then extracting oxygen as it passes over the gills. Instead of having a single opening with a hard protective plate on each side of the head, as in bony fishes, their gills are found on five pairs of gill arches (some more primitive species have six or seven pairs) that form the walls of the external gill slits. The heart pumps oxygen-depleted blood to capillary beds in the gill arches and, as water is pumped over the gills, oxygen diffuses into the blood.

The popular perception that sharks must keep swimming in order to breathe is partly true, but only for some species under certain conditions. When they are swimming, the forward motion does indeed force water into their mouths and over the gills and, consequently, highly mobile species such as shortfin makos and blues suffocate fairly quickly if they stop moving (for example, if they are caught in a fishing net). But bull sharks, lemon sharks and many other species can actively pump water over their gills by opening and closing their mouths, and some bottom-dwellers do this as a matter of course.

Sharks also have holes behind their eyes (one on each side of the head) called spiracles. These are particularly large in many bottom-dwelling species, and may be used as intake valves for breathing. If they were to use their mouths, which lie very close to the seabed, they could choke their gills with debris or sand particles. In most other species, the spiracles are barely visible and serve no known purpose. An interesting exception is the whale shark, which has very large spiracles that are used as hiding places by its accompanying community of small fishes.

Sharks tend to have relatively large brains. At least, the ratio of brain to body weight is normally higher than in most bony fishes and is more comparable with small mammals. Although this does not necessarily mean that they are particularly intelligent, experiments suggest that some sharks can learn surprisingly quickly.

Sensing the environment

Sharks use a combination of powerful senses, including some unavailable to humans, to find their way around, hunt prey and avoid predators.

In many species, each sense comes into play at a particular distance from the potential food source. Initially, sharks use sound, which travels much farther and five times faster in water than it does in air. If they hear something interesting, perhaps several kilometres away, they will investigate. Then they are likely to pick up a scent trail, which might be blood or another body fluid, and follow it until they are within visual range at a distance of tens of metres. They might bump the target to obtain some tactile information and, if it seems to be edible, attack. They roll back their eyes or cover them with special protective membranes, and switch to a 'sixth sense' that detects weak electrical signals and guides their jaws to the target. Finally, they take an exploratory bite and, if the prey tastes satisfactory, keep feeding.

There is strong evidence that no single sense works in isolation. When lemon sharks are captured and released several kilometres away, they are able to find their way back to the capture site even if their eyes are covered, their nostrils blocked or their electroreceptors disrupted with magnets.

Sharks do not have vocal cords and have no way of vocalizing underwater (they communicate with one another primarily by scent and body language), but they do have an acute sense of hearing. It is one of their longest-range senses and enables them to detect sounds from hundreds of metres or even several kilometres away. They can hear a wide range of sounds, including those within our own hearing range, but are most attracted by the low-frequency sounds produced by struggling or injured fish (and, indeed, by healthy people when they are playing in the water). The sound of a struggling fish works like a dinner bell and can attract sharks over a wide area within minutes. Sharks do not have external ear flaps, which would create turbulence and noise while swimming, but do have inner ears that open to the outside through tiny holes on the top of the head. Their ears detect sound, of course, but also help the sharks to keep their balance.

In a way, sharks can 'hear' or, at least, detect vibrations passing through the water, with their whole bodies. They have special organs, lying just below the skin and running all the way from the head to the tail on each side of the body, called lateral lines. These are fluid-filled canals with tiny 'hair cells' that are triggered by the slightest changes in water pressure. They enable the sharks almost to feel the presence of an object in the water – in a way that has been described as touching at a distance. The lateral-line system probably plays an important role for a hunting shark within about 100 m/328 ft.

Smell is the ability to detect dissolved molecules, whether they are in the air or in water, and for a shark it is effectively a form of long-distance tasting. The main difference is that the water is 'tasted' by special receptor cells in the nostrils rather than by taste buds inside the mouth.

It is strange for us to think of smelling underwater because, if we tried to do it, we would drown. But a shark's nostrils are not connected to the respiratory system. They are adapted exclusively for smelling and are packed with odour-detecting cells. Sharks also have very large olfactory centres in their brains and, not surprisingly, have some

impressive smelling abilities. It has even been claimed that certain species, such as grey reef sharks, can detect one part fish extract in 10 billion parts water. Even if their smelling ability is 1000 times less than this particular calculation, it is still the equivalent of detecting a few drops of blood in an average-sized swimming pool (although, of course, this is different to an open water setting and is dependent on other conditions being just right – but it gives an idea of their extraordinary abilities). In moving water they are able to detect blood and other body fluids from at least hundreds of metres away. They immediately swim up-current to investigate, often taking a zigzag course to sample the water for areas of greatest concentration. Some sharks are also believed to smell the air in their constant search for a meal.

Sharks also have good eyesight, with an excellent field of vision, the ability to see in very dim light and, in many species, even colour vision. Some have a 'third eye' as well – a thin area on top of the skull leading to the pineal gland in the brain. This cannot form an image, but is sensitive to light and may help the sharks to regulate their biological clocks and activity cycles.

They can see in almost all directions, because their eyes are set wide apart and they swing their heads from side to side while swimming. They also have binocular vision immediately in front, enabling them to judge distances fairly accurately. Open-ocean species are believed to be relatively far-sighted, while reef dwellers are probably a little short-sighted, although recent research suggests that lemon sharks (and possibly some other species) can focus on near and distant objects.

Sharks' eyes are adapted to cope well in low light and, on average, are roughly 10 times more sensitive to light than our own eyes. Their night vision is so good that some experts believe they are able to hunt by starlight. Like mammals, they can dilate their pupils, but they also have a reflective mirror-like layer in each eye to boost the available light still further. This 'tapetum lucidum' is located behind the retina and effectively doubles the amount of light reaching the photo-receptors in the eye. It is the tapetum that makes a shark's eyes shine when it is caught in torchlight on a night dive. When the light gets too bright, many sharks are able to protect their eyes by covering the tapetum with mobile, melanin-filled cells known as melanoblasts. Species living near the surface also have special pigments in their lenses, which are believed to help screen out harmful ultraviolet radiation. Deep-water species do not need such protection, and have exceptionally large eyes to help them see in the near-total darkness of the ocean depths. Since there is no colour in deep water, they can only see in black and white, but most species can probably see in colour. They are believed to be most sensitive to the blue-green end of the spectrum, which accounts for most of the light in the sea.

Sharks use a combination of powerful senses, including some unavailable to humans, in their constant search for food.

Most sharks have upper and lower eyelids that do not move, but requiem sharks and some other species have a unique structure called a nictitating membrane, which is a thick, fleshy third eyelid at the bottom of the eye. This can cover the eye completely and protects it when the shark is feeding or in other potentially hazardous situations. Mackerel sharks such as great whites, which do not have nictitating membranes, protect their eyes by rolling them up into their sockets just before an attack.

A good sense of taste helps a shark to decide what is edible and what is not. As well as taste buds inside the mouth, some species have fleshy, whisker-like structures, called barbels, which may also be taste organs. Taste is important in helping a shark to avoid toxic animals, which are immediately spat out, and it probably helps them to select the most appropriate and beneficial prey.

Perhaps the most intriguing and mysterious sense is the ability to detect the minute amounts of electricity generated by the muscles in all living things. Sharks have special electrical receptors, called the ampullae of Lorenzini, which are small, jelly-filled pores on the snout

The electrical receptors, or ampullae of Lorenzini, are just visible as tiny pores on the snout of this great white shark.

and lower jaw. These are so effective at detecting weak electrical fields – as low as five billionths of a volt per centimetre – that a shark can find a prey animal even if it is completely buried in sand or mud on the seabed. Hammerheads are believed to use their flattened heads like metal detectors (except that they are detecting electrical fields) by sweeping them back and forth over the sand in search of stingrays.

The range of the electroreceptors is about 30 cm/12 in, and they are particularly important in the final split second of an attack. Sharks protect their eyes (because they are vulnerable to damage from struggling prey) and are effectively swimming blind just before they hit – so this is when the electro-sensory system takes over. It might explain why sharks sometimes attack divers in safety cages. Rather than trying to get at the divers themselves, they are more likely to be responding to the weak electrical field generated by the metal of the cage. It might also explain why sharks often repeatedly attack their original victim, even when there are other people in the water nearby. Wherever the skin is broken there is a much stronger electrical 'aura' (and, of course, more olfactory clues) which is precisely where their sixth sense guides them.

Many animals, from bees to whales, are able to use the earth's magnetic field like the contours on a map, to navigate. Research has revealed tiny crystals of a magnetic material (a form of iron oxide known as magnetite) in the soft tissues covering their brains. One theory is that these crystals continually orientate themselves in line with natural magnetic force fields, rather like tiny compass needles, and by sensing changes in the way they are facing, the animals can work out the direction in which they are travelling. Magnetite has not been found in sharks but, because of the close relationship between magnetism and electricity, they may be able to use a similar system to navigate across vast areas of open ocean. An ocean current creates an electrical field as it flows through the earth's magnetic field – so does a shark's body – and it is possible that sharks can read the relative fluctuations in these two fields like a map.

The ultimate predator

Sharks are perhaps best known for their impressive teeth. Their shape, size and number vary enormously from one species to another, depending on their diet. Surface-feeding sharks tend to have sharp teeth to seize and hold soft-bodied, struggling prey, while bottom-feeding sharks have flattened teeth for crushing the shells of shellfish and crustaceans. Great white sharks have large, serrated triangular teeth to saw through the flesh and bones of their mammalian prey, while whale sharks and basking sharks have tiny, vestigial teeth that appear to serve no dietary purpose (they may be used by the male to hold onto the female during mating). In fact, the teeth can be so distinctive that a species can often be identified by a single tooth or even by its tooth marks in a shark-attack victim. A single shark may, however, have several different kinds of teeth, designed for catching, cutting or crushing their food (although they lack both the molars and the musculature that would enable them to chew). In the dusky shark, for example, the teeth in the lower jaw are straight and pointed to grab and hold onto its prey, while those in the upper jaw are serrated, asymmetrical and triangular to cut through the prey.

Sharks' teeth are made of dense, bone-like tissue and are embedded in the gums, rather than in the jaw. They are continually being shed and replaced with new ones – a conveyor-belt process that begins even before the sharks are born. Behind each functional tooth is a replacement, or understudy, ready to move into place as soon as the first one is worn, broken off or lost. Behind the replacement is another developing tooth, and so on. Replacement teeth are usually folded down against the gums and move forward and upright only when they are needed. In most species, the teeth are replaced one by one, rather than all at once, although the cookiecutter shark is a notable exception. The speed of tooth replacement depends upon the species, the age of the individual, the season and environmental factors such as water temperature. A juvenile great white shark's teeth may be replaced as often as once a week, and lemon sharks are believed to produce no fewer than 40,000 teeth in their 50-year lifespan.

A shark's jaws are just as impressive as its teeth. They are only attached to the skull by muscles and ligaments, enabling some species to throw their jaws forward, like an outstretched arm, and open them very wide. Consequently some sharks are able to bite off lumps of flesh that are far too big to swallow: a great white shark can easily cut a 10-kg/22-lb chunk of blubber from a whale carcass in a single bite. The jaws are also powerful, although many of the figures quoted for the force of a shark's bite are nonsense. In studies, the biting force of most species is not much more impressive than it is in humans. The difference, of course, lies in the teeth – a shark's razor-sharp teeth can cause considerable damage. This partly explains how a tiger shark is able to bite through turtle shell.

Sharks are all carnivorous (there are no herbivorous members), but they are not all predators. Many of them prefer small- to medium-sized fishes and invertebrates such as squid, but there are plenty of exceptions. The large filter-feeders such as basking sharks prefer microscopic plankton; bottom-dwellers feed mainly on crustaceans and molluscs; large mackerel sharks such as the great white feed, at

least part of the time, on marine mammals; and parasitic cookiecutter sharks bite plugs of flesh out of their victims while they are still alive. Some sharks are surprisingly fussy about what they eat and many have their favourite foods – several hammerhead species have a particular penchant for stingrays, for example. But most sharks are quite flexible in their diets, and a few will take anything from sea snakes to sea birds. The ultimate scavenger and opportunist is the tiger shark, which will swallow almost anything it can get into its mouth, including boat cushions and old boots.

Cooperative feeding has been reported in sandbar sharks, threshers, porbeagles and some other species, although whether this is true cooperation or not is still a matter of debate, and most just happen to come together at a good source of food and compete with one another instead. There appears to be a distinct hierarchy in many species, with smaller individuals waiting for their larger relatives to eat their fill, but there may be some threatening and biting if the competition becomes too intense. When they are really excited a 'feeding frenzy' may develop, during which the participants will bite anything within reach and may even eat one another.

Despite their ravenous reputation, most sharks are not particularly big eaters. They seem to be adapted to a 'feast or famine' regime and gorge themselves when they can, but then might go for days, weeks or even months without another meal. A typical shark will eat its own weight in food roughly once a month, whereas a carnivorous bony fish is more likely to take just three or four days to eat the equivalent amount.

Blue sharks feeding on northern anchovies off the coast of southern California.

Most sharks digest their food relatively slowly (often over several days), partly because they are cold-blooded. Their body temperatures vary with the temperature of the surrounding water. However, some mackerel sharks, such as the thresher, great white and shortfin mako, have a sophisticated modification of their circulatory system that effectively makes them warm-blooded (the extremities remain cool, but the core temperature is warmed) and this results in much faster digestion. The higher temperature increases the activity of the digestive enzymes, enabling the sharks to feed again rapidly, should the opportunity arise.

Sharks often swallow indigestible matter, such as bones and shells. This can all be regurgitated by turning the stomach inside out (it literally emerges from the mouth like an inverted balloon) until it has been washed into the sea.

Although sharks are the ultimate predators, many have surprisingly friendly associations with other fishes – even if they are roughly the same size as their normal prey. Some, such as pilot fish, travel with sharks and feast on their parasites or eat the scraps left over from their meals. Remoras literally attach themselves to their predatory hosts, with the help of special suckers, and ride the oceans for free. Others wait at 'cleaning stations', where sharks queue up for a professional manicure, and some even dare to feed around the predators' mouths. The cleaners get an easy meal and a guarantee of safety, in return for removing all their customers' parasites. Whitetip reef sharks and jack fish may even work together in hunting smaller schooling fishes: the jacks attack first and, when their victims attempt to hide in the reef, the sharks probe them out or drive them into the jaws of their waiting comrades. Sharksuckers even gather on pregnant lemon sharks as they approach full term and, when the pups are born, not only eat the afterbirth but may also assist by breaking and eating the umbilical cord.

Sharks are not immune to predation themselves. The juveniles fall prey to a wide variety of other predators, from crocodiles to seals, and are hunted by many types of larger sharks. As they grow in size, the risk of predation greatly decreases, but even adults can fall prey to orcas and the larger open-ocean sharks. They are also susceptible to cookie-cutter sharks, which are only about 50 cm/20 in long, but are so daring that they have even been known to attack nuclear submarines.

One problem with living in the sea is that animals with a lower salt content than their surroundings tend to lose water by osmosis. But sharks maintain a high concentration of minerals in their body tissues by retaining large quantities of urea (derived from the digestion of protein) and by producing an organic compound called trimethylamine oxide. This keeps them roughly in osmotic balance with the sea, although a small amount of water may diffuse into their bodies. They get rid of excess salt (which is ingested incidentally with food) by excreting salt ions through a special organ called the rectal gland, which is like a third kidney.

Making more sharks

In bony fishes, the female lays thousands or even millions of tiny eggs and these are fertilized by the male outside her body. This is a process known as spawning. Some species look after their fertilized eggs, but most allow them to drift off into the ocean, where only a fraction of one per cent manage to survive long enough to grow up and produce offspring of their own. Sharks use a very different strategy. They mate rather than spawn (in other words, fertilization is internal), rely

In the Andaman Sea, a juvenile silvertip shark swims alongside an adult of the same species – some experts believe that this may be evidence of parental care.

on a smaller number of larger eggs and in many species keep the eggs safely inside the female's body. This system produces far fewer offspring, but they have a much higher survival rate.

Relatively little is known about courtship and mating in sharks. It has only been described for about a dozen species and, even then, most of the observations have been on captive animals in aquariums and marine laboratories. Males and females do not appear to form long-term bonds, but limited evidence suggests that the females are quite particular about which males they will accept as mates. Perhaps as a result, the males seem to take part in dominance displays and will even attack their subordinates. It is unclear how the females signal that they are ready to mate, but they probably release a chemical message into the water. As soon as they have done so, they may be pursued by several different males.

Mating can be a brutal affair. The male bites the female on the back, flanks or fins – perhaps to stimulate her – and frequently inflicts quite severe wounds. In some species the females have particularly thick skin (up to three times thicker than in the male), but even this extra protection does not always save them from injury.

The male shark has two external reproductive organs, known as claspers, which develop from medial folds in the pelvic fins and are analogous to the penis in mammals. The term 'clasper' was originally coined by Aristotle, who mistakenly believed that males used them to clasp, or grab, the females. While biting his mate, the male flips the female over or wraps his tail around her, inserts one of his claspers into her cloaca (a slit that also contains the urinary and anal openings) and discharges the seminal fluid. In many species the clasper is firmly anchored inside the cloaca by spines or hooks. After mating, female sharks sometimes store the sperm for many months or even years before the eggs are fertilized, and might even use the sperm from a single mating over several breeding seasons.

Sharks use two main strategies for dealing with the fertilized egg: oviparity, which is the most 'primitive' method and involves laying eggs; and viviparity, which is the most 'advanced' method and involves live birth. There are two main forms of viviparity: yolk-sac viviparity or lecithotrophy (which used to be termed ovoviviparity), in which the eggs develop inside the mother's uterus and obtain their nutrients exclusively from the yolk; and matrotrophy, in which the mother provides the nutrients (in some cases via a placenta).

Horn sharks, swell sharks, cat sharks and some other species package each egg in a special case or pouch. Many egg cases have tendrils, which safely anchor them to rocks or seaweed on the seabed; some have sticky sides, providing a Velcro-like attachment; and others are corkscrew-shaped, ready to be anchored in the sand or wedged into a crevice. A female horn shark will actually pick up the soft, freshly laid egg cases in her mouth and deposit them in crevices so that, when they harden, they are firmly wedged. Each developing embryo lives off the egg yolk, inside its case, and when it is fully developed it struggles out into the open sea. Empty egg cases often wash ashore, and these are the so-called 'mermaid's purses' found by beachcombers.

In tiger sharks, nurse sharks, makos and other viviparous species, the eggs develop inside the relative safety of the mother's uterus. Each pup has its own yolk sac for nourishment and it 'hatches' out of a membranous covering before being born. It is believed that the embryos receive no nutrition directly from the mother, although the females of mackerel sharks continue to ovulate unfertilized eggs after the first embryos have hatched, to provide an additional source of food. The egg-eating embryos are known as oophagous. In sand tiger sharks, the first-hatched pups also feed on their smaller siblings – so only two pups are born, one from each of the two uteri. This is known as uterine cannibalism.

As soon as this young lemon shark was born, off the coast of the Bahamas, striped sharksuckers moved in to feed on the birth-sac membrane.

In the most advanced strategy (relatively speaking), requiem sharks and their relatives have developed a system that is quite remarkable for fishes. Viviparity in these more modern sharks is almost identical to our own live-bearing strategy, although it evolved millions of years earlier. Inside the mother the embryos are connected to a tissue called the yolk-sac placenta, which serves exactly the same function as the placenta in mammals, providing nourishment directly from the mother's bloodstream to the developing embryos. When the pups are born, the mother expels an afterbirth, consisting of the placenta and embryonic membranes.

Gestation periods vary enormously, with some smaller sharks taking as little as five to six months and most large ones nine to twelve months. The gestation period in tiger and blacktip sharks may be as long as 16 months, while in basking sharks it could be two years. The size of the newborn pup also varies, from a few centimetres in some lantern sharks to 1.2 m/4 ft in great whites, and as much as 1.8 m/6 ft in basking sharks. The pups are small versions of their parents and are able to swim and feed almost immediately after birth or hatching.

Some sharks migrate hundreds or thousands of kilometres to suitable breeding grounds. Blue sharks are believed to migrate the farthest, and specimens caught and tagged off the east coast of the USA have been recovered 6000 km/3736 miles away off the coast of Brazil and the west coast of Africa. Limited evidence suggests that some individuals may travel even further. Many species give birth in special nursery areas, often in shallow lagoons, bays or estuaries, where there is plenty of food for their newborn pups and where they are relatively safe from larger sharks. Some species, however, give birth in the open ocean, far offshore, or on the ice-cold, deep-sea floor. The number of youngsters produced varies considerably from species to species, from as few as one in each uterus of the bigeye thresher to as many as 307 discovered inside one particular whale shark. Many of the larger sharks seem to reproduce every other year, with a mating and resting year followed by a pregnancy year.

It has long been thought that parental care for most baby sharks is nonexistent after they have been born, but there is limited evidence to suggest that there may be exceptions. Adult scalloped hammerheads have been observed apparently forming protective shields around their youngsters; and at Ningaloo Reef, in Western Australia, a female whale shark was observed from the air, by a shark expert in a light aircraft, surrounded by what appeared to be 14 baby whale sharks. Sharks are slow-growing animals and take a long time to reach maturity. Some larger species are not ready to breed until they are in their late teens – and there is even a population of spiny dogfish in which the females do not reach sexual maturity until they are at least 35 years old.

Shark research

After years of studying captive sharks in marine laboratories, and dead ones brought ashore by fishermen or collected by scientists, we have a reasonable understanding of their anatomy and physiology, but we know surprisingly little about sharks that live wild and free, and many aspects of their lives are still shrouded in mystery.

Studying sharks in the wild can be difficult, not so much because they have sharp teeth, but also because they live in rather inaccessible places and often travel vast distances. But with recent technological advances a number of research techniques have been developed to study them in their natural habitats, and exciting new discoveries are being made all the time.

Some experts have a hands-on approach and enter the water to observe their subjects at close range. One of the most extraordinary pieces of shark behaviour (frequently put to good use by these

Studying sharks in the wild frequently requires a steady nerve: this researcher is attaching a tag to the dorsal fin of a wild tiger shark.

underwater researchers) is 'tonic immobility'. If an active shark is turned over on its back, it goes into a kind of trance and can be handled with little fear of being bitten. It remains in its temporary coma for a minute or more, then revives fairly quickly and swims away as if nothing has happened.

One of the most intriguing and productive areas of study involves tagging. Rather like bird ringing, this is an invaluable and cost-effective way of learning more about shark movements, growth rates and activities over days, weeks, months or even years. Researchers secure or hold the shark alongside their vessel; attach a tag to its dorsal fin or to the body just below the base of the fin; collect relevant data, such as length and gender, the presence of mating scars and the water temperature; then release it as quickly and efficiently as possible. Sometimes blood and tissue samples are also taken, for genetic analysis. Long-term studies have shown no detrimental effects from tagging; besides, sharks do considerably more damage to each other when they are mating or feeding.

The most basic tags are surprisingly simple: each one has a sequential number and contact information for the tagging agency. But they are only useful if the animals are caught later on in their lives, and so the more sharks tagged, the better the chance of some being recovered. This research would be difficult without the help and support of fishermen. Many sports fishermen have now stopped catching and killing sharks in favour of catching, tagging and releasing them, while commercial fishermen frequently send the tag information of sharks caught in their nets to the researchers (sometimes claiming special rewards in the process).

The largest tagging agency is the Cooperative Shark Tagging Program, sponsored by the United States National Marine Fisheries Service. Since it began work in 1962, more than 100,000 sharks of nearly 50 different species have been tagged off the eastern seaboard of North America. Nearly 4000 of them have been recovered.

Such tagging programmes have begun to solve some of the mysteries surrounding sharks. For example, we now know that blue sharks mate off the east coast of North America, but that their pupping grounds are thousands of kilometres away off the coasts of southern Europe and Africa.

Some tags are far more sophisticated: acoustic tags emit ultrasonic beeps that are beyond the hearing range of both sharks and humans, but can be heard with an underwater microphone; satellite tags send signals to satellites orbiting the earth, which are then beamed back down to powerful receiving stations on the ground. These tags can transmit an incredible amount of information beyond the mere location of the sharks – including their depth and compass headings, the temperature of their muscle tissues and the pH (acidity or alkalinity) of their stomachs, plus the temperature of the surrounding water.

A variety of tags is being used by the Hawaii Institute of Marine Biology to study tiger sharks. The sharks are captured just off Honolulu Harbour, by setting lines baited with fish-market scraps, and individuals under 3 m/10 ft in length are fitted with simple numbered tags, while larger ones are fitted with acoustic tags. The more sophisticated tags are about the size of a beer can and are surgically implanted into the peritoneal cavity (the space containing the liver and other organs). The researchers are able to recognize individual sharks by their transmitter bleeps and can then track them by boat and with the help of special monitors placed by divers on the seabed. So far, more than 130 tiger sharks have been tagged and released during the study, which is already gaining valuable insights into tiger-shark movements and home ranges.

Just like all good scientific research, most shark studies are throwing up more questions than they are able to answer. There is still so much to learn, but they are helping to piece together the jigsaw and, more than satisfying our quest for knowledge, they are critically important if the world's dwindling shark populations are to be managed wisely.

5 Shark Conservation

According to the most widely accepted scientific estimate, more than 100 million sharks are killed by people every year. Many experts believe that even this figure may be an underestimate. No shark species has yet been declared extinct, although it is very likely that some have disappeared without our knowledge; several species are critically endangered and a number of regional stocks have definitely become extinct.

Sharks face many threats but two, in particular, account for the majority of deaths:

- Incidental capture by fisheries targeting other species. Drift nets, purse-seine nets and longlines set for other fishes catch many millions of sharks every year.

- Commercial fisheries targeting sharks for their fins, meat, liver oil, skin, cartilage, gill rakers, teeth and jaws. Demand for these products has varied over the years, partly because of technological and cultural changes, but these days the greatest threat by far is the escalating trade in shark fins to make shark-fin soup.

Sharks are also killed deliberately by commercial fishermen determined to eliminate competition for 'their' stocks or to protect their nets, and by sports fishermen willing to pay large sums of money to catch fierce-looking 'trophy' sharks – there is a considerable demand for their jaws and teeth. Several thousand sharks also die every year in the nets set around certain South African and Australian bathing beaches; designed to protect bathers, these do not form complete barriers to keep sharks out, but merely reduce the number of sharks in the area by killing them (along with a lot of other marine wildlife).

We know so little about most shark populations that the consequences of this dreadful slaughter are largely unknown. What we do know is that shark populations have a habit of crashing very quickly when they are targeted and then take many years to recover – if they recover at all. The reason is that 'sharks barely replace themselves', as Professor Samuel Gruber, former Chairman of the World Conservation Union Shark Specialist Group, once commented. They reproduce very slowly: some species are not sexually mature until they are in their mid-teens, a few have one- or two-year gestation periods and others produce as few as one or two pups per year. Sharks are naturally

A sad reminder of the impact of fisheries on sharks: this grey reef shark was caught on a longline set in the Marshall Islands, in the South Pacific.

A set of powerful jaws and large, triangular teeth belonging to a great white shark.

accustomed to conditions of low natural mortality and simply cannot adapt by producing larger numbers of young to replace the huge numbers now being killed by fishermen. Worse still, for much of their lives, many shark species are segregated according to their age or sex, and so heavy fishing can completely eradicate an entire generation or all the females or males, frighteningly quickly.

Some biologists believe that shark populations are so fragile, so biologically vulnerable, that they should never be exploited at all. Yet governments frequently encourage fishermen to take sharks (usually when more traditional species have been overfished and are no longer commercially exploitable) and even offer loans, subsidies and other financial or logistical support to help them make the change. Sharks have become the 'salvation' fishery of the past two decades – and they are being overfished as quickly as the traditional resources. To make matters worse, while most economically important fisheries are now controlled by catch and size limits, closed seasons, gear restrictions and other management practices, only a handful of the 125 countries involved in shark fishing and international trade have even the most minimal control measures in place.

This near-total lack of awareness and management includes a failure to compile shark-catch records in most parts of the world. Specific and consistent monitoring of the catch and trade in sharks is urgently needed to fill the gap. The little information that does exist demonstrates a strong 'boom and bust' tendency – which does not bode well. The porbeagle shark fishery in the North Atlantic, for example, peaked at 8060 tonnes/7931 tons in 1964 but has failed to exceed 100 tonnes/98 tons since the late 1970s; similarly, the soupfin shark fishery in California lasted for only eight years, but in that time it expanded so rapidly that the population was almost fished out and may never recover.

Sharks also suffer from habitat degradation as a result of coastal development and pollution. Habitat requirements vary from species to species and during different stages of their life cycles, but critical shark habitats include shallow estuaries, coastal bays, coral reefs, kelp forests, mangrove swamps and the open ocean. Many sharks – even some open-ocean species – use inshore pupping and nursery grounds. The juveniles may remain in these shallow waters year-round, taking advantage of abundant food, and shelter from predators, and without them many shark populations are doomed. More than half the salt marshes and mangrove swamps in the USA were lost by the mid-1970s, for instance, and a similar story of destruction is being repeated all over the world. Sharks' reliance on such threatened inshore habitats has become a major liability for them in recent years.

But does it really matter if shark populations, or even shark species, are allowed to disappear? Of course it matters, and there are several compelling arguments for shark conservation.

Since sharks are such an integral component of marine eco-systems, their disappearance would disrupt the whole ecology of the oceans. For example, predators control their prey populations in a beneficial way, by stabilizing population fluctuations and removing diseased or genetically defective individuals, and their disappearance can cause havoc. There is some evidence from field research and computer modelling work that this has already happened in some parts of the world.

It also matters from an economical point of view. In many parts of the world, sharks are now worth more alive than they are dead. Divers pay substantial sums of money to see many species of sharks, and shark diving has become a multimillion-dollar business. Sharks that specifically attract divers to a particular coral reef (or any other dive location) are worth much more to the local economy than the relatively small one-off payment a fisherman would receive for their fins. In the summer of 1994, for example, the world-famous sharks of Sha'ab Rumi reef in the Sudanese Red Sea were caught by Yemeni fishermen working their way up the Red Sea reefs. Instead of providing a substantial income for a whole community for life, they provided a few fishermen with a small income for a day.

Last but not least, the loss of such spectacular creatures would make the world's oceans much poorer places. This is an unquantifiable argument, but an ocean without sharks is unthinkable: like the Serengeti without lions, or Vancouver Island without killer whales.

There are signs that some governments, at least, are beginning to take shark conservation seriously. A major breakthrough came in April 1991 when South Africa became the first country in the world to protect the great white shark; Australia, Israel, Namibia, the Maldives, the USA and other countries have since followed suit by affording great whites varying degrees of protection. It was a small step on a world scale, but if the most feared shark in the world can be given official protection, there is hope for the future. Indeed, during the past two years alone several critical laws have been passed to protect everything from basking sharks in the waters around Britain to whale sharks in the Philippines, Western Australia, the Maldives, India, Honduras, the US Atlantic/Gulf of Mexico and most other range states.

There is still a very long way to go – and introducing official protection is one thing, enforcing it quite another. Like whaling, past experience has demonstrated that shark fishing can be incredibly difficult to control and there are cases where shark populations have declined dramatically, even after they have gained legal protection. The next challenge is to ensure that the world's sharks really do receive all the protection that they deserve – at sea, as well as on paper.

Shark finning

The finning trade is by far the greatest threat facing the world's sharks. While shark meat, skin, liver oil, cartilage and other products have an inherent value, it is shark fins that drive the market. In fact, they are so much more valuable than the rest of the shark that, as soon as they have been removed, the whole of the animal is normally thrown overboard to save storage space on the boat for more valuable fishes. Demand substantially exceeds supply, and pressure on sharks for their fins has now spread to virtually every corner of the shark-inhabited world.

Fishermen are being approached by traders and offered good prices for fins and, not surprisingly, inshore shark populations are being targeted and fished out for rapid, but short-lived, profits. A great many fins also come from sharks caught 'accidentally' during other fishing operations. Until recently, sharks were often thrown back alive and intact (one study estimated that 86 per cent of blue sharks caught and thrown back managed to survive), but now they are no longer seen as 'trash' fishes and die because they have become a profitable sideline.

The fins comprise only a tiny proportion of a shark's body weight, and so finning wastes 95–98 per cent of each animal. It is also incredibly cruel – the fins are frequently removed from the sharks while they are still alive. Dumped overboard, the sharks are left to die slow, agonizing deaths from their terrible injuries or from starvation.

The fins are air-dried, and then the supporting collagen fibres are extracted, cleaned and processed to make shark-fin soup. This is a traditional Chinese dish dating back thousands of years – it was an essential part of formal banquets during the Ming Dynasty (1368–1644). The fibres take on a consistency similar to noodles, but have little flavour or nutritional value, so chicken or vegetable stock is added to improve the taste. But the soup is considered a delicacy and sells for a high price in Asia. In Hong Kong, which is the biggest market, a single bowl of shark-fin soup now costs as much as US$100 or more.

Demand for shark-fin soup has increased dramatically since the mid-1980s and there is now an insatiable market for shark fins of almost any size or type. This is partly a result of the explosive growth of the Chinese economy and the rapid expansion of trade with the outside world, witnessed during the 1980s and 1990s. More and more people in mainland China, Hong Kong and Taiwan can now afford luxury food items. There has also been a huge increase in oriental restaurants worldwide, adding to the demand. Meanwhile, improvements in shipbuilding and navigational electronics have exacerbated the problem by enabling shark-fishing boats to go to almost every corner of the globe: these days, few shark populations are too remote to be exploited by modern fishing fleets.

Data on the fin trade are incomplete, because many countries do not report fin exports, but from the relatively few figures available it involves more than 125 countries around the world. The scale of the known trade alone is staggering. The main centre is Hong Kong, which imported, or reimported, 6400 tonnes/6297 tons of shark fins in 1999 – representing the deaths of more than 28 million sharks.

Much of the international trade in shark fins is based in Hong Kong and Taiwan. Like the international trade in other wildlife products, it is ruthless, and the traders are not the kind of people easily persuaded by conservation arguments. There are claims that many traders have already made huge profits smuggling rhino horn, elephant ivory, bear gall bladders, tiger bone and turtle shells. They have simply added shark fins to their inventory, or switched all their efforts to the shark-fin trade. There are huge profits to be made (shark fins are among the most expensive fish products in the world, selling for as much as US$250 per kg/2.2 lb) and shark fins do not even have to be smuggled. No one seems to be as interested in the fate of sharks as they are in rhinos, elephants, bears, tigers and turtles, so the traders probably cannot believe their luck.

A major breakthrough came on 6 June 2000, when the US House of Representatives passed the Shark Finning Prohibition Act by a landslide

OVERLEAF
The body of a grey reef shark, killed for its fins, lies on the bottom of the Andaman Sea.

vote of 390–1. Shark finning had already been banned, since 1993, in the US Atlantic and the Gulf of Mexico, but sharks in the US Pacific remained unprotected. A major concern was the number of blue sharks being killed by Hawaiian longline fishermen targeting tuna and swordfish, which climbed from 2289 in 1991 to 60,857 in 1998 – an astonishing 2500 per cent increase. The sharks were caught incidentally but were being killed for their fins. The Act, which was formally passed by the US Senate on 7 December 2000, now makes finning illegal in all US waters. It prohibits the landing or possession of shark fins without the carcasses and, since whole shark carcasses would compete for freezer space with much more valuable tuna and swordfish, this should make finning uneconomical for the fishermen.

Prior to the US ban, shark finning was already banned in the waters of South Africa, Oman and Brazil, and it has recently been banned by Costa Rica and India. Meanwhile, a finning ban (including a package of measures such as methods of enforcement and new ways of monitoring the fin trade) is likely to be proposed by the EU Fisheries Commission in 2002.

But with so many countries involved in the shark-fin trade, and so many sharks migrating across international borders or living in international waters, there is an urgent need for a global agreement to protect and manage them properly. With this in mind, an International Plan of Action for the Conservation and Management of Sharks has been developed by the Food and Agricultural Organization (FAO). But participation is voluntary and, although it includes many strong conservation recommendations, the Plan is designed primarily to ensure the long-term sustainable use of sharks.

Shark fins drying outside a fish market in Trincomalee, Sri Lanka.

Shark skin, meat, liver oil, cartilage and other products

Sharks have been hunted for a variety of products since time im-memorial and, at one time or another, every part has been used for some purpose. The teeth of Greenland sleeper sharks were used by Inuit people to make knives; European artisans used shark skin to cover books, jewellery boxes and spectacle cases; Tasmanians chopped up the whole bodies to fertilize their orchards; and sponge fishermen in Florida threw the liver oil on to the surface of the water to help them see the bottom more clearly.

Dried, but untanned, shark skin is called shagreen. Before the invention of sandpaper, it was used by carpenters to smooth and polish wood; and it was used to cover sword handles to provide a grip that would not become slippery when soaked in blood. After the denticles have been removed, shark skin can also be turned into high-quality leather with several times the tensile strength of pig skin or cow hide; Texas and Arizona are major markets for shark leather, where it goes into the manufacture of cowboy boots.

Shark meat is highly prized in some parts of the world (French chefs love the white, flaky, boneless meat of mako and porbeagle sharks) and is traditionally eaten dried, salted and smoked by many coastal communities. But it is considered inferior and even unpalatable food by many people, especially in the developed world. Some shark meat is also difficult to process, because the high urea content in the muscles gives it a strong ammonia taste and smell, if it is not bled, rinsed and processed quickly. However, its popularity has grown significantly in recent years, and it is becoming a significant part of the fresh fish trade. The advent of shark hysteria may have helped to make it a trendy menu item in some parts of the West, and there have been many marketing campaigns to overcome consumer resistance. It is even sold under different names to disguise its true identity – dogfish are sold in the USA as grayfish and in Britain as rock salmon.

During the nineteenth and early twentieth centuries the huge, oil-filled livers of sharks sustained a large and important industry. The oil content of the liver varies from zero to more than 90 per cent, depending on the species and the maturity of the shark, and a single basking shark can yield up to 500 kg/1100 lb. The oil is rich in vitamin A and, during the 1930s and 1940s, many children gagged for their own good when they were forced to eat shark-oil extract. The market collapsed in the 1950s, when Dutch chemists introduced a high-potency synthetic vitamin A, which could be manufactured on demand in great quantity and at a fraction of the cost of the original shark-derived product. Shark oil also contains a colourless hydro-carbon, called squalene, which has been likened to ambergris (the

This mako shark was caught off the coast of New Zealand – just one more to add to the horrifying world statistics.

waxy substance regurgitated by sperm whales and once used as a fixative in the perfume industry). Squalene was once used to light lanterns and has many commercial applications – for lubricating fine machinery such as watches and clocks; as a skin rejuvenator in the cosmetics industry; and for pharmaceutical products requiring a non-oily base. Petroleum-based products have driven most of their shark-oil competitors from the market, although some cosmetics manufacturers prefer squalene, and small quantities are still used in certain products.

Sharks have attracted a great deal of attention in medicinal research, because they seem to be particularly healthy animals and rarely get sick. Shark corneas have been transplanted to humans, and the cartilage is a primary source of the compound chondroitin sulphate, a viscoelastic material used as a buffer in corneal transplants and cataract operations. Shark cartilage pills – sold as dietary supplements in health-food shops to bypass the usual government controls on new medicines – have also been widely promoted as a miracle cure for cancer. But scientists conducting the research on which these products are based have publicly denounced them, and a study by the independent Cancer Treatment Research Foundation, published in the *Journal of Clinical Oncology* in November 1998, concluded that shark cartilage did nothing to improve the quality of life or to slow the disease in terminally ill cancer patients. It is true that sharks suffer a remarkably low incidence of cancerous tumours, but this probably has nothing to do with their cartilaginous skeletons and is more likely to be related to their powerful immune systems.

How divers can help

One of the greatest challenges in shark conservation is reversing, or at least mollifying, the traditional 'man-eating shark' image. A single person attacked by a shark makes headline news all over the world, but the relentless slaughter of millions of sharks attracts little attention. Whereas whales and dolphins have oodles of public sympathy on their side, sharks are still seen as the bad guys, to be reviled and destroyed. This attitude not only hampers conservation efforts but actively encourages anti-shark measures – it has even been argued that fishermen are doing the world a favour by killing sharks and thereby making the oceans safer.

Scuba-divers are in a unique position to help. We are among the fortunate few who have the opportunity to see wild sharks in their natural environment, and we are in a privileged position to tell other people the truth about these magnificent creatures. More than that, we have a moral obligation to speak up for them.

If you would like to support shark conservation measures around the world, here are some useful website addresses:

American Elasmobranch Society
www.flmnh.ufl.edu/fish/organizations/aes/aes.htm

The Basking Shark Society
www.isle-of-man.com/interests/shark/index.htm

European Elasmobranch Association
www.dholt.demon.co.uk/elasmo.htm

Fiona's Shark Links Galore
www.postmodern.com/~fi/sharklinks/links.htm

The Shark Trust
www.sharktrust.org

WildAid
www.wildaid.org

6 Shark Directory

There are approximately 410 known species of living sharks. This figure is continually increasing because, on average, several new species are identified and added to the list every year. Taking into account all the sharks that have been photographed or collected, but not yet scientifically described or named, there could be as many as 450–500 species altogether. In addition, there are unknown numbers yet to be discovered.

Many of the world's sharks are quite small, have a limited range or occupy depths beyond the reach of human divers – so relatively few species are commonly encountered, or actively sought, on organized shark dives. This directory covers all the species on the 'must-see' list of most divers and many of the other stars of shark-diving hotspots around the world.

Shark identification

When trying to tell one species from another, scientists working with dead or captured sharks have the advantage of being able to use characteristics that are beyond the scope of recreational divers. These include the size, shape and number of teeth, the type of denticles on the skin, the number of vertebrae, the presence or absence of spiracles and nictitating membranes, and the exact proportion of fin height to total body length. In some circumstances, such precise measurements and detailed observations are the only way of making a positive identification.

Identifying living sharks in the wild can be an even greater challenge. While scientists can spend weeks examining every detail of a specimen, divers may encounter a shark for only a few seconds or minutes. Many species look alike, and one individual may not be identical to the next. There are, however, relatively few species in any one area and, with some background knowledge and a little practice, it is quite possible for anyone to recognize the more common and distinctive species and, eventually, some of the more difficult ones as well.

The key to successful shark identification underwater is a process of elimination, based on a mental checklist of the main features to look for in every animal encountered. One feature alone is rarely enough for a positive identification, and so the golden rule is to gather information on as many features as possible before drawing any firm conclusions.

The oceanic whitetip is one of the easiest sharks to identify, with its enlarged first dorsal fin and long, paddle-shaped pectoral fins.

There are 12 main points on the checklist:

1 **Size**: it is extremely difficult to estimate the exact size of a shark underwater, even if there is something with which to make a direct comparison. One major problem is that *actual* distances underwater differ from *apparent* distances by about 30 per cent – which makes everything seem much closer than it is in reality. With sharks, there is also an understandable tendency to overestimate their length. Therefore, for easy use, this directory adopts four simple size categories: small (up to 1.5 m/5 ft); medium (1.5–2.5 m/5–8 ft); large (2.5–3.5 m/8–11½ ft); and very large (over 3.5 m/11½ ft). Using these categories is much more effective for identification than trying to make an accurate estimate.

2 **Unusual features**: does the shark have any immediately obvious characteristics? The protruding, needle-sharp teeth of the sand tiger, the incredibly long tail fin of the thresher, the cavernous, diamond-shaped open mouth of the basking shark and the unmistakable cephalofoil (flattened hammer-shaped head structure) of the hammerhead are all sufficiently distinctive to make identification, at least to generic level, relatively straightforward.

3 **Colour**: note the main background colours of both the upperside and underside, as well as any distinctive markings. Many sharks are similar in colour, which makes subtle differences all the more important, but the unique coloration of a few species makes them almost instantly recognizable. The tiger shark, for example, was actually named for the dark stripes on its back (although they become paler with age), and the distinctive leopard shark looks striking, with lots of dark spots and blobs all over its body. But bear in mind that colours vary considerably from one individual to another, especially in species with relatively drab markings.

4 **Body shape**: look at the shark's overall shape. Judge whether its body is spindle-shaped, as in the shortfin mako; relatively flattened, as in the whale shark; or long and slender, as in the blue shark.

5 **Head shape**: the head shape, and the main features of the head, can be very important for identification. Is the snout blunt, rounded or pointed? Is the mouth at the end of the snout, as in plankton-feeders such as basking sharks, or underneath, as in bottom-feeders such as nurse sharks? If you are close enough, have a look at the size and position of the spiracles and the size of the nostrils.

6 **Dorsal (back) fins**: the shape and position of the first and second dorsal fins can be invaluable. How large are they in relation to one another and to the size of the shark's body? Do they have broad or narrow bases? Are they curved or upright? Are they falcate (sickle-shaped)? Are the tips rounded or pointed? What is the position of the first dorsal fin on the shark's back – does it begin immediately over the pectorals, behind them, or in front? Are there any dorsal fin spines? What is the background colour of the fins? Do they have any distinctive markings, especially at the tips or along the margins? Some species have very distinctive dorsal fins – the first dorsal fin of the oceanic whitetip, for instance, is huge, rounded and conspicuously marked with a mottled white tip.

7 **Caudal (tail) fins**: what is the overall shape of the tail? Is it almost symmetrical, with the upper and lower lobes roughly equal in length, as in the great white shark? Or is the upper lobe longer, as in the scalloped hammerhead?

Naming the parts of a shark

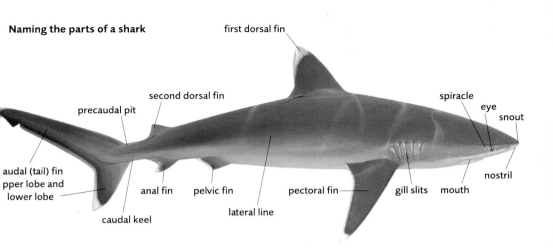

first dorsal fin

second dorsal fin

precaudal pit

spiracle

eye

snout

audal (tail) fin
pper lobe and
lower lobe

anal fin   pelvic fin

pectoral fin

gill slits   mouth

nostril

caudal keel

lateral line

8 **Pectoral fins**: the size and shape of the pectoral fins vary greatly from species to species, as does their position in relation to the first dorsal fin. Are they broad or narrow? Are the tips rounded or pointed? Do they have any distinctive markings, especially at the tips or along the margins?

9 **Pelvic and anal fins**: what shape and size are the two ventral fins? How do they compare with the dorsal fins? Is an anal fin present (in some species, such as cookiecutter sharks, it is absent)?

10 **Gill slits**: most shark species have five gill slits – in fact, all the species in this directory have five – but some species have six or seven instead. Check the position and length of the slits, because they are on the underside in some species and vary considerably in length. The gill slits of an angel shark are on the underside, while those of a basking shark almost encircle the creature's head.

11 **Behaviour**: what is the shark doing? Is it shy, curious or behaving agonistically? Is it lying on the seabed, cruising around in mid-water or staying near the surface? Is it on its own, or in a large school? Unfortunately it is difficult to use behaviour for identification purposes – just because a shark is lying on the seabed does not necessarily mean that it is a bottom-dwelling species, such as a nurse shark – but it can be used to support other evidence.

12 **Location**: the geographical location and habitat provide invaluable clues to a shark's identity, because they help to narrow down the possible species. All sharks are restricted in their range in one way or another. Whitetip reef sharks are found only in the Pacific and Indian Oceans (including the Red Sea), for example, while bull sharks are found virtually worldwide but only in tropical and sub-tropical waters. The habitat can also be a distinguishing feature – Caribbean reef sharks occur mainly around island reefs, whereas oceanic whitetip sharks are more common farther offshore in oceanic waters.

Sand tiger shark *Carcharias taurus*

The sand tiger or ragged-tooth shark is a fierce-looking shark. It swims slowly with its mouth open to reveal several rows of needle-sharp teeth and, as underwater photographer Marty Snyderman once observed, 'It is large enough to get your undivided attention.' Sadly, it has suffered for its appearance. Many sand tigers (originally called sand sharks) have been killed by spearfishermen or caught for display in aquariums. They are also targeted by fisheries, because the time and location of large mating aggregations can easily be predicted. The sand tiger became the first ever shark species to receive official protection, in New South Wales, Australia, in 1984, and has since been protected in other parts of the world – but some populations have declined severely and are already endangered.

Reproduction in this species is better understood than in many others. The sand tiger readily adapts to captivity and will breed in a suitable tank, and major courtship and mating grounds have been studied in the wild for nearly 20 years.

Sand tigers are unusual for several reasons. There are reports of them hunting cooperatively, surrounding and corralling their prey before feeding. They also have a unique ability to swallow air and hold it in their stomachs to maintain near-neutral buoyancy. This works like a swim bladder in bony fishes and enables them to hover motionless, despite being denser than water.

IDENTIFICATION CHECKLIST (ADULT)

- large size
- light golden-brown or bronze upperside, paler underside
- may have darker reddish or brownish spots scattered over body
- high 'hunched' back on stout body (more pronounced in female)
- flattened, conical snout
- long mouth with several rows of large, needle-sharp teeth protruding
- large and broad-based dorsal and anal fins of equal size
- first dorsal fin closer to pelvic fins than to pectoral fins
- elongated tail with long upper lobe

ALTERNATIVE NAMES

ragged-tooth shark, raggie, raggy, spotted ragged-tooth shark, grey nurse shark, sand shark

ORDER	Lamniformes
FAMILY	Carchariidae
MAXIMUM LENGTH	3.2 m/10½ ft; possibly up to 4.3 m/14 ft
REPRODUCTION	yolk-sac viviparous; uterine cannibalism; 1–2 pups (95–105 cm/37–41 in)
DIET	bony and cartilaginous fishes, squid, crustaceans

Danger to divers

Minimal to moderate risk. Has a bad reputation in some areas, but is probably confused with other species. When unprovoked, is normally inoffensive and unaggressive, but has attacked under duress. It feeds voraciously at night and has been known to steal fish from spearfishermen. Its sheer size and protruding teeth should instil caution.

Distribution

Warm temperate to tropical waters worldwide. Absent from the eastern Pacific. Mainly coastal (frequently in the surf zone and shallow bays) or around coral reefs or rocky outcroppings farther offshore. From the surface down to at least 190 m/ 625 ft, though normally in mid-water or near the seabed. Year-round in some regions, but strongly migratory in others (in the northern and southern extremes of its range it will migrate to higher latitudes in summer and lower latitudes in winter).

Good places for a close encounter

(most trips in season): *USA:* Papoose, Caribsea and Atlas Wrecks, North Carolina (p.168); *South Africa:* Sodwana Bay, KwaZulu-Natal (p.207); Aliwal Shoal, KwaZulu-Natal (p.207); Protea Banks, KwaZulu-Natal (p.208); Plettenberg Bay, Western Cape (p.209); *Lebanon:* Shark Point, Beirut (p.214); *Japan:* Ogasawara Islands (p.233); *Australia:* Fish Rock, South West Rocks, New South Wales (p.258); Forster/Tuncurry, New South Wales (p.258).

Thresher sharks *Alopias vulpinus, Alopias pelagicus* and *Alopias superciliosus*

Threshers are instantly recognizable by their enormous scythe-like tails. It is the upper lobe of the tail that is exceptionally long, and may equal the length of the rest of the body. It is used as a weapon, like a whip, to herd or stun prey animals such as fishes or squid. The sharks swim around a shoal in ever-decreasing circles and lash out to herd their prey together. Then they rush in, swatting and swiping, before turning back to swallow their stunned or dead victims. Their jaws are relatively small but, with their sharp teeth, are very efficient at capturing slippery prey. There are three described species: the common thresher (*Alopias vulpinus*), which is distinguished from the others by the position of the first dorsal fin, with its leading edge situated above the trailing edge of the pectoral fins; the pelagic thresher (*Alopias pelagicus*), which is the smallest (up to 3.5 m/11½ ft) and is now seen regularly at sites in The Philippines and Egypt; and the bigeye thresher (*Alopias superciliosus*), which is readily identifiable by the deep grooves above its huge eyes. There is also evidence of a fourth species, from Baja California in Mexico, which is yet to be described and named.

Like the great white, shortfin mako and some other mackerel sharks, the thresher has a sophisticated modification of its circulatory system that effectively makes it warm-blooded. The system is sufficient for the shark to remain active and react quickly even in cold water, and results in much faster digestion, enabling it to feed again rapidly, should the opportunity arise.

IDENTIFICATION CHECKLIST (ADULT)

- very large size
- dark blue-grey above, white underside (ragged break in between)
- white colour of underside extends over pectoral fin bases
- spindle-shaped body
- relatively short, conical snout
- large eyes placed well forward on head
- first dorsal fin considerably larger than second (which is minute)
- enormous upper lobe of caudal fin (about as long as rest of shark)
- slightly falcate, pointed and narrow-tipped pectoral fins

ALTERNATIVE NAMES

thrasher shark, swingletail, swiveltail fox shark, whiptail shark, sailfish shark

ORDER	Lamniformes
FAMILY	Alopiidae
MAXIMUM LENGTH	3–5.5 m/10–18 ft; possibly up to 6.1 m/20 ft (common thresher)
REPRODUCTION	yolk-sac viviparous; uterine cannibalism; 2–4 pups (114–50 cm/45–59 in)
DIET	small schooling fishes, squid, octopuses, pelagic crustaceans

(Illustration shows common thresher)

Danger to divers

Moderate risk. Does not appear to act aggressively in the company of divers, but its large size and powerful tail make it an animal to approach with caution. Some attacks on boats have been reported. There is one anecdotal account from 30 years ago of a fisherman off the eastern seaboard of the USA who was decapitated by a tailstroke from a big adult.

Distribution

Warm temperate to tropical waters virtually world-wide. Mainly an open-ocean shark, though occasionally encountered near reefs, and commonly feeds near rocky drop-offs or kelp beds. Juveniles frequently come inshore and even enter shallow bays. From the surface down to at least 360 m/ 1180 ft.

Good places for a close encounter (pelagic thresher)

(most trips in season): *The Philippines:* Malapascua Island, Cebu (p.224); **(many trips in season):** *Egypt*: Daedalus Reef (p.216).

Basking shark *Cetorhinus maximus*

This is the second-largest fish in the sea, after the whale shark. Essentially an industrial-sized mouth with fins, it feeds on tiny planktonic animals and can filter the equivalent of a 50-m/164-ft swimming pool every hour.

Its skin is unique for being coated with a thick, foul-smelling mucus. It also has a massive liver, containing up to 2300 litres/500 gallons of oil and filling a substantial part of the body cavity, which serves as a float to help maintain neutral buoyancy.

The basking shark is shrouded in mystery and we do not even know where it goes for much of the year. It spends the summer months feeding near the surface and then, as winter arrives and the density of plankton falls, it disappears for at least four or five months. Basking sharks can be observed easily from above the surface. They cruise slowly through the water at the speed of about two knots, sometimes with their huge first dorsal fins, the upper lobes of their tail fins and even their snouts protruding high into the air. They have also been reported jumping out of the water.

IDENTIFICATION CHECKLIST (ADULT)

- very large size
- irregular shades of greyish-brown to black
- swims slowly at surface (sometimes with first dorsal fin and upper lobe of caudal fin exposed)
- enormous gill slits almost encircle head
- conical, pointed snout (sometimes bulbous tip) – less pronounced with age
- huge mouth (diamond-shaped when open) with minute hooked teeth
- small eyes
- high, erect and angular first dorsal fin (up to 2 m/6½ ft tall)
- second dorsal and anal fins less than half size of first dorsal fin
- long, relatively broad pectoral fins

ALTERNATIVE NAMES
basker, sun fish

ORDER	Lamniformes
FAMILY	Cetorhinidae
MAXIMUM LENGTH	10 m/33 ft; some reports up to 15.2 m/50 ft
REPRODUCTION	yolk-sac viviparous; probably uterine cannibalism; 2–6 pups (est. 150–70 cm/59–67 in – the largest size at birth of any known shark)
DIET	small plankton, including fish eggs and crustacean larvae, possibly small schooling fish

Danger to divers

Minimal risk. Unaggressive and does not object to close approach, but its large size should inspire some caution, and its skin may cause abrasive injuries if touched. No attacks on swimmers or divers reported, although has sunk hunter boats.

Distribution

Cool temperate waters worldwide. Occurs very close to land (even in enclosed bays), as well as offshore. Noteworthy for its seasonal appearance in known localities and subsequent disappearance.

Good places for a close encounter
(most trips in season): *UK:* Isle of Man (p.202); Cornwall (p.202).

Shortfin mako shark *Isurus oxyrinchus*

The shortfin mako is a highly prized gamefish and featured in Ernest Hemingway's novel *The Old Man and the Sea*. But surprisingly little is known about its biology and natural history. It is a pursuit predator that actively chases down its fleeing prey, and is probably the fastest of all sharks. Determining how fast a shark (or any other fish) can swim is notoriously difficult, and all sorts of exaggerated claims have been made, but it can probably reach speeds of 35–56 kmh/22–35 mph. The shortfin mako is a spectacular jumper and has been known to launch itself more than 6 m/20 ft into the air when hooked.

Like the great white, the thresher and some other mackerel sharks, the shortfin mako has a sophisticated modification of its circulatory system that effectively makes it warm-blooded. By retaining body heat, the muscles are bathed in warm blood (about 5–7 °C above the temperature of the surrounding water), which is an adaptation for fast, efficient swimming and gives the mako an advantage over its cold-blooded prey. In contrast, the body temperature of other pelagic sharks is no more than a fraction of a degree above the sea temperature.

The closely related longfin mako (*Isurus paucus*), which has longer pectoral fins and a blunter snout, seems to be the least common of the two species.

IDENTIFICATION CHECKLIST (ADULT)

- large to very large size
- dark blue upperside, white underside
- spindle-shaped body
- long, conical and pointed snout
- long, slender, needle-like teeth visible even when mouth closed
- large black eyes
- crescent-shaped tail (upper and lower lobes of equal length)
- minuscule second dorsal fin and anal fin
- short, broad, narrow-tipped pectoral fins
- keel present

ALTERNATIVE NAMES
bonito shark, blue pointer

ORDER	Lamniformes
FAMILY	Lamnidae
MAXIMUM LENGTH	4 m/13 ft; most smaller
REPRODUCTION	yolk-sac viviparous; probably uterine cannibalism; 4–16 pups (60–70 cm/24–28 in)
DIET	bony and cartilaginous fishes, including swordfish and other billfishes and other sharks; very large individuals may feed on marine mammals

Danger to divers

Potentially high risk. Its predominantly open-ocean habitat limits contact with people, and so real risk is largely unknown. Some attacks reported, and its speed, power and quick determination in the presence of a feeding stimulus instil caution among experienced divers. Large individuals may actively feed on marine mammals and probably pose the greatest threat; smaller individuals have been hand-fed by divers and, although they are bold and fast, are probably not high risk.

Distribution

Warm temperate to tropical waters worldwide. Mainly an open-ocean shark, but sometimes encountered inshore. From the surface down to at least 480 m/ 1580 ft. In extreme northern and southern parts of its range it tends to migrate to higher latitudes in summer. Seems to have a strong preference for waters in a precise temperature range (17–22 °C /

63–72 °F) and will migrate geographically and between depths to stay within this range.

Good places for a close encounter

(most trips in season): *New Zealand:* Tutukaka, North Island (p.248); Gisborne, North Island (p.248); Hawkes Bay, North Island (p.249); open ocean, Marlborough Sounds (p.249); Kaikoura, South Island (p.250); **(many trips in season):** *USA:* San Clemente Island, California (p.164); 9-Mile Bank, San Diego, California (p.165); *Portugal:* Cape St Vincent and The Canyon, The Algarve (p.203); *New Zealand:* Whatuwhiwhi, North Island (p.248).

Great white shark *Carcharodon carcharias*

This is the quintessential shark. Its enormous size, powerful jaws that can extend almost like an outreaching hand, rows of large, triangular teeth and jet-black eyes make it the most feared creature on the planet. It is the ultimate super-predator. Yet it does have a predator of its own: a few years ago a killer whale was observed catching and killing a 3-m/10-ft great white at the Farallon Islands, off the coast of California.

Great whites seem to be strongly visual predators and are the only fish known to spyhop – lifting their heads out of the water, apparently to look around for prey. They will hunt deep-diving elephant seals, but many attacks take place on the surface – without warning, from below and behind. Sometimes they leap right out of the water in pursuit. Their teeth hit first and they protect their eyes from the prey's flailing teeth and claws by rolling them back into their sockets.

Once believed to be solitary, the great white is actually quite a social animal. There seems to be a distinctive pecking order, especially around food sources such as a dead whale, with smaller individuals giving way to their larger relatives. Body posturing helps to avoid too many hostilities, but numerous individuals have the scars to prove that fighting is not uncommon.

After years of sports fishing and persecution, the great white is quite rare, but it is now one of the most widely protected sharks in the world.

IDENTIFICATION CHECKLIST (ADULT)

- large to very large size
- slate-grey or bronze-grey upperside, white underside (separated by a distinct line)
- stout, spindle-shaped body
- long, conical snout
- large mouth (rarely closed) with protruding, triangular serrated teeth
- large, jet-black eyes
- long gill slits
- crescent-shaped tail almost symmetrical
- large first dorsal fin
- minuscule second dorsal fin and anal fin
- pectoral fins tipped in black on underside

ALTERNATIVE NAMES

white shark, white pointer, white death

ORDER	Lamniformes
FAMILY	Lamnidae
MAXIMUM LENGTH	6.4 m/21 ft; rarely more than 5.5 m/18 ft
REPRODUCTION	yolk-sac viviparous; uterine cannibalism; 2–10 pups (120–150 cm/47–59 in)
DIET	seals, sea lions, dolphins, bony and cartilaginous fishes, invertebrates, carrion (will 'taste test' almost anything)

Danger to divers

Potentially high risk. Believed to be responsible for nearly a quarter of all reported attacks on swimmers, divers and surfers – and for considerably more attacks than any other species (although this may change as more attacks are attributed to bull sharks). A willingness to hunt in surf brings it into regular contact with people. Approximately a quarter of all attacks prove fatal. Great whites have, however, investigated divers very closely indeed without causing harm. Boats may be attacked, especially where there is a feeding stimulus, and on rare occasions have even been sunk.

Distribution

Mainly cold to warm temperate waters worldwide. Primarily within a 14–22 °C/57–72 °F temperature range, but now known to tolerate a broader range from 5–26 °C/41–79 °F or more, and larger individuals are known to penetrate the tropics. Mainly coastal (will enter the surf and shallow bays), but also around offshore continental islands. Large individuals travel across open ocean and occasionally appear around oceanic islands. Often found near land where seals and sea lions congregate. From the surface down to the seabed at depths of at least 1280 m/4200 ft. Most populations are small and highly localized, with the greatest concentrations in California, South Africa and Australia, and a significant population in the Mediterranean.

Good places for a close encounter

(most trips in season): *Mexico:* Guadalupe Island, Baja California (p.173); ***South Africa:*** Mossel Bay, Western Cape (p.210); Dyer Island, Western Cape (p.211); False Bay, Western Cape (p.212); ***Australia:*** Dangerous Reef (p.260); North & South Neptune Islands (p.261); **(many trips in season): *USA:*** Farallon Islands, California (p.159).

Scalloped hammerhead shark *Sphyrna lewini*

Like all members of the Sphyrnidae family, the scalloped hammerhead has the uniquely flattened hammer-shaped head structure known as a cephalofoil, the leading edge of which (in this species) is shaped rather like a scallop.

There is nothing else like it in the animal kingdom. Formed from the front of the skull, which is expanded laterally, the cephalofoil is believed to serve several functions: it improves hydrodynamic efficiency, by adding lift during swimming; it increases the surface area for sensory systems such as electroreception and separates the receptors for systems such as sight; and it may even be used to pin stingrays and other slippery prey against the seabed.

Scalloped hammerheads are best known for schooling in enormous numbers around seamounts (submarine mountains). Several hundred may gather together. This behaviour has puzzled scientists for many years. Unlike schooling in bony fishes, it is unlikely to be a defence strategy against predators, because mature and near-mature hammerheads have little to fear; nor does it appear to be a feeding strategy, since no feeding has been reliably witnessed during daytime; and it is unlikely to be predominantly for repro-duction, because hammerhead schools are composed mainly of females, with considerable numbers of juveniles, and there is little obvious sexual behaviour. Recent research suggests that a seamount may serve as a naviga-tional centre – quite literally, as a magnet. The hammerheads spread out at night to feed, then use the earth's magnetic field to navigate their way back to the seamount to spend the day socializing.

IDENTIFICATION CHECKLIST (ADULT)

- large to very large size
- light grey, bronze or reddish-brown upper-side appears greyer at depth, pale or white underside
- broad, narrow-bladed head
- leading edge of head has prominent median indentation (two smaller lobes on either side)
- first dorsal fin high and moderately falcate
- second dorsal fin smaller than anal fin
- dusky or black-tipped pectoral fins with straight or slightly concave trailing edges
- long upper lobe of caudal fin

ALTERNATIVE NAMES

kidney-headed shark, bronze hammerhead

ORDER	Carcharhiniformes
FAMILY	Sphyrnidae
MAXIMUM LENGTH	4.2 m/13½ ft; most under 3 m/10 ft
REPRODUCTION	viviparous; 12–38 pups (42–55 cm/16–22 in)
DIET	bony and cartilaginous fishes, rays, small sharks, cephalopods, crustaceans

Danger to divers

Potentially moderate risk. Most attacks by hammerheads have not been reliably attributed to a single species, and so there is little information. In large schools normally timid and difficult to approach, especially when divers on scuba are blowing bubbles, but may make close passes to observe divers. Larger and solitary individuals may be dangerous.

Distribution

Warm temperate to tropical waters worldwide. Probably the most abundant and widely distributed of the large hammerheads. May enter enclosed bays and estuaries, but also in deep water adjoining continental shelves. In some areas it aggregates around seamounts during the daytime. From the surface down to at least 275 m/900 ft. Some populations believed to migrate to higher latitudes in summer, but others appear to be resident.

Good places for a close encounter

(most trips in season): *USA:* Flower Garden Banks, Texas (p.165); *Mexico:* Revillagigedo (Socorro) Islands, Baja California (p.170); El Bajo Seamount and Las Animas Island, Baja California (p.172); *Costa Rica:* Cocos Island (p.180); *Ecuador:* Wolf Island and Darwin Island, Galápagos Islands (p.183); *Colombia:* Malpelo Island (p.184); *Tanzania:* Mtangani Reef, Pemba Island (p.205); *Mozambique:* Pinnacle, Ponta D'Ouro (p.206); *South Africa:* Protea Banks, KwaZulu-Natal (p.208); *Egypt:* The Brothers (p.215); *Sudan:* Pfeiffer Reef (p.218); Abington and Angarosh Reefs (p.218); Sha'ab Rumi (p.219); *The Maldives:* Fotteyo (Hurahu) Channel, Felidhoo (Vaavu) Atoll (p.244); Hammerhead Point, Rasdhoo-Madivaru Island, Rasdhoo Atoll (p.247); *Papua New Guinea:* Point P, Jay's Reef and Craig's Ultimate, Eastern Fields (p.263); *Melanesia:* Wakaya Island, Fiji (p.273); *French Polynesia:* The Hammerhead Sentry Point, Eiao and Hatutu, Marquesas Archipelago (p.275).

Great hammerhead shark *Sphyrna mokarran*

This is the biggest member of the hammerhead family and one of the largest predatory sharks in the world. It has a particular penchant for stingrays and it is not uncommon to see a great hammerhead covered in their barbs – one individual was reputed to have no fewer than 96 of them embedded in its head, mouth and throat. The hammerhead uses its broad, flattened head to pin a stingray against the seabed, and then twists around and cleanly bites off a large chunk of the animal's pectoral fin or 'wing'. Once the stingray has been immobilized, the shark takes more leisurely bites.

Great hammerheads also seem to be undeterred by the poisons found in pufferfish and trunkfish, and will take much larger prey. Other sharks frequently appear on their menu and one individual in the Bahamas, measuring some 4.5 m/15 ft long, had a 2.7 m/9 ft lemon shark in its stomach.

It is fairly easy to tell the great hammerhead apart from the scalloped hammerhead, by the relatively straight leading edge of its head and the enormous size of its first dorsal fin, which appears to be out of all proportion compared to the rest of the body. Also, while scalloped hammerheads are frequently found in large schools, the great hammerhead is usually solitary.

The cephalofoil is believed to result in a 'blind spot' directly in front of the shark which could be why it swings its head from side to side as it swims; or, it could be 'scanning' with its electroreceptors, rather like a person with a metal detector.

IDENTIFICATION CHECKLIST (ADULT)

- large to very large size
- bronze, light grey or grey-brown upperside, whitish underside
- no markings on adult fins (second dorsal tip may be dusky in juveniles)
- stout body
- first dorsal fin extremely high, pointed and falcate
- second dorsal, pelvic and anal fins large, with deeply concave rear margins
- base of anal fin much longer than base of second dorsal fin
- pelvic fins have pronounced concave curve to rear edge
- anterior head margin nearly straight with slight median indentation
- extremely long upper lobe of caudal fin

ALTERNATIVE NAMES

horned shark

ORDER	Carcharhiniformes
FAMILY	Sphyrnidae
MAXIMUM LENGTH	6 m/20 ft; most under 4 m/ 13 ft
REPRODUCTION	viviparous; 12–42 pups (50–70 cm/20–28 in)
DIET	mainly stingrays, but also other bony and cartilaginous fishes

Danger to divers

Potentially high risk. Unlike other members of the hammerhead family, which are considered relatively harmless, the great hammerhead should be treated with considerable caution. Has been known to harass spearfishermen, and large, apparently fearless individuals will approach divers closely. Actual hammerhead attacks have not been verified to species, but this species is the most likely culprit.

Distribution

Warm temperate to tropical waters virtually world-wide. Found from shallow coastal waters to the open sea and favours both inshore and offshore reefs. Most often encountered near coral reef drop-offs and adjacent sandy habitats. From the surface down to at least 80 m/260 ft. Some populations appear to be resident, others nomadic and a few (including Florida and China) have seasonal migrations involving a movement to higher latitudes in summer.

Good places for a close encounter

(most trips in season): *Papua New Guinea:* Point P, Jay's Reef and Craig's Ultimate, Eastern Fields (p.263); **(many trips in season):** *The Bahamas:* Orange Creek Wall, Cat Island (p.194); *Turks and Caicos:* French Cay (p.197); *Dominican Republic:* Catalinita Island and Saona Island (p.198); *South Africa:* Protea Banks, KwaZulu-Natal (p.208); *New Zealand:* Whatuwhiwhi, North Island (p.248); *Australia:* Predator's Playground, Holmes Reef, Queensland (p.254); Marion Reef, Queensland (p.256); *Papua New Guinea:* Milne Bay (p.263); *French Polynesia:* Avatoru Pass and Tiputa Pass, Rangiroa Atoll (p.277).

Caribbean reef shark *Carcharhinus perezi*

A common species around coral reefs in tropical and sub-tropical waters of the western North Atlantic, the Caribbean reef shark is familiar to divers in shallow waters close to shore. But its biology and natural history are still poorly understood.

Caribbean reef sharks are probably best known for 'napping' on the seabed. This behaviour was first observed near Isla Mujeres, near the Yucatan Peninsula in Mexico. The sharks were in caves some 20 m/66 ft down, completely motion-less and apparently so tranquil that they could be lifted and handled. Resting Caribbean reef sharks have since been observed throughout their range; indeed, similar behaviour has been witnessed in the whitetip reef shark and some other species. Lying in caves or under ledges, usually during the day, they genuinely appear to be resting. In the Bahamas and other parts of their range, Caribbean reef sharks are easily conditioned to accept fish handouts. They are present all year round and half-day shark-feeding dives, provided by the local dive centres, virtually guarantee sightings. Not surprisingly, these have become some of the most-watched sharks in the world.

Caribbean reef sharks can be fairly difficult to distinguish in the field from a number of similar species, particularly bull sharks, which are occasional visitors to these underwater feeds. But the bull shark tends to be larger, with a stockier body, a slightly broader, more rounded snout and an even more sharply pointed first dorsal fin.

IDENTIFICATION CHECKLIST (ADULT)

- medium to large size
- grey to grey-brown upperside fading to white underside
- may be bronze-coloured on sides
- dusky markings on dorsal and underside of ventral fins and lower lobe of caudal fin
- stocky body
- short, blunt, rounded snout
- sharply pointed first dorsal fin
- long, narrow pectoral fins

ALTERNATIVE NAMES
sleeping shark

ORDER	Carcharhiniformes
FAMILY	Carcharhinidae
MAXIMUM LENGTH	3 m/10 ft; most under 2.5 m/6½ ft
REPRODUCTION	viviparous; 4–6 pups (60–75 cm/24–30 in)
DIET	bony and cartilaginous fishes, squid, octopus

Danger to divers

Minimal risk. Not particularly aggressive, but often has a bold disposition in the presence of food and very occasionally bumps divers. Comes into frequent conflict with spearfishermen, and some injuries reported during shark-baiting dives.

Distribution

Tropical and sub-tropical waters of the western North Atlantic, the Caribbean and the Gulf of Mexico. The most abundant reef shark within its range, particularly common on island reefs. May also be encountered near drop-offs on outer reef edges. From the surface down to at least 30 m/100 ft.

Good places for a close encounter

(most trips in season): *USA:* Palm Beach – Fort Lauderdale, Florida (p.167); *Mexico:* Sleeping Sharks' Cave, Quintana Roo (p.170); *Belize:* Blue Hole, Lighthouse Reef (p.176); Shark's Cave, Tobacco Caye (p.177); Shark Point, Glover's Reef (p.177);

The Bahamas: Shark Rodeo/Spiral Cavern, Walker's Cay (p.187); Shark Alley, Grand Bahama Island (p.189); Shark Junction, Grand Bahama Island (p.190); Bull Run/Shark Reef, Bimini (p.190); Shark Runway, New Providence Island (p.192); Shark Arena/Shark Wall, New Providence Island (p.193); Danger Reef/Amberjack Reef, Danger Cay, Exuma Cays (p.193); Shark Reef, Long Island (p.195); *Turks and Caicos:* West Caicos (p.196); French Cay (p.197); *Cayman Islands:* Shark Alley, East End Wall, Grand Cayman (p.200); *Tobago:* Diver's Dream, Diver's Thirst, Flying Reef and Sisters Rocks (p.201); **(many trips in season):** *Belize:* Gladden Spit (p.178); *The Bahamas:* Shark Hole/Little Hole, Cay Sal Bank (p.187); Lost Ocean Blue Hole, New Providence Island (p.191); Fernandez Bay, Long Bay and French Bay, San Salvador (p.195); *Turks and Caicos:* Shark Hotel, Providenciales (p.196); Shark Point, Salt Cay (p.198).

Oceanic whitetip shark *Carcharhinus longimanus*

The impressive oceanic whitetip is one of the easiest sharks to identify, by its enlarged first dorsal fin and long, paddle-shaped pectoral fins. Its common name refers to the blotchy white tips on its dorsal and most other fins, while its scientific name refers to the length of the pectorals (*longimanus* meaning 'long hands'). It is quite unlike the much smaller whitetip reef shark (*Triaenodon obesus*), despite their similar common names.

The oceanic whitetip roams the open ocean, usually far from shore, and is possibly the most numerous large shark in the world. Some enormous schools have been observed, but lone individuals are more common. They can sometimes be seen cruising at the surface, with their huge pectoral fins conspicuously outspread, and they have even been observed raising their snouts high into the air. Russian scientists have discovered that, by sniffing the air, they can respond to the smell of food much more quickly, and from a greater distance, than if they relied on the 'odour message' reaching them underwater. Once they have found food, they can be very aggressive and will dominate other shark species joining in the feast.

Oceanic whitetips are often seen in association with other species, including dolphin fish and tuna. They are also known to follow several different whale species. They travel with pods of short-finned pilot whales, perhaps taking advantage of the whales' remarkable ability to find squid by echolocation or even feeding on injured individuals.

IDENTIFICATION CHECKLIST (ADULT)

- medium to large size
- brown, grey or grey-bronze upperside, white underside (blotchy intermediate area on sides)
- blotchy white tips on first dorsal fin, pectoral fins, pelvic fins and lower lobe of caudal fin (sometimes also upper lobe)
- stocky body
- enormous, rounded first dorsal fin
- very long, broad, paddle-shaped pectoral fins with rounded tips
- short, blunt snout
- often accompanied by up to several dozen black-and-white pilot fishes

ALTERNATIVE NAMES

whitetip whaler, white-tipped shark

ORDER	Carcharhiniformes
FAMILY	Carcharhinidae
MAXIMUM LENGTH	3.9 m/12³/₄ ft; most under 3 m/10 ft
REPRODUCTION	viviparous; 1–15 (normally 6–9) pups (60–75 cm/24–30 in) – litter size increases with size of mother
DIET	oceanic bony fishes (some cartilaginous fishes), squid and occasionally seabirds, turtles and marine mammal carrion

Danger to divers

Potentially high risk. Considered one of four sharks responsible for most attacks on humans (others are the great white, tiger and bull). Thought to be the main culprit for attacks on survivors of air and sea disasters in tropical waters. Can be nervous, but inquisitive, in the presence of divers and is so persistent it may not even move away when pushed or hit. Warns by 'gaping' (opening its mouth without projecting its jaw) if divers get too close.

Distribution

Warm temperate to tropical waters worldwide. Most abundant between 20 °N and 20 °S and prefers water above 20 °C/68 °F. Mainly an open-ocean shark and most common far from land, but may be seen off deep-water coastal reefs and occasionally in coastal waters. From the surface (which it favours) down to depths of at least 150 m/490 ft. Considered one of the most abundant oceanic sharks.

Good places for a close encounter

(most trips in season): *USA:* Kona Coast, Hawaii (p.156); **(many trips in season):** *Egypt:* Shark Reef and Jolanda Reef, Ras Muhammad (p.214); The Brothers (p.215); *Sudan:* Abington and Angarosh Reefs (p.218); *Australia:* Jervis Bay, New South Wales (p.259).

Silky shark *Carcharhinus falciformis*

Named after the smooth, silky texture of its skin, this shark is an agile predator. It is a fast swimmer, capable of quick, darting movements, and is often encountered at sea with marine mammals.

The silky is believed to be one of the three most common oceanic sharks, along with the blue shark and oceanic whitetip, although it is less abundant beyond the continental shelf. The silky's more energy-dependent speed-swimming habits, and its pursuit-predator lifestyle, may be better suited to offshore areas close to land masses where there tends to be a higher productivity of prey species. Blue and oceanic whitetip sharks tend to have more opportunistic feeding habits. Although it can be quite stubborn, the silky seems to defer to the more persistent oceanic whitetip.

There is little detailed information on the silky's population structure or segregation, and what is known comes largely from fisheries data. There does not appear to be a strong tendency for the sexes to stay apart, but there may be segregation according to size.

In the eastern tropical Pacific, where it is associated with schools of tuna, the silky has been dubbed the 'net-eater' shark because of the damage it causes to purse-seine nets and catches.

IDENTIFICATION CHECKLIST (ADULT)

- large size
- grey, dark grey, bronze or grey-brown upperside, whitish underside
- no conspicuous markings on body or fins
- relatively long and slender body
- long pointed snout (when viewed from side)
- relatively low, slightly rounded first dorsal fin
- very low second dorsal fin
- long, narrow pectoral fins

ALTERNATIVE NAMES

sicklefin shark, net-eater shark, sickle shark

ORDER	Carcharhiniformes
FAMILY	Carcharhinidae
MAXIMUM LENGTH	3.3 m/10³/₄ ft
REPRODUCTION	viviparous; 2–14 pups (70–87 cm/27¹/₂–34 in)
DIET	bony fishes, squid, pelagic crabs

Danger to divers

Potentially high risk because of its large size and tendency to approach divers boldly, but very few attacks reported. May make a threat display to anyone approaching too closely, with back arched, head raised and caudal fin lowered, and has been known to force divers to abort night dives on coral reefs because of its unwanted attentions. Probably not as dangerous as the oceanic whitetip shark, because it has a more easy-going temperament and a more restricted diet.

Distribution

Warm temperate to tropical waters worldwide. Some evidence suggests a water temperature of 23–24 °C/73–75 °F is preferred. Mainly an open-ocean shark, especially near the edge of continental and insular shelves, but also farther offshore and occasionally in shallow water inshore. Frequently found over deep-water reefs. From the surface down to at least 500 m/1640 ft.

Good places for a close encounter

(most trips in season): *USA:* Flower Garden Banks, Texas (p.165); ***Mexico:*** Revillagigedo (Socorro) Islands, Baja California (p.170); ***Costa Rica:*** Cocos Island (p.180); ***The Bahamas:*** Shark Buoy, New Providence Island (p.191); ***Cuba:*** Jardines de la Reina, Júcaro (p.199); **(many trips in season): *Ecuador:*** Wolf Island and Darwin Island, Galápagos Islands (p.183); ***Sudan:*** Sha'ab Rumi (p.219).

Dusky shark *Carcharhinus obscurus*

There are relatively few places where sightings of dusky sharks are virtually guaranteed, but their habit of following ships makes them a familiar sight in some parts of the world.

Like many sharks they have been overfished, but conservationists are particularly concerned for the dusky because, even by shark standards, it is a slow breeder (males reach maturity at about 21 years, females at 17–24 years) and it is therefore likely to take a depleted population a long time to recover.

Like some other sharks, the dusky has different teeth in its upper and lower jaws, designed for the distinct roles of grabbing and holding or cutting through prey. The teeth in the upper jaw are broad, triangular and strongly serrated, while those in the lower jaw have erect, serrated cusps.

Studies in Florida and South Africa have revealed significant numbers of bottlenose dolphins with healed scars and open wounds caused by shark bites. Four species of shark have been implicated: dusky, tiger, great white and bull in South Africa, and dusky, tiger and bull in Florida. Dusky sharks have been found with dolphins in their stomachs (although these might have been scavenged) and large individuals would certainly be capable of preying on medium-sized dolphins. The two animals hunt similar schooling fishes, and the sharks are likely to inflict slash-type wounds on any of their competitors – whether dolphins or other sharks. So whether the dolphins are being attacked as prey or as competitors remains uncertain.

IDENTIFICATION CHECKLIST (ADULT)

- large size
- grey-brown, grey or dark grey upperside, white underside
- pale band along each side of body (to pelvic fins)
- tips of most fins dusky in juveniles (less distinct in adults)
- fairly slender body
- relatively broad, rounded snout with fairly large eyes
- slightly falcate, moderate-sized first dorsal fin
- small, low second dorsal fin
- large, falcate pectoral fins
- long upper lobe of caudal fin

ALTERNATIVE NAMES

dusky whaler, black whaler, bay shark, shovelnose shark, dusky ground shark

ORDER	Carcharhiniformes
FAMILY	Carcharhinidae
MAXIMUM LENGTH	3.7 m/12 ft; possibly up to 4 m/13 ft
REPRODUCTION	viviparous; 3–14 pups (69–100 cm/27–39 in)
DIET	bony and cartilaginous fishes, crustaceans, squid, octopuses, starfish, barnacles, occasionally carrion

Danger to divers

Moderate risk. Sometimes considered dangerous to people and has a bad reputation in several parts of the world, although its behaviour in the company of divers is poorly documented, and few verified attacks have been recorded. Data are limited because of possible confusion with the Galápagos shark.

Distribution

Warm temperate to tropical waters virtually world-wide. Found close to shore, even in the surf zone, but more often above coastal shelves in offshore waters adjacent to the open ocean. From the surface down to at least 400 m/1312 ft, with a tendency to move into deeper waters during cooler months. Normally avoids estuaries and other areas where water salinity is reduced. Strongly migratory in at least parts of its range, moving to higher latitudes during the summer.

Good places for a close encounter

(most trips in season): *Mexico:* Revillagigedo (Socorro) Islands, Baja California (p. 170).

Galápagos shark *Carcharhinus galapagensis*

The Galápagos shark was originally described in 1905, from a specimen found in the Galápagos Islands, off the coast of Ecuador, and for some time was believed to occur only in the Pacific. It is now known to live in tropical and sub-tropical waters virtually worldwide, but its name has persisted.

Although Galápagos sharks do not appear to form properly coordinated schools, small gatherings are not unusual and they have been observed in mixed groups with other shark species. In the Galápagos Islands, over a two-week period in May 1997, an incredible school of more than 10,000 hammerheads was found to contain large numbers of Galápagos and silky sharks.

In the presence of divers, and some other sharks, Galápagos sharks sometimes use a distinctive 'hunch' threat display similar to the grey reef shark's well-documented display. While swimming in a twisting, rolling motion, they arch their backs, raise their heads and lower their pectoral and caudal fins. Silky sharks have since been observed showing a similar display, while bonnethead and blacknose sharks adopt the body posture without the erratic swimming. We are only just beginning to understand what they are trying to say, but threat displays have helped to overturn the traditional image of sharks as empty-headed monsters.

A large, uniformly grey or brownish-grey shark, the Galápagos can be difficult to distinguish from several similar species. But, the lack of distinctive markings on its body or fins is, in itself, an important identification feature.

IDENTIFICATION CHECKLIST (ADULT)

- medium to large size
- dark grey to brownish-grey upperside, whitish underside
- fin tips and edges mostly dusky (but not black)
- inconspicuous white band on flanks
- moderately long, broadly rounded snout
- large first dorsal fin with straight rear edge
- distinctive ridge between dorsal fins (invisible except at very close range)
- upper caudal lobe longer than lower

ALTERNATIVE NAMES
grey reef whaler

ORDER	Carcharhiniformes
FAMILY	Carcharhinidae
MAXIMUM LENGTH	3.7 m/12 ft; most under 3m/10 ft
REPRODUCTION	viviparous; 6–16 pups (60–80 cm/24–32 in)
DIET	bottom-living bony fishes, squid, octopuses, sometimes also garbage

Danger to divers

Moderate risk. Usually wary at first and will circle on the edge of visibility, but then likely to rush in and investigate divers closer. A fast, frisky swimmer, and quite unnerving, but generally curious rather than aggressive. Unprovoked attacks on swimmers have, however, been reported, and it can be threatening. Its large size and fast movements make experienced divers treat it with extra caution.

Distribution

Sub-tropical to tropical waters virtually worldwide. Normally associated with oceanic islands, where it occurs inshore, but also in the open ocean nearby. Prefers clear water with coral reefs and sandy bottoms. From the surface down to at least 80 m/ 260 ft, but often swims just a few metres above the substrata, sometimes in water as shallow as 2 m/6^1/$_2$ ft. Juveniles seem to be restricted to shallow waters (maximum 25 m/80 ft), perhaps to avoid predation by adults.

Good places for a close encounter

(most trips in season): *USA:* Midway Atoll, Hawaiian Islands (p.158); *Mexico:* Revillagigedo (Socorro) Islands, Baja California (p.170); *Ecuador:* Wolf Island and Darwin Island, Galápagos Islands (p.183); *Australia:* Lord Howe Island, New South Wales (p.257).

Grey reef shark *Carcharhinus amblyrhynchos*

In some parts of the world, the grey reef shark has a reputation for its short temper. What it lacks in size it makes up for in belligerence, and its threat display is one of the most spectacular and best-documented natural behaviours in all the world's sharks. When it feels threatened, it arches its back, raises its snout, points its pectoral fins straight down and begins an erratic writhing motion. The display intensifies according to the shark's level of agitation and, ultimately, it will twist its entire body into a distinctive S-shape. If that fails, the shark will attack fast and vigorously, with its mouth agape, slashing the victim.

Grey reef sharks have been known to threaten other sharks much larger than themselves and have even attacked a research submersible. The threats may be a form of anti-predator behaviour, but are more likely to be a form of territorial defence (of their own personal space rather than a particular site). In most parts of the world, if divers respect this personal space, they are easy-going and show no sign of such a short temper.

The sharks patrol their home reefs alone or, more commonly, in loosely organized groups. Typically 20–30 of them will spend the day together, swimming around the deeper part of the reef. At dusk the school breaks up and the sharks glide over the reef looking for food.

IDENTIFICATION CHECKLIST (ADULT)

- small to medium size
- grey upperside, white underside
- first dorsal fin may have irregular, narrow white edge or tip
- second dorsal, anal, pelvic and pectoral fins have blackish or dusky tips
- pronounced black posterior margin to caudal fin
- broadly rounded snout

ALTERNATIVE NAMES

blacktail shark, longnose blacktail shark, grey whaler

ORDER	Carcharhiniformes
FAMILY	Carcharhinidae
MAXIMUM LENGTH	2.5 m/8 ft; rarely over 1.5 m/5 ft
REPRODUCTION	viviparous; 1–6 pups (45–60 cm/18–24 in)
DIET	bony fishes, squid, octopuses, crustaceans

Danger to divers

Minimal to moderate risk. An inquisitive shark, likely to investigate divers (often soon after they have entered the water), even when there is no food stimulus. Quite placid in many parts of the world, but can be aggressive, especially when feeding at dusk, and may react to being approached too closely. Discharging a flash unit during a threat display can also elicit an attack. The threat display is instantly recognizable, but if the warning signs are ignored, it may attack.

Distribution

Tropical waters in the Pacific and Indian Oceans (where it is one of the most common reef sharks), and the Red Sea. Found inshore and offshore, but particularly around coral reefs and in clearer, deeper waters near drop-offs. Will enter shallow lagoons, especially in areas with strong currents. From the surface down to at least 100 m/330 ft (possibly to 280 m/920 ft).

Good places for a close encounter

(most trips in season): *USA:* Molokini Crater, Maui (p.157); *Brazil:* Laje Dois Irmãos, Fernando de Noronha (p.185); *Cayman Islands:* Little Cayman Bloody Bay Marine Park, Little Cayman (p.200); *Egypt:* Shark Reef and Jolanda Reef, Ras Muhammad (p.214); The Brothers (p.215); Elphinstone Reef (p.216); Daedalus Reef (p.216); Rocky Island (p.217); *Sudan:* Pfeiffer Reef (p.218); Abington and Angarosh Reefs (p.218); Sha'ab Rumi (p.219); Sanganeb (p.219); *The Philippines:* Shark Ridge, Apo Reef (p.221); Maricaban Strait (p.222); *Malaysia:* Pulau Sipadan, Sabah (p.226); *India:* Andaman Islands (p.232); *Mauritius:* Shark Pit, Shark Point, Shark Place, Belle Mare and Whale Rock (p.234); *Seychelles:* Marie Anne (Marianne) Island (p.235); *The Maldives:* many sites (pp.238–47); *Australia:* many sites (pp.251–61); *Papua New Guinea:* many sites (pp.262-67); *Melanesia:* many sites (pp.268–74); *French Polynesia:* many sites (pp.275–79); *Micronesia:* many sites (pp.280–86).

Silvertip shark *Carcharhinus albimarginatus*

The silvertip shark was named after the distinctive white tips and margins on its first dorsal, pectoral and caudal fins, which are subtly different to other white-tipped sharks and make it easily recognizable in the field.

Although it is a swift and powerful predator, it tends to become rather lethargic and laid-back as it grows older and larger. Aged silvertips frequently supplement their normal diet of tuna, bonito, flying fish and other open-water fishes by feeding on stingrays and generally slower-moving animals close to the reef or along the seabed. But they often seem to injure themselves in the process and, after close encounters with stingray barbs and collisions with coral, can become heavily scarred as they grow older.

Underwater experiments have confirmed that silvertips will travel long distances to investigate low-frequency sounds, probably because these frequencies are very similar to those emitted by injured fish.

IDENTIFICATION CHECKLIST (ADULT)

- medium size
- grey to dark grey or bronze upperside, white underside
- conspicuous white tips and posterior margins on all fins (may be absent or thinner on second dorsal, anal and pelvic fins)
- sturdy but fairly slender body
- long, rounded snout
- long, semi-falcate and pointed pectoral fins
- long upper lobe of caudal fin
- older individuals may be heavily scarred

ALTERNATIVE NAMES

silvertip whaler

ORDER	Carcharhiniformes
FAMILY	Carcharhinidae
MAXIMUM LENGTH	3 m/10 ft; most under 2.5 m/8 ft
REPRODUCTION	viviparous; 1–11 (usually 5–6) pups (65 cm/25½ in)
DIET	bony fishes, sometimes stingrays and octopuses

Danger to divers

Moderate risk. Has a reputation for being aggressive towards other sharks and will harass divers in some areas (at other dive sites they will investigate divers closely but show no signs of aggression). Can be dangerous if overstimulated or provoked, and should be treated with caution.

Distribution

Tropical waters of the Pacific and Indian Oceans (absent from the Atlantic). Common over continental shelves inshore and offshore. Usually in deep-water drop-offs at open-water reefs, but also around offshore islands, over banks, and in open water far from land. From the surface down to about 800 m/2625 ft.

Good places for a close encounter

(most trips in season): *Mexico:* Revillagigedo (Socorro) Islands, Baja California (p.170); *Costa Rica:* Cocos Island (p.180); *Sudan:* Pfeiffer Reef (p.218); Abington and Angarosh Reefs (p.218); Sha'ab Rumi (p.219); *Myanmar (Burma):* Silvertip Bank, Burma Banks (p.231); *Australia:* Rowley Shoals, Northern Atoll Reefs, Western Australia (p.252); Predator's Playground, Holmes Reef, Queensland (p.254); Watanabe Pinnacle and Scuba Zoo, Flinders Reef, Queensland (p.254); *Papua New Guinea:* Point P, Jay's Reef and Craig's Ultimate, Eastern Fields (p.263); Milne Bay (p.263); Fairway Reef, Inglis Shoal and Kimbe Island Bommie, Kimbe Bay (p.265); Kavieng Region (p.266); Valerie's Reef (p.267); *French Polynesia:* Avatoru Pass and Tiputa Pass, Rangiroa Atoll (p.277); *Micronesia:* Silvertip City, Palau (p.283).

Blacktip reef shark *Carcharhinus melanopterus*

The blacktip reef shark is famous for entering incredibly shallow water. It sometimes swims around coastal lagoons, where the water may be less than 1 m/39 in deep, with its first dorsal and the upper lobe of its caudal fin clearly visible above the surface. It has even been seen in such shallow water that it has had to wriggle across the seafloor with much of its back exposed.

Unusually among sharks, the blacktip reef has only one kind of photoreceptor in its eyes. Most sharks' eyes have both rods (which function in dim light and detect shapes and shades of grey) and cones (which work better in bright light and are able to detect colour). The majority have more rods than cones, although the actual ratio varies from species to species. Shallow-living blacktip reef sharks and deep-living sixgill sharks are the only two species known to have only rods – and no cones. The reason why two species with entirely different habits should share this feature is still unclear.

The superficially similar blacktip shark (*Carcharhinus limbatus*) is found in warm temperate to tropical waters worldwide and occurs in similar habitats to the blacktip reef (although it is also found farther offshore over the continental shelf). Best known for leaping out of the water and spinning longitudinally before dropping back into the sea, it can be seen on dives at Cocos Island, in Costa Rica, and Kalbarri, Western Australia. Compared with the blacktip reef shark, the blacktip is slightly larger, has a smaller black tip on its first dorsal fin (which may be lacking altogether in some adults) and a longer, more pointed snout.

IDENTIFICATION CHECKLIST (ADULT)

- small to medium size
- brownish-grey to brownish-yellow upper-side, white underside
- large black markings (highlighted with white) on first dorsal and lower caudal lobe
- other fins may be black-tipped
- conspicuous white band on flanks
- short, bluntly rounded snout
- horizontally oval eyes
- falcate first dorsal fin and pectoral fin
- upper caudal lobe much longer than lower

ALTERNATIVE NAMES

blackfin reef shark, blacktip reef whaler, black shark

ORDER	Carcharhiniformes
FAMILY	Carcharhinidae
MAXIMUM LENGTH	1.8 m/6 ft
REPRODUCTION	viviparous; 2–5 pups (33–50 cm/13–20 in)
DIET	bony fishes, squid, octopuses, sea snakes, crustaceans

Danger to divers

Minimal risk. Normally timid and easily frightened by an approaching diver, but can be curious. Tends to be unaggressive, but on rare occasions has bitten the legs or feet of people wading in shallow lagoons. Will attack speared fish and may become agonistic towards spearfishermen.

Distribution

Warm temperate to tropical waters in the Pacific and Indian Oceans. In recent years has also entered the eastern Mediterranean, via the Suez Canal. One of the most common tropical reef species. Prefers shallow lagoons and coral reefs close to shore. From the surface down to 30 m/98 ft and will often enter very shallow and turbid water (commonly in the intertidal zone).

Good places for a close encounter

(most trips in season): *Belize:* Blue Hole, Lighthouse Reef (p.176); Bull Shark Pass, Glover's Reef (p.178); ***The Bahamas:*** Shark Rodeo/Spiral Cavern, Walker's Cay (p.187); ***Tobago:*** Diver's Dream et al. (p.201); ***Mozambique:*** Cabo San Sebastian, Bazaruto Archipelago (p.205); ***Sudan:*** Sha'ab Rumi (p.219); ***The Philippines:*** Shark Ridge, Apo Reef (p.221); Maricaban Strait (p.222); ***Thailand:*** Similan and Surin Islands (p.230); ***Myanmar (Burma):*** Mergui Archipelago (p.231); ***The Maldives:*** Rasfari, North Male (Kaafu) Atoll (p.240); Miyaru (Shark) Channel, Felidhoo (Vaavu) Atoll (p.243); ***Australia:*** Watanabe Pinnacle and Scuba Zoo, Flinders Reef, Queensland (p.254); Marion Reef, Queensland (p.256); Lady Elliot Island, Queensland (p.257); ***Melanesia:*** Solomon Islands (pp.268–70); Beqa Lagoon, Viti Levu, Fiji (p.274); ***French Polynesia:*** many sites (pp.275–79); ***Micronesia:*** Peleliu Corner, Palau (p.280).

Blacktip shark

(most trips in season): *Costa Rica:* Cocos Island (p.180); ***Australia:*** Kalbarri, Western Australia (p.251).

Bull shark *Carcharhinus leucas*

Bull sharks have baffled scientists for many years by thriving in both saltwater and freshwater. They are found as far as 3700 km/2300 miles up the Amazon River in Peru, and are known to occur in rivers in Malaysia, western Africa, southern Africa, North America, Iraq and India, as well as in lakes in Nicaragua, Guatemala and New Guinea and even the Panama Canal.

The bull shark's ability to move freely between habitats of such wide-ranging salinity is an impressive physiological feat. It is probably not a permanent freshwater resident, but appears to migrate between saltwater and freshwater, which makes it all the more astounding.

There has been some confusion over the species status of various bull-shark populations and other sharks found in freshwater. The individuals living in Lake Nicaragua were once thought to be a separate species, but are now known to be bull sharks; conversely, all sharks in the Ganges were once believed to be bull sharks, but the rare Ganges shark is now known to be an entirely separate species. Every spring, during the pupping season, hundreds of females gather in shallow lagoons close to reefs off the Florida coast. No one knows whether this ritual triggers the shut-down of their normal feeding behaviour, gives them safety in numbers or whether there is another explanation. Once they have given birth they quickly return to the sea and the pups are left to fend for themselves.

IDENTIFICATION CHECKLIST (ADULT)

- medium to large size
- silvery to dark grey or brown upperside, white underside
- fin tips may be dusky (but not strikingly marked)
- stocky to very heavy-bodied
- short, blunt, broadly rounded snout
- very small eyes
- large, triangular, pointed first dorsal fin with very wide base

ALTERNATIVE NAMES

Zambezi shark, Lake Nicaragua shark, cub shark, shovelnose shark, freshwater whaler, river whaler, Swan River whaler

ORDER	Carcharhiniformes
FAMILY	Carcharhinidae
MAXIMUM LENGTH	3.4 m/11 ft
REPRODUCTION	viviparous; 1–13 pups (55–81 cm/22–32 in)
DIET	mainly bony and cartilaginous fishes, but also crustaceans, sea turtles, birds, dolphins and marine mammal carrion

Danger to divers

Potentially high risk. Considered one of four sharks responsible for most attacks on humans (others are the great white, oceanic whitetip and tiger) and potentially one of the most dangerous sharks in sub-tropical and tropical waters. It is large and powerful, very common, and its willingness to enter murky water gives it ample opportunity to encounter people. Now widely believed to have been the culprit in some attacks attributed to other species, although regularly encountered by divers in some parts of the world with no incident.

Distribution

Sub-tropical to tropical waters virtually worldwide. Prefers shallow coastal waters, including beaches, lagoons and bays. Mainly in water less than 30 m/ 98 ft deep (sometimes less than 1 m/39 in), but occurs from the surface down to 150 m/492 ft. The only shark known to penetrate far into freshwater.

Good places for a close encounter

(most trips in season): Belize: Shark's Cave, (p.177); Bull Shark Pass, Glover's Reef (p.178); **Costa Rica:** Bat Islands, Gulf of Papagayo (p.181); **The Bahamas:** Shark Beach, Walker's Cay (p.188); **Cuba:** Shark's Point, Playa Santa Lucia (p.199); Jardines de la Reina, Júcaro (p. 199); **Mozambique:** Cabo San Sebastian, Bazaruto Archipelago (p.205); Pinnacles, Ponta D'Ouro (p.206); **South Africa:** Protea Banks, KwaZulu-Natal (p.208); **Melanesia:** Beqa Lagoon, Viti Levu, Fiji (p.274);

(many trips in season): USA: Teneco Towers, Florida (p.166); **Belize:** Blue Hole, Lighthouse Reef (p. 176); Gladden Spit (p.178); **The Bahamas:** The Pinnacle, Eleuthera (p.194); Orange Creek Wall, Cat Island (p.194); **South Africa:** Aliwal Shoal, KwaZulu-Natal (p.207); **Myanmar (Burma):** Western Rocky Island and Black Rock, Mergui Archipelago (p.231); **Mauritius:** Shark Pit et al. (p.234).

Bronze whaler shark *Carcharhinus brachyurus*

Named for its bronze, sometimes greyish-bronze, upperside, the bronze whaler shark is a common warm-water species in many parts of the world, although it is surprisingly poorly known.

Its diet consists mainly of bony fishes and dogfish, stingrays and electric rays. However, it is one of the few sharks known to eat jellyfish – which mostly comprise water and are not particularly nutritious, with little protein and a low fat content. Portuguese man-o'-war remains have also been found in its stomach. Bronze whalers are fairly adaptable predators and will even follow fishing boats and grab fish that fall from their nets. They are believed to migrate with their prey in some parts of the world, travelling to higher latitudes during spring and summer.

IDENTIFICATION CHECKLIST (ADULT)

- medium to large size
- bronze to grey upperside, white underside
- larger fins have inconspicuous darker edges and dusky to black tips (especially pectorals)
- faint white band along flanks (almost to pelvic fins)
- fairly slender body
- moderately long, slightly pointed snout
- large, falcate first dorsal fin with pointed tip
- second dorsal fin small and low
- long, falcate pectoral fins
- long upper lobe of caudal fin

ALTERNATIVE NAMES

New Zealand whaler, cocktail shark, copper shark

ORDER	Carcharhiniformes
FAMILY	Carcharhinidae
MAXIMUM LENGTH	3 m/10 ft; most under 2.5 m/8 ft
REPRODUCTION	viviparous; 13–20 pups (60–65 cm/24–26 in)
DIET	bony and cartilaginous fishes, sometimes squid, sea snakes and jellyfish

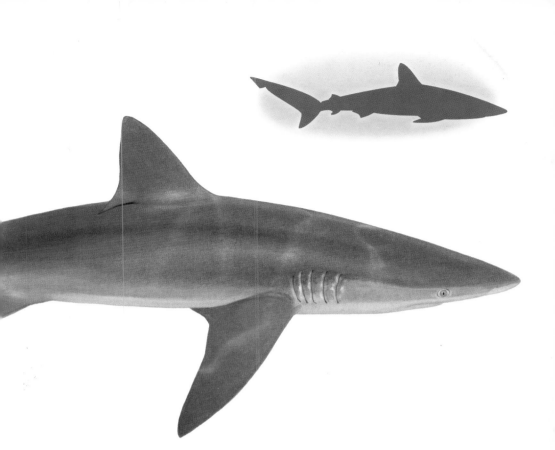

Danger to divers

Moderate risk. Considered dangerous in some parts of the world, and unprovoked attacks have been reported. Problems tend to arise when there is a food stimulus present or when swimmers are splashing about on the surface, but otherwise not a particular danger.

Distribution

Warm temperate to sub-tropical waters virtually worldwide (absent from the north-eastern seaboard of North America and from the northern Indian Ocean). Mainly inshore, especially along rocky reefs and in shallow bays, but also around islands and offshore as far as the continental shelf edge. From the surface down to at least 100 m/330 ft. Some populations migrate to higher latitudes during the summer.

Good places for a close encounter

(most trips in season): *Australia:* Kalbarri, Western Australia (p.251); **Papua New Guinea:** Hammerhead Corner, Shark Alley and Silvertip City, D'Entrecasteaux Islands (p.264); McDonald's Reef and Salamaua Offshore Reefs, Huon Gulf (p.265); **(many trips in season):** *South Africa:* Protea Banks, KwaZulu-Natal (p.208); *New Zealand:* Whatuwhiwhi, North Island (p.248); *Australia:* Lady Elliot Island, Queensland (p.257); Fish Rock, South West Rocks, New South Wales (p.258); Jervis Bay, New South Wales (p.259); *Papua New Guinea:* Bagabag Island, Crown Island, Long Island and Bernie's Wall, Vitiaz Strait (p.262); *Melanesia:* Espiritu Santo and Reef Islands, Vanuatu (p.270); *Micronesia:* Silvertip City, Palau (p.283).

Lemon shark *Negaprion brevirostris*

The lemon shark is named for the hint of yellow in its skin and this, combined with its two nearly equal-sized dorsal fins, makes it easy to identify. The colour provides good camouflage when it is swimming over the sandy seafloor of the shallow water in its coastal home.

Lemon sharks may appear to be sluggish, but they are capable of sudden turns of speed, and can be very determined in pursuit of prey. They are primarily nocturnal, but seem to have peaks of activity during dusk and dawn. Daylight hours are often spent lying quietly on the seabed, where the sharks actively pump water over their gills by opening and closing their mouths. They appear to be resting, but oxygenating the gills in this way uses about nine per cent more energy, and so they may be waiting to be cleaned of parasites by wrasses and other small reef fishes.

Lemon sharks are capable of surviving in extreme conditions, including a wide range of salinity, water with a very low oxygen content and water temperatures of up to 30 °C/86 °F, but they have specific habitat requirements at different stages of their lives. In their first year the pups stay in very shallow inshore waters. When they are two years old they move into other sites within the lagoon, then as adults include the open sandflats and eventually the open reef. At each site only sharks of the same age and size tend to associate with one another. There is a similar species, the Pacific or sicklefin lemon shark (*Negaprion acutidens*), which is found in the Indo-Pacific.

IDENTIFICATION CHECKLIST (ADULT)

- medium to large size
- yellowish-brown upperside, white or yellowish-white underside
- no conspicuous markings
- stocky body (variable – can be long and thin)
- flattened head with short, broad snout
- first and second dorsal fins of nearly equal size
- large anal fin
- upper lobe of caudal fin longer than lower
- long, slightly falcate pectoral fins

ALTERNATIVE NAMES

none known

ORDER	Carcharhiniformes
FAMILY	Carcharhinidae
MAXIMUM LENGTH	3.4 m/11 ft; most under 2 m/ 6½ ft
REPRODUCTION	viviparous; 4–17 (typically 8–12) pups (60–70 cm/24–28 in)
DIET	bony and cartilaginous fishes, squid, octopuses, crustaceans, molluscs and occasionally seabirds

Danger to divers

Minimal risk. Generally considered harmless unless provoked, but can move very fast and inflict a powerful bite. Nearly half of reported attacks on divers and swimmers were provoked. Occasionally bites people wading in shallow lagoons, probably after being trodden on while resting on the seafloor.

Distribution

Warm temperate to tropical waters in the western Atlantic (possibly also the west coast of Africa) and eastern Pacific. Most common in the Caribbean. Mainly clear, shallow coastal waters, especially around reef systems and areas with seagrass and associated mangroves. Will tolerate brackish water of estuaries and is known to enter freshwater at times. Common around docks. From the surface down to at least 90 m/295 ft, but often in very shallow water. Some populations may migrate to higher latitudes in summer.

Good places for a close encounter

(most trips in season): Belize: Shark Point, Glover's Reef (p.177); Bull Shark Pass, Glover's Reef (p.178); **The Bahamas:** Pier 1 Seafood Restaurant, Grand Bahama Island (p.189); **Turks and Caicos:** French Cay (p.197); **(many trips in season): Belize:** Blue Hole, Lighthouse Reef (p.176); Gladden Spit (p.178); **The Bahamas:** Shark Rodeo/Spiral Cavern, Walker's Cay (p.187).

Tiger shark *Galeocerdo cuvier*

The notorious tiger shark is often described as the great white of the tropics. It is a large, powerful shark named for the tiger-like stripes on its back. These distinctive markings are most pronounced in juveniles, and become pale or disappear in large adults.

Tiger sharks were long believed to be nocturnal hunters, spending the day in deep waters offshore, then entering shallow reefs and lagoons after dusk to feed. But recent research suggests that they are more flexible and, given the opportunity, will hunt during the day as well. They are long-distance travellers, at home virtually anywhere in the sea. Individuals around Hawaii were found to patrol regular home ranges of up to 100 sq km/40 sq miles.

The ultimate scavengers and opportunists, tiger sharks probably have the widest-ranging diet of all sharks. They have a large stomach capacity and a wide mouth capable of devouring enormous chunks of food. Their heavily serrated, cockscomb-shaped teeth resemble the teeth in a circular saw and, by moving their mouths in a rolling motion, they can even bite through mammalian bone and the shells of large sea turtles. In season, in some parts of the world, they gather near albatross colonies to feed on young fledglings that fall into the water. There is very little they will not eat; indeed, they will swallow anything that has fallen or been dropped into the sea.

IDENTIFICATION CHECKLIST (ADULT)

- large to very large size
- sandy to grey upperside, creamy-white to white underside
- vertical dark grey to black bars and spots (fade with age)
- body noticeably slimmer behind first dorsal fin
- broad-based first dorsal fin much larger than second dorsal
- massive head with blunt snout and wide mouth
- large, dark eyes
- distinctive flaps over prominent nostrils
- base of tail very slender
- upper lobe of caudal fin longer than lower

ALTERNATIVE NAMES
none known

ORDER	Carcharhiniformes
FAMILY	Carcharhinidae
MAXIMUM LENGTH	5.5 m/18 ft; possibly longer
REPRODUCTION	yolk-sac viviparous (the only non-viviparous requiem shark); uterine cannibalism; 6–82 pups (50–75 cm/20–30 in)
DIET	includes sharks, rays, crustaceans, cephalopods, sea snakes, turtles, seabirds, seals, small cetaceans and carrion

Danger to divers

Potentially high risk. Considered one of four sharks responsible for most attacks on humans (others are the great white, oceanic whitetip and bull) and one of the most dangerous sharks in sub-tropical and tropical waters. Many attacks reported and more than a quarter fatal. Will often circle divers just at the limit of visibility, and occasionally approach for a closer look, but may swim past, with barely a second glance, and the vast majority of encounters pass without incident.

Distribution

Warm temperate to tropical waters worldwide. Probably the most common large shark in the tropics. Can occur anywhere from the surfline to open sea, although mainly inshore at night. Wide-ranging and routinely travels long distances, with limited movement into higher latitudes in summer, then back to the tropics in winter. From the surface down to at least 350 m/1150 ft.

Good places for a close encounter

(most trips in season): *USA:* Midway Atoll, Hawaiian Islands (p.158); **(many trips in season):** *Mozambique:* Cabo San Sebastian, Bazaruto Archipelago (p.205); *Australia:* Raine Island and Shark City, Far Northern Reefs, Queensland (p.253); Jervis Bay, New South Wales (p.259); *French Polynesia:* Rangiroa Atoll (p.277).

Whitetip reef shark *Triaenodon obesus*

The whitetip reef shark is fairly sluggish and seems to spend most of the day lounging around or resting on the seabed or in crevices. Several individuals may lie together in a row or share a bolthole. But when it is time to feed, they go their separate ways and become relentless, competitive predators. They hunt mostly at night, and during slack tides, when many of the smaller reef inhabitants are asleep in holes in the coral. Unlike most other requiem sharks, they are not good at catching prey animals in open water and tend to specialize in extracting them from their resting places. They may break apart coral heads, or wriggle into crevices, to get at reef fishes and invertebrates. Like most reef sharks, whitetip reef sharks have their own predators – other, larger sharks and even large groupers.

Whitetip reef sharks are among the few sharks to have been observed mating in the wild. One researcher in Hawaii saw a male and female lying side-by-side in shallow water, with their heads resting on the seabed and their bodies pointing towards the surface, at an angle of 45 degrees. The male grabbed the female by her pectoral fin and they copulated. Whitetip reef sharks are sometimes confused with the superficially similar silvertip and oceanic whitetip sharks, but these species prefer deeper water, never rest on the seabed, have stockier bodies and smaller second dorsal fins.

IDENTIFICATION CHECKLIST (ADULT)

- small to medium size
- grey to brownish upperside, white or greyish-white underside
- conspicuous white tips on first dorsal fin and upper lobe of caudal fin
- may be white tips on second dorsal fin, lower lobe of caudal fin and underside of pectoral fins
- some individuals have dark spots along the flanks
- noticeably slender body
- broad, flattened, squarish head with short, blunt snout
- prominent nasal flaps
- second dorsal fin relatively large (but still smaller than first dorsal)
- fairly broad, triangular pectoral fins

ALTERNATIVE NAMES

blunthead shark

ORDER	Carcharhiniformes
FAMILY	Carcharhinidae
MAXIMUM LENGTH	2.1 m/7 ft; most less than 1.6 m/5 ft
REPRODUCTION	viviparous; 1–5 pups (50–60 cm/20–24 in)
DIET	bony fishes, crustaceans, sometimes squid and octopuses

Danger to divers

Minimal risk. A small number of incidents have been verified, but it is normally shy and often flees when approached by divers. Curious in some areas, it will follow divers at a distance along a reef before moving off. Like most sharks, can be dangerous if sufficiently agitated and will bite if provoked.

Distribution

Sub-tropical to tropical waters of the Pacific and Indian Oceans (including the Red Sea). One of the most abundant tropical reef sharks. From the surface down to 330 m/1080 ft, but prefers shallow water and rarely occurs deeper than 40 m/130 ft. Rarely ventures into open water away from the reef.

Good places for a close encounter

(most trips in season): *USA:* Kona Coast, Hawaii (p.156); Molokini Crater, Maui, Hawaii (p.157); *Mexico:* Revillagigedo (Socorro) Islands, Baja California (p.170); *Costa Rica:* Cocos Island (p.180); Catalina Islands, Gulf of Papagayo (p.182); Caño Island, Osa Peninsula (p.182); *Ecuador:* Wolf Island and Darwin Island, Galápagos Islands (p.183); *Colombia:* Gorgona Island (p.185); *Egypt:* Ras Muhammad (p.214); The Brothers (p.215); Elphinstone Reef (p.216); *Sudan:* Sha'ab Rumi (p.219); Sanganeb (p.219); *The Philippines:* many sites (pp.221–25); *Malaysia:* Pulau Sipadan, Sabah (p.226); *Thailand:* Similan and Surin Islands (p.230); *Myanmar (Burma):* Silvertip Bank, Burma Banks (p.231); Mergui Archipelago (p.231); *India:* Andaman Islands (p.232); *Japan:* Ogasawara Islands (p.233); *Mauritius:* Shark Pit et al. (p.234); *The Maldives:* many sites (pp.238–47); *Australia:* many sites in Queensland (pp.253–57); *Papua New Guinea:* Madang (p.262); Eastern Fields (p.263); Kimbe Bay (p.265); Kavieng Region (p.266); *Melanesia:* many sites (pp.268–74); *French Polynesia:* many sites (pp.275–79); *Micronesia:* many sites (pp.280–86)

Blue shark *Prionace glauca*

The blue shark is one of the most attractive and graceful of the world's sharks. With its indigo-blue coloration, it is also one of the easiest species to identify. It is often seen at the surface, particularly in higher latitudes, with its pectoral fins outspread and its first dorsal fin and upper caudal lobe out of the water.

Blue sharks have an uncanny ability to turn up at the right place at the right time to gorge on seasonally abundant food, whether it be an annual glut of flying-fish eggs in the Adriatic or mating and spawning squid off California. They are notorious for turning up at the floating carcasses of dead whales, and sailors even used to claim that they would appear alongside a ship when someone had died. They often gorge themselves to bursting, sometimes regurgitating everything and starting all over again.

Blue sharks are great travellers and many individuals tagged by researchers have been rediscovered thousands of kilometres away – sometimes only a matter of weeks later. Little is known of their migrations, although it is clear that there are substantial variations between the movements of adult males, adult females and juveniles. In the Atlantic, for example, most of the long-distance travellers are female and follow the Gulf Stream from the North American coast to Europe (where pregnant females drop their pups), then move south along the African coast before making another transatlantic crossing to the Caribbean, while most of the males simply patrol the eastern seaboard of the USA.

IDENTIFICATION CHECKLIST (ADULT)

- large size
- metallic or indigo-blue upperside, bright blue sides, abruptly snowy-white underside
- slender body
- exceptionally long, narrow, pointed pectoral fins
- first dorsal fin well behind pectorals
- second dorsal fin about half the size of first
- scythe-like tail
- long, conical snout
- large, round eyes centred within a white ring

ALTERNATIVE NAMES

blue whaler, great blue shark

ORDER	Carcharhiniformes
FAMILY	Carcharhinidae
MAXIMUM LENGTH	3.8 m/12½ ft; unconfirmed reports of considerably larger individuals
REPRODUCTION	viviparous; 4–135 pups (35–44 cm/14–17 in)
DIET	bony and cartilaginous fishes, squid, octopuses, crustaceans, mammalian carrion and occasionally seabirds

Danger to divers

Potentially high risk. A number of serious attacks have been verified, and it has been blamed for feeding frenzies on survivors of ship sinkings during the Second World War. Not particularly aggressive, and many encounters are organized for divers without incident, but may circle for long periods, and has been known to test-bite or nip when excited.

Distribution

Temperate to tropical waters worldwide. The most widespread, and one of the most abundant, oceanic sharks, but some stocks seriously reduced by heavy fishing. Mainly an open-ocean shark, but may venture inshore (especially at night) around oceanic islands or in areas with a narrow continental shelf. Will approach kelp forests in temperate waters. From the surface down to at least 220m/720 ft. Prefers relatively cool water and, while common at or near the surface in temperate waters, tends to occur at depth in the tropics. Higher-latitude populations tend to be migratory, but lower-latitude populations are mainly resident.

Good places for a close encounter

(most trips in season): *USA:* Santa Catalina Island, California (p.162); Avalon Banks, California (p.163); San Clemente Island, California (p.164); 9-Mile Bank, San Diego, California (p.165); Rhode Island (p.169); ***Portugal:*** Cape St Vincent and The Canyon, The Algarve (p.203); ***New Zealand:*** Hawkes Bay, North Island (p.249); open ocean, Marlborough Sounds (p.249); Kaikoura, South Island (p.250); **(many trips in season): *New Zealand:*** Whatuwhiwhi, North Island (p.248); Tutukaka, North Island (p.248); Gisborne, North Island (p.248).

Whale shark *Rhincodon typus*

The whale shark is the largest fish in the sea, its maximum size a subject of unending debate. Covered with light-coloured spots, bands and stripes, it is also one of the most distinctive sharks. Its mouth is large enough to take in a person – but though there are more than 300 rows of tiny, hooked teeth, about 2–3 mm/ 0.08–0.12 in long, in each jaw, they are not functional and the shark is completely harmless.

Whale sharks are highly efficient filter-feeders, roaming the world's oceans following seasonal concentrations of food. They either swim slowly through shoals of zooplankton (microscopic animals) with their mouths open, or remain stationary and vacuum up larger, more dynamic prey such as sardines and anchovies. They have a unique sieve-like structure on the inside of the gill rakers, which can filter out objects as small as 1 mm across, before allowing the water to exit through the five large gill slits on either side of the head. But they have relatively small throats and cannot swallow anything larger than a small tuna.

Whale sharks are often accompanied by an entourage of grey or white remoras and other fishes. They are great travellers – a satellite-tagged individual from the Sea of Cortez, in Mexico, travelled 13,000 km/8073 miles to the Marshall Islands, in the central Pacific, over a three-year period.

Whale sharks are officially protected in Western Australia, the Maldives, the Philippines, India, Honduras, along the Atlantic and Gulf of Mexico coasts of the USA and in most other range states, but are still being hunted in some countries – particularly Taiwan.

IDENTIFICATION CHECKLIST (ADULT)

- very large size
- dark grey, bluish-grey or brownish-grey upperside, whitish underside
- alternating light vertical stripes and rows of spots on a dark background
- random spots on head
- pronounced longitudinal ridges along back (one central and three on each side)
- broad, flattened head
- immense, broad mouth at end of snout
- minute, extremely numerous teeth
- small eyes far forward on head
- large, broad-based first dorsal fin (small second dorsal and anal fins)
- upper caudal lobe longer than lower
- very large pectoral fins

ALTERNATIVE NAMES

none known

ORDER	Orectolobiformes
FAMILY	Rhincodontidae
MAXIMUM LENGTH	12.1 m/40 ft; possibly up to 18 m/59 ft
REPRODUCTION	yolk-sac viviparous; 300 or more pups (55–60 cm/ 21³/₄–23¹/₂ in) – the largest number for any known species of shark
DIET	mainly zooplankton, but also small- to medium-sized fishes and squid

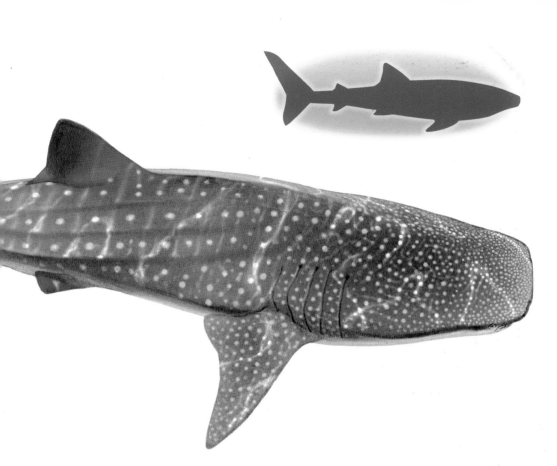

Danger to divers

Minimal risk. A gentle shark that will tolerate divers and snorkellers nearby, without reacting aggressively (although may take avoidance action by diving). Can be very curious and may swim up to divers to investigate.

Distribution

Warm temperate to tropical waters worldwide. Absent from the Mediterranean. Open ocean and coastal, sometimes entering lagoons of coral atolls. Normally encountered close to the surface, but capable of diving to at least 240 m/790 ft. Optimal conditions appear to be a surface temperature of 21–25 °C/70–77 °F, with cold water of 17 °C/63 °F or lower coming from underneath (such upwellings bring nutrients that stimulate plankton growth). Highly migratory, moving according to changes in water temperature and planktonic blooms.

Good places for a close encounter

(most trips in season): *USA:* Flower Garden Banks, Texas (p.165); *Belize:* Gladden Spit (p.178); *The Philippines:* Donsol, Sorsogon (p.223); *Seychelles:* St Anne Marine National Park, Inner Islands (p.235); *Australia:* Ningaloo Reef, Western Australia (p.251); (many trips in season): *Mexico:* many sites in Baja California (pp.170–73); *Belize:* Shark Point, Glover's Reef (p.177); *Honduras:* Utila, Bay Islands (p.179); *Ecuador:* Wolf Island and Darwin Island, Galápagos Islands (p.183) *Cuba:* Jardines de la Reina, Júcaro (p.199); *Tanzania:* Mtangani Reef, Pemba Island (p.205); *Mozambique:* Cabo San Sebastian, Bazaruto Archipelago (p.205); Pinnacles, Ponta D'Ouro (p.206); *South Africa:* Sodwana Bay, KwaZulu-Natal (p.207); *Thailand:* Similan and Surin Islands (including Richelieu Rock) (p.230); *The Maldives:* many sites (pp.238–47).

Nurse shark *Ginglymostoma cirratum*

The nurse shark is probably encountered more than any other shark by divers and snorkellers in the Caribbean. There are many theories about the origin of its name. Some claim that it is a corruption of its original fifteenth-century name, 'nusse', meaning 'large fish'. Others believe it comes from the sucking sound that it makes when feeding. But it is probably derived from the ancient English name for a dogfish: 'huss'. Its scientific name is perhaps more appropriate and translates as 'the shark with the flexible curly mouth'.

It is a strange-looking shark. Spending most of its time on or near the seabed, it can use its long pectoral fins to 'walk' on the bottom, to 'stand up' and even to reverse out of tight spots. Its body is so flexible that it can swim into small holes in the reef in search of hidden prey. In most parts of the world, it is sluggish during the day, typically lying motionless with its head hidden under a ledge or inside a cave, and sometimes even lying on top of other nurse sharks. But it becomes more active at night, feeding with the help of whisker-like barbels on its snout, which detect or 'taste' for the presence of marine invertebrates buried in the sand. If it finds a likely-looking animal hiding out of reach, it cups its mouth over the hole or crevice and then, by expanding its throat, creates a vacuum that sucks the hapless prey out.

The nurse is one of the few sharks for which courtship is relatively well known in the wild. The male swims alongside the female or slightly behind and below, then grabs one of her pectoral fins in his mouth, rolls her over and they mate.

IDENTIFICATION CHECKLIST (ADULT)

- medium to large size
- yellowish-brown to grey-brown upperside
- broad, flat head with blunt snout
- mouth well in front of very small eyes
- moderately long barbels
- large, rounded first and second dorsal fins (similar size)
- large, rounded pectoral fins
- long caudal fin (over 25 per cent of total body length)

ALTERNATIVE NAMES

none known

ORDER	Orectolobiformes
FAMILY	Ginglymostomatidae
MAXIMUM LENGTH	2.8 m/9 ft; longer claims are disputed
REPRODUCTION	yolk-sac viviparous; 20–28 pups (27–30 cm/10½–12 in)
DIET	small fishes, squid, bivalves, crabs, shrimps, lobsters, sea urchins

Danger to divers

Minimal risk. Harmless by nature, and readily approached as it rests on the seabed, but short-sighted and easily scared. Nearly all incidents are provoked. Foolhardy divers who cannot resist the urge to pull on its tail when it is resting are likely to get bitten. Although its teeth are small, its jaws are incredibly strong (designed to crush shellfish) and can deliver a serious bite; worse, it may refuse to release its vice-like grip if it feels tormented.

Distribution

Warm temperate to tropical waters of the Atlantic and eastern Pacific. Most common over inshore coral reefs and along rocky coastlines. Abundant in very shallow water (as little as 1 m/39 in) of the Caribbean and Florida Keys and often found in aggregations. Prefers to swim close to the seabed. Often found in caves.

Good places for a close encounter

(most trips in season): *USA:* Samantha's Ledge/Shark Ledge, Florida (p.166); Palm Beach – Fort Lauderdale, Florida (p.167); *Mexico:* Sleeping Sharks' Cave, Quintana Roo (p.170); *Belize:* Shark-Ray Alley, Ambergris Caye (p.175); Shark Chutes, Gallow's Point (p.175); Shark's Cave, Tobacco Caye (p.177); Bull Shark Pass, Glover's Reef (p.178); *The Bahamas:* Shark Rodeo/Spiral Cavern, Walker's Cay (p.187); Shark Junction, Grand Bahama Island (p.190); Bull Run/Shark Reef, Bimini (p.190); Lost Ocean Blue Hole, New Providence Island (p.191); Danger Reef/Amberjack Reef, Danger Cay, Exuma Cays (p.193); Shark Reef, Long Island (p.195); *Turks and Caicos:* West Caicos (p.196); French Cay (p.197); Shark Point, Salt Cay (p.198); *Cayman Islands:* Bloody Bay Marine Park, Little Cayman (p.200); *Tobago:* Diver's Dream, Diver's Thirst, Flying Reef and Sisters Rocks (p.201).

Zebra shark *Stegostoma fasciatum*

With its long tail and spectacular markings, the zebra shark is one of the most endearing and beautiful of all the world's sharks. It is a harmless creature and can be approached quite closely. Many divers have lain down alongside one as it rests on the seabed, and watched remoras moving about all over its skin.

The zebra shark's name comes from the juvenile markings, which are basically black with yellow stripes and blotches, but these are not particularly zebra-like. Its alternative name – the leopard shark – is more appropriate because the adults are covered in dark brown or black spots. To add to the confusion there is an unrelated species called the leopard shark (*Triakis semifasciata*); found in the cold waters of the eastern Pacific, it is covered in black blobs and saddle-shaped markings.

The zebra shark is similar in body shape and habits to the nurse shark, and lives on or near the seabed. It spends most of the day resting on the sand, usually near large coral heads, but can sometimes be seen propped up on its pectoral fins, facing the current with its mouth open to oxygenate its gills. It hunts for shellfish and other reef creatures, usually at night, and its body is so flexible that it can wriggle into tiny crevices in search of food.

Its large, oblong egg cases are brown or purplish-black and are securely attached to the seabed with lots of hair-like fibres.

IDENTIFICATION CHECKLIST (ADULT)

- medium to large size
- silvery, yellowish or greenish-brown upperside and underside
- body covered in dark brown or black spots
- cylindrical body with prominent longitudinal ridges along the flanks
- elongated upper lobe of caudal fin to form long, low tail (same length as rest of body)
- large, broad head with small barbels on snout
- small mouth and eyes but huge spiracles (as large as eyes)
- first and second dorsal fins close together (first much larger)

ALTERNATIVE NAMES

leopard shark, variegated shark

ORDER	Orectolobiformes
FAMILY	Stegostomatidae
MAXIMUM LENGTH	3.5 m/11½ ft; most under 3 m/10 ft
REPRODUCTION	yolk-sac viviparous; 1–4 eggs (hatch size 20–36 cm/8–14 in)
DIET	molluscs, sometimes crustaceans, small bony fishes and octopuses

Danger to divers

Minimal risk. Generally docile and considered harmless: one of the few large sharks that will allow a close approach without the risk of being bitten. However, it should not be provoked.

Distribution

Warm temperate to tropical waters of the western Pacific and Indian Oceans (including the Red Sea). Mainly over the continental and insular shelves, and most common around coral reefs.

Good places for a close encounter

(most trips in season): *Thailand:* Hin Muang (Purple Rock) and Hin Daeng (Red Rock), Koh Lanta Marine National Park (p.228); Shark Point, Phi Phi Islands (p.229); Shark Point, Koh Phuket (p.229); Similan and Surin Islands (including Richelieu Rock) (p.230); ***Myanmar (Burma):*** Western Rocky Island and Black Rock, Mergui Archipelago (p.231); ***Australia:*** Raine Island and Shark City, Far Northern Reefs, Queensland (p.253); Watanabe Pinnacle and Scuba Zoo, Flinders Reef, Queensland (p.254); Lady Elliot Island, Queensland (p.257); ***Melanesia:*** New Caledonia (p.271); **(many trips in season): *Madagascar:*** Nosy Tanikely et al. (p.213); ***Malaysia:*** Layang-Layang, Borneo Banks (p.227); ***Myanmar (Burma):*** Silvertip Bank, Burma Banks (p.231); ***India:*** Andaman Islands (p.232); ***The Maldives:*** Makunudhu Channel, North Male (Kaafu) Atoll (p.239); Himendhoo Dhekunu Thila, North Ari (Alifu) Atoll (p.245); ***Australia:*** Rowley Shoals, Northern Atoll Reefs, Western Australia (p.252).

Directory of Shark-Watching Sites

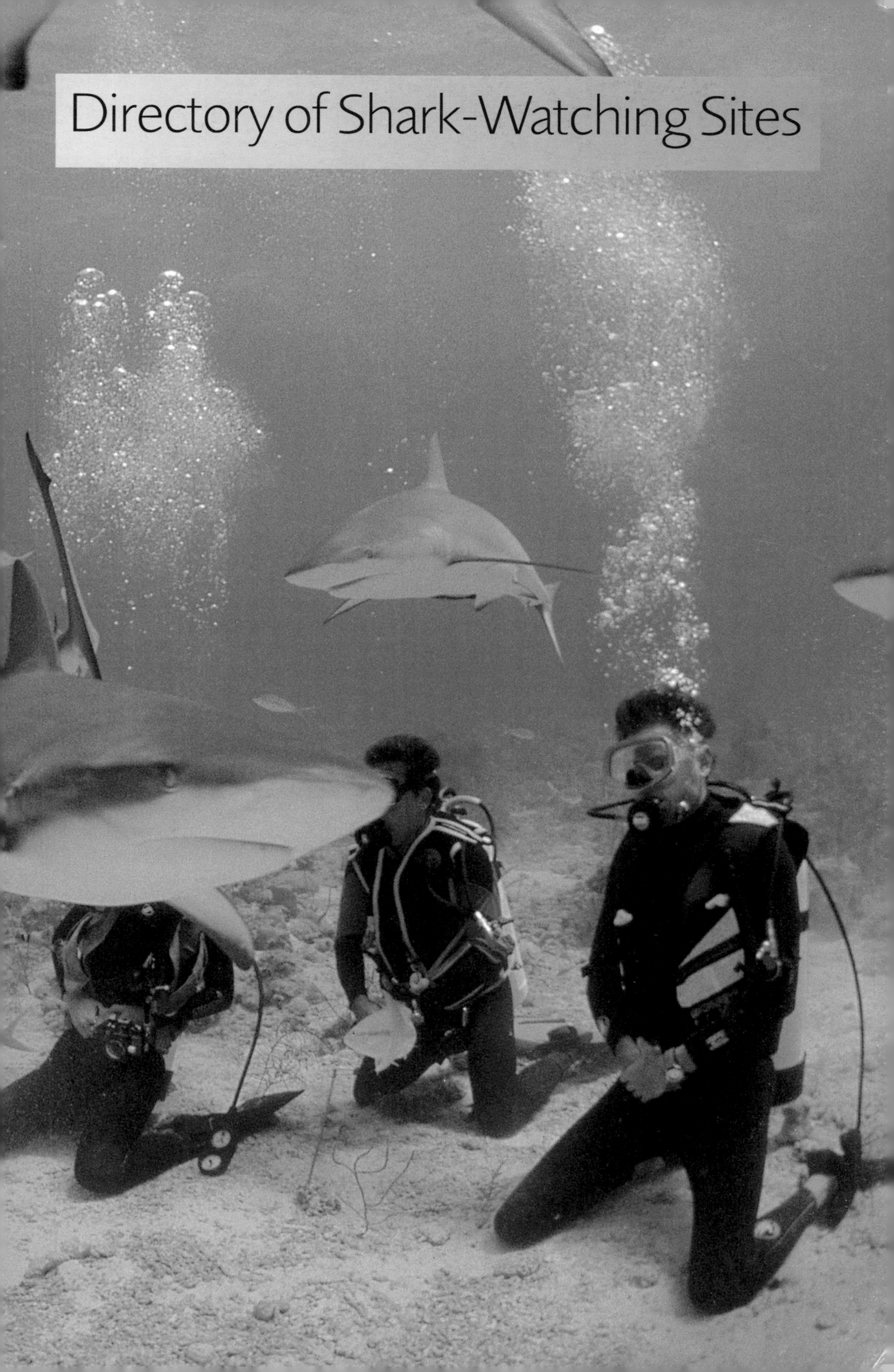

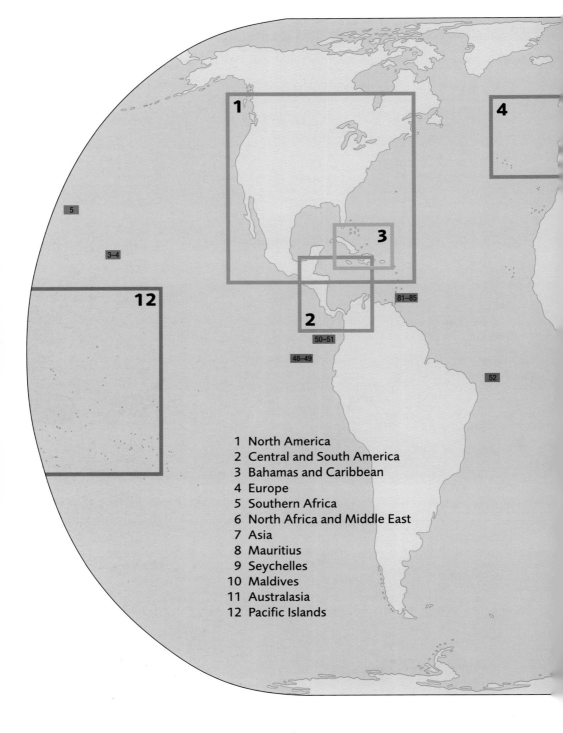

1 North America
2 Central and South America
3 Bahamas and Caribbean
4 Europe
5 Southern Africa
6 North Africa and Middle East
7 Asia
8 Mauritius
9 Seychelles
10 Maldives
11 Australasia
12 Pacific Islands

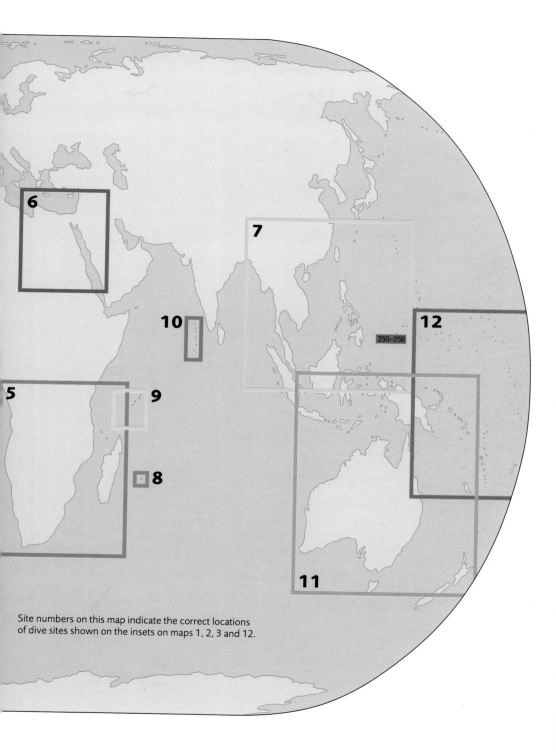

6

7

10

250–256

12

5

9

8

11

Site numbers on this map indicate the correct locations
of dive sites shown on the insets on maps 1, 2, 3 and 12.

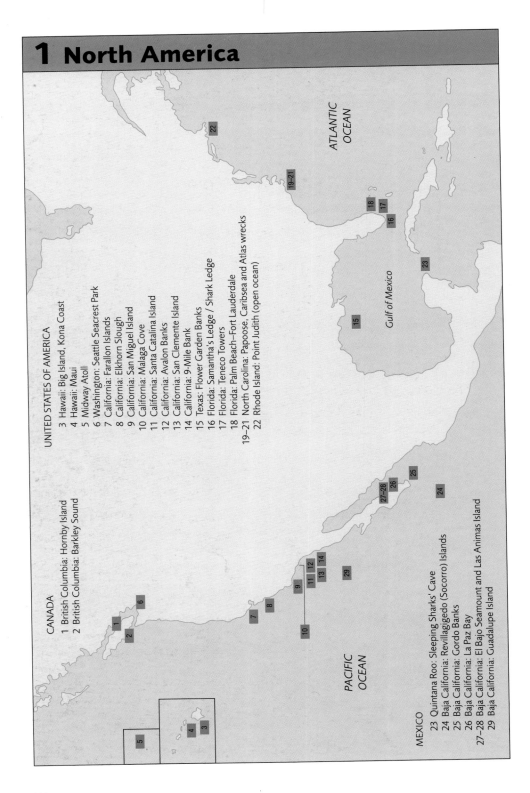

CANADA

1 British Columbia: Hornby Island
2 British Columbia: Barkley Sound

UNITED STATES OF AMERICA

3 Hawaii: Big Island, Kona Coast
4 Hawaii: Maui
5 Midway Atoll
6 Washington: Seattle Seacrest Park
7 California: Farallon Islands
8 California: Elkhorn Slough
9 California: San Miguel Island
10 California: Malaga Cove
11 California: Santa Catalina Island
12 California: Avalon Banks
13 California: San Clemente Island
14 California: 9-Mile Bank
15 Texas: Flower Garden Banks
16 Florida: Samantha's Ledge / Shark Ledge
17 Florida: Teneco Towers
18 Florida: Palm Beach–Fort Lauderdale
19–21 North Carolina: Papoose, Caribsea and Atlas wrecks
22 Rhode Island: Point Judith (open ocean)

MEXICO

23 Quintana Roo: Sleeping Sharks' Cave
24 Baja California: Revillagigedo (Socorro) Islands
25 Baja California: Gordo Banks
26 Baja California: La Paz Bay
27–28 Baja California: El Bajo Seamount and Las Animas Island
29 Baja California: Guadalupe Island

ATLANTIC OCEAN

Gulf of Mexico

PACIFIC OCEAN

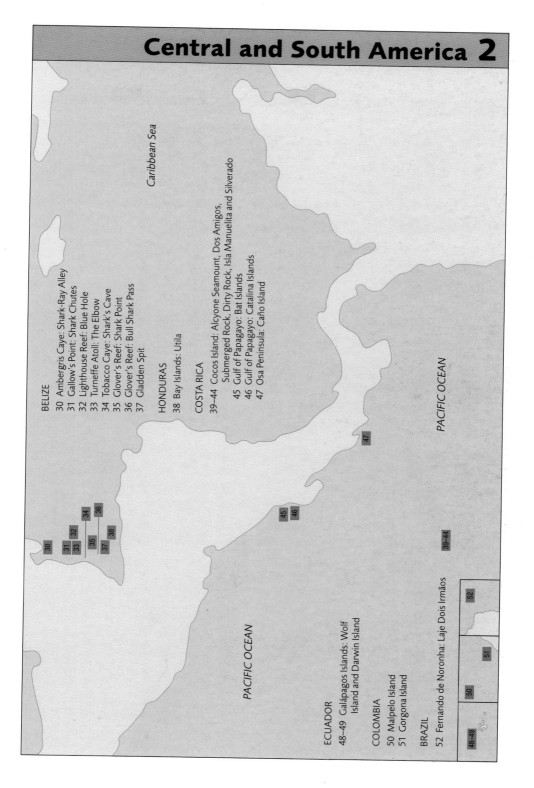

Caribbean Sea

BELIZE
30 Ambergris Caye: Shark-Ray Alley
31 Gallow's Point: Shark Chutes
32 Lighthouse Reef: Blue Hole
33 Turneffe Atoll: The Elbow
34 Tobacco Caye: Shark's Cave
35 Glover's Reef: Shark Point
36 Glover's Reef: Bull Shark Pass
37 Gladden Spit

HONDURAS
38 Bay Islands: Utila

COSTA RICA
39–44 Cocos Island: Alcyone Seamount, Dos Amigos, Submerged Rock, Dirty Rock, Isla Manuelita and Silverado
45 Gulf of Papagayo: Bat Islands
46 Gulf of Papagayo: Catalina Islands
47 Osa Peninsula: Caño Island

PACIFIC OCEAN

PACIFIC OCEAN

ECUADOR
48–49 Galápagos Islands: Wolf Island and Darwin Island

COLOMBIA
50 Malpelo Island
51 Gorgona Island

BRAZIL
52 Fernando de Noronha: Laje Dois Irmãos

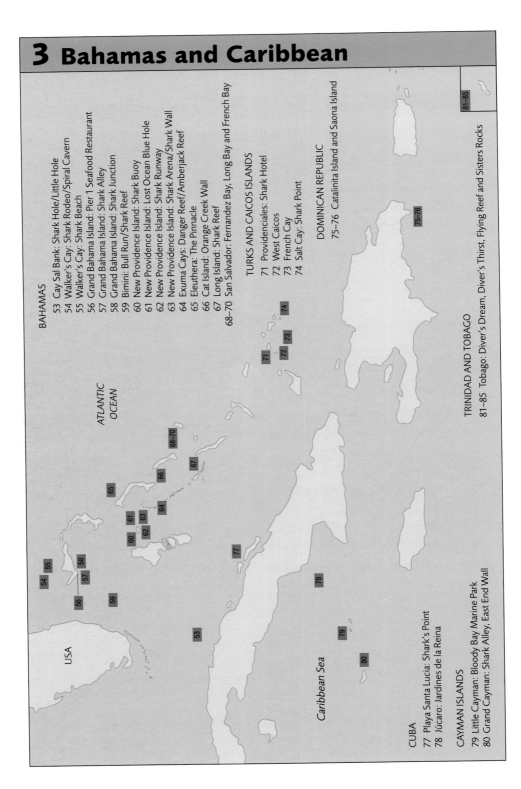

BAHAMAS

53 Cay Sal Bank: Shark Hole/Little Hole
54 Walker's Cay: Shark Rodeo/Spiral Cavern
55 Walker's Cay: Shark Beach
56 Grand Bahama Island: Pier 1 Seafood Restaurant
57 Grand Bahama Island: Shark Alley
58 Grand Bahama Island: Shark Junction
59 Bimini: Bull Run/Shark Reef
60 New Providence Island: Shark Buoy
61 New Providence Island: Lost Ocean Blue Hole
62 New Providence Island: Shark Runway
63 New Providence Island: Shark Arena/Shark Wall
64 Exuma Cays: Danger Reef/Amberjack Reef
65 Eleuthera: The Pinnacle
66 Cat Island: Orange Creek Wall
67 Long Island: Shark Reef
68–70 San Salvador: Fernandez Bay, Long Bay and French Bay

TURKS AND CAICOS ISLANDS

71 Providenciales: Shark Hotel
72 West Caicos
73 French Cay
74 Salt Cay: Shark Point

DOMINICAN REPUBLIC

75–76 Catalinita Island and Saona Island

TRINIDAD AND TOBAGO

81–85 Tobago: Diver's Dream, Diver's Thirst, Flying Reef and Sisters Rocks

ATLANTIC
OCEAN

Caribbean Sea

USA

CUBA

77 Playa Santa Lucia: Shark's Point
78 Júcaro: Jardines de la Reina

CAYMAN ISLANDS

79 Little Cayman: Bloody Bay Marine Park
80 Grand Cayman: Shark Alley, East End Wall

Europe 4

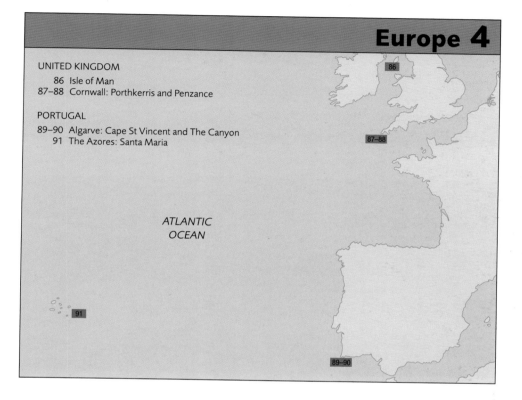

ATLANTIC
OCEAN

86

87–88

91

89–90

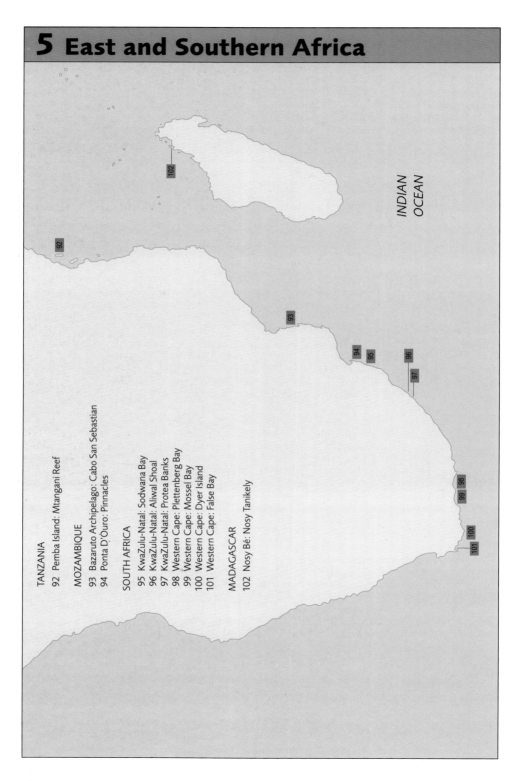

INDIAN OCEAN

TANZANIA

92 Pemba Island: Mtangani Reef

MOZAMBIQUE

93 Bazaruto Archipelago: Cabo San Sebastian
94 Ponta D'Ouro: Pinnacles

SOUTH AFRICA

95 KwaZulu-Natal: Sodwana Bay
96 KwaZulu-Natal: Aliwal Shoal
97 KwaZulu-Natal: Protea Banks
98 Western Cape: Plettenberg Bay
99 Western Cape: Mossel Bay
100 Western Cape: Dyer Island
101 Western Cape: False Bay

MADAGASCAR

102 Nosy Bé: Nosy Tanikely

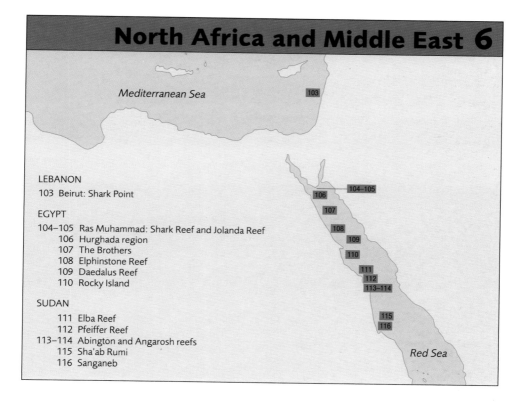

Mediterranean Sea

LEBANON

103 Beirut: Shark Point

EGYPT

104–105 Ras Muhammad: Shark Reef and Jolanda Reef
106 Hurghada region
107 The Brothers
108 Elphinstone Reef
109 Daedalus Reef
110 Rocky Island

SUDAN

111 Elba Reef
112 Pfeiffer Reef
113–114 Abington and Angarosh reefs
115 Sha'ab Rumi
116 Sanganeb

Red Sea

7 Asia

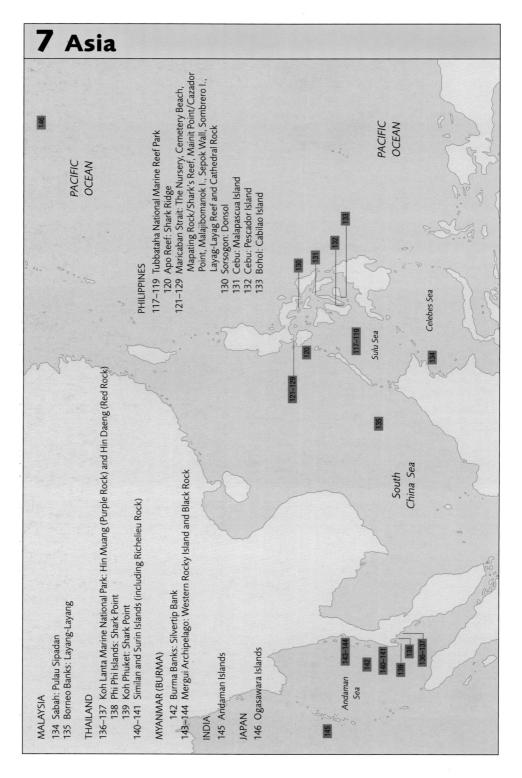

MALAYSIA
134 Sabah: Pulau Sipadan
135 Borneo Banks: Layang-Layang

THAILAND
136–137 Koh Lanta Marine National Park: Hin Muang (Purple Rock) and Hin Daeng (Red Rock)
138 Phi Phi Islands: Shark Point
139 Koh Phuket: Shark Point
140–141 Similan and Surin Islands (including Richelieu Rock)

MYANMAR (BURMA)
142 Burma Banks: Silvertip Bank
143–144 Mergui Archipelago: Western Rocky Island and Black Rock

INDIA
145 Andaman Islands

JAPAN
146 Ogasawara Islands

PHILIPPINES
117–119 Tubbataha National Marine Reef Park
120 Apo Reef: Shark Ridge
121–129 Maricaban Strait: The Nursery, Cemetery Beach, Mapating Rock/Shark's Reef, Mainit Point/Cazador Point, Malajibomanok I., Sepok Wall, Sombrero I., Layag-Layag Reef and Cathedral Rock
130 Sorsogon: Donsol
131 Cebu: Malapascua Island
132 Cebu: Pescador Island
133 Bohol: Cabilao Island

PACIFIC OCEAN

PACIFIC OCEAN

Celebes Sea

Sulu Sea

South China Sea

Andaman Sea

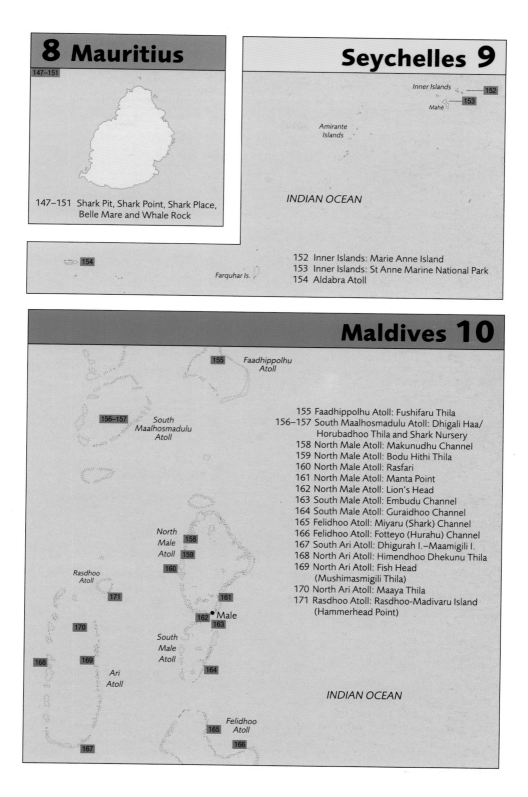

8 Mauritius

147–151

147–151 Shark Pit, Shark Point, Shark Place, Belle Mare and Whale Rock

Seychelles 9

Inner Islands — 152
153
Mahé

Amirante
Islands

INDIAN OCEAN

154

Farquhar Is.

152 Inner Islands: Marie Anne Island
153 Inner Islands: St Anne Marine National Park
154 Aldabra Atoll

Maldives 10

155 Faadhippolhu Atoll

156–157 South Maalhosmadulu Atoll

North Male Atoll 158
159

160

Rasdhoo Atoll

171

170

168 169

Ari Atoll

161

162 •Male
163

South Male Atoll

164

Felidhoo Atoll
165
166

167

155 Faadhippolhu Atoll: Fushifaru Thila
156–157 South Maalhosmadulu Atoll: Dhigali Haa/
Horubadhoo Thila and Shark Nursery
158 North Male Atoll: Makunudhu Channel
159 North Male Atoll: Bodu Hithi Thila
160 North Male Atoll: Rasfari
161 North Male Atoll: Manta Point
162 North Male Atoll: Lion's Head
163 South Male Atoll: Embudu Channel
164 South Male Atoll: Guraidhoo Channel
165 Felidhoo Atoll: Miyaru (Shark) Channel
166 Felidhoo Atoll: Fotteyo (Hurahu) Channel
167 South Ari Atoll: Dhigurah I.–Maamigili I.
168 North Ari Atoll: Himendhoo Dhekunu Thila
169 North Ari Atoll: Fish Head
(Mushimasmigili Thila)
170 North Ari Atoll: Maaya Thila
171 Rasdhoo Atoll: Rasdhoo-Madivaru Island
(Hammerhead Point)

INDIAN OCEAN

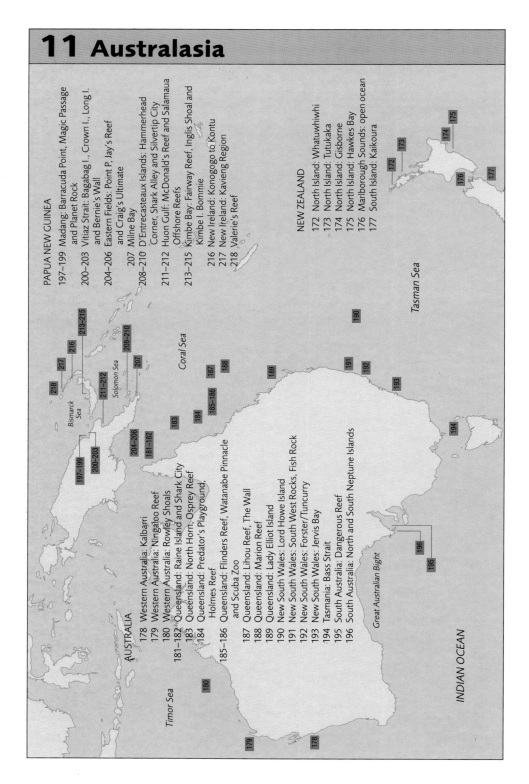

PAPUA NEW GUINEA

197–199 Madang: Barracuda Point, Magic Passage and Planet Rock
200–203 Vitiaz Strait: Bagabag I., Crown I., Long I. and Bernie's Wall
204–206 Eastern Fields: Point P, Jay's Reef and Craig's Ultimate
207 Milne Bay
208–210 D'Entrecasteaux Islands: Hammerhead Corner, Shark Alley and Silvertip City
211–212 Huon Gulf: McDonald's Reef and Salamaua Offshore Reefs
213–215 Kimbe Bay: Fairway Reef, Inglis Shoal and Kimbe I. Bommie
216 New Ireland: Konogogo to Kontu
217 New Ireland: Kavieng Region
218 Valerie's Reef

NEW ZEALAND

172 North Island: Whatuwhiwhi
173 North Island: Tutukaka
174 North Island: Gisborne
175 North Island: Hawkes Bay
176 Marlborough Sounds: open ocean
177 South Island: Kaikoura

AUSTRALIA

178 Western Australia: Kalbarri
179 Western Australia: Ningaloo Reef
180 Western Australia: Rowley Shoals
181–182 Queensland: Raine Island and Shark City
183 Queensland: North Horn, Osprey Reef
184 Queensland: Predator's Playground, Holmes Reef
185–186 Queensland: Flinders Reef, Watanabe Pinnacle and Scuba Zoo
187 Queensland: Lihou Reef, The Wall
188 Queensland: Marion Reef
189 Queensland: Lady Elliot Island
190 New South Wales: Lord Howe Island
191 New South Wales: South West Rocks, Fish Rock
192 New South Wales: Forster/Tuncurry
193 New South Wales: Jervis Bay
194 Tasmania: Bass Strait
195 South Australia: Dangerous Reef
196 South Australia: North and South Neptune Islands

Tasman Sea

Coral Sea

Solomon Sea

Bismarck Sea

Timor Sea

Great Australian Bight

INDIAN OCEAN

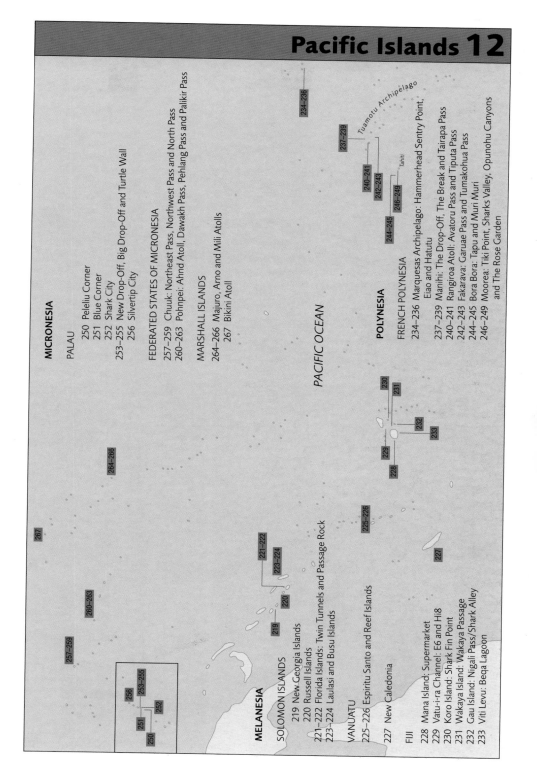

MICRONESIA

PALAU
- 250 Peleliu Corner
- 251 Blue Corner
- 252 Shark City
- 253–255 New Drop-Off, Big Drop-Off and Turtle Wall
- 256 Silvertip City

FEDERATED STATES OF MICRONESIA
- 257–259 Chuuk: Northeast Pass, Northwest Pass and North Pass
- 260–263 Pohnpei: Ahnd Atoll, Dawakh Pass, Pehlang Pass and Palikir Pass

MARSHALL ISLANDS
- 264–266 Majuro, Arno and Mili Atolls
- 267 Bikini Atoll

Tuamotu Archipelago

Tahiti

PACIFIC OCEAN

POLYNESIA

FRENCH POLYNESIA
- 234–236 Marquesas Archipelago: Hammerhead Sentry Point, Eiao and Hatutu
- 237–239 Manihi: The Drop-Off, The Break and Tairapa Pass
- 240–241 Rangiroa Atoll: Avatoru Pass and Tiputa Pass
- 242–243 Fakarava: Garuae Pass and Tumakohua Pass
- 244–245 Bora Bora: Tapu and Muri Muri
- 246–249 Moorea: Tiki Point, Sharks Valley, Opunohu Canyons and The Rose Garden

MELANESIA

SOLOMON ISLANDS
- 219 New Georgia Islands
- 220 Russell Islands
- 221–222 Florida Islands: Twin Tunnels and Passage Rock
- 223–224 Laulasi and Busu Islands

VANUATU
- 225–226 Espiritu Santo and Reef Islands
- 227 New Caledonia

FIJI
- 228 Mana Island: Supermarket
- 229 Vatu-i-ra Channel: E6 and H18
- 230 Koro Island: Shark Fin Point
- 231 Wakaya Island: Wakaya Passage
- 232 Gau Island: Nigali Pass/Shark Alley
- 233 Viti Levu: Beqa Lagoon

Introduction

This directory has been compiled over a period of about two years, with the generous help of more than 2000 dive operators, as well as a great many shark biologists, divers and fishermen, in some 50 different countries. To the best of our knowledge, it includes all the prime shark dives around the world, as well as a broad geographical spread of other places where sharks are encountered on a regular basis.

However, we see this as just the beginning of an ongoing process – in the hope that it will become the reference work for shark divers worldwide – and would welcome any thoughts on other shark-diving sites, or dive operators, that you feel should be included in future editions.

The directory is fairly self-explanatory, but there are a few important points to bear in mind:

Main species wherever possible, the frequency of sightings (*most trips*, *many trips* or *occasional trips*) is based on actual sightings records by the people diving the sites on a daily basis. Where these have not been available, the frequency is subjective and is based on personal experience or on discussions with local operators and divers. More importantly, sightings can change from year to year and depend on a wide range of factors, from individual shark behaviour and complex natural phenomena such as El Niño to local shark-fishing activities. Shark watching, like watching any other form of wildlife, is largely a matter of luck and – with pelagic species in particular – there can be lots of sharks at a site one day, and none at all the next.

Best time of year although we have listed the sharks most likely to be encountered at a particular site, it is important to check this section for any seasonal variation. In many places some shark species may be present only at certain times of the year. Again, this information is based on a combination of actual sightings records, personal experience and discussions with local operators and divers, but bear in mind that it can change according to local conditions.

Contact details the dive operators listed for each site are the ones who have helped us with our research; although they seem to be responsible and knowledgeable, we have not met them all and cannot vouch for their professionalism; and they are not necessarily the only operators working at that site. As with all wildlife trips, we strongly recommend that you speak to dive operators before booking.

Travel we have not commented on political instabilities or such dangers as terrorism or piracy at any of the sites (unless shark diving has actually been suspended) because these situations change constantly. If you are in any doubt at all about local safety, it is advisable to check with the relevant government body before leaving home.

CANADA

1 BRITISH COLUMBIA: HORNBY ISLAND

Location in the Strait of Georgia, midway between Nanaimo and Campbell River, off the east coast of Vancouver Island (British Columbia).

Main species *most trips:* bluntnose sixgill (*Hexanchus griseus*).

Viewing opportunities bluntnose sixgill sharks are widely distributed around the world, but there are few places where it is possible to view them. Adults are usually found at great depth (up to 2500 m/8200 ft) and are thus inaccessible to people under most circumstances. Juveniles are more likely to be found inshore and one particular population, which makes a brief appearance in the Pacific North-West every summer, frequently ventures into much shallower water. There were two ways to see the sixgills around Hornby Island, which forms part of Helliwell Provincial Park: by scuba diving or from a research submersible. The submersible dives have been discontinued, but scuba diving with the sharks is still possible.

There is a steep drop-off at Flora Islet, next to Hornby Island, where the sharks are commonly seen at depths of 30–42 m/100–140 ft (sometimes as shallow as 24 m/80 ft) and, during night dives, they have even been reported as shallow as 10 m/33 ft. This puts them well within the reach of recreational divers. The wall consists of a series of terraces, at 6–25 m/20–66 ft, and then a sheer vertical face that drops to over 75 m/250 ft. The sharks generally hug the terraces and become agitated if they are separated from this point of reference. No one knows why they move into relatively shallow water here during the summer. Local divers have never observed signs of feeding or breeding and the sharks never seem to do anything other than cruise along the ledges of the wall. There may be a clue in the fact that most of them are juveniles: the females are normally less than 4 m/13 ft in length and the males less than 3 m/10 ft; large adults have been reported to be twice as long. They appear to be quite sluggish, at least compared with many other sharks, but it is still impossible for human divers to keep up with them if they are disturbed. Sixgills are large and voracious predators and, although they show little interest in divers and there are no known reports of them attacking humans, should be treated with caution. If they are touched, or a strobe light is fired at close range, some individuals descend quickly out of range – and there are unsubstantiated reports of them snapping. They are generally solitary, although groups of up to 12 have been observed in the area. With the onset of autumn, the number of sightings decreases, but research suggests that the sharks stay relatively close by and simply move into deeper water.

More sixgills can be found at depths of 120–220 m/400–700 ft throughout the summer, and for a short period, there was a unique opportunity at Hornby Island to view them from deep-water submersibles. There were lectures about the practicalities of the dive and presentations by local scientists before taking a short boat ride to the 'mission-control' barge. Twilight enveloped the submersible as it descended, but in the lights it was possible to see the ghostly white masses of huge cloud sponges clinging to the rock face. Tiny maroon and white-striped juvenile rockfish flitted into the openings of the sponges, and orange and purple Puget Sound king crabs wandered among them. Best of all, there were grey forms taking shape against the pale glow: sixgill sharks. As the dive progressed, it was easier to see them properly in the submersible lights. The expeditions used three-person *Aquarius* and two-person *Dual Deep Worker 350* submersibles, both of which were capable of descending to a depth of 300 m/1000 ft. Certified for deep diving and piloted by experts who had been leading scientific expeditions for many years, they were comfortable and dry inside, maintained an atmospheric pressure similar to that on land, were in constant contact with the support vessel on the surface and had a life-support capacity of 72 hours. They were inspected annually and hydrostatically tested every five years. In the *Dual Deepworker 350*, which was just over 3.7 m/12 ft long and 1.4 m/4.5 ft high, the single participant was seated in front in a chair similar to an airline seat. In the *Aquarius*, which was nearly 4.1 m/14 ft long and 2 m/7 ft high, the two participants were also in the front and sat or lay down on benches. There were large viewing spheres, with excellent clarity for observation and photography.

Bait/feed no.

Cage no.

Other wildlife Steller's sea lion, California sea lion, bald eagle, giant Pacific octopus, king crab, sunstar, cloud sponge.

Best time of year May–Sep (scuba), Jul–Sep (submersible – currently out of operation).

Dive depth 24–42 m/80–140 ft (scuba), 120–220 m/400–700 ft (submersible – currently out of operation).

Typical visibility 6–30 m/20–100 ft (In sixgill season best near end of summer or between plankton blooms).

Water temperature 20 °C/68 °F at the surface in

summer; constant 8–10 °C/46–50 °F at 25 m/80 ft year-round.

Weather and sea notes difference between ebb and flow tides in the Strait of Georgia is up to 5 m/16 ft, but not strong enough to impact on dives to a great extent; some strong currents locally.

Contact details Hornby Island Diving (www.hornbyislanddiving.com), Ocean Explorers Diving (www.oceanexplorersdiving.com).

Travel national and international flights to Seattle, Vancouver or Victoria; journey from Victoria (southern tip of Vancouver Island) involves 3½-hour drive north to Buckley Bay, 10-min ferry to Denman Island, 15-min drive to Gravelly Bay, ferry to Hornby Island; also accessible by seaplane; limited choice of accommodation on the island.

2 BRITISH COLUMBIA: BARKLEY SOUND

Location south-west coast of Vancouver Island (British Columbia), approximately 40 km/25 miles from Port Alberni.

Main species *occasional trips:* bluntnose sixgill (*Hexanchus griseus*), blue.

Viewing opportunities Barkley Sound, with its prolific and pristine waters, is widely considered to be one of the premier dive sites in North America. It has spectacular kelp forests, a living treasure of starfish and an amazing variety of marine life around its reefs and wrecks. Dedicated shark diving in the area is relatively new, although it is rapidly becoming a popular site for encountering sixgill sharks in relatively shallow water. The main location for these dives is a pinnacle known as Tyler Rock, which drops to sand at a depth of about 27 m/90 ft and then slopes off to much deeper water. The sharks are typically found at 21–27 m/ 70–90 ft during the day, but can rise to within just 3 m/ 10 ft of the surface at night. They are usually slow-moving, curious and non-threatening towards divers, and will allow themselves to be approached quite closely, altering their course just enough to avoid an actual collision. They should never be touched, however, because they have a habit of whipping round and snapping. Some divers have been able to attract them closer by 'clinking' two rocks together, although this does not always work. The sixgills in this area are 1.5–4.5 m/5–15 ft long and a mixture of adults and juveniles of both sexes. It is unclear why they congregate here, but it is possible that the younger animals arrive for the seasonal salmon run and the adults are breeding (fresh scars appear on the napes of many sub-adult and adult females – perhaps induced by males as a prelude to mating). On dedicated

shark dives as few as none and as many as seven sharks are typically encountered, with an average sightings success of about 20 per cent during the summer season.

Bait/feed no.

Cage no.

Other wildlife grey whale, California sea lion, bald eagle; black bear.

Best time of year sharks present Jun–mid-Oct; peak sightings Aug–Sep.

Dive depth 3–36 m/10–120 ft.

Typical visibility averages 10 m/33 ft (range 2–30 m/ 6½–100 ft).

Water temperature 10 °C/50 °F; drysuits recommended.

Weather and sea notes a surface current at Tyler Rock is quite common.

Contact details Rendezvous Dive Ventures (www.rendezvousdiveventures.com).

Travel national and international flights to Seattle, Vancouver or Victoria; ferries to Victoria or Nanaimo; trips leave from Port Alberni; accommodation at Rendezvous Retreat on Barkley Sound.

USA

3 HAWAII: KONA COAST

Location various sites within 50 km/30 miles of Kailua-Kona (tourist town on the west coast of Big Island).

Main species *many trips:* whitetip reef; Galápagos, oceanic whitetip; *occasional trips:* grey reef, blacktip reef, scalloped hammerhead, tiger, whale.

Viewing opportunities the west coast of Hawaii, or Big Island, is a mecca for divers. Known as the Kona Coast, it has a well-deserved reputation for calm, clear waters and abundant marine life. It is most famous for its 'manta mania' and manta rays can easily be seen on night dives and snorkels, or from glass-bottomed boats. Shark diving is relatively new along the Kona Coast and, at the moment, most dedicated trips are on request only. The main problem is that the best places to see sharks are not great dive sites, but sharks are common in the region and the potential is enormous. Whitetip reef sharks are found in caves and lava tubes at a number of well-known sites and can be virtually guaranteed on several regular dives. Galápagos sharks are frequently found in mid-water at a site just outside Honokohau Harbour (where the bottom depth is about 60 m/200 ft); there is little else to see here and the dives are conducted specifically for the sharks. They tend to be present for just a few hours (approximately 11.00 am until 1.00 pm) each day – but the success rate for finding them is better than 80 per cent. Sightings of scalloped hammerheads are not uncommon but they are unpredictable; they tend to be seen in schools of up to 50 individuals and are occasionally encountered at Ule Rock, Au'Au Canyon, Hammerhead Point, Kaiwi Point, Suck'em Up, Golden Arches and Pipe Dreams. Oceanic whitetips appear to be resident in the area and are sometimes encountered in very deep water 2–6 km/1⅓–4 miles offshore; week-long charters on Kona Aggressor II, specifically to cage-dive with them, have a good success rate year-round. They are often found following pods of short-finned pilot whales and there is sometimes an opportunity – on an *ad hoc* basis – to snorkel with them if they are near the surface. Whale sharks are rarely seen more than a dozen times a year, but some dive operators will take clients out to snorkel with them when they do appear. Grey reef sharks are a relatively new discovery in the area and can be seen at A Touch of Grey – a deep drop-off exposed to strong currents.

Bait/feed no.

Cage no.

Other wildlife humpback whale (Nov–Apr), short-finned pilot whale, long-snouted spinner dolphin, green turtle, manta ray (manta night dives are a year-round event at the Garden of Eels – only accessible by boat – and at Manta Ray Village), eagle ray.

Best time of year most sharks present year-round (scalloped hammerheads mostly winter and spring).

Dive depth surface to 30 m/100 ft (depending on site and encounter).

Typical visibility 15–40 m/50–130 ft.

Water temperature 23–25 °C/74–77 °F (winter), 26–29 °C/78–84 °F (summer).

Weather and sea notes Kona Coast is sheltered from the prevailing trade winds by two enormous volcanoes (Mauna Kea and Mauna Loa) and the sea is usually calm; some sites have windier conditions, bigger waves and swifter currents; best conditions May–Oct (warmer water and less rain).

Contact details Jack's Diving Locker (www.jacksdivinglocker.com), Kona Coast Divers (www.konacoastdivers.com), Kona Aggressor II (www.aggressor.com/ka_home.html), Sea Paradise Scuba (www.seaparadise.com).

Travel international flights to Honolulu; connecting flights to Big Island; wide choice of accommodation in and around Kailua-Kona.

Note a series of buoys, installed by the state of Hawaii every 8 km/5 miles off the coast of Kona, are now becoming popular with shark divers. The buoys have been installed as fish-aggregating devices (dubbed FADS) for the benefit of fishermen looking for marlin and tuna. Their purpose is to attract small fish that, in turn, attract larger predatory fish. But the FADS attract all manner of marine life – from whales to sharks – and have turned out to be goldmines for divers. These blue-water dives are not easy, due to strong currents, but they are all the more exciting because almost anything can turn up.

4 HAWAII: MAUI: MOLOKINI CRATER

Location 5 km/3 miles from Makena, on the south-west coast of Maui.

Main species *many trips:* grey reef, whitetip reef; *occasional trips:* whale.

Viewing opportunities the dramatic crescent-shaped islet of Molokini is the partial rim of an extinct volcano and sits in nearly 100 m/330 ft of crystal-clear water. Its sharks have been fished in the past, but the islet was declared a marine preserve in 1977 and, fortunately, enough tourist boats have been visiting since then to deter poachers. Nowadays the shark population seems to have recovered well – it may even be approaching its original size – and whitetip reef or grey reef sharks are seen by divers almost anywhere here (both inside the crater and around the outer slopes of the cone) virtually every day. One particular site, near the eastern tip of the crescent, has been dubbed Shark Ledges or Shark Condos because there are nearly always a few whitetips hiding under the lava ledges at a depth of about 40 m/130 ft. Reef's End and Back Wall are also good for large whitetip reef sharks (Back Wall is rated the premier wall dive in the US; it is normally conducted as a gentle drift). Every year, during August and September, grey reef sharks congregate around Enenue to mate and give birth, and there are sometimes loose schools of juvenile sharks around at this time. The crater can get busy with snorkellers and divers, but Molokini offers some beautiful dives with a variety of walls, gentle slopes, sand patches, pristine corals and a diverse reef community.

Bait/feed no.

Cage no.

Other wildlife various cetaceans (including humpback whales: present Nov–Jun, but best Feb–Mar), manta and eagle rays, moray eel, jack, wide variety of reef fish (many endemic to Hawaii), spiny lobster.

Best time of year sharks present year-round (grey reef most concentrated Aug–Sep).

Dive depth 12–40 m/40–130 ft.

Typical visibility 30–50 m/100–165 ft (reputed to have the clearest waters in Hawaii).

Water temperature 22 °C/72 °F in Feb, 27 °C/81 °F in Sep.

Weather and sea notes currents variable, but can be strong (especially around full moon); typically calm in the mornings, windy in the afternoons.

Contact details Mike Severns Diving (www.mikesevernsdiving.com), Maui Dive Shop (www.mauidiveshop.com).

Travel international flights to Honolulu; connecting flights to Maui; Molokini is a 20–40-min boat ride (depending on departure point) from Maui; wide choice of accommodation.

5 HAWAII: MIDWAY ATOLL

Location north-west end of Hawaiian archipelago; 2000 km/1250 miles north-west of Honolulu.

Main species *most trips:* Galápagos, tiger (above the surface, not while diving); *occasional trips:* grey reef, whitetip reef, blacktip (from lagoon piers, not while diving).

Viewing opportunities Midway Atoll consists of three islands surrounded by a beautiful shallow lagoon and sheltered by a circular reef. Best known for being the location of the pivotal naval battle of World War II, it was opened up to non-military visitors in 1997 and is currently the only north-western Hawaiian island open to recreational divers. There are three islands within the atoll (Sand, Eastern and Spit): Sand Island is the largest and, with about 150 residents, the only one that is inhabited.

There are large numbers of sharks at Midway and they can be seen at many dive sites both inside and outside the lagoon. Galápagos sharks are virtually guaranteed at several key dive sites as they patrol the outskirts of the lagoon. Fish Hole is a shallow dive, outside the atoll in the south, with lots of Galápagos sharks; visibility is best during low tide. There are many of them at Pitt Stop, and outside the atoll in the south-west; and nearby Chromis offers some great photo opportunities when the sharks approach divers during safety stops. But perhaps the best place for Galápagos sharks is the Channel, a man-made cut through the reef originally created by the US Navy to allow large ships to enter the lagoon, where it is not uncommon to see more than 20 sharks and up to a dozen spotted eagle rays during a single dive; visibility here is best when there is an incoming current. Whitetip reef sharks can sometimes be found within snorkelling range, close to shore, and can be seen at Cargo Pier.

Tiger sharks are rarely encountered by divers, but large numbers of them move into the lagoon for a few weeks every summer to feed on newly fledged albatrosses. Midway is a refuge for the world's largest colony of Laysan albatrosses, or gooney birds as they are more popularly known, and nearly half a million pairs breed on the atoll. Their incessant calling is an integral part of life here. When the albatross chicks are fledging in July and early August, at an age of about 18–21 weeks, they begin to practise flying. Many of them are unsuccessful the first time and crash into the sea. Their downy feathers become waterlogged and, when they cannot take off again, they have little choice but to sit on the water and wait. This is when the lagoon becomes an albatross smorgasbord for tiger sharks, which arrive en masse to feed on the hapless fledglings. Some of the tigers are 4 m/14 ft or more in length. It is not permitted to dive or snorkel in the area when this is happening, but visitors are taken out in small boats to watch the feast safely.

Bait/feed no.

Cage no.

Other wildlife long-snouted spinner dolphin (250 inhabit the lagoon during the day and exit to feed in deeper waters each evening) and other cetaceans, Hawaiian monk seal (45–55 individuals readily seen but rarely encountered underwater), Laysan albatross, black-footed albatross, variety of petrels, boobies, terns and frigatebirds, green turtle, manta ray, spotted eagle ray, many endemic reef fish.

Best time of year Galápagos present year-round; tiger best Jul–early Aug (coinciding with peak albatross fledging period); best diving Jul–Sep.

Dive depth 4.5–27 m/15–90 ft (depending on site).

Typical visibility 6–7.5 m/20–25 ft inside lagoon; 18–37 m/60–120 ft outside lagoon; visibility changes rapidly during tidal shifts.

Water temperature 18–29 °C/65–84 °F; warmest in summer; cold-water upwellings frequently encountered.

Weather and sea notes sheltered inside the lagoon with no strong currents; outside lagoon currents range from mild to strong; some southern sites subject to easterly swell; warm and slightly humid in summer, cooler with some wind and rain in winter.

Contact details Midway Atoll National Wildlife Refuge (http://midway.fws.gov), Midway Phoenix Corporation (www.midwayisland.com), Oceanic Society Expeditions (www.oceanic-society.org), Waikīkī Aquarium (www.mic.hawaii.edu/aquarium/class/travel.html), Destination Pacific (www.fishdive.com/midwayatoll.htm).

Travel accessible via three-hour flight from Honolulu; private air-charter services and cruise ships visit periodically; limited to 100 visitors in residence at any one time; comfortable accommodation in the renovated Naval Bachelor Officer Quarters on Sand Island.

Notes tiger sharks can also be seen hunting albatross fledglings around Laysan Island and French Frigate Shoals, both at the north-west end of the Hawaiian archipelago; access is difficult via small chartered aircraft (French Frigate Shoals) or boat (Laysan). The season is slightly earlier than at Midway (best time mid-Jun to early Jul). On Midway, Waikīkī Aquarium offers an opportunity to join shark researchers working on a shark tagging and tracking programme. At the time of going to press, diving at Midway was about to be suspended – please check the websites for further details.

6 WASHINGTON STATE: SEATTLE SEACREST PARK

Location west side of Elliott Bay, in Puget Sound.

Main species *many trips:* bluntnose sixgill (*Hexanchus griseus*).

Viewing opportunities Seattle may be one of the least-likely places for an exceptional shark dive, but it offers one of the best chances anywhere in the world to see little-known sixgill sharks. In fact, there is probably nowhere better for shore diving with these deep-water animals. Puget Sound has several locations where it is possible to dive with sixgills from shore, but three coves near the Seacrest Fishing Pier in Seacrest Park are the best known and certainly the most readily accessible. Number one lies to the south, near Salty's Restaurant, and coves two and three are immediately south and north (respectively) of the pier itself. The fact that the sharks – which, when adult, are normally found at great depths of up to 2500 m/8200 ft – can be seen in such shallow water and so close to shore offers an incredible opportunity to study them without having to incur the expense of deep-ocean research. Biologists from the Seattle Aquarium have documented sightings for more than 30 years, but these have increased significantly since the mid-1990s and the waters around Seacrest have become a major hotspot in the past two years. This does not necessarily signify an increase in the population, and is probably more an indication that more divers have learnt where and when to look. The sharks seem to enter Elliott Bay to feed on dogfish, ratfish and squid and reach a maximum length here of about 5 m/16 ft (large adults from else-where in the world have been reported to reach lengths of half as much again). Divers simply walk about 12–21 m/40–70 ft for a surfless entry into the water and then swim along the gently sloping, silty

seabed for another 70 m/230 ft until the depth is about 21 m/70 ft. Although they have been seen in water as shallow as 10 m/33 ft, the sharks are normally found at 21–27 m/70–90 ft. Most sightings are at dawn and dusk (during twilight), but they may be seen at any time of the day and will often investigate divers quite closely.

Bait/feed no (local divers strongly discourage baiting attempts).

Cage no.

Other wildlife Pacific spiny dogfish, giant octopus, lingcod.

Best time of year peak sightings Jul–Oct, but encounters reported year-round.

Dive depth 10–30 m/33–100 ft.

Typical visibility 1–12 m/3–40 ft (average 6 m/20 ft).

Water temperature 10 °C/50 °F year-round.

Weather and sea notes mild currents (diveable regardless of tide conditions – a rarity in Puget Sound); seas generally calm (protected from all but easterly winds) year-round.

Contact details Northwest Sports Divers (www.nwsportsdivers.com), ScubaSET Adventure Center (walt@scubaset.com), Seattle Aquarium (www.seattleaquarium.org), Seattle Parks and Recreation (www.ci.seattle.wa.us/parks/).

Travel national and international flights to Seattle; short drive to the site; wide choice of accommodation.

Note there is a campaign to stop fishing for sixgill sharks off West Seattle's Seacrest Fishing Pier. After fishermen caught a number of 2–3 m/7–10 ft sharks, a howl of protest from local divers and biologists resulted in a 120-day temporary ban on killing sixgills, from 15 August 2000. Anglers could continue to fish for them, but had to release the animals alive. Local experts are concerned that too much fishing could harm the shark population in Puget Sound, and the Washington State Department of Fish and Wildlife is working with experts from a variety of organizations to study sixgills in the area before considering further regulations.

7 CALIFORNIA: FARALLON ISLANDS

Location approximately 43 km/27 miles west of the Golden Gate, San Francisco.

Main species *many trips:* great white; *occasional trips:* blue.

Viewing opportunities the group of windswept, wave-eroded outcroppings forming the Farallon Islands are bathed in nutrient-rich upwelling currents and few marine areas are as bountiful in marine wildlife. Contiguous with the Monterey Bay National

Marine Sanctuary, the region has itself been declared a National Marine Sanctuary. Large great whites forage for immature northern elephant seals and other pinnipeds in the waters around the islands each autumn. They have been studied, particularly around South East Farallon (often known as SEFI – the largest island in the group) since the late 1960s and have put the islands on the world map. Researchers watch for shark attacks from the lofty peak of Lighthouse Hill, which offers a superb vantage point, and then launch a small Boston whaler for a closer view of the feeding activity. One-day shark-watching trips are conducted in the same area, over a boulder-strewn seabed in some 6–12 m/20–40 ft of water. Decoys are used, rather than bait, and participants can observe the sharks from the boat or from a sturdy two–person cage. During the 2000 season, great whites were encountered on more than 80 per cent of trips (although there was often a long wait for them to arrive) and participants observed many breach attacks above the surface and a small number had close encounters from the cage. There are no more than six divers per trip. Visitors are not allowed to land on the islands.

Bait/feed no (decoys only).

Cage yes.

Other wildlife grey whale (mainly Apr–May and Oct–Nov), blue and humpback whales (Jun–Nov), Risso's dolphin, Pacific white-sided dolphin, Dall's porpoise, northern elephant seal, California sea lion, Steller's sea lion, many seabirds (as many as 12 species, with up to 250,000 birds).

Best time of year Sep–Nov (peak period for white shark predation at the Farallon Islands).

Dive depth cage floats at the surface.

Typical visibility 3–12 m/10–40 ft (average 6 m/20 ft).

Water temperature 10–13 °C/50–55 °F.

Weather and sea notes heavy fog common during summer; cool temperatures with frequent rain showers Oct–Nov; cage diving can be difficult when small storms pass through.

Contact details Golden Gate Expeditions (www.goldengateexpeditions.com).

Travel trips leave from Alameda, in San Francisco Bay; national and international flights to San Francisco; wide choice of accommodation in and around the city.

Notes researchers and shark divers may be out with the sharks simultaneously and there is some friction between the two (the researchers being concerned that the presence of shark watchers may be disruptive).

Location 5.6 km/3½ miles east of Moss Landing, approximately halfway between Santa Cruz and Monterey.

Main species *most trips*: leopard (*Triakis semifasciata*), brown smooth-hound (*Mustelus henlei*), gray smooth-hound (*Mustelis californicus*).

Viewing opportunities this important coastal wetland area of tidal creeks and restored salt marshes is best known for its spectacular bird life, but Elkhorn Slough is also a great place for watching sharks. During the spring, summer and autumn, sharks and rays are abundant here and can easily be seen from the elevated wooded boardwalks or from shore. Many people enjoy watching them from tour boats or kayaks, as well. Adult leopard sharks – among the most beautiful of all sharks – can reach an impressive length of about 2 m/7 ft. They feed mainly at night in the main channel (which winds inland for nearly 11 km/7 miles), then gather in the shallows of the Slough during the day. Younger animals (less than 1.2 m/4 ft) are found in the shallower lagoons at any time of the day or night. Their main diet is fat innkeeper worms, which they find in the mud, and bottom-dwelling fish. They also use Elkhorn Slough as a pupping ground. The best time to see them is at high tide and on an incoming tide, when it is possible to watch large numbers of them swarming in such shallow water that their dorsal fins break the surface. Leopard sharks sometimes mix with much smaller brown smooth-hound sharks (1 m/3 ft) and gray smooth-hound sharks (75 cm/30 in) in these shallows. The smooth-hounds do not breed here, but can be seen cruising the bottom looking for crabs, shrimps and small fish. There are no particular viewing areas, but the Elkhorn Slough National Estuarine Research Reserve footbridge is good and there is an excellent 1.6 km/1 mile walking trail at nearby Kirby Park Public Access, which runs alongside the Slough (a portion of it is elevated) in an area where sharks can be seen very close to shore at high tide.

Other wildlife harbour seals and sea otters in the main slough channels; wide variety of birds year-round (greatest variety spring and autumn, but large numbers of waterfowl and waders in winter); bat ray, stingray.

Best time of year sharks present year-round, but greatest numbers mid-summer to early autumn.

Contact details Elkhorn Slough Foundation (www.elkhornslough.org), Elkhorn Slough National Estuarine Research Reserve (www.members.cruzio.com/~dchase/), Elkhorn Slough Safari Nature Boat Tours (www.elkhornslough.com).

Travel head north of Moss Landing on Highway 1,

then at the power plant take Dolan Road east 5.6 km/
3½ miles, left into Elkhorn Road, 3.5 km/2¼ miles to
the reserve entrance and visitor centre; closest town
Moss Landing with a wide choice of accommodation.

Note there have been problems with archers at
Elkhorn, who use the smooth-hound sharks for target
practice; anyone seen doing this should be reported
to the authorities.

9 CALIFORNIA: SAN MIGUEL ISLAND

Location westernmost and northernmost of the
North Channel Islands; 72 km/45 miles west of Santa
Barbara, 89 km/55 miles west of Ventura.

Main species *occasional trips:* blue, shortfin mako,
great white.

Viewing opportunities there is no dedicated shark
diving at San Miguel, but it is home to blues, shortfin
makos and great whites and has enormous potential
for regular sightings. It is an exciting place to dive
(rarely without the company of California sea lions or
harbour seals) although it can be difficult to reach in
bad weather. San Miguel supports an exceptionally
high density of pinnipeds – northern elephant seals,
California sea lions, northern fur seals and harbour
seals are all common breeders on the island, while
Steller's sea lions and Guadalupe fur seals occur occasionally. It is the seals that attract great whites, which
are known to hunt at Point Bennett on the western
end of the island. In 1995 a great white is believed to
have been responsible for the death of a commercial
urchin diver using a 'scooter' along the reef here.
Great whites are occasionally seen during dive trips
and, although there have been no verified attacks on
recreational divers, everyone is advised not to make
long surface swims in the area. Blues and shortfin
makos are sometimes seen off the north shore, along
the 11-km/7-mile chain known as the Front Side
Seamounts. Wilson Rock and Richardson Rock
(10 km/6 miles north-east and 11 km/7 miles north-
west of Point Bennett respectively) are the best
known of these seamounts and the only two rising
a few metres above the surface. The others, hidden
18–27 m/60–90 ft beneath the surface (their exact
depth depends upon the tide), are Boomerang and
Skyscraper. Wilson and Richardson are surrounded by
churning boilers and have dramatic sheer rock walls
plunging into the deep. Diving folklore suggests that
sharks do not go to Wilson and divers do not go to
Richardson but, of course, this is far from true and
shark sightings are made at both sites. There is also
a small island called Castle Rock, whose reef is almost
contiguous with Point Bennett Reef to the south-west,
which has a growing reputation for shark sightings.

Dubbed the Shark Park, it lives up to its name when
the visibility is good by rewarding divers with occasional sightings of great whites and shortfin makos.
The sharks are probably around more often than
records suggest because, in poorer visibility, they
may simply remain beyond normal vision.

Bait/feed no.

Cage no.

Other wildlife various cetaceans; northern elephant
seal, harbour seal, California sea lion and northern
fur seal (common breeders); Guadalupe fur seal and
Steller's sea lion (occasional visitors); electric ray; rich
variety and huge numbers of invertebrates.

Best time of year May–Oct.

Dive depth 9–30 m/30–100 ft (depending on site).

Typical visibility 6–18 m/20–60 ft (occasionally
up to 24 m/80 ft, especially in open water); plankton
blooms above the thermocline can dramatically
reduce visibility near the surface; water clearest
Sep–Oct.

Water temperature 10–18 °C/50–65 °F during
summer (warmest Aug–Oct); influenced by cooler,
nutrient-rich California current, which results in cooler
water temperatures than some other Channel Islands.

Weather and sea notes subject to high winds and
fog, even during summer (stronger winds and bigger
seas in winter); strong currents and surge normal; dive
trips may be cancelled when bad weather prevents
crossing from the mainland.

Contact details Cal Boat Diving
(www.calboatdiving.com), Truth Aquatics
(www.truthaquatics.com).

Travel accessible only via multi-day trips on live-
aboards from San Pedro, Ventura or Santa Barbara;
national and international flights to Los Angeles; wide
choice of accommodation in southern California.

Note there are limits to how close boats are allowed
to approach the island (to protect breeding seals and
nesting seabirds): 275 m/900 ft within the San Miguel
Ecological Reserve and 90 m/300 ft (15 Mar–30 Apr
and 1 Oct–15 Dec) elsewhere. Shark feeds do not
take place at San Miguel for fear of attracting and
aggravating great whites, which could cause
problems for the commercial diving community as
well as for sports.

10 CALIFORNIA: MALAGA COVE

Location 1 km/½ mile from Torrance Beach on
north coast of Palos Verdes Peninsula (approximately
16 km/10 miles south of LA Airport) in Los Angeles
County.

Main species *many trips:* swell (*Cephaloscyllium ventriosum*), horn (*Heterodontus francisci*), Pacific angel (*Squatina californica*), leopard (*Triakis semifasciata*).

Viewing opportunities this unlikely site, in a busy residential area facing Santa Monica Bay, is surprisingly good for shark watching. Sharks of no fewer than four species can be found in and around the shallow reef directly in front of Malaga Cove School. Enter the water below the bluff at Malaga Cove. If the visibility is sufficiently good, this is a site that can be enjoyed by snorkellers as well as divers, but bear in mind that it is quite a climb from the shore back to the parking area by the school, so it is not for everyone.

Bait/feed no.

Cage no.

Other wildlife bat ray, shovel-nosed guitarfish, lobster.

Best time of year sharks present year-round, but best diving May–Oct.

Dive depth 4.5–11 m/15–35 ft.

Typical visibility 3–12 m/10–40 ft.

Water temperature 16–21 °C/61–70 °F during summer (warmest Aug–Oct); falls to around 13 °C/55 °F Dec–Jan.

Weather and sea notes seas generally calm during summer (stronger winds and bigger seas in winter), but unprotected in prevailing winds.

Contact details The Sand Eaters (www.geocities.com/sandeaters).

Travel accessible from shore (approaching Palos Verdes from the north on US1, turn right on to Palos Verdes Boulevard, right on to Via Corta, then merge with Via Almar, right on to Via Arroyo to Paseo del Mar – access to Torrance Beach behind the school); national and international flights to San Diego or Los Angeles; wide choice of accommodation.

Note blue sharks are also common here and, indeed, along the entire coast of LA County. They are rarely seen by divers but, according to local lifeguards and surfers, are cruising just outside the surf break much of the time.

11 CALIFORNIA: SANTA CATALINA ISLAND

Location 40 km/25 miles south of Long Beach and San Pedro; 130 km/80 miles north-west of San Diego.

Main species *most trips:* blue; *many trips:* Pacific angel (*Squatina californica*), horn (*Heterodontus francisci*), leopard (*Triakis semifasciata*); *occasional*

trips: shortfin mako, swell (*Cephaloscyllium ventriosum*), soupfin (*Galeorhinus galeus*).

Viewing opportunities there are many different shark-watching opportunities around Santa Catalina Island, the largest of the South Channel Islands, ranging from open-water cage dives to shallow-water snorkels. The main attraction is cage diving with blue sharks, which has been conducted here for decades at several open-water sites around the island. One popular site is 15 Mile Bank (24 km/15 miles off the coast of Newport Beach between the mainland and Santa Catalina), but there are others. The captain cuts the engines and, while the boat drifts with the winds and currents, chumming begins. The favourite chum is mackerel – an oily fish that creates a lot of scent when dispersed in the water. Twenty years ago it was not uncommon to attract 100 blues or more, but so many sharks have been killed in recent years by gill-netting and for their fins that their numbers have dramatically declined. However, at least some blues usually appear within an hour or so. Most range in size from 1.2–3 m/ 4–10 ft. As soon as they are around the boat, the crew feeds them larger pieces of fish to keep their interest while the divers enter the cage. Some operators hang the cage 3–4.5 m/10–15 ft underwater; others float it at the surface, which enables snorkellers with no scuba qualifications to take part. The cages vary in size according to the operator, but some hold as many as six people, allowing maximum time with the sharks. When everyone is settled, the guide hand-feeds the sharks in front of the cage, offering some fabulous photo opportunities. Many divers prefer to swim freely with the sharks, outside the cage, and although the blues are curious and approach very closely they are not aggressive. Shortfin makos appear on about 25 per cent of dives (blue sharks outnumber makos here by about 20:1) and will stay around if they are fed entire fish. Makos have never harmed a diver at Catalina and are usually relatively small (in the 2 m/ 7 ft range) here. But they are faster than the blues, and behave a little more boldly (some would say aggressively) and many people prefer to enter the cage for these heart-thumping encounters. Lucky divers may also witness California sea lions taunting the sharks – blues and makos – by nipping their fins and stealing their food. Sea lions are sometimes killed and eaten by both species, but they seem to get away with these antics by being faster and more agile.

Catalina Island is justly famous for its spectacular forests of giant kelp and this is where, in recent years, soupfin sharks have been spotted. Sharks in the 1.5–2 m/5–6 ft range are believed to move into the kelp during the latter part of the summer (Jul–Sep) and are now being seen with some regularity. The best place to see angel sharks is probably Ship Rock, a seamount that rises 20 m/65 ft above the surface off the north-west coast outside Isthmus Harbour. On the north side, facing the channel, the seamount drops to the sandy seabed at a depth of about 37 m/120 ft and this is a well-known resting place for the sharks. They were once very common, and it was not unusual to see 20 or more in a single dive, but their numbers have declined dramatically in recent years – perhaps because they are a popular target for spearfishermen. Some dive operators actually send a guide to look for an angel shark and then put a marker near it (they are bottom-dwellers and stay still for long periods) to help their clients find it later. Swell sharks can also be found near Ship Rock, hiding in the caves and crevices (they are more active at night); it is sometimes possible to find their strange egg cases here, too. Horn sharks are particularly common around Catalina, and leopard sharks school in very shallow water here; in places like Fisherman's Cove, leopards can be found in just 1 m/ 40 in of water and, although they are quite nervous around bubble-blowing scuba divers, they are easy to approach on snorkel. The muddy bottom at Fisherman's Cove is also very popular with angel sharks.

Great whites are known to occur around Santa Catalina, and are occasionally encountered by divers (there were a number of sightings in 2001), but have never caused any problems.

Bait/feed yes (cage diving only).

Cage yes (cage diving only).

Other wildlife various cetaceans, California sea lion, northern elephant seal, harbour seal, ocean sunfish.

Best time of year May–Oct (when open-water shark sites are readily accessible); best in spring and autumn when fewer fishing tournaments.

Dive depth cage suspended at the surface or 3–4.5 m/10–15 ft; angel sharks at 37 m/120 ft.

Typical visibility 9–24 m/30–80 ft (occasionally up to 30 m/100 ft especially in open water); closer to shore, and away from currents, plankton blooms can dramatically reduce visibility near the surface; water clearest Sep–Oct.

Water temperature 18–24 °C/65–75 °F in summer (warmest Aug–Oct).

Weather and sea notes seas generally calm during summer (strong winds and big seas in winter); fairly strong currents at some sites.

Contact details Psalty Adventures (www.psaltyadventures.com), Team Shark Inc. (www.teamshark.com), Catalina Scuba Luv (www.scubaluv.com), Great Escape Charters (www.diveboat.com).

Travel day trips from mainland California and Catalina or multi-day trips on live-aboards; national and international flights to San Diego or Los Angeles; wide choice of accommodation in southern California and on the island.

12 CALIFORNIA: AVALON BANKS

Location 11 km/7 miles off Avalon, south-east Catalina Island (35 km/22 miles off Long Beach).

Main species *most trips:* blue; *occasional trips:* shortfin mako.

Viewing opportunities this is a fabulous opportunity for snorkellers and divers alike to experience active sharks in the open ocean. It is a 2½-hour ride to Avalon Banks, in the San Pedro Channel, where male and female blue sharks are present year-round. On arrival it is too deep to anchor (approximately 400 m/1300 ft), so the boat simply drifts with the wind and current. Mackerel and skipjack tuna are used as chum to attract the sharks close to the boat – which may take as little as a few minutes or as long as five hours. A rectangular, welded aluminium cage, measuring 5 m/16 ft long, 2.5 m/8 ft wide and 1.2 m/4 ft deep and covered with vinyl-encased steel mesh, has been designed specially to give snorkellers an opportunity to encounter the sharks in safety. There are floats to keep it at the surface and it is tied to the side of the boat. Participants enter using a swim ladder and as many as 10 can use the cage at any one time. No dive qualifications are required and everyone gets unlimited time in the cage. Experienced divers with a minimum of 20 logged dives are able to enter the water outside the cage (in the company of a safety diver wearing a chainmail suit) using drop lines attached to the swim step on the stern of the boat. Each diver gets a minimum of one 20-minute dive at a depth of about 4.5 m/15 ft. Participants are not allowed to touch or feed the sharks, which range in length from 0.6–2.7 m/2–9 ft, although they come extremely close and may bump into underwater cameras and video housing. As few as one and as many as 20 sharks (mainly blues) are seen on some 90 per cent of trips. These dives are also sometimes conducted at night, using the cage for safety and a powerful 1400-watt lighting system, when the metallic blue of the sharks looks even more dramatic.

Bait/feed yes.

Cage yes (snorkellers, inexperienced divers during the day and all divers at night); no (experienced divers during the day).

Other wildlife grey whale (winter–spring), fin whale, long-finned pilot whale, Risso's dolphin, common dolphin, long-snouted spinner dolphin, California sea lion, ocean sunfish.

Best time of year sharks present year-round, but best conditions for chumming Oct–Mar.

Dive depth surface (snorkellers), 4.5 m/15 ft (divers).

Typical visibility minimum 10 m/33 ft in winter/spring, 18 m/60 ft in summer/autumn.

Water temperature 14–22 °C/57–72 °F depending on season.

Weather and sea notes storms and big swells can pass through the area year-round and 10–15-knot winds are typical, even in summer.

Contact details Dive Aquatica (www.diveaquatica.com).

Travel national and international flights to Los Angeles; wide choice of accommodation in and around the city; vessel based in Los Angeles harbour (30 mins from LAX airport or 10 mins from Long Beach) and journey time to shark dive site is about 2½ hours.

Notes there is a strong educational emphasis to the trips, with informative presentations on everything from shark chumming to shark biology. Participants are also given the opportunity to assist with collecting, tagging, documenting and releasing juvenile sharks, as part of a research programme investigating their movement patterns.

13 CALIFORNIA: SAN CLEMENTE ISLAND

Location southernmost of the South Channel Islands; 97 km/60 miles west of San Diego.

Main species *most trips:* blue; *many trips:* shortfin mako, horn (*Heterodontus francisci*), swell (*Cephaloscyllium ventriosum*), leopard (*Triakis semifasciata*).

Viewing opportunities San Clemente is well known to Californian divers for having lots of superb all-weather dive sites (especially in Pyramid Cove) with spectacular canyons, arches, walls and kelp forests. It is possible to find horn and swell sharks hiding among the rocks during the day or actively feeding in the open at night. Literally dozens of leopard sharks also congregate here during the summer, mainly in the shallows off the front side of the island; they range in size from 1–1.8 m/3⅓–6 ft and gather to mate along the sand and gravel bottoms in about 6 m/20 ft of water or less. But the best shark diving takes place in open water several kilometres offshore and the calm lee of the island is used merely for practice. Participants have the opportunity to remove all extra gear and hoses that might entangle in the shark cage and then swim from the stern of the boat to the cage, work the latches on the door and adjust their weight and buoyancy to anchor themselves to the floor – before doing it for real while surrounded by hungry sharks. When everyone is ready, the boat makes for open water, where it drops a sea anchor and drifts in the

gentle current. The sharks are attracted by chumming and, when there are enough of them, the cage is lowered into the water. Secured to a mooring line, while the air from the ballast tanks is slowly released, it sinks to the desired depth of about 3–4.5 m/10–15 ft. The depth of the water here is at least 600 m/2000 ft. A chainmail-suited leader escorts each diver, one by one, into the cage. There are four divers in the cage for 45–60 minutes at a time and, by taking turns, everyone gets at least two dives (sometimes more, depending on how quickly the sharks appear). The leader stays outside the cage, with a bag of bait, and encourages the sharks to come very close. As many as 40–50 blue sharks may appear on a good day, sometimes with a few makos as well, ranging in size from less than 1 m/3⅓ ft to over 2.1 m/7 ft. Divers are permitted to leave the cage at their own discretion. However, when the sharks get excited (especially after prolonged chumming) they tend to snap repeatedly at anything in the water – from the boat's dive platform to the bait bag – so it is sometimes necessary to return to the sanctuary of the cage, just in case. When the food has gone and the scraps have been dispersed by the ocean current, the sharks begin to slip away and the divers return to the boat.

Bait/feed yes.

Cage yes.

Other wildlife ocean sunfish (open water); harbour seal, California sea lion, moray eel, bat ray, garibaldi, octopus (close to shore).

Best time of year May–Oct (when open-water shark sites are readily accessible).

Dive depth cage suspended at 3–4.5 m/10–15 ft; island dives 18–30 m/60–100 ft.

Typical visibility 9–24 m/30–80 ft (occasionally up to 30 m/100 ft in open water); closer to shore, and away from currents, plankton blooms can dramatically reduce visibility near the surface; water clearest Sep–Oct.

Water temperature 18–24 °C/65–75 °F in summer; warmest Aug–Oct.

Weather and sea notes swell and surge common, even during the summer (stronger winds and bigger seas in winter).

Contact details San Diego Shark Diving Expeditions (www.sdsharkdiving.com).

Travel day trips from mainland California or multi-day trips on live-aboards from San Diego; national and international flights to San Diego or Los Angeles; wide choice of accommodation in southern California.

Note San Clemente is owned and controlled by the US Navy and sometimes parts of the island are closed to boat traffic due to live firing exercises. Assume that any bomb or artillery shell found on the seabed is live and report its location to the authorities.

14 CALIFORNIA: 9-MILE BANK

Location 16–32 km/10–20 miles offshore from San Diego.

Main species *most trips:* blue; *many trips:* shortfin mako.

Viewing opportunities this is a thrilling one-day trip to encounter active sharks in the open ocean. It takes about 90 minutes to travel to an offshore underwater mountain range known as 9-Mile Bank and, since anchoring is impossible in such deep water, the boat simply drifts with the wind and current. After a detailed briefing there is a practice dive (which all participants must take) to ensure that everyone is correctly weighted and that all the equipment is working properly, to get used to the sense of vertigo that often comes with diving in more than 1000 m/3300 ft of deep-blue sea, to experience getting in and out of the cage without sharks present, and to see the hand signals that the expedition leader will use to communicate with everyone. The rectangular, welded aluminium cage is covered with vinyl-encased steel mesh and is suspended from floats at a depth of about 5 m/16 ft. It is tethered to the dive vessel, at a distance of about 8 m/25 ft, and rubber shock absorbers are attached to the tether and float lines to dampen the surface chop in order to provide a smoother ride. After the practice dive, chumming begins to attract sharks to the boat. This can take anything from a few minutes to several hours; as soon as the sharks are actively feeding, each diver is escorted to the cage, one by one, by the expedition leader, who wears a chainmail suit and headphones to maintain verbal communication with the boat crew on the surface. There are four people in the cage at any one time and each diver has an individual window that is opened to give an unobstructed view of the action. The leader then takes up position in front of the cage and baits the sharks right up to the divers and their cameras. Although he does not allow himself to be bitten by the makos (their needle-sharp teeth easily go through the chainmail suit), the blues frequently bite both him and the cage. On a typical day some 10–30 blue sharks and 1–2 makos put in an appearance, but there could be as few as 5–6; on a couple of memorable occasions more than 100 have turned up. There are no more than eight divers per trip and they are rotated in the cage until sunset to give everyone two or three dives of 30–60 minutes each.

Bait/feed yes.

Cage yes.

Other wildlife blue whale (Jun–Sep), bottlenose and common dolphins, California sea lion, ocean sunfish.

Best time of year Apr–Nov (high season Sep–Oct); trips tend to avoid the strong winds and big seas of winter.

Dive depth 5 m/16 ft.

Typical visibility 10–30 m/33–100 ft.

Water temperature 18–21 °C/65–70 °F.

Weather and sea notes site exposed in open ocean, so a 1 m/39 in swell is typical.

Contact details San Diego Shark Diving Expeditions (www.sdsharkdiving.com).

Travel trips leave in season from Mission Bay, near Sea World, San Diego; direct domestic and international flights to San Diego (or via Los Angeles); wide choice of accommodation in and around the city.

15 TEXAS: FLOWER GARDEN BANKS

Location 185 km/115 miles south of Texas/Louisiana border (260 km/160 miles south-east of Houston) in north-western Gulf of Mexico.

Main species *most trips:* scalloped hammerhead, whale, silky; *many trips:* nurse.

Viewing opportunities the Flower Garden Banks National Marine Sanctuary harbours the northernmost coral reef system in the continental United States. It consists of three submarine banks bulging out of the seabed at a depth of some 120 m/400 ft and rising to within about 18 m/60 ft of the surface. Shark sightings are virtually guaranteed at the right time of year although, frustratingly, scalloped hammerheads and whale sharks are found here in different seasons. West Flower Garden rises to within 20 m/65 ft of the surface and its colourful coral meadow stretches over an area of 40 ha/100 acres; East Flower Garden, which is about 19 km/12 miles away and lies just 17 m/55 ft beneath the surface, covers an area of 162 ha/400 acres. Stetson Bank, or Stetson Rock as it is sometimes known, lies 72 km/45 miles closer to shore; added to the sanctuary in 1996 and barely larger than a couple of baseball fields, it is quite different in character (many divers describe it as a moonscape) with no corals but plenty of sponges and colourful fish. Literally hundreds of scalloped hammerheads gather in Flower Garden Banks every winter and it is not unusual to see dozens of them, their fins slicing the surface of the water, as you make your giant stride entry. Whale sharks can be seen at all three reefs throughout the summer. Their behaviour towards divers and snorkellers varies enormously from one individual to another: many of them merely swim past, but others will hang around for an hour or more. Juvenile silky sharks can also be seen in the area every autumn and early winter. Large numbers of 1–1.2 m/ 3⅓–4 ft youngsters congregate at the natural-gas platform near the East Flower Garden (gas and oil platforms throughout the Gulf of Mexico serve as nurseries for silkies) and divers frequently encounter them exploring the reef.

Bait/feed no.

Cage no.

Other wildlife Atlantic spotted dolphin, loggerhead turtle, spotted eagle ray, manta ray, mobula ray, mass coral spawning takes place on the eighth night after Aug or early Sep full moon.

Best time of year diving year-round; peak season May–Oct, but best months Aug–Sep; scalloped hammerhead late Dec to early Apr; whale Jun–Sep; silky Sep–Apr.

Dive depth 17–30 m/55–100 ft (though pelagics often spotted near the surface).

Typical visibility 15–38 m/50–125 ft (averages 30 m/100 ft).

Water temperature 19–22 °C/66–72 °F in winter, 27–29 °C/81–84 °F in summer.

Weather and sea notes boats sometimes unable to make the crossing in bad winter weather; currents common, but generally limited to the top 12 m/40 ft of water.

Contact details Rinn Boats (www.rinnboats.com), Sea Searcher II (www.seasearcherii.com).

Travel accessible only via live-aboard from Freeport, Texas (6–7 hours one-way); national and international flights to Houston (less than 90-min drive from Freeport); wide choice of accommodation in Freeport.

Notes during the hammerhead season, in 2001, sand tiger sharks were spotted by divers on many occasions (very unusual for this area); they left after the hammerheads had gone. The same year was also unusual for having few whale shark sightings.

16 FLORIDA: SAMANTHA'S LEDGE/ SHARK LEDGE

Location Samantha's Ledge is a few kilometres east of Marathon (a central Florida Keys island, accessible via the Overseas Highway, about 80 km/50 miles from Key West).

Main species *most trips:* nurse; *occasional trips:* Caribbean reef.

Viewing opportunities Samantha's Ledge is a delightful dive in its own right, with its shallow reef and a lush collection of soft corals and prolific fish life. But it is best known for its resident population of about half a dozen nurse sharks. Sightings are virtually guaranteed. Most of the sharks are juveniles (the site appears to be a nursery area where they are born and grow large enough to fend for themselves) and range from 1–2 m/3–7 ft in length. Each individual is known to local divers – Taz, for example, appears to be a bit of a troublemaker (Taz is short for Tasmanian Devil) and seems intent on winding up the other sharks; Snuggles lives up to his name by lying in front of the divemaster for a head rub. Although there is a no-touching policy for participating divers, the sharks are extremely friendly and will approach very closely. They used to be offered ballyhoo and squid by the divemaster and, although they are normally nocturnal bottom-feeders, adapted well to this artificial food source and would feed at any time of the day and at any depth. However, on 1 January 2002, Florida became the first state in the US to prohibit divers from feeding sharks, and food is no longer offered during this dive. The sharks are normally waiting when the boat arrives although, on rare occasions, they remain fast asleep under the coral ledges with only their tails visible. This is a trip that can be enjoyed by divers and snorkellers alike, and there are typically 12–18 participants.

Bait/feed no.

Cage no.

Other wildlife moray eel.

Best time of year sharks present year-round.

Dive depth 4.5–7.5 m/15–25 ft.

Typical visibility 10–30 m/33–100 ft (averages 12 m/40 ft in winter, 15 m/50 ft in summer).

Water temperature 21–32 °C/70–90 °F.

Weather and sea notes best diving conditions (calmer, clearer water) May–Sep; hurricane season Jun–Oct.

Contact details The Diving Site (www.divingsite.com), Abyss Dive Center (www.abyssdive.com).

Travel national and international flights to Miami or Key West; choice of accommodation on Marathon.

17 FLORIDA: TENECO TOWERS

Location 2.8 km/1¾ mile off Hallandale (between Fort Lauderdale and Miami), just north of the Dade County line.

Main species *many trips:* bull, nurse.

Viewing opportunities Teneco Towers is a spectacular artificial reef established by the Teneco Oil Company in 1985, by sinking two oil-production platforms and a section of a third. They lie in 30–58 m/ 100–190 ft of water with some sections rising to within 18 m/60 ft of the surface. The structures are covered with a colourful jungle of sponges, gorgonians and invertebrates and the fish life around them is exceptionally rich. Bull sharks are seen here throughout the winter, and many divers have really good encounters, but the best time to see them is January and February. At this time of year large numbers of grouper gather at the Towers and half a dozen or more bull sharks turn up to meet them. They are big, stocky individuals (typically approaching 3 m/10 ft in length), but can be quite skittish among divers. They rarely approach closer than about 3–4.5 m/10–15 ft, although the sharks are so impressive they appear to be much closer. No food is provided at the site because it is considered unnecessary and too dangerous (and, since 1 January 2002, feeding has been illegal). The shark dives are conducted in 33–37 m/110–120 ft of water, but most divers prefer to wait on the main platform at a depth of 24 m/80 ft and let the sharks come to them, rather than go in chase. It is worth checking with the operators before booking a dive, because some years the bulls leave early if commercial shark fishermen have been operating in the area.

Bait/feed no.

Cage no.

Other wildlife wahoo, amberjack, orange cup coral.

Best time of year Jan–Feb (when sharks congregate to feed on grouper); sharks present Nov–Apr.

Dive depth 24–37 m/80–120 ft.

Typical visibility average 18 m/60 ft (range 6–37 m/ 20–120 ft).

Water temperature typically 21 °C/70 °F in winter.

Weather and sea notes some current around the artificial reef is not uncommon.

Contact details H2O Scuba (www.h2oscuba.com), Dixie Divers (www.dixiediver.com).

Travel national and international flights to Miami and Fort Lauderdale; wide choice of accommodation in and around Hallandale.

18 FLORIDA: PALM BEACH–FORT LAUDERDALE

Location Shark Reef is north-east of Palm Beach Inlet off Riviera Beach; Shark Canyon is north-east of Riviera Beach; Shark Ledge is 6.5 km/4 miles north-east of Boca Raton Inlet (between Delray Beach and Pompano Beach); Shark Feed is south of West Palm Beach; Shark Reef is off Pompano Beach; exact location of some sites kept secret because of shark fishermen.

Main species most trips: Caribbean reef, nurse; occasional trips: bull, tiger.

Viewing opportunities the Sunshine State is home to a wide variety of sharks and has huge potential for shark watching. But, in the past, every time an operator has found a good place for shark encounters and the sharks have become used to divers, commercial fishermen have moved in for the kill. At some sites the sharks have disappeared literally overnight. This happened at Grouper Hole, off Boca Raton: once one of the best and most famous shark dives in Florida, thanks to nine resident Caribbean reef sharks that turned up at every feed, it was ruined by longline fishermen who killed them all. But there are still some great shark dives along the 60-km/37-mile stretch between Palm Beach and Fort Lauderdale. The latest change, however, is a total ban on shark feeding in Florida waters, which took place on 1 January 2002 and, at the time of writing, it is unclear how this will affect shark watching. Historically, shark feeds used to take place at a beautiful dive site known as Shark Canyon at a depth of about 20–23 m/65–75 ft. A frozen 'chumsicle' (a block of frozen fish pieces – like the one used at Walker's Cay in the Bahamas) was lowered into the water and divers knelt on the seabed or swam around with the sharks. A typical dive lasted 30–40 minutes and 10–25 Caribbean reef and nurse sharks attended. Several shark species, including occasional bulls, were fed at Pompano Beach's Shark Reef in about 18 m/60 ft of water. Another feed took place in the Pompano/Fort Lauderdale Beach area at a depth of just 5.5 m/18 ft. There is a small coral ledge that rises 1.2 m/4 ft from the sand and divers knelt on the sand, with their backs to this wall, while hungry nurse sharks were fed in front. This dive was also suitable for snorkellers with no scuba qualification. Dives at Riviera Beach's Shark Reef begin in the sand at a depth of 26 m/85 ft and take participants along a ridge with several deeply undercut ledges. These are used on a regular basis by several shark species (mainly Caribbean reef and nurse, but with occasional bull and tiger near the deeper wrecks offshore) and it is possible to find many of them apparently resting on the ledges. Shark Ledge is an impressive 4.5–6 m/ 15–20 ft ledge starting at 15 m/50 ft and dropping to 20 m/65 ft with lots of crevices and undercuts. Caribbean reef sharks, which are resident at this site, are seen on virtually every dive.

Bait/feed no (feeding took place until it was banned from 1 January 2002).

Cage no.

Other wildlife green turtle, jewfish, green moray eel, Atlantic spadefish.

Best time of year sharks present year-round; best conditions May–Sep.

Dive depth average 12–26 m/40–85 ft (depending on site).

Typical visibility averages 18 m/60 ft (range 6–37 m/20–120 ft).

Water temperature 23–29 °C/74–84 °F May–Sep.

Contact details Dixie Divers (www.dixiediver.com), Coral Island Charters (www.coralislandcharters.com), Rampage Dive Charters (www.diverampage.com), Jim Abernethy's Scuba Adventures (www.scuba-adventures.com).

Travel national and international flights to Miami, Fort Lauderdale, Orlando or Palm Beach; wide choice of accommodation.

19–21 NORTH CAROLINA: *PAPOOSE*, *CARIBSEA* AND *ATLAS* WRECKS

Location 50 km/32 miles south of Cape Lookout (nearest town Morehead City).

Main species *most trips:* sand tiger; *occasional trips:* nurse.

Viewing opportunities the treacherous waters along the North Carolina coastline have claimed so many ships since the sixteenth century that it has been dubbed the Graveyard of the Atlantic. Warmed by the Gulf Stream and blessed with surprisingly good visibility, this area is world-renowned for wreck diving and provides divers with a rare opportunity to explore a four-century-long chronicle of maritime history. It is also one of the best places to see sand tiger sharks. These fierce-looking sharks, dominated by row after row of needle-sharp teeth, are a familiar sight at several wrecks in the area.

Traditionally they have congregated around the *Papoose*, a 125.6-m/412-ft oil tanker that was struck by a German torpedo and sank on 18 March 1942. The ship lies intact and virtually upside down in 40 m/ 130 ft of clear water, with its enormous flat keel rising to within 26 m/85 ft of the surface. Why the sharks have chosen this particular wreck is a mystery, but it may be because it lies perpendicular to the prevailing currents and acts as a wall that magnifies the current flow. Divers follow the anchor line of the dive boat down to the wreck, descending through schools of amberjack and Atlantic spadefish, and normally begin to see sharks about 18 m/60 ft above the seabed. Some people choose to continue down to the bottom and just kneel in the sand at 37–40 m/120–130 ft to watch the sharks for the duration of the dive. Varying in length at 1.2–3 m/4–10 ft, they swim slowly near the wreck or hover motionless just above the seabed. They regard divers with idle curiosity, frequently approaching to within 1 m/3⅓ ft or so, but show no sign of aggression. Until recently, on a typical dive, there were 10–25 sharks around the wreck and it was not uncommon to see as many as 20 at once. Some were alone, but most seemed to be in pairs. The wreck was probably both a feeding and breeding area for sand tigers: the females were present year-round and were joined by the males for the summer (males migrate along the Eastern Seaboard, moving north-wards in the spring and returning south in the autumn). The males bite the females in front of the first dorsal fin before copulation, leaving substantial bite marks on their mates and frequently losing some teeth in the process, and there are numerous teeth on the wreck and in the surrounding sand to testify to this. Sadly, an incident in the summer of 2001 had a great impact on the sand tiger sharks of the *Papoose* in particular, and of the North Carolina wrecks in general, and the future of shark watching at the *Papoose* is now uncertain. On 8 July 2001 three dive operators found a 1.8–2.1-m/6–7-ft pregnant female critically injured with a gunshot wound in the head. No one knows exactly what happened, but it is believed to have been shot by a fisherman with a handgun. Within a week of the wounding and subse-quent death of the sand tiger, every single shark around the *Papoose* disappeared (although, just before going to press, it appears that they may be starting to return).

Currently, the other good places to see sand tigers in this area are the *Atlas* and *Caribsea* wrecks. The *Atlas* is a tanker that sank in 1942 and lies in 40 m/ 130ft of water (although its upper deck lies at about 24 m/80 ft); the *Caribsea* is a freighter sunk in 1942, which now lies in 26 m/85 ft of water. They have both rewarded divers with more and more sightings of sand tigers in recent years, and both have had particularly large numbers since the *Papoose* group departed. Sand tiger sharks can also be seen at several other wrecks along this stretch of coast. One of the better known is the *Tarpon*, an American submarine that sank in 1957 and now lies in 40 m/130 ft of water, although sightings have become increasingly sporadic. Others include the *City of Houston*, an iron steamship that sank in 1878 and whose scattered remains lie in 27 m/90 ft of water; and the *Aeolus*, sunk in 1988 as part of the North Carolina artificial reef programme and lying in 34 m/110 ft of water. However, the sharks at these three sites have suffered from over-fishing. Commercial longline shark fishermen were attracted to the area in the late 1980s, when the sharks received their first blaze of publicity, and virtually wiped them out almost overnight. Thanks to the recent ban on fishing for sand tigers off the coast here, however, divers can hope to see more in years to come.

Great white sharks turn up at the wrecks very occasionally, although not enough to include in the list of regular sightings; the most recent encounter took place on 21 July 2001 at the *Caribsea*.

Bait/feed no.

Cage no.

Other wildlife moray eel, southern stingray.

Best time of year sharks present year-round; best diving Jun–Sep.

Dive depth 24–40 m/80–130 ft (*Papoose*); other wrecks vary from 24 m/80 ft (*Caribsea*) to 40 m/130 ft (*Tarpon*).

Typical visibility surface visibility varies from 12–15 m/40–50 ft (Nov–May) to 21–40 m/70–130 ft (Jun–Oct; best Aug–Sep); visibility around the wrecks is generally reduced (3–40 m/10–130 ft, depending on site); visibility at *Papoose* usually good (15–40 m/50–130 ft).

Water temperature 13–27 °C/55–81 °F; coldest Jan–Mar, warmest Jul–Sep.

Weather and sea notes most sites susceptible to ocean swells; *Papoose* currents can be strong, but currents around most other wrecks relatively mild.

Contact details Diveocean Dive Center (www.divocean-dive-center.com), Diver Down (www.diverdownscubadiving.com), Pelican Divers Inc. (www.diveguideint.com/p0408a.htm).

Travel international flights to Washington or Atlanta; national flights to Wilmington; *Papoose* accessible from Hatteras, Ocracoke, Beaufort and Morehead City; wide choice of accommodation.

22 RHODE ISLAND: POINT JUDITH (OPEN OCEAN)

Location 30–65 km/20–40 miles south-east of Point Judith.

Main species *most trips:* blue; *occasional trips:* shortfin mako, dusky, thresher, great white, basking.

Viewing opportunities Rhode Island is a great place for both divers and snorkellers to encounter blue sharks in the open ocean. It takes about two-and-a-half hours to get to an area known as the Fingers, about 65 km/40 miles offshore and on the edge of the continental shelf, although the dive is sometimes conducted closer to shore. The water here is about 60 m/200 ft deep and a sea anchor is used, so the boat may drift several kilometres during the dive. A chum mixture of fish chunks, blood and oil is used to attract the sharks and the wait can last anything from 10 minutes to four hours (about an hour is average). Two different cages are used and, with both in operation at the same time, six people can comfortably view the sharks while three wait on the boat. Made of 2.5 cm/1 in anodized aluminium pipe, the first cage is a three-person construction measuring 1.5 m/5 ft wide, 2 m/6½ ft long and 2.3 m/7½ ft high. It hangs a few metres below the surface and some 3–4.6 m/10–15 ft from the stern of the boat. Divers have to swim the gap between the boat and the cage unprotected. Everyone gets two 30-minute turns in the cage during a typical day trip. It is not compulsory to stay in the cage and many divers choose to roam around outside for the entire dive, usually armed with shark sticks (plastic snow shovels with the blades removed) to push over-inquisitive sharks gently away. The sharks can be quite excitable and may nip one another and make tight passes to check out divers. If they become too agitated and threatening (which can happen on the second day of a rare two-day trip) or if there is a large mako present, it is advisable to stay inside the cage. The second cage has been dubbed the 'playpen' and is actually a floating platform, surrounded by protective aluminium piping, designed for non-certified divers. Participants simply lie on the platform and peer underwater with a mask and snorkel. On a typical dive dozens of blues turn up, most in the 1.8–2.4 m/6–8 ft range, and it is common to see as many as four in the water at the same time.

Bait/feed yes.

Cage yes.

Other wildlife various cetaceans, Portuguese man-o'-war.

Best time of year peak numbers late Jun to mid-Jul, but blues present Jun to mid-Sep; basking in Jun.

Dive depth 3–3.5 m/10–12 ft.

Typical visibility 9–12 m/30–40 ft (ranges from 4.5–24 m/15–80 ft).

Water temperature 16–18 °C/61–65 °F Jun; 21–22 °C/70–72 °F Sep.

Weather and sea notes open-sea conditions with a swell typical.

Contact details Snappa Charters (www.snappacharters.com).

Travel international flights to Boston and New York or national flights to Providence; trips leave Galilee (near Point Judith, midway between Newport and New London); choice of accommodation in town.

MEXICO

23 QUINTANA ROO: SLEEPING SHARKS' CAVE

Location 6.5 km/4 miles north-east of Isla Mujeres (which is 7 km/4 miles north of Cancún) off the Yucatan Peninsula.

Main species *many trips:* Caribbean reef, nurse; *occasional trips:* tiger, lemon, blue, bull, whale.

Viewing opportunities discovered in 1969 by local fisherman Carlos Garcia Castilla while free-diving for lobsters, and first described by Eugenie Clark in the mid-1970s, Sleeping Sharks' Cave has become one of Mexico's best-known shark dives. Despite its name, the site is actually a limestone arch (about 8 m/26 ft wide, 3 m/10 ft high and 10 m/33 ft long) off the coast of Isla Mujeres. The number of sharks varies daily, but it is not uncommon to find as many as 30. Caribbean reef sharks are most frequently encountered, but nurse sharks are also very common. Tiger, lemon and blue occur with some regularity; bull sharks have been reported (local people always say there are many of them in the area) and undoubtedly occur here, but there is some confusion over the identification of some individuals. Sharks of one species or another used to be seen on about 70 per cent of dives, although their numbers are definitely declining because of overfishing. Local operators and con-servationists are putting pressure on the Mexican government to take action (in the meantime, the sightings success rate is only 10–20 per cent). Why the arch is popular with so many sharks is still a mystery and, indeed, the name of the site is a misnomer for another reason – because the sharks are not actually sleeping. Their eyes follow divers intently as they move about inside the arch. It is likely that they are attracted by the high oxygen content and low salinity of the water, caused by freshwater from underground springs seeping up through the seabed. The extra oxygen may help them to remain still for long periods while expending relatively little energy (they have to pump water over their gills to breathe); another theory is that it produces a narcotic effect that is enjoyed by some sharks. At the same time, the reduced salinity may loosen the grip of skin parasites, allowing remoras to remove copepods, leeches and other ectoparasites more easily. Whatever the reason, the sharks remain in the arch for hours at a time and come and go throughout their lives. Their attitude towards divers varies from day to day, perhaps depending on the presence of commercial fishing boats in the area, and they can be quite nervous or completely unperturbed. Whale sharks occasionally appear in deeper water around Isla Mujeres.

Bait/feed no.

Cage no.

Other wildlife manta ray.

Best time of year sharks present year-round, but best time winter.

Dive depth 20–22 m/65–70 ft.

Typical visibility 20–30 m/65–100 ft.

Water temperature 24–29 °C/75–84 °F; cooler in winter.

Weather and sea notes conditions normally calm; medium current typical, but can be strong.

Contact details Coral Scuba Dive Center (www.coralscubadivecenter.com), Mundaca Divers (www.prodigyweb.net.mx/airemundaca).

Travel national and international flights to Cancún; ferry from Puerto Juarez (suburb of Cancún) to Isla Mujeres (25 mins); wide choice of accommodation on the island.

24 BAJA CALIFORNIA: REVILLAGIGEDO (SOCORRO) ISLANDS

Location 355 km/220 miles south-south-west of Cabo San Lucas (southern tip of Baja California) at their nearest point.

Main species *most trips:* scalloped hammerhead, silvertip, dusky, silky, Galápagos, whitetip reef; *occasional trips:* grey reef, tiger, oceanic whitetip, porbeagle, whale, thresher.

Viewing opportunities the Revillagigedo Islands, or Socorro Islands as they are commonly called, are famous for big fish encounters. Frequently compared to Costa Rica's Cocos Island, they seem to act as a magnet to an impressive variety of pelagics. They are best known for their enormous manta rays, which seem positively to enjoy interacting with divers here, but are also superb for sharks. In some areas it is hard to get into the water without immediately being in the company of sharks, and one operator reports encoun-tering no fewer than seven different species during a single dive. Volcanic in origin, and rugged both above and below the surface, the islands are uninhabited apart from a small naval base on the island of Socorro. There are three main islands in this widely spaced archipelago: Socorro is the largest (18 × 15 km/11 × 9 miles); 50 km/30 miles to the north is San Benedicto; and 460 km/285 miles to the west is Clarión. There is also a tiny islet, called Roca Partida, just over 100 km/60 miles to the west of Socorro (one-third of the way to Clarión). There are many excellent dive sites in the area, and some superb pinnacle diving, with sharks appearing almost anywhere. Silky sharks are nearly always present and can be very curious; their close approaches can be quite unnerving for the first few days and, especially late in the afternoons, they may even nudge divers. But schooling scalloped hammerheads are the main draw. They are particularly common around Socorro Island itself – Roca O'Neil, off the western end, is a good place to start. Socorro is good for sightings of other shark species, too, and even tiger sharks are sometimes seen cruising over its impressive underwater lava formations. San Benedicto has some super caverns that are large enough for one or two divers to get inside with resting whitetip reef sharks. Off the western coast of the island is a small, flat-topped seamount called The Boiler; rising to within about 5 m/16 ft of the surface, its name comes from the water turbulence created by passing swells. The Boiler is probably the best place for mantas (especially during the late morning or early afternoon when they gather to be cleaned by resident barberfish and angelfish) and is as good a place as any to see occasional whale sharks. Roca Partida is a wonderful open-ocean pinnacle, dropping almost straight down to 75 m/250 ft and from there, beyond its base, to the ocean depths; it is small enough to circumnavigate in one dive and, although shark sightings vary enormously from day to day, can reward divers with huge numbers of several different species (particularly Galápagos, silvertip and schooling scalloped hammerhead).

Bait/feed no.

Cage no.

Other wildlife humpback whale (Feb–Mar; can be heard singing on almost every dive during this period), bottlenose dolphin, manta ray (it is common to be in the water with 5–12, with 4–6 m/13–20 ft wingspans; seen on every dive at The Boiler), dorado, yellowfin tuna, marlin, wahoo, clarion angelfish (endemic), Socorro spiny lobster.

Best time of year Nov–May (weather conditions too bad outside this period).

Dive depth 10–40 m/33–130 ft.

Typical visibility 15–30 m/50–100 ft.

Water temperature 26–28 °C/78–82 °F Nov–early Jan and late Apr–May; 21–23 °C/70–74 °F late Jan–early Apr.

Weather and sea notes these are unprotected oceanic islands, so a large swell is common; surge on north shores can be heavy; currents variable, but can reach 0.5–1.5 knots and many dives are conducted as drifts; surge at some sites can reach nearly 2 m/7 ft; storms and strong winds make Revillagigedo largely inaccessible Jun–Oct.

Contact details Solmar V (www.solmar.com), Poseidon's Mistress (www.poseidons-mistress.com).

Travel flights from several US cities or Mexico City to Cabo San Lucas; crossing from Cabo to Revillagigedo takes 22–24 hours.

Note heavy fishing in the supposedly protected waters around Revillagigedo has depleted the shark population in recent years.

25 BAJA CALIFORNIA: GORDA BANKS

Location 13 km/8 miles east of San José del Cabo (near the southern tip of Baja), 44 km/27 miles north-east of Cabo San Lucas.

Main species *many trips:* scalloped hammerhead, whale; *occasional trips:* bull.

Viewing opportunities this is one of the most challenging shark dives in the region. Gorda Banks (sometimes spelt Gordo) is a huge seamount situated roughly at the meeting place of the Pacific and the Sea of Cortez. Lying about 33 m/110 ft below the surface at its highest point, it is well known to sports fishermen because it is teeming with fish. On calm days, the water literally boils with schools of horse-eye jacks and grunts feeding at the surface and they attract large numbers of game fish. It is also a rich gathering ground for pelagic sharks and cetaceans, making it a popular location for divers and whale watchers. Divers descend down the anchor line – frequently engulfed by massive schools of jacks spiralling in the upper water column – and hide among the pinnacles and rocks to view schooling hammerheads. Sometimes there are hundreds passing nearby, sometimes a few dozen and sometimes none. Solitary bull sharks occasionally turn up as well. Whale sharks can be seen anywhere in this area, although most encounters are down to luck rather than judgement. The chances of success are greatly increased by some companies that use spotter planes to find both whale sharks and manta rays, and then direct their dive boats straight to the animals.

Bait/feed no.

Cage no.

Other wildlife variety of cetaceans, California sea lion, manta ray, devil ray, moray eel, striped marlin, mahi mahi, yellowfin tuna, sailfish.

Best time of year hammerheads present Feb–Nov (best Aug–Nov); whale sharks present May–Nov (best end of May–Jun and Oct).

Dive depth 30–40 m/100–130 ft; surface snorkelling with whale sharks.

Typical visibility 10–30 m/33–100 ft (best late summer/early autumn).

Water temperature 18–29 °C/65–84 °F; warmest Aug–Nov.

Weather and sea notes open-ocean conditions; strong currents fairly common (less strong Jun–Aug); tropical hurricanes *(chubascos)* affect the area May–Nov (peaking Aug–Sep); short but severe storms sometimes encountered during periods of persistent southerly winds in summer.

Contact details Solmar V (www.solmar.com), Amigos del Mar (www.amigosdelmar.com), Baja Dive Scuba Expeditions (www.caboland.com/bajadive/index.html), Aerocalafia (www.aerocalafia.com/whaleshrk.htm).

Travel flights from several American cities or Mexico City to Cabo San Lucas; boats from Cabo San Lucas (1½ hours); wide choice of accommodation in Cabo.

Note heavy fishing in the area had an impact on the hammerheads and, for some years, they appeared to be getting rarer. However, Gorda Banks is one of the few places in this region where hammerhead populations seem to have increased in the past two or three years.

26 BAJA CALIFORNIA: LA PAZ BAY

Location immediately north of La Paz, in southern Baja, facing the Sea of Cortez.

Main species *many trips:* whale.

Viewing opportunities whale sharks appear in La Paz Bay for several months every year. There is considerable confusion about their arrival and departure times and no particular pattern to their visits and movements within the bay. They first appear in the spring, when the warming waters spur massive plankton blooms, and then occur in large numbers again when the water temperatures reach a peak in the late autumn. Several reports suggest that most of them disappear in the summer, but in some years there have been consistent sightings throughout the entire period. Recent studies suggest that summer visits are transient and, indeed, the animals around at this time do not appear to be feeding. Some of them, at least, appear to be pregnant females. Little is known about where they go for the winter. One individual, tagged in the Sea of Cortez, travelled all the way to the other side of the North Pacific – a distance of 22,500 km/ 14,000 miles. Most dive operators will stop for their clients to snorkel with whale sharks if they encounter them, on an opportunistic basis, but several offer dedicated trips. A mixture of juveniles and adults can be seen within minutes of leaving La Paz and it is not unknown to encounter as many as 10–12 in a single day. However, sightings are unpredictable and it is best to use an operator with a spotter plane, which can find the sharks more easily and then direct the dive boats straight to the right place. Most dive operators adhere to strict guidelines for hands-off underwater encounters, causing as little disturbance as possible to the sharks, but beware of those that do not.

Bait/feed no.

Cage no.

Other wildlife wide variety of cetaceans, California sea lion, manta ray.

Best time of year whale sharks present Apr–Nov, but peak numbers May–June and Oct–Nov (sightings Jul–Sep are unpredictable).

Dive depth surface snorkelling.

Typical visibility 6–12 m/20–40 ft Apr–Jun, 15–37 m /50–120 ft Jul–Nov (highly variable from day to day and year to year).

Water temperature 19–21 °C/66–70 °F Dec–Apr, 21–24 °C/70–75 °F May–Jun, 24–29 °C/75–84 °F Jul–Nov at surface (several degrees colder below thermocline).

Weather and sea notes bay is normally quite sheltered; tropical hurricanes *(chubascos)* can affect the region May–Nov; short but severe storms *(cordonazos)* sometimes encountered during periods of persistent southerly winds in summer; strong northerly winds Nov–Mar.

Contact details Baja Expeditions (www.bajaex. com), Cortez Club (www.cortezclub.com), Baja Quest (www.bajaquest.com.mx).

Travel accessible by day boats or live-aboard; flights from several US cities or Mexico City to La Paz or Cabo San Lucas (2½-hour drive to La Paz); choice of accommodation in La Paz.

Note in 2001 whale sharks were given official protection from commercial fisheries under Mexican law.

27–28 BAJA CALIFORNIA: EL BAJO SEAMOUNT AND LAS ANIMAS ISLAND

Location El Bajo is 56 km/35 miles north of La Paz (13 km/8 miles north-east of Los Islotes); Las Animas is 112 km/70 miles north of La Paz (14 km/9 miles east of Punta Calabozo on the northern tip of Isla San José).

Main species *most trips:* scalloped hammerhead; *many trips:* whale; *occasional trips:* great hammerhead, silky, bull.

Viewing opportunities El Bajo and Las Animas have been on the world diving map for many years and are well known for their scalloped hammerheads. This is where much of the research on the schooling behaviour of hammerheads has been done. Sadly, heavy fishing in the region has had such an impact on the sharks of El Bajo, in particular, that the population has dwindled dramatically in recent years. Las Animas is a small, steep-sided island, with some spectacular caves off the north and east coasts and a series of pinnacles off the east, and is surrounded by deep water. Also known as Animas Sur, it is rich in sea fans and gorgonians, teeming with schooling jacks, and is still one of the best-known hammerhead dives in the region. Dive boats have to use sonar to locate the system of pinnacles that form El Bajo ('The Shallow'), or the Marisla Seamount as it is sometimes called. There are three pinnacles along a 300 m/1000 ft line running north-west to south-east – the north pinnacle peaks at 25 m/83 ft below the surface, the centre pinnacle at 17 m/55 ft and the south pinnacle at 20 m/65 ft. Hammerheads of both sexes are present year-round. Their school sizes range from a handful to several hundred, and their typical depth varies from 15–40 m/50–130 ft or more, depending on the season. Their habits seem to have changed in recent years. In the early 1990s they gathered in large schools throughout the summer (May–Nov), but during the past three years the schools have contained fewer than 60 individuals during Jul–Sep, but hundreds during Oct–Nov. Local fishermen have a theory that they gather to mate in the area in late Oct–Nov. As far as depth is concerned, they are within about 12 m/40 ft of the surface during winter and then drop to 40 m/130 ft during autumn (reaching their deepest in Oct, when the thermocline is deepest). They spend the daytime travelling around El Bajo – always in a clockwise direction – and then spread out, as far as 20 km/12 miles away, to hunt as solitary predators. It is believed that the pinnacles have a strong magnetic field and act as a beacon to hammerheads from far and wide, although why they school in the area is still a mystery. Whale sharks, ranging in length from 2 m/7 ft to 12 m/39 ft, are fairly common and are often found by chance.

Bait/feed no.

Cage no.

Other wildlife wide variety of cetaceans, California sea lion (a popular snorkel with them occurs at nearby rookery on Los Islotes), manta ray, marlin, sailfish, dorado, green moray eel (more at El Bajo than any other known dive site).

Best time of year hammerheads best Jul–Nov, but numbers and depth vary (in recent years deeper, but in larger schools Oct–Nov); whale sharks present late May–Dec (best late May to early Jun and Oct–Nov; unpredictable Jul–Sep).

Dive depth 15–40 m/50–130 ft; surface snorkelling with whale sharks.

Typical visibility 12–18 m/40–60 ft (winter), 18–37 m/60–120 ft (summer).

Water temperature 18–29 °C/65–84 °F; warmest in summer.

Weather and sea notes normally calm conditions Jul–Oct; stronger north winds (lasting several days) can make access to El Bajo difficult Nov–Mar; currents common and particularly strong during spring tides; big swell common in winter and early spring; tropical hurricanes (*chubascos*) may affect region Aug–Oct; short but severe storms (*cordonazos*) sometimes encountered during periods of persistent southerly winds in summer; southerly breeze (the *coromuel*) blows around La Paz almost daily during summer (normally late afternoon, overnight and early morning).

Contact details Baja Expeditions (**www.bajaex.com**), Baja Quest (**www.bajaquest.com.mx**).

Travel accessible by day boats or live-aboard (El Bajo approximately 2½ hours from La Paz, Las Animas about 4 hours); flights from several US cities or Mexico City to La Paz or Cabo San Lucas (2½-hour drive to La Paz); choice of accommodation in La Paz.

29 BAJA CALIFORNIA: GUADALUPE ISLAND

Location 340 km/210 miles south-south-west of San Diego; 240 km/150 miles off San Quintin (Pacific coast of Baja California).

Main species *most trips:* great white, *many trips:* horn (*Heterodontus francisci*); *occasional trips:* oceanic whitetip, shortfin mako.

Viewing opportunities the remote island of Guadalupe is a brand-new shark-diving destination. A small number of divers (fewer than 100 each year) have visited the island in the past, and have been rewarded with spectacular underwater scenery, seals and sea lions and some enormous schools of mackerel. The island has long had a reputation as a haven for great white sharks, but there have been very few underwater encounters. Then, in 1999, long-range sportfishing vessels from San Diego began to report regular sightings. Great whites had begun to compete with them for tuna and yellowtail, sometimes surging out of the water right next to their boats. Experts from San Diego Shark Diving Expeditions went to investigate in October 2000 and, using chum as an attractant, found numerous great whites – including one measuring an estimated 5.5 m/18 ft. The first of many proposed cage-diving trips took place in autumn 2001 (the first great white was actually seen on the day of arrival when a 4 m/13 ft individual made several passes within 10 minutes of dropping the cages) and Guadalupe is now considered to be among a handful of places around the world where great whites can be seen on a regular basis. In addition, horn sharks (which are normally hiding in caves and crevices during the day) are frequently seen roaming around during night dives; and oceanic whitetip and shortfin mako sharks are occasionally seen as well (although no other diving takes place during dedicated great white shark trips).

Bait/feed yes.

Cage yes.

Other wildlife various cetaceans, Guadalupe fur seal, California sea lion, northern elephant seal, bat ray, bluefin tuna, yellowfin tuna, wahoo.

Best time of year great white shark trips conducted Sep–Nov (sharks present Aug to at least Jan).

Dive depth cage suspended at surface or down to 3 m/10 ft.

Typical visibility 24–30 m/80–100 ft; occasionally down to 12 m/40 ft, if affected by El Niño.

Water temperature 17–21 °C/63–70 °F Sep–Nov.

Weather and sea notes Guadalupe is remote and open-ocean conditions prevail; however, the island is large (255 sq km/98 sq miles) and there are many calm anchorages.

Contact details San Diego Shark Diving Expeditions (**www.sdsharkdiving.com/guadalupe.htm**), Horizon Charters (**www.horizoncharters.com**).

Travel national and international flights to San Diego; accessible only via multi-day live-aboard; journey time from San Diego approximately 20 hours; wide choice of accommodation in San Diego.

BELIZE

30 AMBERGRIS CAYE: SHARK-RAY ALLEY

Location 7 km/4.5 miles south of Ambergris Caye, (northern end of the Belize Barrier Reef, which runs the entire 300 km/185 mile length of the country).

Main species *most trips:* nurse; *occasional trips:* tawny, grey reef, lemon, blacktip reef, whale.

Viewing opportunities this is one of the most popular shark-watching sites in the Caribbean – partly because it can be enjoyed by snorkellers and partly because nurse sharks are virtually guaranteed year-round. An equal number of southern stingrays usually turn up as well, adding to the excitement. The dive site is within Hol Chan Marine Reserve, on the land-ward side of the coral reef, where it is protected from ocean swells and heavy wave action. Close to the Mexican border, Hol Chan ('little channel' in Mayan) is next to a small trench in the reef that gives it its name. It has a flat sandy bottom at a depth of 2–3 m/6–10 ft (depending on the tide) with some eel grass and a few large coral heads. Until the early 1990s the site was used by local fishermen for cleaning their fish and, since they dumped all their unwanted scraps overboard, large numbers of sharks and rays were attracted to the area. Shark watching began here in 1995. The site is now frequented by sub-adult (1–1.7 m/3–6 ft) nurse sharks – and most of them appear to be female. No one knows why, or where the males go, but it seems that when they reach adult size they move into deeper water outside the barrier reef. After a 15–20-minute boat ride from Ambergris Caye, snorkellers and divers enter the water with a dive-master, who handfeeds the sharks with whole sardines, ballyhoo or fish scraps. Only the divemaster is allowed to do the feeding because, although these sharks are remarkably tame and have relatively small mouths, they do have teeth and powerful jaws. As few as eight or as many as 30 participate in the feed and frequently approach divers to within a few centi-metres. The food has all gone within about half an hour, but the nurse sharks remain in the area for some time afterwards.

Bait/feed yes.

Cage no.

Other wildlife southern stingray, spotted eagle ray, green moray eel.

Best time of year sharks present year-round.

Dive depth snorkelling in 2–3 m/6–10 ft of water.

Typical visibility 15–30 m/50–100 ft (varies depending on the tide – incoming is clearer, outgoing less clear).

Water temperature 25–30 °C/77–86 °F depending on season.

Weather and sea notes dry season Feb–May; can be wet and stormy Jun–Aug; light showers common Nov–Jan; during rainy season, run-off reduces water visibility along the coast; site fairly sheltered by reef, so shark watching rarely troubled by bad weather.

Contact details Gaz Cooper's Dive Belize (www.divebelize.com), Ramon's Village Resort Dive Center (www.ramons.com).

Travel international flights to Belize City; Ambergris Caye is the largest of Belize's 200 cayes, where most tourists base themselves, and lies about 56 km/ 35 miles north-east of the capital (a short flight to Ambergris's tiny San Pedro Airport); there are many hotels in the area.

31 GALLOW'S POINT: SHARK CHUTES

Location just south of Gallow's Point, near Belize City.

Main species *most trips:* nurse.

Viewing opportunities this is a recently discovered site on the Belize Barrier Reef, where it is possible to see large numbers of good-sized nurse sharks on almost every dive. They rest in a series of narrow sand chutes next to the big ocean drop-off.

Bait/feed no.

Cage no.

Other wildlife hawksbill, loggerhead and green turtles, spotted eagle ray, southern stingray.

Best time of year sharks present year-round.

Dive depth 9–12 m/30–40 ft.

Typical visibility 15–30 m/50–100 ft.

Water temperature 26–30 °C/78–86 °F; warmest in summer.

Weather and sea notes little or no current with generally calm sea conditions (can be choppy, depending on wind speed); dry season Dec–May, wet season Jun–Nov; strong winds possible (especially Nov–Mar and throughout hurricane season of Jun–Oct).

Contact details SeaSports Belize (www.seasportsbelize.com).

Travel international flights to Belize City; wide choice of accommodation locally.

32 LIGHTHOUSE REEF: BLUE HOLE

Location 89 km/55 miles east of Ambergris Caye, 13 km/8 miles north of Half Moon Caye, in Lighthouse Reef Atoll.

Main species *most trips:* Caribbean reef, blacktip reef; *many trips:* bull, grey reef, lemon; *occasional trips:* great hammerhead.

Viewing opportunities this is an exceptional shark encounter, largely because it takes place in one of the most spectacular dive sites in the world. The Blue Hole is undoubtedly the most famous dive in Belize. A sinkhole created by a collapsed underwater cavern, and apparently the only structure of its kind visible from space, it measures 90 m/295 ft in diameter and about 145 m/475 ft deep. It is surrounded by a near-perfect ring of coral and beyond that the water is no more than 4.5 m/15 ft deep. An eerie cavern at a depth of 30–45 m/100–150 ft, with a huge upside-down forest of stalactites hanging from its ceiling, is one of the main attractions. But the site is also a popular shark dive and a number of species can be seen year-round. There are large numbers of Caribbean reef sharks, as well as blacktip reef sharks, and several others turn up on a regular basis. It is actually a good site for bull sharks and, although they are not seen on every dive, sightings are frequent. Some operators feed the sharks, simply throwing bait over the side of the boat; others do not. The feed itself rarely lasts for more than a few minutes, but the sharks hang around afterwards and it is possible to mingle with them for the remainder of the dive. As few as eight or as many as 20 adults of both sexes are typically present and will often come to within a metre or so of divers.

Bait/feed depends on operator.

Cage no.

Other wildlife barracuda, eagle ray.

Best time of year sharks present year-round.

Dive depth 5–45 m/16–150 ft.

Typical visibility 20–50 m/65–165 ft.

Water temperature 27–31 °C/81–88 °F.

Weather and sea notes dry season Feb–May; can be wet and stormy Jun–Aug; light showers common Nov–Jan.

Contact details Gaz Cooper's Dive Belize (www.divebelize.com), Hamanasi (www.hamanasi.com), Blue Hole Dive Center (www.bluedive.com).

Travel international flights to Belize City; live-aboards and day boats from Belize City, Ambergris Caye and Lighthouse Reef go to the Blue Hole; there are many hotels in the capital and Ambergris Caye (accessible by a short flight to the caye's tiny San Pedro Airport) and just one on Lighthouse Reef Atoll (Lighthouse Reef Resort).

33 TURNEFFE ATOLL: THE ELBOW

Location southern tip of Turneffe Atoll (45 km/ 28 miles south-east of Belize City).

Main species *many trips:* grey reef, nurse; *occasional trips:* lemon, Caribbean reef, blacktip reef, great hammerhead, bull.

Viewing opportunities Turneffe is one of only four atolls in the Western Hemisphere (most of these roughly circular rings of coral, rising from deep water and enclosing a central lagoon, are found in the tropical Pacific and Indian Oceans) and is some 50 km/30 miles long and 16 km/10 miles wide. The Elbow is one of its best-known dive sites. Named for the shape of the reef, which sweeps round in an arc as it descends into deeper water, it offers a challenging but very rewarding shark encounter. The site is exposed and lies at the point where several currents converge, but is the permanent home of a resident population of blacktip reef, grey reef and nurse sharks. Nurse are seen on about every second dive, grey reef every third or fourth, and blacktip reef only occasionally. The dive is conducted as a drift, beginning in the shelter of Belize's largest atoll, floating south along the wall, and ending in the deep blue water beyond. There are often enormous schools of cubera snapper, dog snapper, black snapper, horse-eye jacks, permit and other fish feeding in mid-water above the reef, and small numbers of patrolling sharks. Three or four sharks are encountered during a typical dive and may approach divers to within 1.5 m/5 ft or even closer. Some fortunate divers are also rewarded with sightings of lemon, Caribbean reef and great hammerhead sharks. The stronger the current, the more sharks and the better the action. Sightings of bull sharks and others sometimes occur during the safety stop at the end of the dive (off the reef in blue water).

Bait/feed no.

Cage no.

Other wildlife bottlenose dolphin, hawksbill and loggerhead turtles, green and spotted moray eels, spotted eagle ray (school of 50 or more on good days), marlin, sailfish, grouper; inner lagoon of Turneffe Atoll is home to saltwater crocodiles and West Indian manatees.

Best time of year sharks present year-round.

Dive depth 18–40 m/60–130 ft.

Typical visibility 30–40 m/100–130 ft.

Water temperature 26–30 °C/78–86 °F; warmest in summer.

Weather and sea notes strong swirling currents (2 knots) and significant ocean swell typical; dry season Dec–May, wet season Jun–Nov; strong winds (especially Nov–Mar and throughout hurricane season of Jun–Oct) can make this site difficult to dive.

Contact details Hugh Parky's Belize Dive Connection (www.belizediving.com), Seasports Belize (www.seasportsbelize.com), Tobacco Caye Diving (www.tobaccocayediving.com), Hamanasi Dive & Adventure Resort (www.hamanasi.com).

Travel international flights to Belize City; wide choice of accommodation on the mainland, in the Turneffe Islands or in nearby Tobacco Caye.

34 TOBACCO CAYE: SHARK'S CAVE

Location 18 km/11 miles east of Dangriga, 14 km/9 miles north of Tobacco Caye.

Main species *most trips:* Caribbean reef, bull, nurse; *occasional trips:* great hammerhead, tiger.

Viewing opportunities also known as Shark Pit, Shark Hole or Hell's Hole, this is a really unusual and atmospheric dive site. Shark Cave is a vast, domed cavern located in the shallow lagoon between the Belize Barrier Reef and the mainland coast. The entrance is a large 3 × 8-m/10 × 25-ft rectangular hole in the cave's roof, in a large sand field at a depth of about 16 m/53 ft. There is a coral head the size of a football field to the west of the cave entrance. Descending through the hole is like entering another world and it takes a few moments for your eyes to adjust to the dark. A shaft of sunlight illuminates the entrance, but the cave stretches away into darkness all round. More than 120 m/400 ft in diameter, and some 50 m/165 ft below sea level at its deepest point, the cave is unusual because there is a large mound of sand in the middle of the floor. This rises to within 18 m/60 ft of the entrance and gives the cave a bell-jar shape. Everyone descends to a depth of around 25 m/80 ft, where numerous clusters of stalactites are suspended from the ceiling, and then slowly spirals around the sand mound back towards the entrance. There is usually a considerable number of sharks of several different species swimming near the ceiling, or around the mound, and between four and ten are seen on a typical dive. It is unclear exactly what attracts them to the cave. They may be there for its cool waters, which are richer in oxygen than the warmer water in the main lagoon, but it is more likely that they are taking advantage of the opportunity to ambush the large shoals of fish gathered around the entrance. Their

behaviour varies from species to species: the bulls, tigers and great hammerheads tend to maintain a distance of 3–5 m/10–16 ft from divers, the Caribbean reef sharks frequently approach to within 1–3 m/3–10 ft and the nurse sharks (some of which are nearly 4 m/14 ft long) will come to within touching distance. Most of them tend to be wary and, once they have taken a good look at the divers, normally retreat into the dark extremities of the cavern or make their exit.

Bait/feed no.

Cage no.

Other wildlife hawksbill and green turtles; large schools of Atlantic spadefish, cubera and snapper; spotted eagle ray, southern stingray.

Best time of year sharks present year-round.

Dive depth 21–24 m/70–80 ft.

Typical visibility 5–30 m/16–100 ft around entrance; up to 46 m/150 ft inside cave, though storms can reduce visibility to 10–20 m/33–65 ft.

Water temperature 27–30 °C/81–86 °F.

Weather and sea notes current mild or absent; small chop inside the reef; dry season Dec–May, wet season Jun–Nov.

Contact details Tobacco Caye Diving (www.tobaccocayediving.com), SeaHorse Dive Shop (www.belizescuba.com).

Travel international flights to Belize City; 15-min flight to Dangriga and 30-min boat ride to Tobacco Caye; choice of accommodation in Tobacco Caye.

35 GLOVER'S REEF: SHARK POINT

Location 60 km/37 miles east of Dangriga, north-east of North Caye, on the north-eastern tip of Glover's Reef.

Main species *most trips:* Caribbean reef, lemon; *many trips:* nurse, whale; *occasional trips:* blacktip, great hammerhead, tiger, oceanic whitetip.

Viewing opportunities the most southerly of Belize's three offshore reef systems, and one of the more remote dive destinations in the country, Glover's Reef has relatively little diver traffic along its 80 km/50 mile stretch of reef. Shark Point is particularly out-of-the-way and is so exposed to the elements that it is very much a fair-weather dive site. Perhaps not surprisingly it is often neglected by divers, and yet it has a well-deserved reputation for sharks. It is best known for great hammerheads and tiger sharks, which can occasionally be seen on the same dive, but several other species are seen far more often. They are probably attracted by the large numbers of grouper and jewfish that spawn around the exposed point. As many as four different species can be seen together on the sloping white sand channels and coral hills. This is essentially a wall dive, beginning on the reef crest at a depth of 9–12 m/30–40 ft and then descending gently down the slope to 27 m/90 ft, from where it drops to more than 600 m/2000 ft in the deep blue. At certain times of the year Glover's Reef is good for whale sharks and Shark Point is as good a place as any to see them.

Bait/feed no.

Cage no.

Other wildlife green turtle, manta and spotted eagle rays, southern stingray, sailfish, marlin, grouper, jewfish, brain coral.

Best time of year sharks present year-round; whale sharks mainly Apr–Jun and Sep–Dec.

Dive depth 9–27 m/30–90 ft.

Typical visibility 20–40 m/65–130 ft.

Water temperature 26–30 °c/78–86 °F.

Weather and sea notes exposed site, so high swell common; current variable from none to strong; dry season Dec–May, wet season Jun–Nov.

Contact details Dive Hamanasi (www.hamanasi.com), Manta Resort (www.mantaresort.com), Glover's Atoll Resort (www.glovers.com.bz).

Travel accessible by day boat or live-aboard; international flights to Belize City; bus or plane to Dangriga, then boat to Glover's Reef Atoll; limited choice of accommodation on the atoll.

36 GLOVER'S REEF: BULL SHARK PASS

Location just off North East Caye, one of five surviving cayes in Glover's Atoll (approximately 115 km/70 miles south-east of Belize City).

Main species *most trips:* bull, nurse, blacktip reef, lemon.

Viewing opportunities Glover's Reef is the most southerly of Belize's three atolls. It is also the most remote and, according to a survey conducted in the 1970s, the most biologically rich of all the Caribbean atolls. The lagoon is utterly idyllic, within a UNESCO World Heritage Site, and has no fewer than 700 coral patches. It is surrounded by 80 km/50 miles of sheer drop-offs – wall diving begins on the reef crest at a depth of about 10 m/33 ft and from there the walls drop straight down to 800 m/2600 ft. Bull Shark Pass, just off North East Caye, is a shallow pass in the coral reef and can be enjoyed by divers and snorkellers alike. An impressive 3 m/10 ft long bull shark

frequents the site and has become friendly and inquisitive, regularly approaching divers very closely indeed. Small numbers of nurse, blacktip reef and lemon sharks (a mixture of adults and juveniles) are also encountered on most dives. All four species are seen year-round. Dives are typically conducted as a simple swim through the pass and, as soon as sharks are encountered, the small group of divers stays put. Shark feeding is prohibited in the area, but the sharks appear to be resident and are nearly always present. In the evenings, however, they visit the nearby resort to eat scraps thrown from the docks – and this is a great opportunity to view them from shore.

Bait/feed no.

Cage no.

Other wildlife bottlenose dolphin, Atlantic spotted dolphin, manta ray, eagle ray, hawksbill turtle, logger-head turtle.

Best time of year sharks present year-round.

Dive depth surface to 8 m/26 ft.

Typical visibility 50 m/165 ft.

Water temperature 27–31 °c/81–88 °F.

Weather and sea notes light showers common Nov–Jan; site rarely affected by bad weather (sea normally calm year-round).

Contact details Glovers Atoll Resort (www.glovers.com.bz),

Travel international flights to Belize City; North East Caye is a 3.5-ha/9-acre privately owned island with a small resort and diving centre.

37 GLADDEN SPIT

Location 42 km/26 miles east of Placencia Village (on Placencia Peninsula, approximately 115 km/70 miles south of Belize City).

Main species *most trips:* whale; *many trips:* bull, lemon, Caribbean reef, grey reef, blacktip reef; *occasional trips:* scalloped hammerhead, tiger.

Viewing opportunities a promontory on the Belize Barrier Reef, known as Gladden Spit, is the site of one of the densest and most predictable aggregations of whale sharks anywhere in the world. Here, in an area no larger than 1 sq km/½ sq mile, at least 25 whale sharks congregate during the mass spawning of reef fish. They gather around the time of the full moon in April, May and June each year – several days after the full moon is normally the peak period – although they are recorded every month. Since 1999, there have been very good sightings in March and fewer in June (there is some evidence that other biological seasons in the area have also moved a month earlier).Huge, swirling clouds of jacks and snapper gather in the water and spiral towards the surface to release their spawn, and the sharks are there to feast upon the bounty. The ecotourism potential of this extraordinary phenomenon was realized only a couple of years ago and it was not until 2000 that the area was designated Gladden Spit Marine Reserve. Only licensed whale shark guides who have successfully completed a dedicated training programme are permitted to conduct tours. The main site is over the edge of a drop-off at the outer edge of the barrier reef. It is possible to snorkel or dive with the sharks – some operators encourage snorkelling, while others allow diving. Both are being encouraged by the Gladden Advisory Board until further research is done to find out which is the least intrusive. Divers are told to stay in a tight group, as their bubbles are believed to resemble spawn and may actually attract the sharks. At the right time of year there are very good sightings about 10–14 days per month, so it is important to allow a few days to be sure of getting a close encounter. There is a good chance of seeing three or four sharks at any one time, although as many as 25 have been encountered in a single dive. The majority are juveniles (one recent study revealed a mean length of 5.5 m/18 ft), although there are also adults of both sexes. Strict regulations govern all encounters: the emphasis is very much on non-intervention and no one is allowed to touch the sharks or to approach closer than 2 m/7 ft. Ironically, the sharks themselves are often remarkably inquisitive and may come much closer.

Bait/feed no.

Cage no.

Other wildlife bottlenose dolphin, loggerhead turtle, blackfin tuna; kilometre-wide schools of mutton.

Best time of year Apr–Jun (or Mar–May – see main text) for whale sharks (to coincide with mass spawning of reef fish); other sharks present year-round.

Dive depth surface to 30 m/100 ft.

Typical visibility 20–30 m/65–100 ft.

Water temperature 25–30 °C/77–86 °F.

Weather and sea notes open-ocean site, so can be rough at times.

Contact details Kevin Modera Guide Services (www.kevinmodera.com), Seahorse Dive Shop (www.belizescuba.com), Soulshine Resort & Spa (www.soulshine.com), Glover's Atoll Resort (www.glovers.com.bz).

Travel international flights to Belize City; Placencia is a 45-minute flight from the capital; operators from many parts of Belize visit the site.

Note there are several other spawning sites away from Gladden Spit, such as Breeze's Secret near Glover's Atoll, where whale shark watching is also possible during the same season. In Aug, Sep, Oct, Dec and Jan whale sharks can be found a few kilometres from the Gladden Spit drop-off, feeding on large schools of bait fish.

HONDURAS

38 BAY ISLANDS: UTILA

Location 30 km/19 miles off the north coast in the western Caribbean Sea.

Main species *many trips:* whale; *occasional trips:* blacktip reef, shortfin mako, bull, tiger, hammerhead, nurse.

Viewing opportunities this is one of the few places in the world where it is possible to see whale sharks year-round. Utila is the smallest, flattest and most westerly of the three main Bay Islands (the other two are Roatan and Guanaja) and sits on the edge of a deep trench, with the Belize Barrier Reef on the other side. A variety of pelagics gather to feed on smaller fish off the north coast, where the wall of the continental shelf drops from only 5 m/16 ft to depths of more than 300 m/1000 ft. Local skippers are adept at spotting schools of prey 'boiling' at the surface (or they look for feeding seabirds) and then go to see if whale sharks are present. Snorkellers enter the water near the bait fish and are able to observe single sharks, or small groups, rising to the surface open-mouthed as they consume their prey. There are both sub-adults and adults of both sexes in the area. In the region between Utila and Roatan there are reputed to be more whale shark sightings than anywhere else in the western Caribbean, and the statistics suggest that half of all visitors staying on Utila for a week or more get to see one. There are likely to be blacktip reef sharks and manta rays in the area during these encounters, but if large bull, tiger or mako sharks appear snorkellers are requested to leave the water. There are many nurse sharks around the island as well, although they are not seen during the open-water whale shark encounters.

Bait/feed no.

Cage no.

Other wildlife rough-toothed dolphin, long-snouted spinner dolphin, hawksbill turtle, green turtle, manta ray, marlin, wahoo, tuna, ocean sunfish.

Best time of year whale sharks present year-round.

Dive depth snorkelling in water 300 m/1000 ft deep.

Typical visibility 30 m/100 ft.

Water temperature 26–27 °C/78–81 °F in winter; 27–30 °C/81–86 °F in summer.

Weather and sea notes dry season Mar–Sep; wet season Oct–Feb (most rain Oct–Dec); at sea, 0.5–1 m/ 2–3 ft swells are the norm, though periods of calm occur periodically; northerly winds may cause trips to be cancelled at any time of year.

Contact details Utila Lodge Resort and Bay Islands College of Diving (www.dive-utila.com), Bay Islands Aggressor IV (www.aggressor.com).

Travel international flights to Tegucigalpa or San Pedro Sula; regular flights to Utila from San Pedro Sula and La Ceiba; also regular ferry service between La Ceiba and Utila; wide choice of accommodation on Utila; Bay Islands Aggressor IV is a live-aboard based at Parrot Tree Plantation Resort on the neighbouring island of Roatan.

Note the Utila whale sharks are being studied by the Shark Research Institute, based in the USA and hosted in Honduras by Utila Lodge Resort, and they run a series of seminars and field trips throughout the year for anyone interested in whale shark research.

COSTA RICA

39–44 COCOS ISLAND: ALCYONE SEAMOUNT, DOS AMIGOS, SUBMERGED ROCK, DIRTY ROCK, ISLA MANUELITA AND SILVERADO

Location 480–600 km/300–375 miles south-west of the Pacific coast of Costa Rica.

Main species *most trips:* scalloped hammerhead, whitetip reef, silky, silvertip, blacktip; *occasional trips:* whale, Galápagos.

Viewing opportunities diving around Cocos Island is often described as 'high voltage' or 'on the edge'. It is a challenging dive location and, as shark photographer Jeff Rotman once commented, the 'shark equivalent of Piccadilly Circus'. It is often claimed that there are more sharks per cubic metre around Cocos than anywhere else on earth, and sharks of one species or another are encountered on every dive – frequently in breathtaking numbers. Cocos is a single volcanic outcrop rising sharply from the ocean floor and, although most dive sites are adjacent to small islets or rocks, it offers predominantly open-ocean diving (although not blue water diving). It is one of the largest uninhabited islands in the world (measuring 6.5 × 3.2 km/4 × 2 miles), and no one except the staff of the Park Ranger's Station lives here. Featured in the opening sequences of the movie *Jurassic Park*, it has sheer 100-m/330-ft cliffs topped with tropical rainforest

and streaked with waterfalls plunging into the sea. It is one of the most isolated and sought-after dive destinations anywhere in the world. Fed by a network of ocean currents, with upwellings of nutrient-rich cold water, it is a great meeting place for wandering pelagics from all over the Pacific. Many sharks visit to feed and, since it is the only land for hundreds of kilometres, to be cleaned by barberfish, angelfish and other parasite-eaters. Scalloped hammerheads are the local speciality and form an ever-present backdrop to almost every dive (especially at Manuelita, Alcyone and Dirty Rock). It is said that, if you want to see hammerheads bouncing off your mask, go to Cocos Island – and it ably lives up to its reputation. It is one of the few places in the world where it is possible to dive among literally hundreds of hammerheads and, although they are notoriously skittish and easily spooked, close encounters are virtually guaranteed, if you have a little knowledge and patience. Better still, unlike most other hammerhead sites, they are present year-round. Silkies are more curious, especially when schooling, and there are sometimes so many of them that it is impossible to estimate their numbers. There are also vast schools of whitetip reef sharks – Stan Waterman calls it 'an embarrassment of whitetips' – and in some places it is almost impossible to dive without having at least one in sight most of the time. They are typically found swimming or resting on reefs, or along the reef-sand interface. Many other species occur on a regular basis and, as a treat between dives, it is occasionally possible to snorkel with blacktip sharks in Wafer and Chatham Bays on the north-west coast.

ALCYONE SEAMOUNT a submerged mountain 180 m/600 ft long, and rising to within 25 m/80 ft of the surface, about 1.6 km/1 mile off the south-east corner. Also known as Cousteau's Seamount (Jacques Cousteau discovered it during an exploratory visit), it is best known for its schooling scalloped hammer-heads, which are sometimes present in overwhelming numbers.

DOS AMIGOS there are two main islets (known imaginatively as I and II or Big Dos Amigos and Small Dos Amigos) in this cluster of rocky outcrops off the south-west coast. Big Dos Amigos has sheer cliff walls, broken up by ledges, and a dramatic 14 m/45 ft archway at a depth of about 29 m/95 ft. Small Dos Amigos is a little farther offshore and has similar cliff walls, but they descend much deeper. Hammerheads are frequently seen in the area and it also has a reputation for Galápagos sharks, which seem to be encountered here more often than anywhere else around Cocos (although by no means regularly).

SUBMERGED ROCK approximately 1.6 km/1 mile off the south coast, this rock only just breaks the surface. It is a good place to see large numbers of whitetip reef sharks (some of the females here have mating scars inflicted by the males) and silkies are fairly common. Few divers venture farther out from the rock, where hammerhead sharks are reputed to school, because the current is very strong.

DIRTY ROCK this rugged little rock, about 1 km/ 0.6 miles off the north-west coast, is widely regarded as one of the premier sites for encountering large schools of hammerheads. Dives normally begin on the south side, where divers wait quietly on a barnacle-covered rock at a depth of about 24 m/80 ft. They are frequently rewarded with dozens, if not hundreds, of scalloped hammerheads all around them. There are also large numbers of whitetip reef sharks resting on the sandy areas between boulders at about 24–43 m/ 80–140 ft. Whale sharks seem to be encountered in shallower water near Dirty Rock more often than anywhere else in Cocos.

ISLA MANUELITA lying off the north-east coast, this is another famous site for schooling hammer-heads. Divers descend down Manuelita's west wall, typically to a depth of 35–40 m/115–130 ft, looking across the 200 m/650 ft channel towards the main island. Then everyone hides among VW Beetle-sized boulders on the sandy bottom and waits, safely out of the current, for the sharks to come within a few metres. Hammerheads can also be seen outside the shallow bay on the east side of the island. This site is also popular for snorkelling with the multitudinous whitetip reef sharks lying on the sandy bottom near the reef.

SILVERADO this is a finger-shaped rock outcropping from the main island, at a depth of about 9 m/30 ft, with running freshwater from a nearby waterfall. It is a great place to see 2.5–3 m/8–10 ft silvertip sharks as they come in to a cleaning station at the tunnel entrance. Divers simply kneel on the seabed to watch. Sadly, quite a few of the sharks in this area trail fishing lines from their mouths.

Bait/feed no.

Cage no.

Other wildlife manta ray, devil ray, eagle ray, marbled stingray, sailfish, marlin, barracuda, yellowfin tuna; occasional humpback and pilot whales and bottlenose dolphins (underwater encounters rare).

Best time of year sharks present year-round; whale sharks most commonly seen Jun–Aug.

Dive depth surface to 40 m/130 ft (most shark dives are 30 m/100 ft or more).

Typical visibility highly variable, but averages 15–30 m/50–100 ft; has reached 90 m/300 ft during El Niño in 1998 (although there were no sharks present at the time).

Water temperature averages 25–28 °C/77–82 °F; warmest Nov–Apr; widely fluctuating thermoclines can result in great temperature variation (plus or minus 5 °C) during a single dive.

Weather and sea notes Cocos Island is perpetually cloudy and continuously bathed in torrential down-pours (there is 7–8 m/23–26 ft of rain annually in the centre of the island); there tends to be slightly less rain Nov–Apr; seas can be rough; currents intermittent like gusts of wind; most dives have to be conducted as gentle drifts. The water movement in some areas feels like a current, a surge and a swell rolled into one and can send you spiralling up or down for short distances without warning.

Contact details Undersea Hunter and Sea Hunter (www.underseahunter.com), Okeanos Aggressor (www.aggressor.com), HMS The New Inzan Tiger (www.theinzantiger.com), Scuba Tours Worldwide (www.scubascuba.com).

Travel access by live-aboard only (no accommoda-tion onshore); international flights to San José; boats leave from the small fishing village of Puntarenas, about 2 hours' drive from the capital on the west coast of Costa Rica; 30–40 hours by boat to Cocos.

Notes Cocos Island is protected by the Costa Rican government and was declared a World Heritage Site by UNESCO, and there is a 15-km/9-mile exclusion zone for commercial fishing boats, but the surrounding seas still support a large shark fishery which will even enter the exclusion zone.

45 GULF OF PAPAGAYO: BAT ISLANDS

Location northern end of the Gulf, on the Pacific coast between Puntarenas and the Nicaraguan border.

Main species *most trips:* bull; *many trips:* nurse, whitetip reef, blacktip reef; *occasional trips:* hammer-head, tiger, whale.

Viewing opportunities this is a great place for close encounters with large bull sharks against a spectacular rugged backdrop of caves, arches and tunnels. The Bat Islands (Islas Murciélagos) form a group of islands and outcrops within the Santa Rosa National Park. The westernmost outcrop in the archipelago, a rocky pinnacle known as Big Scare, is the site for the shark dive. On entering the water everyone is expected to go headfirst, to stay together as a group and to follow the sloping wall of the pinnacle down towards the sandy seabed. Anyone unable to equalize has to abort the dive. Different operators have different approaches but, typically, everyone hovers for about 15 minutes to view the sharks at a depth of some 15 m/ 50 ft and then the group continues to about 30 m/

100 ft. A healthy population of bull sharks is resident year-round and as few as two or as many as 20 are seen on a typical dive (usually 10–12). They are mostly adults, of both sexes, and range between 3 m/10 ft and 5 m/16 ft in length. Very close encounters are common, with the sharks approaching divers to within 2 or 3 metres. Several other species occur around Big Scare from time to time. Another pinnacle nearby, known as the Arches or Los Arcos, has a short passageway (8 m/26 ft in length) that is also frequented by bull sharks and has some resident nurse sharks. The best way to experience Big Scare is on an overnight charter, although day trips are also possible.

Bait/feed no.

Cage no.

Other wildlife humpback whale, short-finned pilot whale, long-snouted spinner dolphin, manta ray, eagle ray, cow-nosed ray (sometimes thousands present), large schools of horse-eye jacks, sailfish, marlin, yellowfin tuna, wahoo.

Best time of year all sharks present year-round.

Dive depth 15–30 m/50–100 ft.

Typical visibility 4–25 m/13–80 ft (varies greatly according to plankton abundance); most sharks seen when visibility less than 18 m/60 ft.

Water temperature 20–30 °C/68–86 °F; coolest Dec–Mar.

Weather and sea notes dry season Dec–Mar (northerly winds during this season sometimes result in trip cancellations); best conditions for diving in rainy season May–Nov (higher water temperature and better visibility).

Contact details El Ocotal Beach Resort (www.ocotalresort.com), Rich Coast Diving Co. (www.richcoastdiving.com), Mario Vargas Expeditions (www.divexpeditions.com), Resort Divers de Costa Rica (www.resortdivers-cr.com), Bill Beard's Diving Safaris (www.billbeardcostarica.com).

Travel international flights to San José; domestic flights to Liberia near Gulf of Papagayo or 4 hours (280 km/175 miles) by road; wide choice of accommodation.

46 GULF OF PAPAGAYO: CATALINA ISLANDS

Location southern end of the Gulf, on the Pacific coast between Puntarenas and the Nicaraguan border.

Main species *most trips:* whitetip reef; *occasional trips:* tiger, whale, nurse.

Viewing opportunities the 50 km/31 mile wide Gulf of Papagayo has many dive sites for viewing whitetip reef sharks. Coastal sites include Punta Gorda, Bajo Tiburon and Tortuga, where they can readily be found on sand patches between rocks at various depths of 6–25 m/20–80 ft. But none is as good as the Catalina Islands, lying a few kilometres off the coast. The two main sites are Shark Alley and La Punta, where whitetips are encountered on virtually every dive (when the water is warm), sleeping in sand patches among the rocks at depths of 10–30 m/33–100 ft. As few as two and as many as 20 sharks are seen on an average dive (typically 7–9) and they are nearly all very approachable.

Bait/feed no.

Cage no.

Other wildlife long-snouted spinner dolphin, bottlenose dolphin, sea turtles, manta ray (mainly Jan–Apr), eagle ray, bat ray, southern stingray, schools of golden ray.

Best time of year sharks present year-round; best May–Oct for whitetip reef.

Dive depth 6–30 m/20–100 ft.

Typical visibility 4–25 m/13–80 ft.

Water temperature 20–30 °C/68–86 °F.

Weather and sea notes dry season Dec–May (northerly winds during this season can affect diving conditions); rainy season May–Nov; surge and some current likely.

Contact details El Ocotal Beach Resort (www.ocotalresort.com), Rich Coast Diving Co. (www.richcoastdiving.com), Mario Vargas Expeditions (www.divexpeditions.com), Resort Divers de Costa Rica (www.resortdivers-cr.com), Bill Beard's Diving Safaris (www.billbeardcostarica.com).

Travel international flights to San José; domestic flights to Liberia near Gulf of Papagayo or 4 hours (280 km/175 miles) by road; wide choice of accommodation.

47 OSA PENINSULA: CAÑO ISLAND

Location 16 km/10 miles west of the Osa Peninsula, on the southern Pacific coast.

Main species *most trips:* whitetip reef; *many trips:* bull; *occasional trips:* whale, hammerhead.

Viewing opportunities the Osa Peninsula, projecting 50 km/30 miles into the Pacific, is well known for harbouring the largest area of virgin rainforest in Central America. But there is another jewel in its natural crown: the volcanic Caño Island. With its complex underwater architecture of canyons, pinnacles, caves and arches, Caño Island Biological Reserve is home to a large number of whitetip reef sharks and an abundance of other marine life. Access to the reserve is limited to 10 divers at any one time, and diving is permitted only at a small number of sites. Sharks can be seen almost anywhere in the area, but a few key places are particularly good. El Bajo del Diablo (Devil's Rock) is a large area with submerged mountains, valleys and a variety of weird and wonderful rock formations rising from a depth of about 50 m/165 ft to just 6 m/20 ft below the surface. It is usually patrolled by small groups of up to five whitetip reef sharks (sometimes as many as 25 males are observed circling small caves, if there are females resting inside) and quite often by bull sharks. At the same time literally hundreds of mobula rays may be seen circling over-head and manta rays often visit. At a depth of around 15 m/50 ft, Cueva del Tiburon (Shark Cave) is a cavern some 2.5 m/8 ft high and 13 m/43 ft long, which is frequented by some particularly large whitetip reef sharks as well as diamond stingrays. Nearby there is a cluster of rocks where young whitetips (typically only about 50 cm/20 in long) are seen on virtually every dive. Paraiso is also consistently good for shark watching, particularly an area known as 'Shark Lair', where as many as 15 adult whitetips can be seen lying on the sand underneath rock overhangs and groups of up to 35 congregate to feed with almaco jacks. Whale sharks are occasionally seen around the island, although not with any regularity.

Bait/feed no.

Cage no.

Other wildlife humpback whale (Dec–Apr), short-finned pilot whale, Pantropical spotted dolphin, olive ridley sea turtle, sailfish, diamond stingray, spotted eagle ray, manta ray (Feb–May), mobula ray (vast numbers).

Best time of year sharks present year-round.

Dive depth 6–25 m/20–80 ft.

Typical visibility 15–30 m/50–100 ft.

Water temperature 20–30 °C/68–86 °F.

Weather and sea notes dry season Jan–Apr; heavy rain Oct–Dec (though rain rarely diminishes visibility); best diving conditions Dec–Aug.

Contact details Costa Rica Adventure Divers – Jinetes de Osa (www.costaricadiving.com), Aguila de Osa Inn (www.aguiladeosa.com), Drake Bay Wilderness Resort (www.drakebay.com).

Travel international flights to San José; main departure point for shark dives is Drake Bay on the north-western coast of Osa Peninsula; chartered flights to nearby airport, then taxi to Sierpe River and boat to accommodation.

ECUADOR

48–49 GALÁPAGOS ISLANDS: WOLF ISLAND AND DARWIN ISLAND

Location north-west Galápagos Archipelago; 1000 km/620 miles west of mainland.

Main species *most trips:* scalloped hammerhead, Galápagos, whitetip reef; *many trips:* silky, whale; *occasional trips:* Galápagos horn or bullhead (*Heterodontus quoyi*).

Viewing opportunities an isolated group of volcanic islands lying on the Equator, the Galápagos Archipelago is world famous for its unique and fearless wildlife. It was here, during a five-week visit in 1835, that Charles Darwin gathered important evidence for his theory of evolution. But for shark watchers it is the vast squadrons of scalloped hammerheads that are the main draw. They are best seen around Darwin and Wolf Islands, although these and other species can be seen almost anywhere among the 13 major islands, six small ones and scores of islets. Another species familiar to anyone who has dived here is the Galápagos shark, which was named for a specimen collected in the islands in 1904, but is now known to occur throughout the tropical world; this species can be seen anywhere, but Gordon Rocks (off the north coast of Santa Cruz) during the warm season is particularly good. Galápagos is also con-sidered to be outstanding for close encounters with whale sharks and is the home of an endemic species called the Galápagos horn or bullhead shark, which lives on the bottom or in rocky crevices only around the islands and the nearest stretch of South American coastline. The diving in Galápagos is challenging, with strong currents, exposed conditions and fairly cold water, but is undeniably rewarding. Its isolated posi-tion in the middle of the Pacific, at the convergence of no fewer than seven different ocean currents, ensures that it acts like a magnet to sharks and other pelagics.

Darwin is the northernmost and most isolated island in the archipelago, about 18–20 hours by dive boat from the main group. If you want scalloped hammerheads on every dive, *the* place to go is Darwin Arch (sometimes known simply as 'The Arch'). Although it is more common to see 40–50 hammer-heads in a single dive, huge schools of hundreds are sometimes encountered and there have been reports of several thousand. However, their appearances do seem to be cyclical and there may be huge aggrega-tions one day followed by much smaller ones just a week or two later. The boat anchors at the foot of a towering cliff, then everyone is transferred by inflatable skiff to this unique rock formation some 30 m/100 ft tall. The extraordinary thing is that some of the hammerheads literally appear to escort the boat as it approaches The Arch. It is a wonderful sight to see their dorsal fins cutting through the surface. Once the divers have entered the water, the sharks patrol back and forth, from the surface down to below 30 m/100 ft, and are shy but curious. Everyone descends down a steep, boulder-strewn slope and then hides among the largest boulders at a depth of about 18–24 m/ 60–80 ft, which is the best place to wait for the sharks to cruise overhead.

Wolf is also in the north-west of the archipelago. The main shark site here is, appropriately, Shark Bay on the east side of the island. Large numbers of hammerheads can be seen at any time of year – typically 40–50 adults and juveniles, males and females, on a single dive. On a good day, if everyone is keeping calm and quiet, they may approach to within a couple of metres of divers. As at Darwin, the size of their aggregations seems to be cyclical.

Wolf and Darwin are also popular with divers because the sharks around these two remote islands tend to be less nervous of people than those in the central archipelago.

Bait/feed no.

Cage no.

Other wildlife bottlenose dolphin, Galápagos sea lion, Galápagos fur seal, Galápagos penguin, green and hawksbill turtles, marine iguana, manta, eagle and golden rays; approximately a quarter of all inshore marine species here are unique to this archipelago; huge variety of (mainly endemic) wildlife on shore.

Best time of year sharks present year-round; tend to be larger numbers in warmer months; whale sharks best Jun–Dec (peak Sep); whitetip reef best in mating season (Nov–Jun), when as many as 40 can be seen chasing one another in circles.

Dive depth 12–30 m/40–100 ft (depending on site).

Typical visibility 10–25 m/33–82 ft; best Dec–May.

Water temperature 21–28 °C/70–82 °F Dec–May, 16–24 °C/61–75 °F Jun–Nov; surface water temperatures vary greatly according to the currents; marked thermoclines.

Weather and sea notes strong currents (1–3 knots) and surge common; warm and rainy season with little wind and calm seas Dec–May; colder, drier and mistier with wind and choppier seas Jun–Nov.

Contact details Galápagos Aggressors I and II (www.aggressor.com), Galápagos Adventures (www.galapagosadventures.com), DivingGalápagos.com (www.divinggalapagos.com), Quasar Nautica Galápagos Expeditions (www.quasarnautica.com).

Travel international flights to Quito or Guayaquil; overnight on mainland before flight to islet of Baltra in Galápagos; live-aboard vessels depart from Baltra or

Santa Cruz (2-hour boat transfer between the two); limited hotels and guesthouses, with no diving facilities.

Note commercial netting in the Galápagos Marine Preserve is illegal, but local and foreign fishing boats continue to exploit sharks here, safe in the knowledge that no funding has been provided for enforcement; the fins are often sold to a foreign factory ship sitting outside the protection zone. 2001 was a superb year for whale sharks at both Wolf and Darwin, with as many as 12 sightings per week, and dives with two or three sharks at once.

COLOMBIA

50 MALPELO ISLAND

Location open ocean 385 km/240 miles west of Buenaventura; 540 km/335 miles south of Golfito, Costa Rica.

Main species *most trips:* scalloped hammerhead; *many trips:* whitetip reef, silky; *occasional trips:* blacktip reef, Galápagos, sand tiger, oceanic whitetip, whale, tiger ragged-tooth (possible new species).

Viewing opportunities Malpelo is one of the most inaccessible, dramatic and exciting dive destinations in the world. It is widely recognized as the best place to see large schools of scalloped hammerheads in warm, shallow water. Malpelo National Park consists of Malpelo Island itself, which is volcanic in origin and has dramatic sheer cliffs rising high above sea level, as well as 10 isolated crags and islets. Visits to the park are strictly limited by a permit system. Malpelo lies at the meeting point of two currents and this contributes to the richness and abundance of its marine life. The resident scalloped hammerheads are certainly the biggest draw and cruise around the island in large groups of mixed sex and age. There are rarely fewer than 20 individuals together and sometimes more than 100. Unlike Cocos Island, where the hammerheads tend to congregate at depths of more than 30 m/ 100ft (inevitably limiting dive time and frequency), the Malpelo sharks inhabit shallower depths. The best time to encounter them near the surface is during the morning. There are many dive sites around the island where hammerheads can be seen, making it possible to encounter sharks on every dive. These include Hammer/Freezer Wall and Tiger Mount/Castaway Wall (both undersea cliffs), Three Mexicans/Three Musketeers (a group of pinnacles off the northern end) and Altar of the Virgin (a plateau on the top of a seamount at a depth of only 8 m/25 ft). The hammerheads tend to be uninterested in divers – and, although some are skittish, others will sometimes approach to within a metre or so. They can also be observed at established cleaning stations, where they receive the attentions of white-striped angelfish, and at night when they are feasting upon the free-swimming green morays that gather in vast numbers at certain sites. Many other shark species turn up around Malpelo on a regular basis, including whale sharks – the island's relatively small size means they are seen quite often during their visiting period of December and January. One intriguing local species that may be new to science is the so-called tiger ragged-tooth shark, which has recently been recorded from a seamount at Malpelo. It attains a length of up to 6 m/20 ft and has been observed only in water deeper than 40 m/130 ft. Silky sharks are seen infrequently, but when they do appear they are often in large numbers.

Bait/feed no.

Cage no.

Other wildlife humpback whale, bottlenose dolphin, manta ray, eagle ray, green moray, yellowfin and bonito tuna, barracuda.

Best time of year scalloped hammerheads present year-round, but best time for diving Dec–Sep; whale sharks mainly Dec–Jan.

Dive depth surface to 40 m/130 ft.

Typical visibility 10–20 m/33–65 ft.

Water temperature 18–28 °C/65–82 °F.

Weather and sea notes dry season Dec–Mar; wet season Apr–Nov; strong currents likely year-round; storms can slow down or even prohibit the trip from the mainland.

Contact details Pisces Diving Center (www.telesat.com.co/malpelo), Undersea Hunter (www.underseahunter.com), HMS The New Inzan Tiger (www.theinzantiger.com).

Travel accessible only by live-aboard; international flights to San José or Bogotá; 30-hour trip from Costa Rica or Colombia; Pisces Diving Center from Buenaventura, Undersea Hunter from Puntarenas in Costa Rica, HMS The New Inzan Tiger from Golfito in Costa Rica.

Note HMS The New Inzan Tiger recently started special trips to see the possible new species, tiger ragged-tooth shark, and so far has been having an excellent success rate.

51 GORGONA ISLAND

Location 55 km/34 miles off the Pacific coast.

Main species *most trips:* whitetip reef; *occasional trips:* scalloped hammerhead.

Viewing opportunities Gorgona is a remote oceanic island, covered with lush vegetation and teeming with wildlife. It is well known among herpetologists for its abundance of terrestrial snakes, but has only recently started to attract international attention for its marine life. Permits are required to visit Gorgona National Park and access is only by sea. The best places for shark watching are La Tiburonera, La Cazuela and Las Montanitas – all rocky sites around the main island. At each location divers descend to the seabed and take up position to watch the resident whitetip reef sharks. Individuals of both sexes and all ages are encountered and will usually approach divers to within a metre or so.

Bait/feed no.

Cage no.

Other wildlife humpback whale (Jul–Nov), sperm whale, bottlenose dolphin.

Best time of year sharks present year-round.

Dive depth surface to 30 m/100 ft.

Typical visibility 10–20 m/33–65 ft.

Water temperature 18–25 °C/65–77 °F.

Weather and sea notes dry season Dec–Mar; wet season Apr–Nov (wettest Sep–Oct).

Contact details Pisces Diving Center (www.telesat.com.co/malpelo).

Travel international flights to Bogotá or Cali; island accessible by boat from Buenaventura, Colombia; simple accommodation onshore at the Visitor's Centre; Pisces Diving Center operates live-aboard trips Jan–Dec.

BRAZIL

52 FERNANDO DE NORONHA: LAJE DOIS IRMÃOS

Location 360 km/225 miles north-east of Natal on mainland Brazil (Laje Dois Irmãos is off the western end of the main island).

Main species *most trips:* grey reef, nurse; *occasional trips:* blue, lemon, tiger, shortfin mako, whale, great hammerhead, scalloped hammerhead, smooth hammerhead, Caribbean reef, dusky, silky, bronze whaler, oceanic whitetip, sandbar.

Viewing opportunities Fernando de Noronha is a beautiful mountainous archipelago of 21 islands and islets in the tropical South Atlantic. The largest and only inhabited island, from which the group gets its name, boasts spectacular beaches and stunning coral reefs. No fewer than 16 coastal and pelagic shark species are seen in the area. The entire archipelago was declared a Marine National Park in 1988 and visitor numbers are limited by a permit scheme. There are eight recognized shark dives (including Cabeço da Sapata, Pedras Secas, Canal da Rata, Buraco do Inferno, Caieiras, Ponta das Caracas and Praia do Leão), but Laje Dois Irmãos is the best known and most popular. The site consists of a pair of rocky outcrops off the western end of the main island and is the home of a breeding ground and nursery for grey reef sharks. Divers descend to a sandy seabed at a depth of about 20 m/65 ft and wait for the sharks to arrive. Typically, 5–10 juvenile grey reefs appear and slowly spiral in towards the divers until they become so bold that they readily approach to within a metre or so.

Bait/feed no.

Cage no.

Other wildlife long-snouted spinner dolphin (large resident population of 600 can be viewed in Golfinho Bay from shore, but swimming with them is prohibited); large seabird colonies; hawksbill turtle, green turtle, sailfish, manta ray.

Best time of year sharks present year-round.

Dive depth 20 m/65 ft or more.

Typical visibility 20–35 m/65–115 ft.

Water temperature 26–30 °C/78–86 °F.

Weather and sea notes rainy season Jan–Aug (heaviest rains Mar–Jun); dry season Sep–Dec; hottest Dec–Feb.

Contact details Atlantis Divers (www.atlantisnoronha.com.br), Aguas Claras (www.aguasclaras-fn.com.br).

Travel international flights to Recife or Rio de Janeiro; short flights from Recife and Natal on the mainland; basic hotel on Fernando de Noronha (Hotel Dolphin) and simple pousadas (private homes with a small number of rooms available for tourists).

THE BAHAMAS

53 CAY SAL BANK: SHARK HOLE/ LITTLE HOLE

Location 50 km/30 miles north of Cuba (between Cuba, the Florida Keys and Grand Bahama Banks).

Main species *most trips:* Atlantic sharpnose (*Rhizoprionodon terraenovae*); *many trips:* Caribbean reef, blacktip reef, nurse; *occasional trips:* whale.

Viewing opportunities Cay Sal Bank is a shallow plateau surrounded by deep-blue sea and is remote compared to most other dive sites in the Bahamas. It has one of the highest concentrations of blue holes anywhere in the world. Blue holes are so-called because, when viewed from above, the water in them really does appear deep blue next to the surrounding shallows. Typically they begin at a depth of about 10 m/33 ft and then drop vertically downwards. Little Hole – or Shark Hole, as it is more popularly known – has a 60 m/200 ft wide circular opening and resembles a huge well-shaft. At a depth of about 18 m/60 ft the walls taper sharply inwards, creating a pronounced ledge, and the bottom is believed to be around 75 m/ 250 ft. The dive is quite an experience in its own right, with abundant gorgonians, whip corals and sponges in a spectacular twilight world. But it is also one of the best places in the world to see Atlantic sharpnose sharks, which live in considerable numbers right inside the hole. Although normally quite shy, sometimes they gather in huge numbers and look really spectacular as they swim in opposing circles and at different depths.

Bait/feed no.

Cage no.

Other wildlife vibrant coral gardens.

Best time of year Atlantic sharpnose best spring and summer; other sharks present year-round.

Dive depth 18 m/60 ft or more.

Typical visibility 30 m/100 ft.

Water temperature 21–24 °C/70–75 °F in winter, 28–31 °C/82–88 °F in summer.

Weather and sea notes winter months considered high season for tourism (less hot and humid), but divers prefer summer (water temperature higher, winds drop, flat calm seas more common, and water clarity better); tropical storms do occur in summer (May–Oct), but rarely last longer than a couple of hours; official hurricane season Jun–Oct but, based on recent years, Sep is the most likely time for a hurricane to occur.

Contact details Sea Fever Diving Cruises (www.seafever.com), Nekton Diving Cruises (www.nektoncruises.com), Bottom Time Adventures (www.bottomtimetwo.com).

Travel international flights to the capital Nassau (New Providence Island) from Europe and North America (with connecting flights to other islands); Cay Sal is accessible only from live-aboard dive boats.

Note nearby Big Hole (400 m/1300 ft across and with a recorded depth of 90 m/300 ft) has a substantial population of Caribbean reef sharks and some blacktip reef sharks. They frequently follow a wide ledge that runs for more than 100 m/330 ft down the wall of the hole. Shark feeds are often conducted in Big Hole (a weighted tag line is laced with fish and anchored in front of the divers as they gather on a large sandy ledge inside the hole), so there are often more sharks here than in other blue holes. Even without feeding, there can be as many as a dozen Caribbean reef sharks and sometimes a few nurse sharks, which frequently approach divers closely.

54 WALKER'S CAY: SHARK RODEO/SPIRAL CAVERN

Location At the extreme northern tip of the Bahamas, 15 minutes north-west of Walker's Cay.

Main species *most trips:* blacktip reef, Caribbean reef, nurse; *many trips:* lemon; *occasional trips:* bull, great hammerhead, tiger, silky, dusky.

Viewing opportunities once described as 'the sharkiest dive in the world', the Walker's Cay Shark Rodeo is a must for shark aficionados. It can even be snorkelled – and, indeed, as many snorkellers as divers participate. Everyone is taken to a natural underwater arena, called Spiral Cavern, which is surrounded on most sides by massive coral formations and yet is close to the deep waters of the open ocean. Gary and Brenda Adkison started shark feeding here in 1991 and now some 80–200 sharks of several different species (although the vast majority are blacktip reef sharks) gather for their twice-weekly feed. On arrival, the boat does several turns of the area, noisily revving its engines, and the sharks begin to appear from nowhere. Divers descend to the sandy seabed, at a depth of about 12 m/40 ft, and wait with their backs to one of the coral walls. Then a dustbin-sized block of frozen fish pieces (known as a 'chumsicle' – like a giant fishy ice lolly or 'popsicle') is suspended in mid-water, about 3 m/10 ft off the seabed, anchored to the bottom with steel wire and hanging from a float at the surface. As soon as the feed is under way, divers are encouraged to leave their positions and swim among the sharks (though some choose to keep their backs against the wall). The only rule is to stay away from the 'zone of competition': an area about 5 m/16 ft from the chumsicle itself. The sharks completely ignore the divers, perhaps regarding them as fellow predators rather than potential sources of food, and being surrounded by huge numbers of sharks feels surprisingly safe. However, wearing gloves and a hood is strongly recommended to cover up any white flesh that might accidentally be regarded as a tasty morsel. After about 20–25 minutes, when the food has been eaten and the sharks begin to disperse, divers are given the opportunity to swim into the centre of the arena to look for shark teeth that may have fallen to the seabed. Photographers frequently choose to dive Spiral Cavern without the bait, when it is possible to encounter 50–60 sharks in much clearer water. With scientists from the Aquarium of the Americas and the National Marine Fisheries Service, Adkison is pioneering the use of electronic Passive Injectable Transponders to track some of the sharks frequenting Spiral Cavern. These PITs are similar to the tags some people have implanted beneath the fur of their household pets and can be read like a bar code when a reading instrument is passed nearby.

Bait/feed yes.

Cage no.

Other wildlife black grouper.

Best time of year most sharks present year-round; bull sharks mainly Aug–May (then follow tuna migration for a couple of months).

Dive depth 12 m/40 ft.

Typical visibility 15–30 m/50–100 ft (less near the seabed during the shark feed).

Water temperature 21–24 °C/70–75 °F in winter, 28–31 °C/82–88 °F in summer.

Weather and sea notes surface frequently choppy; winter months considered high season for tourism (less hot and humid), but divers prefer summer (water temperature higher, winds drop, flat calm seas more common, and water clarity better); tropical storms do occur in summer (May–Oct), but rarely last longer than a couple of hours; official hurricane season Jun–Oct but, based on recent years, Sep is the most likely time for a hurricane to occur.

Contact details Walker's Cay Hotel & Marina (www.walkerscay.com), Walker's Cay Undersea Adventures (www.nealwatson.com/WalkersCay.html).

Travel national and international flights to Miami or Fort Lauderdale; direct flight to Walker's Cay from Fort Lauderdale; there is a small hotel and diving centre at Walker's Cay (a tiny 40-ha/100-acre island).

Note a deeper shark dive near Walker's Cay is Shark Canyon, about 20 mins due north of the marina; it is a sloping V-shaped valley dropping to a small tunnel system at 28 m/90 ft. Sleeping Caribbean reef sharks are frequently found at the bottom of the gulleys here, with occasional sightings of lemon, bull and tiger sharks.

55 WALKER'S CAY: SHARK BEACH

Location At the extreme northern tip of the Bahamas, a shallow bay on Walker's Cay.

Main species *most trips:* bull; *occasional trips:* lemon.

Viewing opportunities Shark Beach is such a special encounter site that Gary Adkison, the Manager of Walker's Cay Hotel & Marina, is determined that it should be experienced only by select groups with an emphasis on education. It is one of the few places in the world where you can reliably see bull sharks up close. Until recently, bull sharks have had a fearsome reputation – alongside tiger sharks and great whites – and yet these big, full-grown adults show absolutely no sign of aggression towards snorkellers during such close encounters. As many as 15 congregate in the murky water of a shallow bay near the Walker's Cay runway, where fishermen have been cleaning their catches for generations. The bay is so shallow that it is possible to stand up in the grassy sandflats beyond the rocks, and the dorsal fins of the patrolling sharks often break the surface. Snorkellers simply slip off the rocks into the water and are surrounded by sharks almost immediately. A dustbinful of unwanted fish parts collected from the marina's fish-cleaning room (Walker's Cay is primarily a game-fishing destination) is sometimes used to bring the sharks in closer.

Bait/feed yes (sometimes).

Cage no.

Best time of year bull sharks present Aug–May (then follow tuna migration for a couple of months).

Dive depth snorkelling in shallow water.

Typical visibility up to 10 m/33 ft.

Water temperature 21–24 °C/70–75 °F in winter, 28–31 °C/82–88 °F in summer.

Weather and sea notes winter months considered high season for tourism (less hot and humid), but divers prefer summer (water temperature higher, winds drop, flat calm seas more common, and water clarity better); tropical storms do occur in summer (May–Oct), but rarely last longer than a couple of hours; official hurricane season Jun–Oct but, based on recent years, Sep is the most likely time for a hurricane to occur.

Contact details Walker's Cay Hotel & Marina (www.walkerscay.com), Walker's Cay Undersea Adventures (www.nealwatson.com/walkerscay.html).

Travel international flights to the capital Nassau (New Providence Island) from Europe and North America (with flights to Walker's Cay via Freeport) or direct flights to Walker's Cay from Fort Lauderdale; there is a small hotel and diving centre at Walker's Cay (a tiny 40-ha/100-acre island).

56 GRAND BAHAMA ISLAND: PIER 1 SEAFOOD RESTAURANT

Location Freeport Harbour.

Main species *most trips:* lemon.

Viewing opportunities anchored on stilts in Freeport Harbour, Pier 1 is certainly one of the most unusual places to see wild sharks – and it is ideal for anyone who does not want to get their feet wet. It is unlike any other restaurant in the world because, while you are eating your meal inside or on the wooden veranda outside, the waiters are feeding wild lemon sharks in the sea 6 m/20 ft below. Several dozen sharks swim around under the restaurant each evening and squabble over the kitchen scraps. For photography, the earlier 6.30 pm sitting is best, although the whole scene is floodlit during the 8.30 pm sitting. It is a great concept, but is spoiled by the fact that while some sharks are feeding in the sea below, others are being eaten in the restaurant above. The menu includes everything from bull shark stuffed with crabmeat and cheese to lemon shark in a white wine sauce, which does seem rather hypocritical. Advance reservations are essential – especially if you want to sit on the outside patio where all the action takes place.

Contact details Pier 1 Seafood Restaurant (tel: 352-6674 or fax: 352-6583).

Travel international flights to the capital Nassau (New Providence Island) from Europe and North America (with connecting flights to Freeport) or direct flights to Freeport from Miami and Fort Lauderdale; wide choice of hotels in Freeport.

57 GRAND BAHAMA ISLAND: SHARK ALLEY

Location 1.6 km/1 mile offshore from Freeport.

Main species *most trips:* Caribbean reef; *many trips:* nurse.

Viewing opportunities this is the original home of the famous Xanadu Trance, which forms an integral part of a regular shark feed. Divers descend to the sandy seabed, at a depth of about 14 m/46 ft, next to an old recompression chamber and surrounded by coral reef. Everyone kneels in a semicircle, with a safety diver in position at each end, and the feeder stands in front. The staff are all wearing chainmail suits, although participants are in normal wetsuits. Some 10–30 Caribbean reef sharks (mostly females in the 1.5–2.5 m/5–8 ft size range) gather for the feed. They circle patiently, waiting for their turn to move in and take a fish from the feeder's hand. The bait is kept securely inside a PVC tube, with a diaphragm opening, and if the feeding becomes unruly the food is with-held until things calm down. Later the feeder may take hold of a shark and stroke its head and sides. The animal stops swimming, settles gently on the seabed and lies there in a trance-like state. It can then be lifted and literally carried to the semicircle of divers for closer inspection: with the shark lying still, it is even possible to see the tiny ampullae of Lorenzini that form its electro-magnetic sensory organ. After a few moments, the shark shakes its head and swims off at normal speed, apparently none the worse for its experience – neither lethargic nor agitated. The same site is also worth diving outside feeding times, because sharks are still present and the visibility tends to be better.

Bait/feed yes.

Cage no.

Other wildlife stingray, green moray eel.

Best time of year sharks present year-round.

Dive depth 14 m/46 ft.

Typical visibility 6–15 m/20–50 ft (short periods of poor visibility after heavy rain washes muddy water from the island).

Water temperature 21–24 °C/70–75 °F in winter, 28–31 °C/82–88 °F in summer.

Weather and sea notes winter months considered high season for tourism (less hot and humid), but divers prefer summer (water temperature higher, winds drop, flat calm seas more common, and water clarity better); tropical storms do occur in summer (May–Oct), but rarely last longer than a couple of hours; official hurricane season Jun–Oct but, based on recent years, Sep is the most likely time for a hurricane to occur.

Contact details Xanadu Undersea Adventures (www.xanadudive.com).

Travel international flights to the capital Nassau (New Providence Island) from Europe and North America (with connecting flights to Freeport) or direct flights to Freeport from Miami and Fort Lauderdale; wide choice of hotels in Freeport.

Note Xanadu also offers a one-day Shark Awareness Course (including one shark dive and one shark-feeding dive).

58 GRAND BAHAMA ISLAND: SHARK JUNCTION

Location 3 km/2 miles offshore from Port Lucaya, near Freeport.

Main species *most trips:* Caribbean reef, nurse.

Viewing opportunities this is the site of one of the best-known and most popular shark feeds in the world. The Underwater Explorers Society (UNEXSO) has been feeding as many as 30 Caribbean reef sharks here every day since the late 1980s. Approximately a dozen divers descend to the sandy seabed, at a depth of about 14 m/45 ft, and kneel in a wide semicircle with their backs against a rusty old recompression chamber. They are accompanied by four dive masters wearing protective chainmail suits: an underwater videographer; two safety divers armed with billy sticks to keep a watchful eye on proceedings and make regular checks on the air consumption of participants; and a professional shark feeder. The feeder and videographer wear protective chainmail suits weighing about 6.5 kg/14 lb (making them look like medieval warriors), but the safety divers and participants wear normal wetsuits with no extra protection. Very quickly the sharks begin to swim around the feeder in ever-decreasing circles. One by one, he (or she) pulls out entire herring or mackerel from a black PVC tube with a diaphragm opening and literally hands them to each passing shark in turn. Although the animals inevitably get excited, the feeding is carefully controlled. The feeder may also kneel down on the seabed, with one of the sharks laying its head gently in his lap, and then stroke the creature for a minute or two, as if stroking a cat. When the feed has finished, the feeder moves away, the sharks follow and the divers are then permitted to return to the surface. Experienced photographers can be granted special permission to move around more freely during the dive – provided they pay for their own private safety diver. The dive typically lasts about 40 minutes.

Bait/feed yes.

Cage no.

Other wildlife stingray.

Best time of year sharks present year-round.

Dive depth 14 m/45 ft.

Typical visibility 6–15 m/20–50 ft (short periods of poor visibility after heavy rain washes muddy water from the island).

Water temperature 21–24 °C/70–75 °F in winter, 28–31 °C/82–88 °F in summer.

Weather and sea notes site prone to choppy conditions; winter months considered high season for tourism (less hot and humid), but divers prefer summer (water temperature higher, winds drop, flat calm seas more common, and water clarity better); tropical storms do occur in summer (May–Oct), but rarely last longer than a couple of hours; official hurricane season Jun–Oct but, based on recent years, Sep is the most likely time for a hurricane to occur.

Contact details UNEXSO (www.unexso.com).

Travel international flights to the capital Nassau (New Providence Island) from Europe and North America (with connecting flights to Freeport) or direct flights to Freeport from Miami and Fort Lauderdale; UNEXSO operates from nearby Port Lucaya, where there is a wide choice of hotels.

Note UNEXSO also offers a shark-feeder course, during which participants wear a chainmail protective suit and learn how to handfeed the sharks themselves.

59 BIMINI: BULL RUN/SHARK REEF

Location south of Cat Cay, approximately 32 km/20 miles south of Bimini (80 km/50 miles east of Miami).

Main species *most trips:* Caribbean reef, nurse; *occasional trips:* whale.

Viewing opportunities dedicated shark dives have been conducted in Bimini since 1992. Caribbean reef and nurse sharks are seen on almost every dive here, but for a really close encounter Bull Run is the place to go. This would be a nice dive even without the sharks (the coral grows on high mounds with swim-throughs and overhangs) and can be enjoyed by divers and snorkellers alike. The sharks are fed on a flat, sandy area with a tall coral ridge on one side and a seagrass meadow on the other. There are normally five to 10 sharks on a typical dive and they often start circling the divers before the feed begins. Then a 'shark kebab' of bait fish is lowered into the water and the sharks go into a 'safe feeding frenzy' for a minute or two – the feed does not last long compared with other shark feeds in the Bahamas, but it is certainly of high intensity. After the food has gone, the sharks usually stay in the area and swim casually among the divers for the remainder of the dive. Whale sharks are rarely encountered at Bull Run itself – but are occasionally seen offshore.

Bait/feed yes.

Cage no.

Other wildlife Atlantic spotted dolphin (occasionally), black grouper, stingray, eagle ray.

Best time of year all shark species present year-round; best conditions May–Sep.

Dive depth 15–18 m/50–60 ft.

Typical visibility 20–40 m/65–130 ft (best in winter).

Water temperature 21–24 °C/70–75 °F in winter, 28–31 °C/82–88 °F in summer.

Weather and sea notes winter months considered high season for tourism (less hot and humid), but divers prefer summer (water temperature higher, winds drop, flat calm seas more common, and water clarity better); thunderstorms do occur in summer (May–Oct), but rarely last longer than a couple of hours; official hurricane season Jun–Oct, but hurricanes rare; Oct–Mar brings stronger winds.

Contact details Blackbeard's Cruises (www.blackbeard-cruises.com).

Travel shark trips conducted from live-aboard based in Miami, Florida; international flights to Miami.

60 NEW PROVIDENCE ISLAND: SHARK BUOY

Location offshore north-east of Fresh Creek, between New Providence and Andros Islands in an area known as the Tongue of the Ocean.

Main species *most trips:* silky; *occasional trips:* Caribbean reef.

Viewing opportunities this is a most unlikely dive site but one of the best places in the world to encounter pelagic silky sharks. It is quite an experience – being surrounded by 2–10 of these exquisite sharks in limitless blue water and with superb visibility. Some 19 km/12 miles off the south-west coast of New Providence Island is a United States Naval Buoy. Anchored to the seabed in 1800 m/5900 ft of water in a deep oceanic trench that cuts into Great Bahama Bank, it is officially known as Deer Island Buoy and is used for submarine tracking and various NATO exercises. Although only about 6 m/20 ft in diameter, like all floating objects in open oceanic waters the buoy has its own mini-ecosystem ranging from algae and planktonic animals near the bottom of the food chain to silky sharks at the top. The sharks may also be attracted by the vibrations of the buoy's cable as the current passes through this natural deep-water trench. Divers enter the water at the buoy and normally descend to a depth of around 25 m/80 ft. The silkies here are smaller and sleeker than the Caribbean reef sharks encountered on most other Bahamian shark dives. They are not aggressive, and the ones around the buoy rarely exceed 1.5–1.8 m/5–6 ft, but they frequently pass close to divers (with the help of a little food) and offer some wonderful opportunities for photography.

Bait/feed yes.

Cage no.

Other wildlife dolphinfish (mahi-mahi) occasionally.

Best time of year sharks present year-round.

Dive depth 6–30 m/20–100 ft.

Typical visibility 40–50 m/130–165 ft.

Water temperature 21–24 °C/70–75 °F in winter, 28–31 °C/82–88 °F in summer.

Weather and sea notes since the buoy is exposed, choppy seas are common, but the dive is rarely done in anything but flat, calm conditions; fairly strong currents sometimes occur; winter months considered high season for tourism (less hot and humid), but divers prefer summer (water temperature higher, winds drop, flat calm seas more common, and water clarity better); tropical storms do occur in summer (May–Oct), but rarely last longer than a couple of hours; official hurricane season Jun–Oct but, based on recent years, Sep is the most likely time for a hurricane to occur.

Contact details Stuart Cove's Dive Bahamas (www.stuartcove.com).

Travel international flights to the capital Nassau (New Providence Island) from Europe and North America; wide choice of accommodation on New Providence.

Note Stuart and Michelle Cove frequently immobilize silky sharks on this dive to remove fishing hooks and lures from their mouths. They grab a shark by the tail and, with one strong twist, turn it upside down on to its back: it stops moving and becomes almost catatonic as long as it is being held in that position. The sharks do not appear to be harmed or stressed by a minute or two of 'tonic immobility' and, as well as helping them, it gives divers an opportunitiy to examine these beautiful creatures at very close range.

61 NEW PROVIDENCE ISLAND: LOST OCEAN BLUE HOLE

Location south of Rose Island, 18 km/11 miles east of Nassau.

Main species *most trips:* nurse; *many trips:* Caribbean reef, finetooth (*Carcharinus isodon*).

Viewing opportunities this is an unusual shark dive inside a natural hole in the open ocean floor. With an almost perfect circular opening some 30 m/100 ft in diameter, and appearing dark blue against the white sandy bottom, the hole itself is a really impressive sight. It opens at about 12 m/40 ft below the surface, where a few coral heads teeming with fish perch precariously around the edge, and drops straight down to a depth of at least 60 m/200 ft and well below sports-diving limits. There are several interesting caverns and crevices inside (including one at 24 m/80 ft, which is often packed with spiny lobsters) and these provide suitable resting places for a number of nurse sharks. One cavern on the eastern side, some 18–27 m/60–90 ft below the surface, has a large ledge where nurse sharks are seen most frequently. Caribbean reef sharks also seem attracted to the hole and, especially later in the summer, more than 20 can sometimes be seen circling around inside just below the lip. A real bonus, in mid-summer, is a large school of 100-plus finetooth sharks.

Bait/feed no.

Cage no.

Other wildlife southern stingray (lie in sand around the opening), large schools of sergeant major, brown chromis, French grunt and (unusually) grey angelfish, barracuda, Atlantic spadefish, grouper, spiny lobster.

Best time of year summer (mid-summer best for finetooth, late summer for Caribbean reef).

Dive depth 12–27 m/40–90 ft.

Typical visibility 20–30 m/65–100 ft.

Water temperature 21–24 °C/70–75 °F in winter, 28–31 °C/82–88 °F in summer.

Weather and sea notes fairly exposed and surface frequently choppy; winter months considered high season for tourism (less hot and humid), but divers prefer summer (water temperature higher, winds drop, flat calm seas more common, and water clarity better); tropical storms do occur in summer (May–Oct), but rarely last longer than a couple of hours; official hurricane season Jun–Oct but, based on recent years, Sep is the most likely time for a hurricane to occur.

Contact details Divers Haven (www.divershaven.com), Nassau Scuba Centre (www.nassau-scuba-centre.com), Lost Blue Hole – Aqua Cat Cruises (www.aquacatcruises.com), Bahama Divers (www.bahamadivers.com), Out-Island Oceanics (www.seadragonbahamas.com).

Travel international flights to the capital Nassau (New Providence Island); wide choice of accommodation in and around Nassau.

62 NEW PROVIDENCE ISLAND: SHARK RUNWAY

Location near Clifton Bay off the south-western tip of New Providence Island.

Main species *most trips:* Caribbean reef.

Viewing opportunities Shark Runway is one of many dive sites along the 'Tongue of the Ocean' (an 1830-m/6000-ft deep ocean trench) and is certainly one of the best for shark watching. The predominantly male Caribbean reef sharks here are a little 'wilder' than their contemporaries at nearby Shark Alley, perhaps because they are not as well conditioned to hand-feeding. Although local operators confirm that they are all Caribbean reef, some are so large that divers have confused them with bull sharks. The feeder descends to the flat, sand-surrounded patch reef at a depth of about 14 m/45 ft with a bucket of fish and hands them to the sharks, one by one, on the end of a spear (or, when wearing a full chainmail suit, by hand). On a typical dive as many as 40 or 50 sharks arrive for the feast. When they have safely departed (as soon as the food has all gone) the 10–12 divers spend the remainder of the dive searching the area for shark teeth – anyone with reasonable eyesight can expect to find two or three lying on the sandy bottom. The nearby wreck of the *Bahama Mama* (sunk as a dive attraction in 1995) makes an interesting backdrop to the dive and provides some excellent photo opportunities.

Bait/feed yes.

Cage no.

Other wildlife yellowtail snapper, southern stingray, grouper, moray eel, pufferfish.

Best time of year sharks presents year-round.

Dive depth 14 m/45 ft.

Typical visibility 20–40 m/65–130 ft.

Water temperature 21–24 °C/70–75 °F in winter, 28–31 °C/82–88 °F in summer.

Weather and sea notes site has fairly sheltered conditions most of the year; no current; winter months considered high season for tourism (less hot and humid), but divers prefer summer (water temperature higher, winds drop, flat calm seas more common, and water clarity better); tropical storms do occur in summer (May–Oct), but rarely last longer than a couple of hours; official hurricane season Jun–Oct but, based on recent years, Sep is the most likely time for a hurricane to occur.

Contact details Dive, Dive, Dive (www.divedivedive.com), Stuart Cove's Dive Bahamas (www.stuartcove.com), Nassau Scuba Centre (www.divenassau.com).

Travel international flights to the capital Nassau (New Providence Island) from Europe and North America; wide choice of accommodation in and around Nassau.

63 NEW PROVIDENCE ISLAND: SHARK ARENA/SHARK WALL

Location approximately 18 km/11 miles south-east of New Providence Island.

Main species *most trips:* Caribbean reef; *occasional trips:* nurse.

Viewing opportunities most visiting divers experience two rather different shark encounters at this site. The first, along Shark Wall, is designed to whet your appetite for the 'real thing'. It is a wonderful dive in its own right, with spectacular hard and soft corals, but with the added bonus of prowling sharks it is superb. The boat anchors near the edge of the reef, in about 12 m/40 ft of water, where a sheer cliff face drops off into the abyss. Finning away from the edge and psychological safety, over several kilometres of deep-blue sea, is an exhilarating experience – made all the more exciting by the fact that you are likely to be followed by a number of Caribbean reef sharks for the entire dive. The reason the sharks take such an interest in divers is because the feeding site, known as Shark Arena, is just 50 m/165 ft from the ocean drop-off. This is where the second encounter takes place. Divers descend to a natural coral amphitheatre and kneel on the sandy seabed in a semi-circle. The feeder enters the water and positions himself (or herself) in the centre with a large box filled with fish scraps and then pulls them out, one by one, on the end of a long, blunt pole spear. The sharks take the fish from the end of the spear. Some feeders wear full chainmail suits, others prefer to wear only the gloves and arms (just enough to be able to handle the bait if necessary). The trick is to feed the sharks fast enough to keep them interested, but slow enough to prevent a feeding frenzy and to allow photography and detailed observation. Typically about 20–30 Caribbean reef sharks gather in the area. They are mostly large females and frequently jostle and nudge divers. The feeding takes about 20–25 minutes and then the sharks tend to move away of their own accord. Divers have a few minutes to search for shark-tooth souvenirs before returning to the surface.

Bait/feed yes.

Cage no.

Other wildlife nassau grouper, stingray, green moray eel.

Best time of year sharks present year-round.

Dive depth 17 m/56 ft (Shark Arena); 15–23 m/ 50–75 ft (Shark Wall).

Typical visibility 15–30 m/50–100 ft.

Water temperature 21–24 °C/70–75 °F in winter, 28–31 °C/82–88 °F in summer.

Weather and sea notes the site is fairly sheltered and there is no predominant current; winter months considered high season for tourism (less hot and humid), but divers prefer summer (water temperature higher, winds drop, flat calm seas more common, and water clarity better); tropical storms do occur in summer (May–Oct), but rarely last longer than a couple of hours; official hurricane season Jun–Oct but, based on recent years, Sep is the most likely time for a hurricane to occur.

Contact details Stuart Cove's Dive Bahamas (www.stuartcove.com), Nassau Scuba Centre (www.divenassau.com or www.feedshark.com), Dive, Dive, Dive (www.divedivedive.com).

Travel international flights to the capital Nassau (New Providence Island) from Europe and North America; wide choice of accommodation in and around Nassau.

Note nearby Shark Valley, a double wall formation at the end of a sandy plain, is well known for the number of Caribbean reef sharks frequently encountered cruising along the reef. Stuart Cove's Dive South Ocean also offers a Shark Awareness Course (with training in shark identification and biology, conducting a safe encounter, and conservation) and an opportunity to train as a Shark Feeder. Nassau Scuba Centre offers a similar awarness course and the famous 'Shark Suit Adventure' (learning to feed the sharks while wearing a chainmail suit) at Shark Arena.

64 EXUMA CAYS: DANGER CAY: DANGER REEF/ AMBERJACK REEF

Location Danger Cay in Exuma Sound, central Exumas; 90 km/55 miles south-east of Nassau.

Main species *most trips:* Caribbean reef, nurse; *occasional trips:* whale, great hammerhead.

Viewing opportunities this 14 m/45 ft patch of reef is a popular site for shark feeds, conducted by several live-aboard operators, which can be enjoyed by divers and snorkellers alike. A large block of frozen fish, known as a chumsicle, is tethered between the surface and the seabed at a height of about 4.5 m/15 ft off the bottom. This attracts a group of 5–10 resident Caribbean reef sharks and one or two nurse sharks, as well as an equally impressive gathering of 10–15 large groupers. While the predators take turns to feed on the bait, the divers are allowed to swim freely among them (although no one is allowed closer than 6 m/ 20 ft from the chumsicle). The sharks appear unperturbed by their human admirers and are likely to swim very close. The feed typically lasts about 15–20 minutes before they begin to disperse. Farther north, in Allan's Cay, Whale Shark Reef lives up to its name because whale sharks frequent this area each winter.

The chance of seeing them varies enormously from year to year: some winters they are encountered almost every week; in others they fail to materialize at all.

Bait/feed yes.

Cage no.

Other wildlife black and nassau groupers, stingray, eagle ray, pirate blenny.

Best time of year Caribbean reef and nurse sharks present year-round; whale sharks in winter.

Dive depth 15–20 m/50–65 ft.

Typical visibility 25–35 m/80–115 ft.

Water temperature 21–24 °C/70–75 °F in winter, 28–31 °C/82–88 °F in summer.

Weather and sea notes no strong current; winter months considered high season for tourism (less hot and humid), but divers prefer summer (water temperature higher, winds drop, flat calm seas more common and water clarity better); tropical storms do occur in summer (May–Oct), but rarely last longer than a couple of hours; official hurricane season Jun–Oct but, based on recent years, Sep is the most likely time for a hurricane to occur.

Contact details Aqua Cat Cruises (www.aquacatcruises.com), Blackbeard's Cruises (www.blackbeard-cruises.com), Out-Island Oceanics (www.seadragonbahamas.com).

Travel accessible by live-aboard, departing from the capital Nassau (Aqua Cat Cruises and Out-Island Oceanics) or Miami (Blackbeard's Cruises); international flights to Nassau (New Providence Island); wide choice of accommodation in Nassau.

65 ELEUTHERA: THE PINNACLE

Location 10 km/6 miles south-east of Harbour Island, off the north-east coast of Eleuthera (5 km/3 miles offshore); 100 km/62 miles east of Nassau.

Main species *many trips:* blacktip, bull.

Viewing opportunities this is not a particularly easy dive, usually conducted in a strong current and at a depth that severely limits bottom time, but it is frequently rewarded with good open-water shark encounters. A mooring line is attached to the top of a pinnacle, which sits on an undulating seamount, at a depth of about 30 m/100 ft. Divers descend the line and, while some choose to explore the big stands of black coral and huge barrel sponges at greater depth, many choose to remain at the mooring and watch for blue-water pelagics. The seamount is surrounded by very deep water, and a variety of species – most commonly blacktip and bull sharks – frequent the area.

Bait/feed no.

Cage no.

Other wildlife barracuda, wahoo, amberjack, yellowtail snapper, huge barrel sponges and black coral trees.

Best time of year sharks present year-round.

Dive depth 30–40 m/100–130 ft.

Typical visibility 20–30 m/65–100 ft.

Water temperature 21–24 °C/70–75 °F in winter, 28–31 °C/82–88 °F in summer.

Weather and sea notes fairly exposed and surface frequently choppy; current can be strong; winter months considered high season for tourism (less hot and humid), but divers prefer summer (water temperature higher, winds drop, flat calm seas more common, and water clarity better); tropical storms do occur in summer (May–Oct) but rarely last longer than a couple of hours; official hurricane season Jun–Oct but, based on recent years, Sep is the most likely time for a hurricane to occur.

Contact details Valentines Dive Centre (www.valentinesdive.com), Romora Bay Club Dive Shop (www.romorabay.com).

Travel international flights to the capital Nassau (New Providence Island), with daily flights to the north end of Eleuthera or direct flights from Miami and Fort Lauderdale; water taxi to Harbour Island; limited choice of accommodation on the main island or wider choice on Harbour Island.

66 CAT ISLAND: ORANGE CREEK WALL

Location 3 km/2 miles off Orange Creek on the north-west coast of Cat Island; 210 km/130 miles south-east of Nassau.

Main species *many trips:* great hammerhead, bull, blacktip reef, whitetip reef.

Viewing opportunities there are not large numbers of sharks at this little-dived site, but it is noteworthy for its great hammerhead and bull sharks. Midway down the Bahamas, Cat Island (not to be confused with tiny Cat Cay in the Biminis) is one of the least populated islands in the archipelago. Most of the better-known dive sites are in the south, especially around Port Howe, but Orange Creek Wall is in the north. Divers swim down a sloping sandy bank to an impressive wall with rocky pinnacles and ledges, where sharks of several species can be encountered patrolling backwards and forwards. Anywhere between two and five sharks are observed on a typical dive and, when there are small groups of divers in the water, they often approach very closely;

they tend to be more wary of larger groups. The bull sharks, in particular, are unusually uninhibited here and make great subjects for photographers. The best time to see them is later in the afternoon, in winter, when they tend to rise nearer to the surface. In the summer, most of the sharks spend the daytime in deeper water (around 60 m/200 ft).

Bait/feed no (see **Note**).

Cage no.

Other wildlife eagle ray, barracuda, grouper.

Best time of year sharks present year-round, but less accessible (move to deeper water during the day) Jun–Oct.

Dive depth 30 m/100 ft.

Typical visibility 30–60 m/100–200 ft.

Water temperature 20–29 °C/68–84 °F; coolest Dec–Mar.

Weather and sea notes rain more likely May–Oct; Nov–Apr cooler with breezes.

Contact details Dive Deep South (www.diving-in-the-bahamas.com).

Travel international flights to Nassau (New Providence) or Freeport (Grand Bahama); scheduled or charter flights to Arthur's Town; limited choice of accommodation around Orange Creek.

Note Dive Deep South feeds sharks from the dock-side every evening – no one gets in the water, but the sharks can be observed by torchlight from shore.

67 LONG ISLAND: SHARK REEF

Location 11 km/7 miles west of Stella Maris.

Main species *most trips:* Caribbean reef, nurse; *occasional trips:* bull, mako, tiger, whale.

Viewing opportunities Stella Maris Resort was the first operation in the world to start regular shark feeding. In the late 1960s three German friends set up the resort and learnt to dive. Before long, they were feeding sharks in 10 m/33 ft of water at the site now known as Shark Reef. Initially they did so from inside a cage (at the time many people considered even that to be risky), but a year later they ventured outside and cautiously began to swim freely with the sharks. They never looked back. Shark feeds continue at the same site to this day and are fairly representative of the early experiments. The engine noise of the boat is enough to attract the sharks, and divers descend through them before kneeling in a semicircle on the seabed. Unlike most other Bahamian shark feeds, the feeding is largely uncontrolled, so the action tends to be more intense. A bucket of fish is brought down to the bottom by the feeder and, instead of being handfed, the sharks are simply allowed to help themselves. As many as 25 Caribbean reef sharks turn up on a typical dive and, between them, they devour the bait in under a minute. For some time afterwards, though, they continue to race about in search of more food and frequently come very close to the divers – offering outstanding photographic opportunities.

Bait/feed yes.

Cage no.

Other wildlife sea turtle, eagle ray.

Best time of year sharks present year-round.

Dive depth 10 m/33 ft.

Typical visibility 15 m/50 ft.

Water temperature 21–24 °C/70–75 °F in winter, 28–31 °C/82–88 °F in summer.

Weather and sea notes surface can be choppy, but relatively little current; winter months considered high season for tourism (less hot and humid), but divers prefer summer (water temperature higher, winds drop, flat calm seas more common, and water clarity better); tropical storms do occur in summer (May–Oct), but rarely last longer than a couple of hours; official hurricane season Jun–Oct but, based on recent years, Sep is the most likely time for a hurricane to occur.

Contact details Stella Maris Resort Club (www.stellamarisresort.com).

Travel international flights to the capital Nassau (New Providence Island) from Europe and North America (with connecting flights to Long Island) and direct flights from Fort Lauderdale; there are several resorts on the island.

68–70 SAN SALVADOR: FERNANDEZ BAY, LONG BAY AND FRENCH BAY

Location north and west coasts of San Salvador Island.

Main species *many trips:* scalloped hammerhead, Caribbean reef; *occasional trips:* great hammerhead, tiger, bull.

Viewing opportunities this is not a dedicated shark dive, but it has a growing reputation for reliable encounters with schooling scalloped hammerheads. Divers exploring any of the dozens of dive sites along the fabulous wall extending through Long and Fernandez Bays on the north coast of San Salvador, and French Bay along the west coast, frequently have close encounters with schooling hammerheads. The sharks often approach to within about 6 m/20 ft and sometimes even to within a metre or so. They are normally spotted swimming parallel to the wall.

Hammerheads are not seen on every dive, but approximately 1100 out of 1500 divers visiting the resort every year are rewarded with at least one close encounter. The edge of the wall varies from one site to another, but nowhere is shallower than 12 m/40 ft.

Bait/feed no.

Cage no.

Other wildlife sea turtle, southern stingray, Nassau grouper.

Best time of year scalloped hammerheads encountered mainly Nov–Jun (they are present Jul–Oct, but tend to stay deeper at 35 m/115 ft or more).

Dive depth 12 m/40 ft (minimum).

Typical visibility 30–50 m/100–165 ft.

Water temperature 21–24 °C/70–75 °F in winter, 28–31 °C/82–88 °F in summer.

Weather and sea notes sea can be choppy; often a surge over the reef and a slight current along the drop-off; winter months considered high season for tourism (less hot and humid), but divers prefer summer (water temperature higher, winds drop, flat calm seas more common, and water clarity better); tropical storms do occur in summer (May–Oct), but rarely last longer than a couple of hours; official hurricane season Jun–Oct but, based on recent years, Sep is the most likely time for a hurricane to occur.

Contact details Riding Rock Resort and Marina (www.ridingrock.com).

Travel international flights to the capital Nassau (New Providence Island) from Europe and North America with connecting flights to San Salvador (also some direct flights from Miami); choice of accommodation on San Salvador.

short swim then takes you to the edge of the wall at around 14 m/45 ft. You dive over the wall and descend to a coral-covered ledge at 24–30 m/80–100 ft, where there is the entrance to an L-shaped swim-through. Leaving the exit, at 41 m/135 ft, you keep right and slowly follow a series of sand chutes back up the wall towards the surface. These chutes form the 'hotel' – so-called because there are often nurse sharks resting inside its little 'rooms'.

Bait/feed no.

Cage no.

Other wildlife humpback whale (migrating past Jan–Mar; can be heard singing underwater on some dives), bottlenose dolphin, green turtle, hawksbill turtle, spotted eagle ray.

Best time of year sharks present year-round; best dive conditions (calmer waters and optimum visibility) May–Nov.

Dive depth 14–41 m/45–135 ft.

Typical visibility 24–37 m/80–120 ft (less during sponge spawning season Mar–Apr).

Water temperature 23–26 °C/74–78 °F in winter to 28–29 °C/82–85 °F in summer.

Weather and sea notes no strong currents and site relatively sheltered; no recognized rainy season.

Contact details Flamingo Divers (www.provo.net/flamingo), Art Pickering's Provo Turtle Divers (www.provoturtledivers.com), Dive Provo (www.diveprovo.com), Turks & Caicos Aggressor (www.aggressor.com), Peter Hughes Diving (www.peterhughes.com).

Travel flights from Miami or London to Providenciales; wide choice of accommodation.

TURKS AND CAICOS

71 PROVIDENCIALES: SHARK HOTEL

Location off the west coast of North West Point, Providenciales; 925 km/575 miles south-east of Miami.

Main species *many trips:* Caribbean reef, nurse, blacktip; *occasional trips:* great hammerhead, tiger, lemon.

Viewing opportunities Caribbean reef sharks can be seen almost anywhere on this dive (and on almost any other dive around 'Provo' – as Providenciales is better known) and it is always worth peering out into the blue water for pelagics. An intriguing variety of species turns up from time to time. But Shark Hotel's main attraction involves quite a challenging dive at depth. The boat moors in 12 m/40 ft of water and a

72 WEST CAICOS

Location 13 km/8 miles south-west of Providenciales; 925 km/575 miles south-east of Miami.

Main species *most trips:* Caribbean reef, nurse; *many trips:* blacktip reef; *occasional trips:* great hammerhead, bull.

Viewing opportunities the uninhabited island of West Caicos lies on the north-western corner of Caicos Bank. It is well known for its walls, which begin very close to shore at about 15–21 m/50–70 ft and drop sharply to 2000 m/6500 ft in the ocean depths. There are 5–6.5 km/3–4 miles of reef and coral wall running parallel to the western shoreline and there is a good chance of seeing sharks and rays almost anywhere. However, certain sites have a reputation for regular encounters. Single great hammerheads are most frequently seen at Elephant Ear Canyon. As its name suggests, this site also has the largest-known orange elephant-ear sponge in Turks and Caicos, measuring just over 3 m/10 ft in diameter; lying at a depth of about 27 m/90 ft, it has been damaged by disease in recent years and is developing a 'Swiss cheese' appearance. A variety of pelagic sharks can be seen from Land of the Giants, a deep-water channel leading to Caicos Bank and lying between Providenciales and West Caicos. The visibility here is tide-dependent and can be reduced by huge quantities of nutrients in the water, but the best shark encounters often occur in poorer visibility. There are regular sightings of Caribbean reef sharks at Whiteface (named for the steep white cliffs along the nearby shoreline) and, at the time of writing, one particular individual has made a name for itself by approaching divers very closely. Nurse sharks are also a familiar sight along the sand channels at Whiteface and are often seen resting around the large coral heads at Magic Mushroom (named after a distinctive rock formation on the surface). There are frequent shark sightings at Highway to Heaven, near the north end of West Caicos, where there are coral arches and swim-throughs at a depth of 24–30 m/80–100 ft. Driveway, or Yankee Town as it is sometimes called, is also good and pelagics are frequently seen a little farther out at South West Reef. Tiger, silky and whale sharks have been reported, but too sporadically to be included in the list of regular sightings.

Bait/feed no.

Cage no.

Other wildlife humpback whale (migrating past Dec–Mar; can be heard singing underwater on some dives), Atlantic spotted dolphin, loggerhead turtle, hawksbill turtle, eagle ray, stingray, black coral.

Best time of year sharks present year-round; best dive conditions (calmer waters and optimum visibility) May–Nov.

Dive depth 15–40 m/50–130 ft.

Typical visibility 24–37 m/80–120 ft (less during sponge spawning season Mar–Apr).

Water temperature from 25–26 °C/77–78 °F in winter to 28–29 °C/82–84 °F in summer.

Weather and sea notes some sites experience medium currents; some sites exposed and can be rough in winter; no recognized rainy season.

Contact details Art Pickering's Provo Turtle Divers (www.provoturtledivers.com), Flamingo Divers (www.provo.net/flamingo), Big Blue Unlimited (www.bigblueunlimited.com), Dive Provo (www.diveprovo.com), Turks & Caicos Aggressor (www.aggressor.com).

Travel flights from Miami or London to Providenciales; accessible by live-aboard or day boat from Providenciales; no accommodation on West Caicos, but wide choice on Providenciales.

73 FRENCH CAY

Location 32 km/20 miles south of Providenciales on the edge of Caicos Bank; 925 km/575 miles south-east of Miami.

Main species *most trips:* nurse, lemon, Caribbean reef; *many trips:* great hammerhead; *occasional trips:* tiger, bull, bonnethead.

Viewing opportunities for a short period during the summer months (usually in August) literally hundreds of nurse sharks gather in the shallows off French Cay to mate and lay their eggs. Sometimes they are so close to shore that it is possible for paddlers – as well as snorkellers and divers – to watch their antics. This is one of the few places in the world where so many nurse sharks can be observed so easily and with such consistency. A wide variety of other sharks can also be seen around French Cay, which is perched on the very edge of the Caicos Bank, and almost anything can turn up. Rarely seen species such as bonnethead occur fairly regularly, although their presence cannot be guaranteed. After nurse sharks, Caribbean reef and lemon sharks are the ones most commonly encountered. There seems to be considerable confusion over the identification of some species here and, although blacktips are frequently reported, they are extremely rare at French Cay. Large Caribbean reef sharks are also confused with bull sharks, although this species does turn up from time to time. Some of the best sites for sharks include: Dax Canyon, with a sheer wall that has a good sightings record for large great hammerheads (over 3.5 m/12 ft) during winter; Rock & Roll, which is particularly good for Caribbean reef sharks; Double D, named after two large pinnacles rising from the ocean floor; and G Spot, apparently so-called because it can be hard to find. But sharks of one species or another can be seen almost anywhere around this beautiful uninhabited island.

Bait/feed no.

Cage no.

Other wildlife humpback whale (migrating past Jan–Mar; can be heard singing underwater on many dives), bottlenose dolphin, green turtle, hawksbill turtle, manta ray, eagle ray.

Best time of year sharks present year-round; nurse sharks mating Jun–Aug (peak month Aug); great hammerheads most often seen in winter; best dive

conditions (calmer waters and optimum visibility)
May–Nov.

Dive depth surface to 40 m/130 ft.

Typical visibility 18–24 m/60–80 ft (less during
sponge spawning season Mar–Apr).

Water temperature 23–26 °C/74–78 °F in winter
to 28–29 °C/82–84 °F in summer.

Weather and sea notes currents often strong
(particularly dangerous when pulling off the wall at
Dax Canyon); fairly exposed and water can be rough,
so only visited under ideal conditions; no recognized
rainy season.

Contact details Flamingo Divers
(**www.provo.net/flamingo**), Art Pickering's Provo
Turtle Divers (**www.provoturtledivers.com**),
Dive Provo (**www.diveprovo.com**), Turks & Caicos
Aggressor (**www.aggressor.com**), Big Blue
Unlimited (**www.bigblueunlimited.com**).

Travel accessible by live-aboard or day boat from
Providenciales; flights from Miami or London to
Providenciales (as little as 40 mins by boat to French
Cay); wide choice of accommodation.

Note inside the boundaries of the French Cay Nature
Reserve, which is where the vast majority of nurse
sharks gather, recently implemented legislation
prohibits snorkelling or diving within 15 m/50 ft of
the mating animals, to minimize disturbance.

74 SALT CAY: SHARK POINT

Location 11 km/7 miles south of Grand Turk;
1045 km/650 miles south–east of Miami.

Main species *most trips:* nurse; *many trips:*
Caribbean reef; *occasional trips:* great hammerhead.

Viewing opportunities Salt Cay is the southernmost inhabited island in the Turks and Caicos and
is only 8 sq km/3 sq miles in area. The wall running
along its western side is both dramatic and varied,
ranging from a slope to a sheer precipice. Nurse
sharks can be encountered almost anywhere here,
but most frequently at Point Pleasant, or Shark Point,
where they rest in and around a series of caverns at
a depth of 4.5–9 m/15–30 ft. They can readily be seen
by snorkellers as well as divers, and put on an impressive display when they gather to mate during April
and May (although there are larger numbers mating
at Great Sand Cay, 11 km/7 miles to the south). Nurse
sharks can also be seen with some regularity at the
Rookery (12–40 m/40–130 ft) and around HMS
Endymion (an unsalvaged eighteenth-century British
warship lying at 4.5–11 m/15–35 ft). Caribbean reef
sharks are often seen at the Rookery and Turtle

Garden. Small numbers of great hammerheads are
seen at least once a month.

Bait/feed no.

Cage no.

Other wildlife humpback whale (Salt Cay widely
regarded as the best place in the archipelago to watch
humpback whales on their way to and from Silver
Bank in Jan–Mar; they can be heard singing underwater on many dives); loggerhead turtle, hawksbill
turtle, manta ray (mainly Jul–Aug), eagle ray.

Best time of year sharks present year-round; nurse
sharks mating Apr–May; best dive conditions (calmer
waters and optimum visibility) May–Nov.

Dive depth 4.5–40 m/15–130 ft.

Typical visibility 24–37 m/80–120 ft (less during
sponge spawning season Mar–Apr).

Water temperature from 23–26 °C/74–78 °F in
winter to 28–29 °C/82–84 °F in summer.

Weather and sea notes fairly exposed to wind and
mild current; no recognized rainy season.

Contact details Salt Cay Divers
(**www.saltcaydivers.tc**), Oasis Divers
(**www.oasisdivers.com**).

Travel flights from Miami to Providenciales or from
Fort Lauderdale to Grand Turk; local airlines link
Providenciales and Grand Turk with Salt Cay; ferry
from Grand Turk or accessible by day boat in calm
weather; wide choice of accommodation on Salt Cay.

DOMINICAN REPUBLIC

75–76 CATALINITA ISLAND AND SAONA ISLAND

Location 175 km/110 miles east of Santo Domingo;
south-east corner of the Dominican Republic.

Main species *many trips:* blacktip reef, nurse,
great hammerhead; *occasional trips:* whale.

Viewing opportunities there are two main shark
dives in the Dominican Republic: around the small
island of Catalinita and the much larger island of
Saona, both just off the Caribbean coast. Saona is a
beautiful tropical island, complete with swaying palm
trees, but is the most popular day trip in the
Dominican Republic and can get extremely touristy.
The shark dive is normally conducted as a drift, specifically to see nurse sharks resting under a series of
ledges and overhangs. Catalinita is a tiny island in the
channel at the north-east end of Saona. Divers leave
Bayahibe, on the mainland, in a small skiff (because
the water in the channel is very shallow) and head for

Shark Point. This is a good place to see blacktip reef and great hammerhead sharks. Both Saona and Catalinita fall within a 42,000-ha/103,784-acre protected area known as the National Park of the East.

Bait/feed no.

Cage no.

Other wildlife various cetaceans, eagle ray, stingray, wide range of reef fish with corals and sponges.

Best time of year sharks present year-round.

Dive depth 15–30 m/16–100 ft.

Typical visibility 20–30 m/65–100 ft.

Water temperature 26–30 °C/78–86 °F.

Weather and sea notes sheltered locations with fairly calm conditions typical year-round; strong currents possible; rainy season May–Nov.

Contact details Scubafun Dive Center (www.o-markt.de/scubafun/e_info.htm).

Travel international flights to Santo Domingo (or Puerto Plata); choice of accommodation in and around departure point of Bayahibe.

CUBA

77 PLAYA SANTA LUCIA: SHARK'S POINT

Location north-east coast of Cuba; 640 km/400 miles south-east of Havana and 150 km/95 miles north of the city of Camagüey.

Main species *most trips:* bull.

Viewing opportunities bull sharks have been fed at Shark's Point since 1987 and consequently it has become one of the most reliable places in the world for close encounters with these impressive creatures. This is a challenging dive, taking place next to a ship-wreck in the La Boca Channel near Nuevitas, about a one-hour boat ride from a 20-km/12-mile sandy beach known as Santa Lucia. Participants are accompanied by four staff: a divemaster, feeder, safety diver and cameraman. The dive begins with a swim of about 100 m/330 ft in shallow water and then a slow descent to about 26 m/85 ft, where the wreck lies on the edge of a drop-off. The divers spread out along a white sandy bank, on the starboard side of the wreck, and are instructed to lie close together on their stomachs, shoulder to shoulder. The sharks usually appear as soon as the freshly speared fish bait is produced. Normally five or six turn up, but as many as 14 have been encountered on a few occasions. The sharks circle around the divers and, although they are generally slow-moving and cautious, will sometimes approach closely. The divemaster warns, however, that

they tend to react badly to underwater strobes. They will take food from the feeder's hand – no one wears chainmail protection of any kind during this dive and he literally hands fish to the sharks with his bare hands. Most of the bull sharks encountered are 2–3 m/6½–10 ft long, although a few individuals may reach 4 m/13 ft.

Bait/feed yes.

Cage no.

Other wildlife rich bird life.

Best time of year Jul–Dec (for bull sharks).

Dive depth 26–30 m/85–100ft.

Typical visibility 30–50 m/100–165 ft.

Water temperature 24–29 °C/75–84 °F; as low as 20 °C/68 °F in Dec–Feb.

Weather and sea notes dives conducted only at high tide.

Contact details USA Cuba Travel (www.usacubatravel.com), Shark's Friends Dive Center (tel/fax: 53-7-666414).

Travel international flights to Havana or Camagüey; choice of accommodation within easy access of the dive site (Shark's Friend Scuba-Cuba based at Hotel Cuatro Vientos).

78 JÚCARO: LOS JARDINES DE LA REINA

Location approximately 90 km/55 miles offshore (south of Júcaro) in the southern part of the country.

Main species *most trips:* bull, silky; *many trips:* whale, blacktip reef, grey reef, nurse; *occasional trips:* scalloped hammerhead.

Viewing opportunities Los Jardines de la Reina (the Queen's Gardens) is a spectacular archipelago of 250 virgin coral islands. Lying roughly parallel to the coast, and up to 30 km/18 miles wide, it stretches for over 240 km/150 miles from north-west to south-east. Sometimes called the Last Paradise Keys, and known colloquially as the JDR, it was declared a national park in 1996. There are no human inhabitants inside the park and the wildlife both above and below the surface is spectacularly rich. There are many dive sites in the area and, although sharks can be seen almost anywhere, there are a few dedicated dives. Bull and silky sharks are seen most frequently (some dives begin by jumping into a milling crowd of 20–40 silkies that frequently swarm around the back of the boat) and they are some-times fed by Avalon Diving Centre. Both species are normally unaggressive, but will occasionally take a run at divers. Blacktip reef sharks are commonly encountered at Coral Negro 1, and several other species are seen within the park on a regular basis. Whale sharks are fairly abundant during the last few months of each year, and as many as 16 have been found in a single day.

Bait/feed sometimes.

Cage no.

Other wildlife hawksbill turtle, barracuda, large schools of tarpon; rich bird life on the keys.

Best time of year diving year-round; whale sharks mainly Aug–Dec; floating hotel closed Sep–Oct.

Dive depth 24–30 m/80–100 ft.

Typical visibility 30–50 m/100–165 ft.

Water temperature 24–29 °C/75–84 °F.

Weather and sea notes most dive sites within the restricted area are well protected from wind and sea currents.

Contact details Avalon Diving Centre (www.avalons.net).

Travel international flights to Havana or Ciego de Avila (500 km/310 miles from capital); short drive to small coastal village of Júcaro, then boat to Los Jardines de la Reina; can either explore aboard one of two live-aboards (Explorador and Halcon) or stay on the floating houseboat *La Tortuga* (moored in the centre of the park) and explore in short half-day or full-day expeditions.

Note Avalon Diving Centre is the only operator allowed by law to dive in this restricted area and is working on a shark-tagging project in conjunction with Havana University.

CAYMAN ISLANDS

79 LITTLE CAYMAN: BLOODY BAY MARINE PARK

Location north coast of Little Cayman (120 km/ 75 miles north-east of Grand Cayman).

Main species *most trips:* grey reef, nurse; *occasional trips:* Caribbean reef, blacktip reef.

Viewing opportunities sharks are frequently encountered on dives anywhere along the North Shore, but the real hotspot is Bloody Bay Marine Park. The park lies between Jackson Point to the east and Spot Bay to the west and is home to some of the most famous dive sites in the world. It has two separate sections: Bloody Bay Wall and Jackson's Bay. The former is a perfect vertical drop-off, plunging from within 6 m/20 ft of the surface to depths of more than 2000 m/6600 ft. Large pelagics are frequently encountered along the wall itself, and Great Wall West, with its huge coral heads, is particularly good for juvenile nurse sharks. The wall at Jackson's Bay is not as steep

as Bloody Bay, but forms a spectacularly rugged landscape of crevices and tunnels. This area is best known for its exciting swim-throughs, which lead from an inner sandy belt through the patch reef to the open ocean. The sandy belt is good for nurse sharks, which can be seen resting on the seabed, and there are several good sites here for grey reef sharks. The best is probably the outside wall at Mike's Mount, but they can also be seen at The Meadows, Eagle Ray Roundup and Jackson Bight. Caribbean reef sharks are normally seen farther west, at Cumber's Cave and Bus Stop, where they gather outside a large tunnel descending from 25–35 m/80–115 ft. Blacktip reef sharks are sometimes reported at Blacktip Tunnels, along the North Shore east of the park. No feeding or touching of sharks is permitted within the protected area.

Bait/feed no.

Cage no.

Other wildlife hawksbill turtle, Nassau grouper, manta ray, southern stingray, spotted eagle ray, green moray eel; large breeding population of red-footed boobies and some magnificent frigate birds onshore.

Best time of year sharks present year-round; best conditions May–Oct.

Dive depth 6–30 m/20–100 ft.

Typical visibility 25–30 m/80–100 ft (can reach 60 m/200 ft).

Water temperature 24–29 °C/75–84 °F; warmest Jun–Aug.

Weather and sea notes calmest seas Jun–Aug (but watch weather patterns for tropical storms Jul–Sep); there can be strong currents at some sites.

Contact details Reef Divers at Little Cayman Beach Resort (www.littlecayman.com), Southern Cross Club (www.southerncrossclub.com), Paradise Divers (www.paradisevillas.com), Cayman Aggressor IV (www.aggressor.com), Little Cayman Diver II (www.littlecaymandiver.com).

Travel international flights to Grand Cayman; daily transfers by air taxi to Little Cayman (45 mins); limited choice of hotels and some condominiums for rent; sites also dived by live-aboards based on Grand Cayman (Cayman Aggressor IV) or Cayman Brac (Little Cayman Diver II).

80 GRAND CAYMAN: EAST END WALL, SHARK ALLEY,

Location south-eastern corner of East End.

Main species *most trips:* Caribbean reef; *occasional trips:* lemon, blacktip reef, bull, scalloped hammerhead.

Viewing opportunities dedicated shark dives are relatively new to Grand Cayman, but they already have a very high success rate and a strong educational element. During the pre-dive classroom briefing, divers are even encouraged to identify well-known individual sharks by their distinctive scarring and other markings. There is one dedicated shark dive – Shark Alley – although Jack McKennedy's Canyon, Pat's Wall, The Maze, Scubabowl and other dives along East End Wall frequently encounter sharks. The resident Caribbean reef sharks of Shark Alley are both male and female and typically measure 1.5–2.5 m/ 5–8 ft in length. They are relatively easy to find on this section of the wall (which starts at about 15 m/50 ft and drops vertically into the abyss) and as many as 6–15 are encountered on a typical dive. Ocean Frontiers uses squid and fish bait to attract the sharks, although this is not a large-scale feed and the sharks are not handfed. Divers are encouraged to stay still for the first 20 minutes or so, providing an opportunity to observe the sharks, but then everyone is allowed to swim freely among them for another 20–25 minutes before surfacing. Some individuals can be very curious and will pass within 1–2 m/3–7 ft of divers.

Bait/feed yes.

Cage no.

Other wildlife pristine corals and sponges, southern stingray, eagle ray, moray eel.

Best time of year sharks present year-round.

Dive depth 15–18 m/50–60 ft.

Typical visibility 25–30 m/80–100 ft (occasional short periods of poor visibility with tide movement).

Water temperature 24°C/75°F in winter to 29°C/ 84°F in summer.

Weather and sea notes rainy season starts in May (heaviest rainfall usually Oct), but most showers are short and sharp; East End is the windward side of the island, so there is often a 1 m/39 in swell.

Contact details Ocean Frontiers (www.oceanfrontiers.com).

Travel international flights to Grand Cayman from North America and Europe; limited choice of accommodation in East End.

Note Ocean Frontiers is conducting a research tagging programme of the local sharks, under government licence.

TRINIDAD AND TOBAGO

81–85 DIVER'S DREAM, DIVER'S THIRST, FLYING REEF AND SISTERS ROCKS

Location Diver's Dream, Diver's Thirst and Flying Reef are just off the south coast of Tobago; Sisters Rocks are a few kilometres off the north coast.

Main species *most trips:* blacktip reef, Caribbean reef, nurse; *many trips:* scalloped hammerhead; *occasional trips:* whale, tiger, bull.

Viewing opportunities dedicated shark dives have been conducted around Tobago since 1992 with enormous success and a variety of species. Nurse and reef sharks can be seen almost anywhere, but a few sites have a particularly good reputation. Diver's Dream sometimes conducts shark feeds, with a maximum of 12 divers per trip, and usually attracts blacktip reef, Caribbean reef and nurse sharks within about 10 minutes of arrival. The sharks usually stay for about half an hour for the feed and tend to be very inquisitive, often circling each diver quite closely. Tiger and bull sharks are seen on 5–10 per cent of these dives. Flying Reef is good for nurse sharks (seen about 75 per cent of the time). In recent years, scalloped hammerheads have started to appear around the spectacular underwater rock formations at Sisters Rocks. They were once very rare here, but at least one (and sometimes as many as 30) is now encountered on about 50 per cent of dives.

Bait/feed sometimes.

Cage no.

Other wildlife green, hawksbill and leatherback turtles, manta ray (occasionally), spotted eagle ray, southern stingray, electric ray, spotted, green, golden-tail and chain moray eels, barracuda, pufferfish, brain coral (largest in the world at Speyside).

Best time of year sharks present year-round.

Dive depth 15–40 m/50–130 ft.

Typical visibility 10–30 m/33–100 ft (lower visibility during rainy season Jun–Oct).

Water temperature 26–31 °C/78–88 °F.

Weather and sea notes seas tend to be calm year-round; Tobago sits in middle of the Orinoco Guyana Current and there is a continuous current of 2–3 knots along the Atlantic coast; rainy season Jun–Oct.

Contact details Manta Dive Center (www.mantadive.com), Man Friday Diving (www.manfridaydiving.com).

Travel international flights to Crown Point; choice of accommodation around Crown Point, Speyside and Charlotteville.

Europe (Map 4)

BRITAIN

86 ISLE OF MAN

Location Irish Sea midway between mainland Britain and Ireland.

Main species *most trips*: basking.

Viewing opportunities the Isle of Man is home to one of the largest concentrations of basking sharks anywhere in the world. While they can be seen from shore, and occasionally enter harbours along the west coast of the island, they are best viewed from a boat. The Basking Shark Society operates daily tours throughout the summer (full-day, half-day or evening, depending on demand). It is not unusual to have several animals in view at once and large groups of more than 50 individuals are occasionally seen. The sharks are often found within a few minutes of leaving harbour, although it can take several hours, and while sightings are not guaranteed, statistics from recent years demonstrate that they are encountered on most days. The sharks spend much of their time at the surface and some individuals come right alongside the boat, with their mouths wide open, so this trip offers one of the few shark-watching opportunities for young children and non-swimmers. But, if conditions permit, confident swimmers are allowed to enter the water to snorkel with the harmless animals as they feed no more than a metre or two away – one of the world's greatest wildlife encounters. A group of very lucky paricipants were privileged to see the birth of a basking shark in 1998 (only the second birth ever recorded) and courtship and mating on one memorable trip in 1999. There is a detailed dockside briefing and continuous interpretation provided by the Society Director. Tour participants are encouraged to join in with the collection and recording of research data for the society, but this is not compulsory.

Bait/feed no.

Cage no.

Other wildlife grey seal, harbour porpoise, minke whale, Risso's and bottlenose dolphins; occasional common dolphin, killer whale, long-finned pilot whale; wide variety of seabirds, chough, peregrine falcon.

Best time of year mid-May–Sep (when sharks are present and the weather is at its best).

Dive depth surface.

Typical visibility 7 m/25 ft, but may be 4–14 m/15–45 ft.

Water temperature 16–18 °C/61–65 °F.

Weather and sea notes sea conditions tend to be calm (occasional rough days in summer) and the weather is variable, but typically warm and dry.

Contact details Basking Shark Society (www.isle-of-man.com/interests/shark/index.htm).

Travel tours leave the village of Peel, on the west coast of the Isle of Man. 1-hour flight to Castletown from London (less from several other major UK and Eire airports), then a short taxi ride across the island. Regular ferry service from Liverpool, Heysham, Belfast and Dublin. Choice of small hotels, guest-houses or campsite in Peel, and larger hotels in nearby towns.

87–88 CORNWALL: PORTHKERRIS AND PENZANCE

Location south coast of Cornwall, 400 km/250 miles west of London; Porthkerris is near St Keverne on the Lizard Peninsula, Penzance near Land's End.

Main species *most trips:* basking; see **Note** for blue and shortfin mako.

Viewing opportunities basking sharks congregate in the coastal waters of Cornwall for several months every spring and summer. They turn up when the water warms to about 11 °C/52 °F and the plankton blooms, typically arriving in the Porthkerris area first and then moving west towards Penzance. Local lore has it that they first appear in the waters around the Lizard Peninsula on 10 April, but their precise arrival time seems to depend on the water temperature of the previous winter. Where they come from – and where they go at the end of summer – is still a great mystery. It is not uncommon to see 'baskers' here less than 10 m/33 ft from shore, and many people snorkel with them from the various beaches, but they can occur at least 15 km/9 miles offshore and local dive operators run trips to see them through out the season. All encounters are on snorkel, rather than scuba, and once participants have been dropped in the water with the sharks the boats move some distance away to minimize disturbance. Dozens of sharks are frequently seen together and more than 100 have been reported on exceptional occasions.

Bait/feed no (basking), yes (blue).

Cage no (basking), yes (blue).

Other wildlife bottlenose dolphin, harbour porpoise, grey seal, seabirds.

Best time of year basking sharks present off Cornwall from mid-Apr (when the previous winter was warm) or mid-May (when it was cold) until Aug (less common later in the season); blue and shortfin mako sharks present year-round, but numbers peak Aug–Nov (see **Note**).

Dive depth surface (snorkelling with basking sharks); 5 m/16 ft cage-diving with blues and shortfin makos.

Typical visibility highly variable at 4–12 m/13–39 ft (greatly reduced during plankton blooms).

Water temperature 11–16 °C/52–61 °F during spring–summer.

Weather and sea notes sea must be sufficiently calm to find the sharks.

Contact details Porthkerris Dive Centre (www.porthkerrisdiver.demon.co.uk), Undersea Adventures (www.undersea.co.uk).

Travel approximately 5- or 6-hour drive from central London; also accessible by train or plane (Penzance); wide choice of accommodation in the area; Porthkerris Divers operate from Porthkerris, St Keverne, near Helston; Undersea Adventures operate from Penzance.

Note there has been a blue shark fishery off the Lizard Peninsula for many years. Every summer fishermen setting deep-water pots put two baited shark hooks on each riser line (between the pot and the surface buoy) at a depth of 6–9 m/20–30 ft. This is the feeding zone for blue sharks and, almost without fail, they will catch one on each hook. Porthkerris Divers is conducting trials in the area and, if they prove successful, will introduce cage diving with the blues (and occasional visiting shortfin makos) as a regular attraction. There are so many sharks off the Lizard that, with a little chumming, it should be possible to attract them to divers in a cage relatively easily. This will be the first dive operation of its kind in Britain.

PORTUGAL

89–90 THE ALGARVE: CAPE ST VINCENT AND THE CANYON

Location approximately 16–32 km/10–20 miles offshore on the South West Continental Shelf, in the Algarve.

Main species *most trips*: blue; *many trips*: shortfin mako; *occasional trips*: great hammerhead.

Viewing opportunities the strong currents and temperate waters off the southern coast of Portugal attract large numbers of blue and shortfin mako sharks, which are regular visitors with the seasonal sardine runs. Divers are taken to offshore dive sites on

one-day cage-diving trips from various locations in the Algarve. The two main sites are the 700 m/2300 ft deep Canyon and Cape St Vincent, which is the most south-westerly point in mainland Europe. Travel time varies considerably according to sea conditions, but it normally takes 1–2 hours to the Canyon and 3–4 hours to Cape St Vincent. A mixture of sardines and mackerel (the natural diet of sharks in the area) is used as chum to attract sharks to the boat. Divers are required to swim to the cage, which is suspended from a buoy approximately 5 m/16 ft below the surface and tethered by safety lines about 10 m/33 ft from the boat. The cage is large enough to hold three people. Dive times are typically 40–50 minutes and, depending on the shark activity and sea conditions, everyone can normally experience at least two dives per day. Algarve Shark Watch is conducting research on the local blues and makos and it is often possible to assist with their tagging and photo-ID research programme.

Bait/feed yes.

Cage yes.

Other wildlife bottlenose dolphin, blue marlin, white marlin.

Best time of year Jun–Sep; trips can be arranged Apr–Nov but, outside the main season, the sea is much colder and more regular Atlantic storms can make cage diving difficult or impossible.

Dive depth 5 m/16 ft.

Typical visibility 25–50 m/80–165 ft (highly variable, depending on wind and current direction and plankton blooms).

Water temperature 17–21 °C/63–70 °F.

Weather and sea notes generally flat calm in the morning, with winds and swell strengthening throughout the day; currents can be strong.

Contact details Algarve Shark Watch (www.algarvesharkwatch.com).

Travel expeditions depart from selected marinas in the Algarve. Closest international airport is Faro, with choice of transport from there to the Algarve. Wide choice of accommodation in the region (advanced booking advisable during high season, Jul–Aug). Multi-day shark cage-diving safaris are also available.

91 THE AZORES: SANTA MARIA

Location 44 km/27 miles north-east of Santa Maria; 1600 km/1000 miles west of Lisbon.

Main species *occasional trips:* scalloped hammerhead, great hammerhead, blue, Galápagos, shortfin mako.

Viewing opportunities shark watching in the

Azores is rather more hit-and-miss than in many other parts of the world, but it does offer the opportunity to see a number of different pelagic species. It takes about an hour to get to the two main dive sites, called Formigas Rocks and Dollabarat, which lie about 5 km/ 3 miles apart on the same seamount in the middle of the North Atlantic. Formigas Rocks actually breaks the surface and consists of little more than a few rocks and a small lighthouse, while Dollabarat is hidden 5–7 m/16–23 ft beneath the surface. The seamount itself drops to a depth of several hundred metres. It is not unusual for an inquisitive hammerhead shark to appear while the skipper is anchoring but, although it may swim around the 6 m/20 ft boat several times, it tends to disappear as soon as divers enter the water. Once everyone is underwater, it is simply a matter of luck as to which species – if any – turn up. Recent experience, however, suggests that at least one shark is encountered on every dive.

Bait/feed no.

Cage no.

Other wildlife wide variety of cetaceans, manta and eagle rays, stingray, schools of greater amberjacks, yellow jacks and barracuda, wahoo, grouper.

Best time of year Jun–Sep (best sea conditions).

Dive depth 20–40 m/65–130 ft.

Typical visibility 30–50 m/100–165 ft.

Water temperature 22–26 °C/72–78 °F in mid-summer (about 10 °C/50 °F colder in winter).

Weather and sea notes moderate currents are common; site accessible only in good weather conditions (best Jul–Aug).

Contact details Wahoo Diving (www.wahoo-diving.de).

Travel national and international flights to Lisbon; flights from Lisbon to the Azores; trips depart from Baia Sao Lourenco on Santa Maria (southernmost island in the archipelago); wide choice of accommodation.

East and Southern Africa (Map 5)

TANZANIA

92 PEMBA ISLAND: MTANGANI REEF

Location 50 km/31 miles east of Tanga (Tanzanian mainland), 50 km/31 miles north of Zanzibar.

Main species *most trips:* scalloped hammerhead; many trips: whale, whitetip reef; *occasional trips:* tiger.

Viewing opportunities relatively untouched by tourism, Pemba Island is rapidly gaining a reputation as one of East Africa's premier dive destinations. Most established and readily accessible dive sites are on the western (leeward) side of the island and perhaps the best known is Manta Point, renowned for the giant manta rays that gather in quite large numbers. But the best shark dive takes place on the much more exposed ocean side of the island, where pristine shallow reefs give way to sheer drop-offs descending to 600 m/1970 ft or more. Divers visiting Mtangani Reef, on the south-eastern coast of Pemba, are virtually guaranteed sightings of scalloped hammerheads. Small numbers are seen on a typical dive, but on a good day there can be several dozen. Sometimes known as Hammerhead Stretch, this is a blue-water dive and is accessible only by live-aboard. It can be a challenging dive, often with no reef reference, and is usually conducted as a drift at 30–40 m/100–130 ft where the sharks are normally encountered. Whale sharks are often seen around Pemba, and tiger sharks are occasionally seen cruising along the reef walls (Great Southern is probably the best site for tigers).

Bait/feed no.

Cage no.

Other wildlife humpback whale (Sep), long-snouted spinner and bottlenose dolphins (hundreds off Pemba west coast every morning – they are habituated and readily swim with people); hawksbill turtle, manta ray (year-round, but best Dec–Feb), eagle ray, barracuda, kingfish, wahoo, tuna, Napoleon wrasse.

Best time of year sharks present year-round, but best diving Oct–Mar.

Dive depth 30–40 m/100–130 ft.

Typical visibility 20–60 m/65–200 ft; best Oct–Mar and on incoming tide.

Water temperature 24–26 °C/75–78 °F in winter, 27–28 °C/81–82 °F in summer.

Weather and sea notes medium to strong current normal (strongest Apr–Sep); down-current possible at site; exposed open-ocean conditions, with ever-present wind and chop likely; sometimes unsafe in bad weather; hot and dry Dec–Mar, heavy rainfall May–Jul, cool and dry Apr and Aug–Oct, short rains Nov (morning showers).

Contact details African Dive Safaris (www.scubadiving.co.za/pemba.htm), Aquatours (www.aquatours.com/kenya/kisiwani.htm).

Travel international flights to Nairobi; connecting flights to Mombasa; east coast accessible only via live-aboard from Mombasa (Oct–Apr only).

MOZAMBIQUE

93 BAZARUTO ARCHIPELAGO: CABO SAN SEBASTIAN

Location southern extremity of the Bazaruto Archipelago (approximately 10 km/6 miles offshore north-east of Vilanculos); 760 km/470 miles north of Maputo.

Main species *most trips:* bull, blacktip reef; *many trips:* silvertip, grey reef, tiger, whale.

Viewing opportunities the Bazaruto Archipelago consists of four islands (Bazaruto, Benguerra, Margaruque and Santa Carolina or Paradise Island) as well as some rocky outcrops. Declared a national park in 1971, it is one of the most popular tourist destinations in Mozambique and is gradually gaining a reputation among divers for its spectacular coral growth and sharks. This particular dive site, 30 m/100 ft off Cabo St Sebastian Lighthouse, is really attached to the mainland, but lies off the southern tip of Margaruque and is normally considered part of the archipelago. In recent years there have been some exceptional shark encounters here, with bull and blacktip reef turning up on a regular basis. There is also a good chance of seeing a whale shark in the area. The dive is usually conducted as a drift. Other good shark sites in Bazaruto include Lighthouse Point (blacktip reef), Rainbow Runner Reef (bull), and Five-Mile Reef (bull) from Bazaruto Island itself; and Two-Mile Reef and Shark Reef (bull, grey reef, tiger and whale) from Benguera.

Bait/feed no.

Cage no.

Other wildlife bottlenose dolphin, dugong, green and hawksbill turtles, manta, bat and brown ribbon-tailed rays (Nov–Apr), potato cod, red-fanged trigger;

freshwater crocodiles, suni antelope and rich birdlife on shore.

Best time of year sharks present year-round, but by far greatest number and diversity in summer (Nov–Apr).

Dive depth surface to 34 m/112 ft.

Typical visibility 20–30 m/65–100 ft.

Water temperature 21 °C/70 °F in winter to 28 °C/82 °F in summer.

Weather and sea notes strong currents (mainly along east coast); moderate sea breeze most days; rainy season Nov–Feb (highest rainfall Jan–Feb), most settled dry weather Apr–Jun.

Contact details Dive the Big 5 (www.divethebig5.co.za), Dive Africa Discovery (www.divediscovery.com/Africa/YachtSarah.html), Scottlee Resorts (www.travelzim.com/margaruque).

Travel international flights to Johannesburg; charter flights to Vilanculos to meet live-aboards; alternatively fly or take a dhow from Vilanculos to Margaruque for day boats; accommodation on Margaruque currently under development (expected to open for maximum of 44 guests at end of 2002).

94 PONTA D'OURO: PINNACLES

Location 4 km/2½ miles offshore; 650 km/400 miles east of Johannesburg, at the southern extreme of Mozambique, close to the South African border.

Main species *most trips:* scalloped hammerhead, bull; *many trips:* blacktip, whale; *occasional trips:* great hammerhead, smooth hammerhead (*Sphyrna zygaena*), great white, tiger, silvertip, oceanic whitetip, blacktip reef, grey reef, whitetip reef, silky, sand tiger, leopard, zebra.

Viewing opportunities Ponta d'Ouro is often referred to as a shark freeway, because extraordinary numbers of many different species pass through here each summer. The name literally means 'Point of Gold' and refers to the beautiful golden appearance of the sandstone cliffs on the point, as the sun rises first thing in the morning. There are several excellent shark sites, all within 4 km/2½ miles of shore, and it takes approximately 15–25 minutes to reach them in a rigid-hulled inflatable. Northern Pinnacle, which consists of a mound on the seabed rising to within 35 m/115 ft of the surface, is probably the best. The top of Granite Ridge, at 23 m/75 ft, is another very active part of the reef; the seaward side drops down a virtually sheer wall to 50 m/165 ft. The current here flows north–south and the dives are usually conducted as deep drifts. Most of the pelagic species are encountered in mid-water, around 15–25 m/50–80 ft, and almost anything can turn up. Bull sharks (known locally as Zambezis) are probably seen most often, but scalloped hammerheads are very common, too. Early morning and late afternoon tend to be best for shark sightings and activity. While there is no shark feeding, the deep-water site off the reef is very popular for spear-fishing and, in recent years, some sharks seem to have learnt to associate the sound of a speargun with a free meal; sometimes they can be enticed close to divers by twanging rubber or making similar sounds under-water. Whale sharks are often seen on trips out to the reef and back, particularly in high summer (Nov–Mar). They are usually found at the surface, in water less than 20 m/65 ft deep and within 1.5 km/1 mile of shore; there is a 60 per cent chance of snorkelling with them during the peak season and this increases considerably if the local microlight is deployed for the search.

Bait/feed no.

Cage no.

Other wildlife black and white rhino, elephant, hippopotamus, Nile crocodile and rich birdlife in Kosi Bay and nearby reserves; humpback whale (Jun–Sep), long-snouted spinner, common and bottlenose dolphins frequently seen on boat ride to reef and back; hawksbill, green and loggerhead turtles, occasional olive ridley and leatherback turtles, honeycomb and geometric morays, barracuda, bigeye trevally, potato cod, eagle and duckbill rays, blue-spotted ribbontail ray, manta ray (mainly Nov–Apr).

Best time of year sharks present year-round, but by far the greatest number and diversity in summer (Oct–Apr); whale sharks best Nov–Mar; Jun–Aug mainly scalloped hammerhead, with occasional bull, tiger, sand tiger and whale.

Dive depth 12–35 m/40–115 ft.

Typical visibility 20–30 m/65–100 ft (Nov–Apr); 10–15 m/33–50 ft (May–Oct).

Water temperature 26–29 °C/78–84 °F Nov–Apr, 24–25 °C/75–77 °F May and Aug–Oct, 21–22 °C/70–72 °F Jun–Jul; site lies in the main warm Mozambique Current.

Weather and sea notes strong current (2–4 knots) normal; greener water in winter (blue in summer); seas normally calm, but can get rough with cold fronts coming up the coast from the Cape; moderate sea breeze most days from mid-morning onwards (windier Aug–Oct, especially late afternoon).

Contact details Andy Cobb Eco Diving (www.adventurescuba.co.za), Dive The Big 5 (www.divethebig5.co.za), Whale Africa Promotions (www.whaleafrica.co.za), The Dive Travel Centre (www.scubadiving.co.za/ponta/htm).

Travel international flights to Johannesburg, then hire car to border (KwaNganase near Kosi Bay) where operators collect (12 km/7 1/2 miles to Ponta d'Ouro by four-wheel drive); choice of accommodation in Ponta d'Ouro.

SOUTH AFRICA

95 KWAZULU-NATAL: SODWANA BAY

Location 3–15 km/2–9 miles from shore (depending on site), approximately 370 km/230 miles north of Durban and just south of the Mozambique border.

Main species *most trips:* sand tiger; *many trips:* whale, whitetip reef, blacktip.

Viewing opportunities forming part of the St Lucia Marine Reserve, Sodwana Bay is warmed by the Mozambique Current and boasts some of the most southerly tropical reefs in the world. About 80 per cent of South Africa's 1200 species of fish occur here and, not surprisingly, it is one of the country's premier dive sites. The reefs run parallel to the coastline and are unromantically named according to their distances from the launch site at Jesser Point: Quarter-Mile, Two-Mile, Five-Mile, Seven-Mile and Nine-Mile. The launches themselves can be pretty exciting, as the rigid-hulled inflatables run the gauntlet of high breakers close to shore, but most of the dive sites are in relatively calm waters. The main attraction here is the congregation of sand tiger sharks (known locally as raggies) at Quarter-Mile Reef. The site tends to be more popular with females than males and it seems that gestating sharks visit specifically to rest. In the past, as many as 40 have been seen on a single dive, but there are considerably fewer these days. There are fears that their numbers have declined because of diver disturbance, so strict regulations have been introduced to ensure that everyone diving with the raggies is accompanied by a shark guide accredited by the KwaZulu-Natal Nature Conservation Service. Whale sharks are also frequently encountered at Quarter-Mile Reef (and nearby reefs) during the summer. Two-Mile Reef is one of the most popular diving reefs in the area and offers frequent sightings of whitetip reef and blacktip sharks.

Bait/feed no.

Cage no.

Other wildlife humpback whale, bottlenose dolphin, leatherback and loggerhead turtles (nest Dec–Feb), moray eel, potato bass, sea pike, marbled ray.

Best time of year sand tiger present Dec–Mar; whale sharks present Sep–Apr (best Oct–Feb); whitetip reef and blacktip present year-round.

Dive depth 5–30 m/16–100 ft (10 m/33 ft at Quarter-Mile Reef).

Typical visibility 10–40 m/33–130 ft; best in summer.

Water temperature 21–28 °C/70–82 °F; warmest in summer.

Weather and sea notes at Quarter-Mile Reef proximity to shore means a strong surge is common; strong currents possible.

Contact details Amatikulu Tours (www.amatikulu.com), Dive the Big 5 (www.divethebig5.co.za), Coral Divers (www.coraldivers.co.za), Sodwana Bay Lodge Scuba Centre (www.sodwanadiving.co.za).

Travel national and international flights to Durban; local flights to nearby Richard's Bay or 4-hour drive from Durban; choice of accommodation.

Note some operators used to organize shark feeds in Sodwana Bay, but these have now been banned.

96 KWAZULU-NATAL: ALIWAL SHOAL

Location 5 km/3 miles offshore, between Scottburgh and Umkomaas; 50 km/31 miles south of Durban.

Main species *most trips:* sand tiger; *many trips:* bull, scalloped hammerhead; *occasional trips:* great white, tiger, blacktip reef, bronze whaler, shortfin mako, spinner (*Carcharhinus brevipinna*).

Viewing opportunities Aliwal Shoal is an extensive, submerged reef with caves, gullies, ridges, overhangs, towering pinnacles, huge amphitheatres, flat reef plains and surge pools. The topography is more rugged than Protea Banks (100 km/62 miles to the south) and, since the dive sites are shallower and tend to be frequented by fewer potentially dangerous sharks, it is ideal for less experienced divers. Jutting into the Agulhas Current as it runs parallel to the KwaZulu-Natal coast, Aliwal offers a variety of temperate, tropical and migratory shark species. But it is best known for its abundant sand tiger sharks, which are seen on virtually every dive for about five months (Jul–Nov) every year. They congregate all over the reef in such impressive numbers that as many as 60 have been encountered at one time. Most of the shark dives are within a 300 m/1000 ft radius, but two of the best for sand tigers are Raggie Cave and Cathedral. Raggie Cave lies on the eastern side of the Shoal at a depth of about 15–18 m/50–60 ft. Named after the sharks themselves (known locally as raggies) it consists of a large central canyon surrounded by several small caves and chambers, each of which frequently contains several sand tigers. Cathedral is a deeper (27 m/90 ft) but more outstanding dive. The site lies on the outer edge of the reef and consists of a 4 m/13 ft rock arch forming the spectacular entrance to a compact, church-like amphitheatre. The sharks are best observed from outside, because swimming into the amphitheatre risks frightening the sharks (and may cause them to leave the area). After mating, the sexually mature female raggies leave Aliwal Shoal in late November and migrate approximately 300 km/186 miles north to northern Maputaland and southern Mozambique, where they remain while gestating. Most of the dives at Aliwal Shoal are conducted as drifts and, although the water is often chilly, there are so many Indian Ocean fish here that it feels surprisingly tropical.

Bait/feed no.

Cage no.

Other wildlife humpback whale, bottlenose dolphin, hawksbill, green and loggerhead turtles, brown ribbontail ray, marbled electric ray, blue-spotted stingray, honeycomb moray, kingfish, potato bass, moorish idol.

Best time of year sharks present year-round, but sand tiger mainly Jul–Nov (best Aug–Sep).

Dive depth 6–27 m/20–90 ft and deeper.

Typical visibility 6–30 m/20–100 ft (average 15 m/ 50 ft); best visibility May–Sep; visibility can be affected by effluent from the SAICCOR cellulose plant in nearby Umkomaas (although the pipeline has now been extended farther out to sea and this has had a marked effect on the clarity of the water).

Water temperature 18–24 °C/65–75 °F.

Weather and sea notes strong currents typical; occasional rough seas with cold fronts coming up from the Cape.

Contact details Shark Divers South Africa (www.sharkdivers-sa.com), Andy Cobb Eco Diving (www.adventurescuba.co.za), Amatikulu Tours (www.amatikulu.com), Dive the Big 5 (www.divethebig5.co.za), Whale Africa Promotions (www.whaleafrica.co.za), The Whaler Dive Centre (whaler@xnet.co.za), Aliwal Dive Charters (www.aliwalshoal.co.za), Sea Fever Dive Centre (www.seafever.co.za).

Travel national and international flights to Durban; 40-min drive south to Umkomaas; wide choice of accommodation locally.

Note there has been serious concern in recent years that the Aliwal Shoal sand tigers are being disturbed by too many divers. Research coordinated by the Natal Sharks Board (www.shark.co.za) is currently under way to determine the severity of any such impact on the sharks, to ensure the development of a sustainable ecotourism industry at Aliwal Shoal. The results will be used to assist in developing a scientifically-based code of conduct for divers and dive operators. The Aliwal Shoal will soon be declared a Marine Protected Area, which will allow more stringent control over any divers and dive practices causing environmental harm.

97 KWAZULU-NATAL: PROTEA BANKS

Location 7.5 km/4.7 miles off the coast of Shelley Beach, near Margate, 160 km/100 miles south of Durban.

Main species *most trips:* bull, scalloped hammer-head, sand tiger; *many trips:* great hammerhead, bronze whaler, blacktip; *occasional trips:* great white, tiger, shortfin mako, smooth hammerhead (*Sphyrna zygaena*), thresher, dusky, African angel, sandbar, guitar.

Viewing opportunities imagine drifting in a strong current, with more potentially dangerous sharks than fellow divers, at depths of 30 m/100 ft or more – and you begin to understand the appeal of Protea Banks. On a good day, the waters are thick with sharks and the action is so frenetic it is impossible to know where to look next. This is not for the faint-hearted or inexperienced, but it is undoubtedly one of the most exhilarating shark dives in the world. It is exceptional for the sheer variety of its sharks and it is not unknown to encounter as many as seven species in a single dive. Lying near the edge of the continental shelf, Protea Banks is an impressive reef system some 4.5 km/2¾ miles long, lying at depths of 28–45 m/90–150 ft and surrounded by deep water. It is packed with pinnacles, caves, ridges and amphitheatres and, given the less-than-tropical latitude, its fossilized sand-dune substrate is covered with an impressive array of sponges, soft corals and gorgonias. Ironically, though, most divers are so overwhelmed by the sharks that they return to the surface with little or no memory of the local fish and invertebrates.

The species you are most likely to encounter depends upon the time of year. The annual sardine run, in June and July, is when unimaginable numbers of sardines gather over the Banks. They are accompanied by bronze whaler sharks (known locally as coppers), which glide in and out of the huge shoals and sometimes leap high into the air. From a distance, when they are pirouetting, they look more like dolphins than sharks. They are often accompanied by dusky sharks, which are also sardine hunters (one individual was found with 950 sardines in its stomach). In late winter, from June onwards, the sand tigers (known locally as raggies) begin to arrive in their hundreds from colder waters farther south. They crowd into the caves and overhangs for refuge – a single cave may contain as many as 30 sand tigers.

They begin to move away from the end of September, heading towards Cape Vidal for their annual mating jamboree. October is when all the pre-mating activity starts and the females become heavily scarred after their painful encounters with courting males. The fertilized females leave Cape Vidal first, moving north to pup off the coast of Mozambique, and a few weeks later the mature males begin to leave, probably returning south. In the Eastern Cape, these sharks have a reputation for being quite pushy and have even been known to harass spearfishermen, but at Protea Banks they seem relatively docile. By the time all the sand tigers have left, around late October or November, schools of game fish begin to appear over the Banks and they are followed by bull sharks (known locally as Zambezis). By March, the water is packed with huge bulls, which normally stay until June. There are so many of them that, at the end of a dive, everyone is advised to tuck their legs and fins under the boat before scrambling back on board; they are unlikely to attack, but it is best not to tempt fate. The bulls can certainly be a little unnerving and have a habit of cruising towards groups of divers to have a good look, then disappearing beyond the edge of visibility. Interestingly, they have probably been monitoring the divers for some time before they approach so closely. There is an excellent chance of encountering scalloped hammerheads during the summer, from November until May, although they maintain a larger personal space than the bulls and rarely come closer than about 10 m/33 ft. Tiger sharks, which are occasionally seen from January to May, behave in a similar way and tend to approach just close enough to reveal their tiger-striped bodies.

Even the launch is impressive at Protea. The rigid-hulled inflatables head straight out into the surf, reaching near-vertical angles as they dodge through the wave sets. The vessels are fitted with foot straps and ski ropes to ensure that no divers are washed overboard during the launch or the high-speed beaching at the end of the dive. The north–south current here is strong and it is possible to cover several kilometres of the site in a single drift dive. The two main areas are around Northern and Southern Pinnacles. Northern Pinnacle is spectacular with its caves, ledges, overhangs and pristine reef formations. As many as 150 sand tiger sharks can be found here in an area just 100 m/330 ft square. It is also a good place for encountering bull sharks and scalloped hammerheads. Southern Pinnacle is easier to dive, because the current is not as strong, but it is not quite as beautiful. The highlight here is the bull sharks, but it is also good for blacktip reef, scalloped hammerhead and even tiger sharks, and the occasional great white puts in an appearance, too. In fact, the real pleasure of diving anywhere at Protea Banks is that anything can turn up – and often does. Most dives are conducted early in the morning, before the wind picks up too much. It is possible to reach Protea Banks later in the day but, if it is windy, the boat ride can be (as one diver described it recently) like whitewater rafting on the Zambezi River. The journey to the dive sites takes about 20–25 minutes, depending on sea conditions.

Bait/feed no.

Cage no.

Other wildlife humpback whale (Jun–Sep), bottlenose dolphin (during sardine run), loggerhead turtle, manta ray, round ribbontail and eagle ray, potato bass, golden soapfish.

Best time of year sharks present year-round, but many species seasonal (bronze whaler Jun–Jul; sand tiger Jun–Oct; bull and scalloped hammerhead Nov–May; tiger Jan–May).

Dive depth 25–32 m/80–105 ft (Southern Pinnacles), 30–37 m/100–120 ft (Northern Pinnacles).

Typical visibility 6–30 m/20–100 ft (averages 18 m/60 ft).

Water temperature 19–25 °C/66–77 °F; warmest Apr–Jun, coldest Jul–Sep.

Weather and sea notes strong current (3–5 knots) typical in summer (much slower in winter); sea breeze most days from mid-morning onwards (windier Aug–Oct, especially late afternoon).

Contact details Shark Divers South Africa (www.sharkdivers-sa.com/diving.htm), Andy Cobb Eco Diving (www.adventurescuba.co.za), African Dive Adventures (www.cybercraft.co.za/dive), Amatikulu Tours (www.amatikulu.com), Dive The Big 5 (www.divethebig5.com), Whale Africa Promotions (www.whaleafrica.co.za), Ocean Extreme Dive Charters (www.scubanet.co.za).

Travel international flights to Durban or Johannesburg; national flights to Margate (or 1½-hour drive from Durban); surf launch from Shelley Beach; wide choice of accommodation in the area.

Note according to shark expert Andy Cobb, it has been estimated that the sharks on Protea Banks attract tourism money of R50,000 every year. Yet there is still nothing to stop commercial fishermen from killing and dumping as many as they like – and they are sold for export at just R6 per kg.

98 WESTERN CAPE: PLETTENBERG BAY

Location approximately halfway between Cape Agulhas and Port Elizabeth, on the Garden Route.

Main species *most trips:* sand tiger; *occasional trips:* great hammerhead, shortfin mako.

Viewing opportunities this holiday and residential resort (popularly known as Plett) lends its name to one of the most beautiful bays in South Africa. It is a popular diving area and sharks of several different species can be seen at various locations. Shortfin makos are occasionally encountered at Playground, north-east of Plett, and several species of small ground sharks (order Carcharhiniformes) are often spotted at Jacob's Poort, immediately to the south. Sand tiger sharks are occasionally seen around the pinnacles at Shallow Blinders and Dolphin Column, just off the coast, and more frequently among the spectacular rock formations at Groot Bank, to the north-east. The best site for sand tigers is undoubtedly Whale Rock, a beautiful pinnacle covered in sea fans, soft corals and colourful sponges lying just under 1 km/½ mile off the point of the Robberg Peninsula; the Rock is home to considerable numbers of these sharks during the winter although, unfortunately, conditions are rarely good enough to dive. The sand tigers migrate to Plettenberg Bay every year to breed, having ridden the Agulhas Current from northern KwaZulu/Natal and southern Mozambique.

Bait/feed no.

Cage no.

Other wildlife southern right whale (winter but best Sep–Nov), humpback whale (best Jun–Nov), Bryde's whale, bottlenose, common and Indo-Pacific hump-backed dolphins.

Best time of year sand tiger present mainly Jul–Nov.

Dive depth 10–30 m/33–100 ft depending on site (Whale Rock 20–30 m/65–100 ft).

Typical visibility 5–10 m/16–33 ft; best in winter.

Water temperature 14–23 °C/57–74 °F.

Weather and sea notes strong currents and big swell make Whale Rock impossible to dive much of the time; onshore south-easterlies tend to make the sea choppy in summer.

Contact details Beyond the Beach (btb@global.co.za), Dive the Big 5 (www.divethebig5.co.za).

Travel national and international flights to Port Elizabeth or Cape Town; 2-hour (Port Elizabeth) or 5-hour (Cape Town) drive; or fly to George, then 1-hour drive to Plett; wide choice of accommodation in Plett.

99 WESTERN CAPE: MOSSEL BAY

Location 380 km/235 miles east of Cape Town.

Main species *most trips:* great white; *occasional trips:* great hammerhead.

Viewing opportunities Mossel Bay is a seaside town at the beginning of the famous Garden Route and many of its visitors would probably be surprised to know that great white sharks frequently swim very close to their favourite bathing beaches. But the sharks here are more interested in Cape fur seals than in people, and most of them gather around Seal Island, which is 8 km/5 miles to the north-west and some 1.6 km/1 mile offshore. This is the home of about 4000 seals, which are an important prey item for great whites, particularly in winter. The island is about a 30-minute boat ride from the harbour and, after anchoring nearby, the divemaster chums the water and sets a 25 m/80 ft line with hard fish bait attached to a float. The sharks sometimes appear within a few minutes, but it may be several hours before they arrive. Once they are around the boat, a two-person circular steel cage is lowered into the water and securely attached to the dive platform. The top of the cage remains above water and is always open, so that divers can get in and out whenever they like. You stand on the bottom of the cage and peer underwater from the surface. The success rate averages 84 per cent (in a typical year there are just eight trips with no sharks at all) and it is normal to see several sharks during a single trip. The record is 14 different creatures and, on another memorable occasion, there were no fewer than seven around the cage at once. The great whites here occasionally breach, although not as frequently as in False Bay. Small great hammerheads are known to occur in good numbers in the bay, but they are rarely seen on cage-diving trips.

Bait/feed yes.

Cage yes.

Other wildlife southern right whale (winter but best Sep–Nov), Indo-Pacific hump-backed and bottlenose dolphins, Cape fur seal, African penguin, black oyster-catcher.

Best time of year great whites present year-round, but best May–Sep; no launches during the peak holiday period in Dec, by agreement with the local municipality.

Dive depth cage floats at the surface.

Typical visibility 4–10 m/13–33 ft.

Water temperature 16–18 °C/61–65 °F May–Sep; 10–25 °C/50–77 °F Oct–Apr (temperature drops dramatically after a strong south-easter).

Weather and sea notes no strong currents; one of the most sheltered bays in South Africa (calmest seas Dec–May, usually some chop Sep–Nov).

Contact details Shark Africa (www.sharkafrica.co.za).

Travel national and international flights to Cape Town or Port Elizabeth; drive by the N2 to Mossel Bay; wide choice of accommodation in the area.

Location 180 km/110 miles east of Cape Town, 8 km/5 miles offshore.

Main species *most trips*: great white.

Viewing opportunities one of the best places in the world to encounter great white sharks is a narrow channel between Dyer Island and Geyser Rock, near where the Indian Ocean meets the Atlantic Ocean off the southern tip of Africa. Dubbed Shark Alley, or Dyer Straits, the channel is roughly 150 m/500 ft wide and 600 m/1970 ft long. Considerable numbers of great whites patrol the channel while hunting Cape fur seals (there are estimated to be 30–60,000 fur seals on Geyser Rock – the exact number depends on the season). This is where, in 1991, cage diving first started in South Africa. During a half-day or full-day trip the boat anchors in the channel (or nearby, depending on sea conditions) and the crew chums the water with finely minced sardines, tuna or a mixture of shark liver and fish oil. When the sharks appear, the divers can enter a small galvanized metal cage (two people at a time) to view them underwater. The cage is circular, about 3 m/10 ft tall and 1.5 m/5 ft wide, and hangs at the surface with the help of flotation tanks. It is attached to the boat by ropes. Divers take turns in the cage and, depending on the shark activity, typically have one, two or three dives per trip. Some operators will use two cages at the same time, if specially requested, maximizing the number of divers in the water and offering great photo opportunities. Non-divers can enjoy the tours as well, because the 3–5-m/10–16-ft sharks spend a lot of time at the surface, sometimes even leaping clear of the water, and frequently swim alongside the boat. Although the cage is floating, and several operators prefer divers to snorkel rather than scuba, local regulations require everyone to have a minimum scuba-diving qualification. As many as 18 different sharks have been observed in a single day, many coming very close and even test-biting the cages, but the turnout and behaviour are highly variable. In recent years, particularly during the summer months (mid-Sep to mid-Feb), most operators have been working much closer to shore – the channel does not appear to be the prime shark area during this period any more.

Bait/feed yes.

Cage yes.

Other wildlife 8000 jackass penguins, plus several cormorant species, African black oystercatcher and other birds on Dyer Island; tens of thousands of Cape fur seals on Geyser Rock; bottlenose and Indo-Pacific hump-backed dolphins occur in the area; southern right whales may be encountered on the way to the shark site and are common in the bay during Jun–early Dec (de Kelders is one of the best places in the world for shore-based whale watching).

Best time of year great whites present year-round, but some months considerably better than others; the best period is May–Sep, when there is a 90–95 per cent sightings record from the boats and 70–80 per cent from the cages; Oct–Jan has a 70–90 per cent sightings record from the boats, and a highly variable record from the cages (largely depending on water visibility); the worst sightings records are Feb–Mar (20–50 per cent from the boats and 0–30 per cent from the cages; these records do, however, shift slightly from year to year; the best weather is Apr–Jun.

Dive depth cage floats at the surface (channel depth 2–7 m/7–25 ft; site close to shore depth 6–12 m/20–40 ft).

Typical visibility best months Jun–Aug (up to 20 m/65 ft); then May and Sep (7–9 m/23–30 ft); then Oct–Apr (1–4 m/3–13 ft).

Water temperature 9–16 °C/48–61 °F (Nov–Apr), 14–21 °C/57–70 °F (May–Oct).

Weather and sea notes during winter (May–Sep) there is often a heavy swell and as many as two in three trips are cancelled (even getting out of the harbour can be difficult); at any time of year, there can be a swell in the channel, so take seasickness pills as it can be a little uncomfortable at anchor; the weather can change quickly.

Contact details Collaborative White Shark Research Programme (www.sharkresearch.org), The White Shark Trust (www.whitesharktrust.org), Southcoast Seafaris trading as White Shark Adventures (www.whitesharkdiving.com), Marine Dynamics (www.dive.co.za), White Shark Ecoventures (www.sharkdive.co.za), Shark Lady Adventures/ White Shark Expeditions (www.sharklady.co.za), White Shark Projects (www.whitesharkproject.co.za), Shark Diving Unlimited (www.sharkdivingunlimited.com), White Shark Diving Company (www.sharkcagediving.co.za), Great White Shark Tours (www.hermanusinfo.co.za/greatwhite), White Shark Discovery (www.whitesharkdiscovery.com).

Travel easy access (2–3-hour drive) from Cape Town. Tours leave Kleinbaai harbour (2 km/1¼ miles from the village of Gansbaai, where most operators are based). There are several small guesthouses and hostels in Gansbaai but many more in Hermanus, about 30 mins drive away. Half-day or full-day tours and multi-day packages. Some companies offer a pick-up service in Cape Town.

Notes following allegations about incompetent operators, the South African government introduced a code of conduct in 1998. Commercial cage-diving companies must have a permit, issued by Marine and Coastal Management (formerly Department of Sea Fisheries), and there are various permit conditions that legislate how cage diving, and its allied activities, should be conducted. Mammalian products cannot be used as bait or chum, and the sharks must not actually be fed at the cage-dive sites. To operate within 500 m/1650 ft of Dyer Island requires another permit issued by Cape Nature Conservation. There is still concern about some operators running unsafe tours, so do not get on an overcrowded boat and do not accept a cage without a lid. If you feel concerned, walk away and find another operator. Only the Collaborative White Shark Research Programme and The White Shark Trust conduct great white shark research or cooperate with existing research projects. White Shark Adventures has recently introduced a six-person cage (although only four are put in at a time) which is always attached to the boat and is suitable for non-divers without qualifications (snorkelling without a diver's licence is illegal unless the cage is solidly attached to the boat).

101 WESTERN CAPE: FALSE BAY

Location Seal Island about 5 km/3 miles offshore, opposite Strandfontein; on the eastern side of the Cape of Good Hope.

Main species *most trips:* great white.

Viewing opportunities False Bay is one of the best places in the world to observe great white sharks and yet it is just 30 km/19 miles from Cape Town's famous Victoria & Albert Waterfront. The sharks gather around Seal Island, some 15 km/9 miles from Simon's Town, to feed on Cape fur seals. A small, rocky islet just 400 m/1300 ft long and 50 m/165 ft wide, Seal Island has a narrow western shelf (with the seabed dropping to 20 m/65 ft within 5 m/16 ft of the shore) and a broad eastern shelf (dropping to 20 m/65 ft within 20 m/65 ft of the shore). Despite its small size, it is populated by no fewer than 64,000 seals. They are aware of the great whites patrolling the waters around their home and tend to gather in one particular area, dubbed the Launching Pad, until there are enough of them to leave en masse. As few as five seals, or as many as 50, suddenly rush away from the island and swim across the so-called Ring of Peril, an area of deep water to the south, towards their feeding grounds. Their continual jostling for the safest position in the middle of the group probably confuses the sharks, but they risk being attacked on a daily basis. More than 80 per cent of the seals that are attacked are young and inexperienced, but the adults have to be careful, too. Even the local penguins are used as target practice – great whites are often seen hunting penguins here, although they have rarely been known to eat them.

Cage diving started here in 1996. The dive boat anchors close to Seal Island and uses ground-up fish and fish-oil chum to attract the sharks before lowering a one-person galvanised steel cage into the water. The cage is securely attached to the boat and divers can get in and out as often as they like. The sharks normally cruise near the seabed, and spend little time in mid-water, but will often investigate the boat and other objects on the surface. There is a 95 per cent success rate during the winter (May–Sep), which is the prime seal-hunting season when offshore winds chill the water and send the sharks' migratory fish prey up the east coast; that drops to 60 per cent during summer (Oct–Apr). Perhaps the main appeal of the great whites in False Bay is their breaching. They leap out of the water here – often cartwheeling and turning head over heels – more frequently than anywhere else in the world. There is occasional breaching in Mossel Bay, farther east, and they do it with some regularity in the Farallon Islands off San Francisco. However, False Bay is the only place where it is virtually a daily occurrence, as they blast through the water to grab seals between their jaws. Great whites less than 1.7 m/5½ ft in length are conspicuously absent, which suggests that they do not breed in False Bay (they are believed to breed in the Eastern Cape, but details on precise pupping grounds are sketchy). Individuals tagged at Seal Island have been resighted around Dyer Island (175 km/110 miles away) and Mossel Bay (350 km/220 miles). Bronze whaler sharks are relatively abundant in False Bay during Feb–Mar (they are caught in nets and sold locally for food), but have never been seen during cage dives and their numbers appear to be dropping.

Bait/feed yes.

Cage yes.

Other wildlife southern right whale (winter, but best Sep–Dec), humpback whale (Sep–Feb), Bryde's whale, common and dusky dolphins, Cape fur seal, jackass penguin.

Best time of year great whites present year-round, but largest numbers May–Sep; bronze whalers present Feb–Mar.

Dive depth cage floats at surface in 20 m/65 ft of water.

Typical visibility 4–10 m/13–33 ft.

Water temperature 12–14 °C/54–57 °F at surface.

Weather and sea notes no strong currents; north-westerly winds Mar–Sep, south-easterly winds Oct–Feb.

Contact details African Shark Eco Charters (www.ultimate-animals.com), Big Blue Charters (www.bigbluecharters.co.za).

Travel national and international flights to Cape Town; short drive to Simon's Town (where trips depart); wide choice of accommodation in Simon's Town.

Note blue and shortfin mako sharks also occur farther offshore and, in good weather conditions, arrangements can be made to cage dive with them during spring and autumn.

MADAGASCAR

102 NOSY TANIKELY ET AL.

Location Nosy Tanikely south-west of Hell-Ville (Andoany) harbour in Nosy Bé Archipelago, north-west corner of Madagascar; Ifaty near Tulear, south-west corner of Madagascar.

Main species *many trips:* grey reef, whitetip reef, tawny nurse (*Nebrius ferrugineus*), zebra or leopard; *occasional trips:* silvertip, whale.

Viewing opportunities Shark diving is relatively new to Madagascar, but two sites already have a good reputation: Nosy Tanikely (near Nosy Bé) and Ifaty (near Tulear). Nosy Bé is sometimes referred to as the Perfumed Island, because of the ever-present scent from its extensive plantations of vanilla and ylang-ylang, and its name literally translates as 'great island'. This might simply refer to the fact that it is the largest island off the north-west coast, but it is beautiful nonetheless. The best shark diving here takes place just off the coast in the Tanikely Marine Reserve. Consisting of a tiny, uninhabited island (apart from the lighthouse keeper and his family) surrounded by coral reef, this is a good place to see whitetip reef and zebra sharks. Whale sharks are seen in this area with increasing regularity in November and December.

Tanikely itself is rather disappointing, because it is popular with day trippers who tend to leave lots of their rubbish behind, but the diving is spectacular. The second site is Ifaty, where there is a pass through the reef with healthy populations of both grey reef and whitetip-reef sharks. There are other sites, particularly at open-sea banks and drop-offs, that are becoming known for shark encounters – including Banc de l'Entrée and Iranja Drop-off.

Bait/feed no.

Cage no.

Other wildlife wide variety of endemic wildlife onshore; various cetaceans, green and hawksbill turtles, manta ray (Apr–Jun and Oct–Dec), blue-spotted stingray, barracuda, clownfish, parrotfish, angelfish, surgeonfish.

Best time of year whale sharks in Nosy Tanikely mainly Nov–Dec; other sharks present year-round; best diving Apr to mid-Jan.

Dive depth 12–25 m/40–80 ft.

Typical visibility 10–30 m/33–100 ft (reduced by plankton blooms).

Water temperature 24–26 °C/75–78 °F Jun–Sep, 26–30 °C/78–86 °F Oct–May.

Weather and sea notes site fairly sheltered and sea conditions normally calm with no strong current; dry season Apr–Dec, rainy season Jan–Mar.

Contact details Reef and Rainforest Tours (www.reefrainforest.co.uk), Blue Dive Center (www.bluedive-madagascar.com), Tropical Diving (www.madagascar-contacts.com/tropical-diving).

Travel international flights to Antananarivo; direct flight to Nosy Bé (or ferry from Ambohimena) or to Tulear; choice of accommodation on Nosy Bé and around Ifaty.

LEBANON

103 BEIRUT: SHARK POINT

Location 1.6 km/1 mile south-west of the Corniche in Beirut.

Main species *most trips:* sand tiger.

Viewing opportunities this is a fairly challenging dive (as are most dives in Beirut), but is often rewarded with dramatic close encounters with sand tiger sharks. As the site name suggests, sharks have been known in the area for some time, but why they return every other year for just two months (early July to late Aug) is still a mystery. The most likely theory is that males and females use Shark Point as a rendezvous site for reproductive purposes, although no mating has ever been witnessed. Divers descend from the boat to rocks about 15–20 m/50–65 ft below the surface and then drift across the site in the current. The sharks are naturally curious and will often approach quite closely (sometimes within arm's length). Although they look impressive, and reach lengths of up to 3 m/10 ft, aggressive behaviour has never been observed at the site and the sharks are very placid. Most trips last a full day and include two dives.

Bait/feed no.

Cage no.

Other wildlife stingray, eagle ray, moray eel.

Best time of year Jul–Aug (only time of year that sharks are present).

Dive depth 25–30 m/80–100 ft.

Typical visibility 15–20 m/50–65 ft.

Water temperature 23° C/74 °F.

Weather and sea notes site is exposed and un-protected, so is quite choppy in windy weather; currents can be strong; hot and dry during Jul–Aug.

Contact details DivingTravel.Com (www.divingtravel.com).

Travel travel to the site is by speedboat; international flights to Beirut; choice of accommodation (pre-dominantly three- and four-star hotels near the dive centre).

Note the sharks are normally present every second year – it is essential to check if they are present before travelling. The use of Nitrox is highly recommended for qualified divers (obtainable at the dive centre).

EGYPT

104–5 RAS MUHAMMAD: SHARK REEF AND JOLANDA REEF

Location southern tip of the Sinai Peninsula.

Main species *most trips*: grey reef, whitetip reef; *many trips*: blacktip reef, scalloped hammerhead, oceanic whitetip; *occasional trips*: great hammerhead.

Viewing opportunities where the southern tip of the Sinai Peninsula meets the sea at Ras Muhammad, there are spectacular shallow reef flats near the shore-line and then sheer coral walls disappearing into the deep water beyond. This is where Shark Reef and Jolanda Reef form the twin peaks of a single coral seamount, connected by a shallow saddle about 20 m/65 ft deep, and separated from the mainland by a channel. They were named, respectively, after their plentiful sharks and a wrecked freighter that sunk in 1986 after a severe storm. The greatest concentration of sharks normally occurs in deep water off the north-eastern corner of Shark Reef, where there is a steep drop-off and the currents are strong. This is a favourite area for patrolling grey reef sharks, but an impressive number of other species turn up fairly regularly. The two reefs are normally done as drift dives, due to the strong currents, with the boat collecting divers from the shallows beyond Jolanda.

Bait/feed no.

Cage no.

Other wildlife moray eel, black-spotted and blue-spotted stingrays, Napoleon wrasse, yellowbar angelfish.

Best time of year the best diving is Jun–Oct and the sharks are most common Jun to early Sep; in Nov–Feb the visibility is more variable and there is a greater chance of rough seas.

Dive depth 20 m/65 ft.

Typical visibility 20 m/65 ft.

Water temperature 28–29 °C/82–84 °F (summer), 20–23 °C/68–74 °F (winter).

Weather and sea notes very strong currents are common and make shore access difficult.

Contact details Carpe Diem Cruise (www.carpediemcruise.com), Eastern Sea Safaris (www.myrosetta.co.uk), King Snefro Diving & Cruising (www.kingsnefro.com).

Travel Shark and Jolanda Reefs are accessible from shore (although currents can be a problem), by local dive boat from the nearby resort town of Sharm El Sheikh (approximately 15 km/9 miles to the north-east) or its satellite resort, Naama Bay, or from live-aboard boat. There is an international airport and a wide range of accommodation at Sharm El Sheikh.

Note there is another shark site about 1 km/½ mile to the north-east of Shark Reef, known as Shark Observatory. This is a vertical wall with a rugged profile that slopes outwards at the base, and has a good reputation for grey reef sharks (although there have been fewer sightings in recent years). They patrol the wall and frequently circle divers, sometimes investigating closely and occasionally becoming slightly aggressive. Until a few years ago they could be viewed from the local cliffs, but there are too many boats around these days and not as many sharks as there once were. Nearby Ras Z'Aatar, marking the entrance to Marsa Bareika, may be better for sharks these days than the more famous Observatory.

106 HURGHADA REGION

Location 75 km/47 miles south-west of Sharm El Sheikh; approximately midway between Cairo and the border with Sudan.

Main species *many trips:* whitetip reef; *occasional trips:* grey reef, tawny nurse (*Nebrius ferrugineus*).

Viewing opportunities while the more serious shark watching in the Red Sea takes place mainly at offshore sites accessible only by long-range live-aboard, there is also some good shark watching closer to shore. Many of these sites can be enjoyed by snorkellers as well as divers and are conducted as day trips or on 'mini-live-aboards', typically lasting one to three nights. Grey reef, whitetip reef and tawny nurse sharks are encountered on a regular basis. Whitetip reef are seen on many dives at Carless and Shaab El Erg, while grey reef and tawny nurse sharks also turn up at Carless, as well as Shaab Abu Ramada (dubbed 'The Aquarium' because of its phenomenal fish life) and sometimes at Small Giftun. Trips from Hurghada have very occasionally encountered scalloped hammerheads at Abu Ramada, El Fanadir and Carless, and whale sharks at Small Giftun and Hamda.

Bait/feed no.

Cage no.

Other wildlife bottlenose dolphin, manta and eagle rays, stingray, guitarfish, moray eel, parrotfish, pipefish, stonefish, crocodilefish, frogfish, lionfish, triggerfish, barracuda, clownfish, tuna, pufferfish, Napoleon wrasse, octopus, Spanish dancer.

Best time of year sharks present year-round, but best May–Sep.

Dive depth surface (snorkellers) or 15–25 m/50–80 ft (divers).

Typical visibility 20–30 m/65–100 ft.

Water temperature 18–22 °C/65–72 °F Nov–Apr, 25–28 °C/77–82 °F May–Oct.

Weather and sea notes seas tend to be rougher Dec–Mar; little rainfall year-round (usually falls Dec–Jan).

Contact details Sunshine Diving Center (www.sunshinediving.com), Dive Point Red Sea (www.dive-point.com), Diamond Sea Dive Center (www.redseadiamond.com)

Travel international flights to Hurghada (or accessible by ferry from Sharm El Sheikh); wide choice of accommodation in Hurghada.

107 THE BROTHERS

Location 70 km/43 miles north-east of El Quseir, nearly midway between Egypt and Saudi Arabia.

Main species *most trips:* grey reef, whitetip reef, scalloped hammerhead; *many trips:* silvertip, oceanic whitetip; *occasional trips:* tiger, pelagic thresher, blacktip, whale.

Viewing opportunities these tiny islands are actually the exposed tips of two massive reef pillars. They stand alone in the open sea, in the middle of nowhere, and are exposed to powerful ocean currents – making them a meeting point for huge numbers of pelagics and more than a few sharks. Big Brother is about 400 m/1300 ft long and is easily recognized by its Victorian lighthouse, manned by the military, while Little Brother is just 20 m/65 ft long and lies just under 1 km/½ mile to the south. Little Brother looks deceptively small from the surface but, like Big Brother, its coastal reef is quite extensive underwater. Known locally as El Akhawein, the Brothers were off limits to divers for three years (1996–8), by order of the Egyptian authorities, but are now diveable once more (although diving laws restrict the number of divers allowed to visit each year). Probably formed by volcanic action caused by the spreading of the Red Sea rift, they rise from some 300 m/1000 ft on the seabed and are often surrounded by wild currents. Schooling fish can be so dense that they sometimes block out the light, and both pillars attract large numbers of sharks when the conditions are right. Lots of different species have been encountered here over the years, but the most common are grey reef, whitetip reef and scalloped hammerheads. The hammerheads are most often seen around the north plateau of Little Brother and off the south-east corner of Big Brother (wherever the currents are strongest), schooling at depths in excess of 30 m/100 ft. This is one of the few places where oceanic whitetips, which spend most of their time in open water far offshore, come alongside reef walls with any regularity. Some huge threshers, as well as a few tiger sharks, blacktips and whale sharks, have also been encountered in recent years. The wreck of the *Aida II*, a troop-carrier that sank here one night in 1957, can be seen lying in 30–70 m/100–230 ft of water off the north-west side of Big Brother; a much older wreck, the *Namidia*, lies in 9–80 m/30–260 ft of water about 100 m/330 ft farther north.

Bait/feed no.

Cage no.

Other wildlife eagle ray, tuna, barracuda, bigeye trevally, huge schools of snapper, unicorns and jacks, surgeonfish, fantastic coral growth.

Best time of year sharks present year-round, but best May–Sep.

Dive depth 20–40 m/65–130 ft plus.

Typical visibility 15–25 m/50–80 ft.

Water temperature 22–24 °C/72–75 °F in winter, 28–30 °C/82–86 °F in summer.

Weather and sea notes exposed conditions with strong currents likely; can only be dived in good weather; calmest conditions usually Jun–Aug; little rainfall year-round (usually falls Dec–Jan).

Contact details Diving World Fleet (www.diving-world.com), Emperor Divers (www.emperordivers.com), MV Oyster (www.oysterdiving.com), MY Cyclone (www.scubaredsea.com), Sinai Divers (www.sinaidivers.com).

Travel live-aboards based in Hurghada or Safaga; international flights to Hurghada; wide choice of accommodation onshore.

Note it is important to check that your operator has a licence for diving at the Brothers – in the past, a few unscrupulous operators have taken bookings and then cancelled the trip at the last minute because of the 'weather'.

108 ELPHINSTONE REEF

Location 12 km/7½ miles off Marsa Abu Dabab, southern Egypt.

Main species *most trips:* grey reef, whitetip reef; *many trips:* scalloped hammerhead; *occasional trips:* blacktip reef, oceanic whitetip, silvertip, pelagic thresher, great hammerhead.

Viewing opportunities there is probably nowhere farther north in the Red Sea where schools of scalloped hammerheads can be encountered than here at

Elphinstone Reef (although the schools are quite small). This long, narrow reef runs for about 300 m/1000 ft from north to south and is often described as having sheer walls with sloping shoulders. The east and west sides do, indeed, drop to depths of 70–100 m/230–330 ft, while the north and west ends are marked by submerged, shelving plateaux. The most popular dive takes place off the southern plateau, where silvertips, oceanic whitetips and grey reef sharks are sometimes encountered cruising the deep blue beyond (or suddenly appear from nowhere to investigate visiting divers). A thresher is supposed to be resident near an impressive archway that lies beyond the range of sports divers, at 50–60 m/165–200 ft, but is rarely seen. The hammerheads are normally encountered off the northern plateau, especially in the early morning, where the current tends to be very strong. A single great hammerhead has been resident here for some years. Blacktip reef sharks occur over the shallow reef in the north, but are not seen very often.

Bait/feed no.

Cage no.

Other wildlife huge schools of anthias, tuna, snapper, jack, Napoleon wrasse, moray eel.

Best time of year sharks present year-round, but best May–Sep.

Dive depth 15–40 m/50–130 ft plus.

Typical visibility 15–30 m/50–100 ft.

Water temperature 22–24 °C/72–75 °F in winter, 28–30 °C/82–86 °F in summer.

Weather and sea notes currents moderate to strong; seas can be rough; little rainfall year-round (usually falls Dec–Jan).

Contact details Diving World Fleet (www.diving-world.com), Emperor Divers (www.emperordivers.com), Eastern Sea Safaris (www.myrosetta.co.uk), MV Oyster (www.oysterdiving.com), MY Cyclone (www.scubaredsea.com), Sinai Divers (www.sinaidivers.com).

Travel live-aboards based in various ports in Egypt; international flights to Hurghada; wide choice of accommodation onshore.

109 DAEDALUS REEF

Location west of Marsa Alam, in the central Red Sea.

Main species *most trips:* grey reef; *many trips:* pelagic thresher, scalloped hammerhead.

Viewing opportunities known locally as Abu el-Kizan, this small isolated reef is famous for its thresher sharks. They are by no means seen on every dive, but appear to be resident and this is one of the few places with repeated sightings. The reef lies in the open sea, almost halfway to Saudi Arabia, and is less than 500 m/1640 ft across. Its nineteenth-century lighthouse is the only break on the horizon for many kilometres in every direction. Slightly elliptical in shape, with sheer walls dropping to 70 m/230 ft or more on three sides, the reef has a broad, sloping plateau in the west starting at 25 m/80 ft and leading to another impressive drop-off at about 40 m/130 ft. Grey reef sharks can be seen in good numbers off the plateau and, if there is a strong current, off the wall in the north. Scalloped hammerheads can also be encountered off this wall. Most sightings of thresher sharks, however, tend to be in the south – particularly off the south-eastern tip of the reef.

Bait/feed no.

Cage no.

Other wildlife hawksbill turtle, barracuda, jack, rainbow runner, snapper, unicornfish, fusilier, surgeonfish.

Best time of year May–Sep.

Dive depth 20–40 m/65–130 ft plus.

Typical visibility 15–25 m/50–80 ft.

Water temperature 22–24 °C/72–75 °F in winter, 28–30 °C/82–86 °F in summer.

Weather and sea notes only diveable in good weather; exposed conditions with strong currents likely; little rainfall year-round (usually falls Dec–Jan).

Contact details Diving World Fleet (www.diving-world.com), Emperor Divers (www.emperordivers.com), MV Oyster (www.oysterdiving.com), MY Cyclone (www.scubaredsea.com), Sinai Divers (www.sinaidivers.com).

Travel live-aboards depart from Hurghada or Marsa Alam; international flights to Hurghada (or accessible by ferry from Sharm El Sheikh); wide choice of accommodation in Hurghada.

110 ROCKY ISLAND

Location 5.5 km/3½ miles south-east of the larger island of Zabargad; approximately 50 km/30 miles off the Egyptian coast.

Main species *most trips:* grey reef; *many trips:* scalloped hammerhead; *occasional trips:* silky, pelagic thresher, oceanic whitetip.

Viewing opportunities Rocky Island (or Rocky Islet, as it is sometimes called) is a small triangle of rock with a tiny beach in one corner. Marking the border

between Egypt and Sudan, it has sheer walls plunging into the depths on its north, south and west sides and a narrow, sloping sandy shelf at about 25 m/80 ft on the east. The best dive site for sharks is on this exposed eastern shelf. The dive is normally conducted as a drift, since the current howls over the shelf at a rate of knots, and offers a chance to see several different shark species. Dubbed a natural 'shark theatre', the shelf is particularly good for grey reef sharks, but massive scalloped hammerheads occur in the deeper water below and big silkies, threshers and oceanic whitetips turn up on a regular basis. Sharks are also encountered quite often off the north coast, although the prevailing north wind, high swell and fierce current can make this a tricky dive, in which you can feel the surge at 25 m/80 ft or more and often have to swim through rough surface waters to be picked up by the boat.

Bait/feed no.

Cage no.

Other wildlife jack, snapper, surgeonfish, triggerfish, parrotfish, angelfish, barracuda, Napoleon wrasse.

Best time of year sharks present year-round, but best May–Sep.

Dive depth 15–40 m/50–130 ft plus.

Typical visibility 15–25 m/50–80 ft.

Water temperature 22–24 °C/72–75 °F in winter, 28–30 °C/82–86 °F in summer.

Weather and sea notes fierce currents likely; big surge and swell on the eastern plateau; little rainfall year-round (usually falls Dec–Jan).

Contact details Diving World Fleet (www.diving-world.com), Emperor Divers (www.emperordivers.com), MV Oyster (www.oysterdiving.com), MY Cyclone (www.scubaredsea.com), Sinai Divers (www.sinaidivers.com).

Travel live-aboards based in various ports in Egypt; international flights to Hurghada or Sharm El Sheikh; wide choice of accommodation onshore.

SUDAN

111 ELBA REEF

Location 18 km/11 miles offshore, almost on the border with Egypt.

Main species *many trips:* silvertip, grey reef, whitetip reef.

Viewing opportunities Elba Reef is not one of the most outstanding shark sites in the Red Sea, but it does offer frequent sightings of silvertips and has a representative selection of grey reef and whitetip reef sharks. The reef is best known for the wreck of the *Lavanzo*, an Italian ship built in the 1930s, whose massive hull lies keel-up across the drop-off. There used to be a resident silvertip, a battle-scarred female, who had a reputation for being fairly hostile to divers around the wreck, but she has not been seen for some time. Elba probably became known for silvertips because of this lone individual; nevertheless, there appears to be a population of them in deeper water below the wreck, and they will often rise to shallower water (the wreck lies from 18 m/60 ft at the propeller to about 75 m/250 ft at the bow) specifically to investigate divers.

Bait/feed no.

Cage no.

Other wildlife grouper, rich reef-fish population, wide variety of corals.

Best time of year sharks present year-round, but best May–Sep.

Dive depth 20–40 m/65–130 ft plus.

Typical visibility 15–30 m/50–100 ft.

Water temperature 22–24 °C/72–75 °F in winter, 28–30 °C/82–86 °F in summer.

Weather and sea notes current mild to strong; choppy sea conditions common; very little rainfall year-round; extremely hot all year, but cooler (relatively speaking) Nov–Mar.

Contact details Diving World Fleet (www.diving-world.com).

Travel live-aboards depart from Port Sudan; international flights to Port Sudan.

112 PFEIFFER REEF

Location 15 km/9 miles south-east of Marsa Halaka, roughly midway between Port Sudan and the border with Egypt.

Main species *most trips:* silvertip, scalloped hammerhead, grey reef.

Viewing opportunities named after the Hollywood actress Michelle Pfeiffer (the connection being beauty), this wonderful reef offers virtually guaranteed shark encounters. Snorkellers can often see sharks here, although diving is preferable because the best sightings are usually quite deep. Few dives do not include at least one shark sighting and, on a good day, the range and number of sharks can be astounding. The southernmost of three offshore reefs, Pfeiffer is the home of some very large sharks –scalloped hammerheads and silvertips being the biggest draw.

The best dive takes place off the southern end, where the reef slopes from the shallows to a depth of about 40 m/130 ft and then forms a plateau before dropping sharply another 10 m/33 ft. Some of the best shark watching in this part of the Red Sea takes place in the open water beyond this drop-off.

Bait/feed no.

Cage no.

Other wildlife grouper, rich reef-fish population, wide variety of corals.

Best time of year sharks present year-round, but best May–Sep.

Dive depth 25–40 m/80–130 ft plus.

Typical visibility 15–30 m/50–100 ft.

Water temperature 22–24 °C/72–75 °F in winter, 28–30 °C/82–86 °F in summer.

Weather and sea notes current mild to strong; choppy sea conditions common; very little rainfall year-round; extremely hot all year, but cooler (relatively speaking) Nov–Mar.

Contact details Diving World Fleet (www.diving-world.com).
Travel live-aboards depart from Port Sudan; international flights to Port Sudan.

113–14 ABINGTON AND ANGAROSH REEFS

Location 21 km/13 miles (Abington) and 25 km/16 miles (Angarosh) south-east of Ras Abu Shajarah, near Dungunab Bay; roughly midway between Port Sudan and the border with Egypt.

Main species *most trips:* silvertip, grey reef; *many trips:* oceanic whitetip, scalloped hammerhead.

Viewing opportunities these two reef pillars are just 4 km/2½ miles apart and share a healthy population of sharks of several different species. Abington is a small reef, with an unmanned lighthouse on top, and has sheer walls on three sides and a sloping plateau on the fourth (to the south-east of the main reef). Its real draw is the silvertips, which tend to be very inquisitive and will investigate divers closely for a few minutes before disappearing back into the blue. Angarosh lies to the south-west and is similar in design, but with two sloping plateaux (at 25 m/80 ft and 40 m/130 ft) instead of one. 'Angarosh' actually means 'the mother of sharks' in Arabic and it certainly lives up to its name. Like Abington, it is good for silvertips and it is not unusual to see individuals here in excess of 3 m/10 ft in length. But there are also lots of grey reef sharks, which continuously patrol around the pinnacle, while sightings of oceanic whitetip and schools of 5–40 scalloped hammerheads off the north-east point are by no means unusual.

Bait/feed no.

Cage no.

Other wildlife grouper, Napoleon wrasse, barracuda, jack, tuna, triggerfish, unicornfish, snapper, parrotfish.

Best time of year sharks present year-round, but best May–Sep.

Dive depth 10–40 m/33–130 ft plus.

Typical visibility 15–30 m/50–100 ft.

Water temperature 22–24 °C/72–75 °F in winter, 28–30 °C/82–86 °F in summer.

Weather and sea notes current usually moderate to strong; choppy sea conditions common; very little rainfall year-round; extremely hot all year, but cooler (relatively speaking) Nov–Mar.

Contact details Diving World Fleet (www.diving-world.com).

Travel live-aboards depart fromPort Sudan; international flights to Port Sudan.

115 SHA'AB RUMI

Location 40 km/25 miles north-east of Port Sudan.

Main species *most trips:* grey reef, whitetip reef, silvertip; *many trips:* blacktip reef, silky, scalloped hammerhead.

Viewing opportunities ask any Jacques Cousteau fan about Sha'ab Rumi and they will immediately know it as the place where he made his 1963 underwater-habitat experiment. Sha'ab Rumi East is often referred to simply as the Conshelf site (it was the Conshelf II experiment) and it is still possible to see a few remnants of his underwater village. The project's shark cages are still here, too, lying in about 30 m/ 100 ft of water and now encrusted and filled with luxuriant coral. Sharks are frequently seen around the village remains, although Sha'ab Rumi South (commonly known as South Point) is much better. This is a large reef surrounded by very deep water, with its longest sides parallel to the prevailing north–south current. There are sheer walls on either side (east and west), but it is the narrow, gently sloping plateau in the south that produces the most shark encounters. Running from a depth of 20 m/65 ft to about 36 m/ 120 ft before plunging into the depths at 600 m/ 2000 ft or more, the plateau is where the currents meet and produce whirlpools and upwellings that attract large shoals of fish and their predators. The site is best known for its scalloped hammerheads, although they

tend to school in deep water beyond the range of divers and are only seen if they choose to come up to investigate. However, as many as 50 other sharks can be seen patrolling back and forth, especially early in the morning. There are scores of grey reef sharks around – especially when there is bait in the water. Among the other regulars are quite a few silvertips and some rather aggressive, fast-swimming silkies. In fact Sha'ab Rumi is probably one of the best places in the Red Sea for close, nerve-jangling encounters with silky sharks.

Bait/feed sometimes (depends on operator).

Cage no.

Other wildlife stingray, dense reef-fish populations, large schools of jack, snapper and barracuda, tuna, triggerfish.

Best time of year sharks present year-round, but best May–Sep.

Dive depth 20–40 m/65–130 ft plus.

Typical visibility 15–30 m/50–100 ft.

Water temperature 22–24 °C/72–75 °F in winter, 28–30 °C/82–86 °F in summer.

Weather and sea notes current mild to strong; choppy sea conditions common at Conshelf site; very little rainfall year-round; extremely hot all year, but cooler (relatively speaking) Nov–Mar.

Contact details Diving World Fleet (www.diving-world.com).

Travel live-aboards depart from Port Sudan; international flights to Port Sudan.

116 SANGANEB

Location 27 km/17 miles north-east of Port Sudan.

Main species *most trips:* grey reef, whitetip reef; *many trips:* scalloped hammerhead, blacktip, silvertip.

Viewing opportunities scalloped hammerhead schools tend to get larger and larger as you move south through the Red Sea. The smallest schools occur at Elphinstone Reef, in Egypt, and the largest here at Sanganeb. But it is not just the hammerheads that attract divers back to Sanganeb time and again, because there is often a never-ending procession of other shark species as well. With Spanish dancers virtually guaranteed off the lighthouse jetty, after dark, it is also one of the most popular night dives in the Red Sea. This large elliptical reef, complete with a shallow lagoon in its centre, has a number of different dive sites, but two in particular are of interest to shark watchers: North Point and South Point. It is hard to do justice to South Point, which is dived most often. It consists of an incredible, sheer-sided reef plateau of pristine coral rising from depths of around 800 m/ 2600 ft and is literally packed with fish on its shallow reef top. The south-west point is at about 20 m/ 65 ft and from there it slopes steeply and then plunges into the deep from about 55 m/180 ft. Attached to the main reef a little to the south-west of the lighthouse, this plateau seems to act like a magnet for sharks, with whitetip reef on the top, a constant procession of grey reef all over the place, and a few blacktip and silvertip among the species out in the open water where anything can happen. As in many parts of the world, the grey reef sharks have an unnerving habit of swimming straight towards divers and then veering off at the very last moment. They are not being aggressive – just inquisitive. Hammerheads tend to gather at depths greater than 70 m/230 ft, but will often come to have a look at visiting divers in ones, twos or threes before disappearing again into the blue; they tend to be more inquisitive early in the morning. North Point consists of a narrow submerged reef on the opposite side of Sanganeb, where a series of shelves continue to well beyond 60 m/200 ft and then fall away from the reef to incredible depths. There are sharks here (hammerheads are seen quite frequently), but not as many as where the currents converge at South Point.

Bait/feed no.

Cage no.

Other wildlife sea turtles, blue-spotted stingray, moray eel, dense reef-fish populations, large schools of jack, snapper and barracuda, surgeonfish, dogtooth tuna, grouper, parrotfish, titan triggerfish, Spanish dancer.

Best time of year sharks present year-round, but best May–Sep.

Dive depth 15–40 m/50–130 ft plus.

Typical visibility 15–30 m/50–100 ft; sand storms from Ethiopia can reduce visibility in Jul–Aug.

Water temperature 22–24 °C/72–75 °F in winter, 28–30 °C/82–86 °F in summer.

Weather and sea notes currents highly variable from mild to fierce, but likely to be strong; high swell and windy conditions also likely; very little rainfall year-round; extremely hot all year, but cooler (relatively speaking) Nov–Mar.

Contact details Diving World Fleet (www.diving-world.com).

Travel live-aboards depart from Port Sudan; international flights to Port Sudan.

THE PHILIPPINES

117–19 SULU SEA: TUBBATAHA NATIONAL MARINE REEF PARK

Location a remote location in the middle of the Sulu Sea, between the island of Palawan and the rest of the Philippines archipelago, approximately 160 km/100 miles south-east of Puerto Princesa (capital of Palawan).

Main species *most trips:* whitetip reef; *many trips:* grey reef, blacktip reef; *occasional trips:* sand tiger, leopard (*Stegostoma fasciatum*), scalloped hammerhead, shortfin mako, thresher.

Viewing opportunities declared a UNESCO World Heritage Site in 1993, Tubbataha National Marine Reef Park comprises two of the best atolls in the Philippines. The diving here is both varied and spectacular, with a mixture of reef platforms, sandy lagoons and perpendicular walls. A wide range of sharks can be seen almost anywhere. As well as having resident reef sharks, Tubbataha has been described as a 'pit stop on the pelagic superhighway' and huge numbers of pelagics turn up whenever there is a strong current running. The site actually consists of two distinct areas, appropriately called North Tubbataha and South Tubbataha, which are separated by about 8 km/5 miles of water. Their sheer walls rise from depths of up to 3000 m/10,000 ft to just below the surface (their shallow reefs are emergent in some places at low tide). The northern site is a large, oblong reef platform some 16 km/10 miles long and 4.5 km/ 3 miles wide, completely enclosing a sandy lagoon. The southern site is also a reef platform enclosing a sandy lagoon, but is triangular in shape and just 3 km/2 miles long and no more than 2 km/1¼ miles across at its widest. Jessie Beazley lies some 18 km/11 miles to the north-west of North Tubbataha. A small, circular reef topped by sandbars, about 0.5 km/ ⅓ mile in diameter, it rises from the depths almost to the surface. Whitetip reef and blacktip reef sharks are commonly seen here, along with sand tigers resting on the sandy ledge, and a variety of pelagics such as hammerheads, makos and threshers are occasionally seen cruising the blue waters beyond the reef itself. There is also a third site, which is rarely marked on maps, but lies about 90 km/ 56 miles south-west of South Tubbataha. Known as Basterra Reef, or sometimes Meander Reef, it is a massive pinnacle topped by a sandbar and slightly bigger than Jessie Beazley. Also surrounded by very deep water, it has a well-deserved reputation for shark watching. Barracuda Slope is particularly good, with blacktip reef and whitetip reef almost always present, and there is an exciting and very fast drift dive in the company of grey reef sharks at Expressway.

Bait/feed no.

Cage no.

Other wildlife huge numbers of seabirds, green and hawksbill turtles, sea snakes, manta, marbled and eagle rays, shovelnose ray or guitarshark, blue-spotted stingray, mackerel, Napoleon wrasse, huge schools of jacks and barracuda, dogtooth tuna.

Best time of year sharks present year-round, but the area can only be dived Mar–Jun (seas too rough outside this period).

Dive depth 20–40 m/65–130 ft.

Typical visibility 20–40 m/65–130 ft.

Water temperature 24–30 °C/75–86 °F.

Weather and sea notes strong currents (often unpredictable around North Tubbataha) and surface chop fairly normal; dry season Mar–May, rainy season Jun–Feb.

Contact details DiveGurus Philippines (**www.divegurus.com**), Virgin Islands of the Philippines (**www.diveamust.com**), Palawan.Com (**www.palawan.com**), Across Pacific Dive Tours/MY Tristar (**www.acrosspacific.com/Resorts/TRI-select.htm**), Tubbataha.com (**www.tubbataha.com**).

Travel accessible only by live-aboard; international flights to Manila; daily flight to Puerto Princesa for DiveGurus, Palawan.Com and MY Tristar, then 10–12-hour boat trip to site; or daily flight to Lapu-Lapu for Virgin Islands of the Philippines, then boat to site.

120 APO REEF: SHARK RIDGE

Location approximately 30 km/19 miles off the west coast of Mindoro Island, in the Mindoro Strait, where the Sulu Sea meets the South China Sea.

Main species *most trips:* grey reef, whitetip reef, blacktip reef; *occasional trips:* scalloped hammerhead.

Viewing opportunities Apo Reef sprawls across 34 sq km/13 sq miles of ocean, and yet most of its main geographical features are hidden beneath the surface. Three small islands mark its position: Apo Island, Apo Menor or Binangaan, and Cayos del Bajo or Tinang-kapang. It is an atoll-like reef, with two beautiful lagoons (complete with azure blue water and fine white sandy bottoms) divided by a narrow channel.

Twenty years ago Apo was considered one of the top dive sites in Asia but sadly, thanks to dynamite fishermen who destroyed a large part of the coral platform, it has lost much of its former glory. It was given official protection in 1996 and, although fishermen continue to visit the area illegally, the reef is gradually making a comeback. But it is the spectacular walls and drop-offs that make Apo so good for sharks and, fortunately, these were not badly harmed by such destructive fishing methods. When a strong current is running (which is often) lots of sharks and other pelagics can be seen almost anywhere here. Grey reef, blacktip reef and whitetip reef are particularly common, but sightings of scalloped hammerheads seem to have increased in recent years (particularly around the northern, southern and eastern drop-offs at Apo Island itself). The most obvious place to look is at the aptly named Shark Ridge, on the eastern side. The coral here is not particularly impressive, and the bottom slopes away to a rather dull sand and detritus at about 25 m/80 ft, but all three reef-shark species are seen here with considerable regularity. Large pelagics tend to be seen more often in the deep blue around Binangaan, on the opposite side of the reef, but can be seen almost anywhere. Apo 29 is worth a mention, because it is basically a blue-water dive around an underwater pinnacle, which rises to within 25 m/80 ft of the surface, and has a reputation for more inquisitive sharks that readily approach divers. Hunter Rock is another rocky pinnacle, some 20 km/12 miles west of Apo, which is not only good for sharks but also superb for sea snakes. The snakes are literally everywhere – hundreds of them for most of the year, but thousands during the mating season (Jun–Jul). Nearby Merope Reef, about 18 km/11 miles west of Apo and a little north of Hunter Rock, rises to within 15 m/50 ft of the surface and is excellent for open-ocean sharks and other pelagics.

Bait/feed no.

Cage no.

Other wildlife variety of seabirds, green and hawksbill turtles, sea snakes, manta ray, huge schools of jacks, dogtooth tuna, barracuda, batfish, rainbow runner, humphead parrotfish, triggerfish, pyramid butterflyfish.

Best time of year sharks present year-round, but diving best Mar–Jun.

Dive depth 10–40 m/33–130 ft plus.

Typical visibility 15–40 m/50–130 ft.

Water temperature 24–30 °C/75–86 °F.

Weather and sea notes currents tend to be strong (unpredictable at Apo Island and Apo 29) and a surface chop is fairly normal (especially Jul–Jan); dry season Dec–May, rainy season Jun–Nov; tropical storms possible Jul–Sep, but between storms the weather can be balmy for long periods.

Contact details Pandan Island Resort (www.pandan.com), Virgin Islands of the Philippines (www.diveamust.com), DiveGurus Philippines (www.divegurus.com), Action Divers (www.actiondivers.com).

Travel accessible by day boat from Pandan Island or by live-aboard from Puerto Galera or Boracay; international flights to Manila; 3-hour bus trip to Batangas, then ferry or dive boat to Puerto Galera or ferry to San Jose, bus to Sablayan and water taxi to Pandan (or fly direct to Pandan by seaplane); regular scheduled flight to Catican via Cebu or direct to Catican in light aircraft, then boat to Boracay.

121–29 MARICABAN STRAIT: THE NURSERY, CEMETERY BEACH, MAPATING ROCK/SHARK'S REEF, MAINIT POINT/ CAZADOR POINT, MALAJIBOMANOK ISLAND, SEPOK WALL, SOMBRERO ISLAND, LAYAG-LAYAG REEF AND CATHEDRAL ROCK

Location between the southernmost tip of Calumpang Peninsula and Maricaban Island; 120 km/ 75 miles south of Manila.

Main species *most trips:* whitetip reef, blacktip reef, grey reef, tawny nurse (*Nebrius ferrugineus*); *occasional trips:* leopard (*Stegostoma fasciatum*), thresher.

Viewing opportunities there are no dedicated shark dives in the Maricaban Strait, but several different species are encountered on a regular basis. There are also some good opportunities for snorkelling with juvenile whitetip reef and blacktip reef sharks at El Pinoy and Cemetery Beach. The young sharks come into very shallow water, within a few metres of El Pinoy resort, in an area dubbed the Nursery; it is possible to encounter adults of both these species by snorkelling to the reef a little farther out – they are used to people and very approachable. At low tide, during the the typhoon season (Jun–Oct), they can also be seen in water as shallow as 0.6 m/2 ft at Cemetery Beach, on Maricaban Island. Divers can encounter sharks almost anywhere here, but there are a few hotspots. Mapating Rock, south-west of Sepok Point, is an open reef with good numbers of whitetip reef and grey reef sharks. Also known as Shark's Reef, the rock itself is submerged and surrounded by a shallow area with an average depth of less than 12 m/ 40 ft, which drops in stages to much deeper water. Mainit Point, or Cazador Point as it is called on some charts, lies off the southernmost tip of the Calampang Peninsula and has a cave at 7 m/23 ft, where it is often possible to see resting whitetip reef sharks. Blacktip reef sharks are commonly seen farther away at

Malajibomanok Island, off the eastern end of Maricaban Island, which consists of patches of coral heads on sandy slopes from 6 m/20 ft to 24 m/80 ft; the nearby hot springs, at 20 m/65 ft, are another draw. When the currents are running, pelagics can be seen around: Sepok Wall (west of Sepok Point off the north-western tip of Maricaban Island); Sombrero Island (about 1 km/½ mile north of Sepok Point), an uninhabited island which really does look like a hat when viewed from underwater and is also good for whitetip reef sharks; and Layag-Layag Reef (off the north-western tip of Caban Island), an extensive coral formation on a slope that drops steeply to open water on the south side. One of the best-known dive sites in the country is also here – Cathedral Rock. Lying some 23 m/75 ft off Bagalangit Point, on the Calumpang Peninsula, it was named for a cross that was blessed by the Pope and then placed at a depth of 14 m/45 ft by Fidel Ramos (who later became President of the Philippines). This giant underwater rock formation looks like a cavern without its roof and is teeming with fish (largely because there has been a lot of fish-feeding here), but is not particularly good for sharks.

Bait/feed no.

Cage no.

Other wildlife various cetaceans, dugong, green and hawksbill turtles, manta and eagle rays, blue spot and marbled stingrays, seahorses, ghost pipefish, pufferfish, moorish idol, parrotfish, Spanish dancer.

Best time of year sharks present year-round, but best diving Nov–Jun.

Dive depth 3–30 m/10–100 ft.

Typical visibility 10–30 m/33–100 ft; poorer visibility Jul–Sep.

Water temperature 17–30 °C/63–86 °F.

Weather and sea notes currents mild to strong, depending on site and tide (often fierce at Layag-Layag, Mapating Rock, Mainit Point, Malajibomanok Island and during full moon at Sombrero Island); surface conditions can be choppy; dry season Mar–May, rainy season Jun–Feb; tropical storms possible Jul–Sep, with choppy seas, but between storms weather can be balmy for long periods.

Contact details El Pinoy Dive Inn (www.elpinoy@tcs.com.ph), Eagle Point Resort (www.eaglepoint.com.ph).

Travel international flights to Manila; 2½-hour drive by car; wide choice of accommodation in the region.

Note there is a code of conduct for shark diving in the Philippines, published by the World Wildlife Fund.

130 SORSOGON: DONSOL

Location in the Burias Strait, in western Sorsogon; approximately 400 km/250 miles south-east of Manila (550 km/340 miles by road).

Main species *most trips:* whale.

Viewing opportunities the huge gathering of whale sharks at the mouth of the Donsol River had been known to the small coastal community of Donsol for generations. But the outside world did not hear about it until 1997 – and organized shark watching did not begin until the following year. Almost overnight, the sleepy little fishing village was transformed into a major ecotourist destination. The sharks gather in the area for about six months every year (mainly Nov–Jun, with a peak in Feb–May – the best month is Mar) to feed in the plankton-rich waters here, and this is one of the few places in the world where they can easily be spotted in large numbers. There may be 40 or 50 of them in the area at any one time and a study conducted in 1998 counted more than 90 different individuals (mostly females) during a single season (although numbers have decreased in the past two years).

The Philippines has a long tradition of hunting *butanding* (the name for whale sharks in the local dialect). In a joint investigation by WWF-Philippines and Silliman University, in 1996–97, it was found that at least 15 villages were involved and that each was catching an average of 26 whale sharks per year. In the past only five villages had been involved and they were hunting the sharks mainly for their meat, which was sold locally, but recent demand for shark fins in South-East Asia encouraged an export market to Taiwan, as well as Japan, Hong Kong and Singapore. The Donsol fishermen have never been involved, but shark numbers had declined in other parts of the country and hunters from outside moved in for the kill. This prompted three important developments in 1998: under intense public pressure, the national government granted whale sharks special protection from killing, wounding, catching, selling, transporting and exporting; the local council of Donsol passed an ordinance declaring a whale shark sanctuary in their municipal waters, stretching 15 km/9 miles from shore; and centrally coordinated whale interaction tours were set up.

The tours were so popular that conservationists began to express concern about causing too much disturbance. Indeed, a number of whale sharks in the area have propeller gashes on their bodies. So the Donsol Butanding Ecotourism Management Plan has been developed in conjunction with WWF and with financial support from the United Nations Development Programme. The aim is to develop a sustainable tourism industry, as an economic alternative to hunting, without harming the sharks.

Shark watchers have to register with the Donsol Municipal Tourism Council (DTMC) at the Visitor Centre on Donsol pier. Everyone pays a fee and is given a research kit (WWF-Philippines runs a voluntary research programme and asks everyone to help in gathering data) before being assigned to a boat. Traditional *bangkas* or *bancas* (motorized outrigger canoes, typically about 6 m/20 ft in length) are used with a maximum of six passengers on board. Each boat has two Butanding Interaction Officers – the spotter, who may once have been a whale shark fisherman, and the skipper. The aim is for the boat to position itself a few metres ahead of the shark, in preparation for all the snorkellers to ease themselves quietly into the water. Everyone has to be ready and waiting, because it has to take no more than 30–60 seconds between spotting a shark and getting into the water. If you take any longer, you are likely to miss the opportunity for a close encounter. The entire process is governed by strict regulations: no more than one boat is allowed with a whale shark at any one time; there is no jumping, no underwater flash photography, no touching, no scuba, and so on. The regulations are good and, although Donsol is not the easiest place to get to, the experience is breathtaking.

Bait/feed no.

Cage no.

Best time of year Nov–Jun (numbers peak Mar).

Dive depth surface (snorkelling only).

Typical visibility 5–25 m/16–80 ft.

Water temperature 24–30 °C/75–86 °F.

Weather and sea notes dry season Mar–May, rainy season with rougher seas Jun–Feb.

Contact details WWF Philippines (www.wwf-phil.com.ph), Philippines Department of Tourism (www.tourism.gov.ph), Dive Elite (www.diveelite.com/whaletour.html), Kalinga Travel Adventure (www.ktadventure.com/kta_enver/whale_en.htm).

Travel international flights to Manila; 12-hour bus ride or 1-hour flight to Legaspi City, then 1-hour bus ride to Donsol; choice of accommodation in Legaspi, but limited options in Donsol.

Note WWF Philippines does not operate tours.

131 CEBU: MALAPASCUA ISLAND

Location 8 km/5 miles off the north-eastern tip of Cebu, in the Visayan Sea.

Main species *most trips:* pelagic thresher, whitetip reef; *many trips:* silvertip, scalloped hammerhead, bamboo (*Chiloscyllium*); *occasional trips:* whale.

Viewing opportunities this is possibly the best place in the world to see pelagic thresher sharks, or fox sharks as they are known locally. Indeed, with the right sea and weather conditions some operators claim a 95 per cent sightings record. In recent years thresher sharks ranging from 2–4 m/6½–13 ft in length have been using a manta ray cleaning station at Monad Shoal, or Sunken Island. This seamount is just 20–30 minutes by boat to the north-east of the 2 × 1 km/1⅓ × ½ mile Malapascua Island. No other cleaning station is known to be used by thresher sharks on such a regular basis. The station lies on the plateau on top of the seamount, in the soft coral garden at 15–23 m/50–75 ft, and is surrounded by vertical drop-offs down to 50 m/165 ft or more. The site has been dubbed Shark Point. Early in the morning seems to be the best time (operators put their divers in the water at sunrise), when it is possible to see as many as nine or ten threshers having their parasites removed by cleaner wrasse and other small fish. The sharks typically swim about 1 m/3⅓ ft off the top of the seamount, in a figure-of-eight pattern. They are fairly relaxed about divers and often approach quite closely if everyone stays perfectly still. Gato Island, 9 km/5½ miles north-west of Malapascua, is also good for threshers. Best known for its whitetip reef sharks, which rest in some of the numerous underwater caverns around the island and among huge boulders on the sandy bottom at a depth of about 25 m/80 ft, it is also a good place for chance encounters with threshers. Gato's other claim to fame is a large underwater cavern filled with banded sea snakes. Silvertips are encountered quite frequently around Malapascua, and scalloped hammerheads can often be seen on deeper dives. The entire region has suffered tremendously from illegal dynamite fishing (vast areas underwater are covered with coral rubble) and there is now a permanent guard post on Gato Island as part of an effort to tackle the problem. Monad Shoal is also under threat from shark fishermen based on Malapascua Island, who sell thresher fins to buying stations on mainland Cebu. Some dive operators are helping to fund urgently needed conservation efforts and, consequently, there is an ongoing battle between them and the fishermen. There are also proposals to include a 'conservation tax' on all Monad Shoal dives – to invest in community development and to establish the site as a marine reserve (which would include a provision to limit the number of divers there at any one time).

Bait/feed no.

Cage no.

Other wildlife hawksbill turtle, black and white banded sea snake, eagle, marbled and manta rays (especially May–Jan), blue-spotted stingray, moray eel, pufferfish, grouper, frogfish.

Best time of year threshers present year-round.

Dive depth 15–27 m/50–90 ft.

Typical visibility 8–15 m/26–50 ft.

Water temperature 24–30°C/75–86 °F.

Weather and sea notes current highly variable, but can be strong (especially at Gato Island); rainy season with rougher seas Jun–Feb.

Contact details Bubble07 (www.bubble07.com), Dive Elite (www.diveelite.com), Phildivers (www.phildivers.com), Blue Abyss Diving (www.blueabyssdiving.com), DiveGurus Philippines (www.divegurus.com).

Travel international flights to Manila with connecting flights to Cebu City, or direct to Cebu from some destinations; 3-hour bus ride to Maya pier, for 20–30-min boat transfer to Malapascua Island; choice of accommodation on the island.

Note this site is becoming very popular very quickly and there have been a number of incidents recently of divers behaving badly around the sharks – demonstrating an urgent need for controls.

132 CEBU: PESCADOR ISLAND

Location 6 km/4 miles from Moalboal, facing Panagsama Beach, in the Tanon Strait; off the southwest coast of Cebu, in the Visayas.

Main species *most trips:* whitetip reef; *many trips:* scalloped hammerhead (see viewing opportunities); *occasional trips:* blacktip reef, thresher, whale.

Viewing opportunities the tiny, uninhabited island of Pescador is often described as the jewel in the crown of the diving in this part of Cebu. Shaped like a giant mushroom, with just the top visible above the surface, it is small enough to circumnavigate in a single shallow dive. It is surrounded by a shallow reef, varying in depth at 3–8 m/10–26 ft and some 5–20 m/16–65 ft wide, and then there is a steep wall that drops down to 40 m/130 ft and beyond. The whole area is packed with superb drop-offs, buttresses, caverns and overhangs, and more than 650 different species of hard coral have been identified here during studies by Sumilon University. Whitetip reef sharks are encountered on almost every dive, although they are often resting on the seabed at 40–60 m/130–200 ft and have to be viewed from a distance alone. But, until quite recently, scalloped hammerheads were the main draw. Schools of 20–30 of them were common off the north-east edge of the reef, usually at a depth of 30–40 m/100–130 ft, especially during the first few months of the year. They seem to have disappeared in the past two years (no one knows why, although El Niño might be to blame) and it is uncertain whether they will return in their former numbers. Blacktip reef

and thresher sharks occasionally turn up along the wall, and whale sharks can be spotted in open water to the south of the island. Whale shark numbers appear to be increasing here and from three to six are now seen every month in Mar–Oct and two to four every week in Nov–Feb. The best-known dive site here is Pescador Cathedral, a large underwater cavern reached by a 15 m/50 ft wide funnel and descending to 35 m/115 ft. Best dived early in the afternoon, when the light streams down inside, it is not particularly good for sharks, but is so beautiful that several couples have actually been married inside it.

Bait/feed no.

Cage no.

Other wildlife banded sea snake, barracuda, jack, mackerel, bigeye and giant trevally, dogtooth tuna, triggerfish, butterflyfish, humphead wrasse, lionfish, snapper, grouper, scorpionfish, stonefish, frogfish, Spanish dancer.

Best time of year scalloped hammerheads and whitetip reef mainly Nov–Apr (hammerheads best Jan–Mar); whale sharks best Nov–Feb.

Dive depth 15–40 m/50–130 ft (30–40 m/100–130 ft for hammerheads).

Typical visibility 5–35 m/16–115 ft; varies greatly with weather and plankton levels.

Water temperature 24–30°C/75–86 °F.

Weather and sea notes currents vary from mild to strong; best sea conditions during dry season (Mar–May), but can be choppy; rainy season with rougher seas Jun–Feb, but sheltered from full effects of typhoons and monsoons.

Contact details Kon Tiki Divers (www.kontikidivers.com.ph), Savedra Dive Center (www.savedra.com), Quo Vadis Beach Resort (www.moalboal.com), Blue Abyss Diving (www.blueabyssdiving.com).

Travel international flights to Manila with connecting flights to Cebu City, or direct to Cebu from some destinations; 2-hour bus ride or drive over a rugged mountain road to Moalboal; wide choice of accommodation in Moalboal.

133 BOHOL: CABILAO ISLAND

Location 2 km/1¼ miles off the south-west coast of Bohol, 8 km/5 miles west of Tagbilaran, in the Cebu Strait, Western Visayas.

Main species *many trips:* scalloped hammerhead, whitetip reef, blacktip reef, grey reef; *occasional trips:* tawny nurse (*Nebrius ferrugineus*), whale.

Viewing opportunities schooling scalloped hammerheads are the main attraction at Cabilao Island. The best time to see them is immediately after sunrise, or just before sunset. They congregate about 50 m/165 ft from the wall around Cabilao all year, but move up and down in the water column with the seasons and tend to be more accessible to divers from Dec–Jun (the best months are Feb–Apr). At this time they are normally schooling at a depth of about 40–45 m/130–150 ft but, later in the year when the water is a little warmer, they drop to as deep as 75 m/250 ft. Until the last El Niño they were being seen on almost every dive, but there do not seem to be as many of them at the moment. Hammerheads can be seen almost anywhere around this small 8 sq km/3 sq mile island, and just 80 m/260 ft from the beach is a continuous steep wall that is perfect for pelagics. Sharks Point is one of the better-known sites. Lying off the lighthouse on the north-western tip of the island, it is a very pretty dive with a series of overhangs and coral gardens on the edge of a sandflat. The best way to find the sharks is to go down to 30–35 m/100–115 ft and then work along the wall. Lighthouse Wall and House Reef are also good, and several different species of reef shark turn up at these sites. Hammerheads can be seen at a number of other sites near Cabilao Island. Dives at the aptly named Hammerhead Point are normally conducted as drifts along the wall, which drops to about 30 m/100 ft and then drops again to very deep water. The currents here are quite strong and, as well as attracting small schools of as many as 30 scalloped hammerheads, make it a good location for grey reef sharks as well.

Bait/feed no.

Cage no.

Other wildlife various cetaceans, eagle ray, barracuda, jack, mackerel, bigeye and giant trevally, dogtooth tuna, triggerfish, butterflyfish, humphead wrasse.

Best time of year scalloped hammerheads present at diveable depths Dec–Jun (best Feb–Apr); other species year-round.

Dive depth 3–40 m/10–130 ft.

Typical visibility 20–50 m/65–165 ft; varies greatly with weather and plankton levels.

Water temperature 24–30 °C/75–86 °F; coolest Feb–May.

Weather and sea notes currents variable from weak to strong (depending on site and tide); best sea conditions Mar–Jun; dry season Mar–May, rainy season Jun–Feb; tropical storms possible Jul–Sep, with choppy seas, but between storms the weather can be balmy for long periods.

Contact details Polaris Dive Center (www.polaris-dive.com), Virgin Islands of the Philippines (www.diveamust.com).

Travel international flights to Manila or Cebu; regular flights or daily 2-hour ferry from Cebu to Tagbilaran (capital of Bohol) for pick-up, or continue by bus to Mocboc for pick-up; choice of accommodation.

MALAYSIA

134 SABAH: PULAU SIPADAN

Location 35 km/22 miles south of Semporna, off the south-east coast of Sabah (north-east Borneo), in the Celebes Sea.

Main species *most trips:* whitetip reef, grey reef; *many trips:* scalloped hammerhead; *occasional trips:* zebra or leopard (known locally as 'variegated'), thresher, whale, tawny nurse, blacktip reef.

Viewing opportunities the volcanic peak of Sipadan is well known for some of the best shore diving in the world and for guaranteed close encounters with green and hawksbill turtles. Diving from shore is easy, with a 5–10 m/16–33 ft swim (depending on the height of the tide) to a very deep drop–off, and it is not uncommon to see 20–30 turtles in a single dive. But it can also be excellent for sharks and one species or another is seen on almost every dive. Rising 600 m/2000 ft from the seabed, Sipadan is a tiny 12-ha/30-acre mop of rain forest surrounded by a narrow strip of white sand. It takes no more than 20–30 minutes to stroll all the way round the island and nowhere is it more than a few metres above sea level. Sipadan was only really discovered as a potential dive site in the mid-1980s, when Borneo Divers began bringing small groups for overnight camping trips, but now there are several comfortable resorts here and as many as 80 people stay over busy weekends. It can feel a little crowded at times, but its popularity among divers has probably helped to save it from dynamite fishing – which still takes place at coral reefs just a few kilometres away. There are many excellent dive sites, accessible both from shore and on boat dives up to 10 minutes away, and sharks can be seen almost anywhere. The best places are where the currents tend to be strongest, such as Barracuda Point and South Point. Whitetip reef sharks are seen on virtually every dive at both these sites – and are common at the aptly named White Tip Avenue. They are often quite shy and difficult to approach closely, but it is not unusual to see as many as a dozen of them in 5–20 m/16–65 ft of water. There is about an 80 per cent chance of seeing them at other places around the island. Grey reef sharks are the next most common species, seen on about 50 per cent of dives at the same two sites. They tend to be a little deeper, below about 30 m/ 100 ft, but are relatively easy to find. Zebra sharks are usually spotted resting on deep ledges at 25–35 m/ 80–115 ft and are encountered on about 20 per cent of dives. Scalloped hammerheads are probably in the area year-round, but normally stay below 50 m/165 ft. They sometimes rise to 30–40 m/100–130 ft early in the morning and late in the afternoon, though, and some lucky divers have seen as many as 50 in a single school. Various other shark species turn up from time to time, including thresher and whale sharks, and blacktip reef sharks seem to pass by the island every month or two. Juvenile blacktip reef and whitetip reef sharks can be seen relatively easily at any time, by walking through the shallows at first light – where they often patrol in search of food.

Bait/feed no.

Cage no.

Other wildlife green and hawksbill turtles, manta, eagle and blue-spotted rays, huge schools of jack and barracuda, hundreds of species of reef fish, giant clam, 70 genera of corals.

Best time of year sharks present year-round; best chance of scalloped hammerheads and whale sharks late Nov–Jan; best diving Feb–May and Sep–Nov.

Dive depth 3–40 m/10–130 ft plus.

Typical visibility 10–30 m/33–100 ft (average 15 m/ 50 ft); highly variable from day to day; worst late Nov–Jan.

Water temperature 25–29 °C/77–84 °F.

Weather and sea notes calm seas common, but can be choppy (calmest Mar–Aug and Oct–Dec); strong currents (vertical and horizontal) likely at some sites, but unpredictable and may change direction during a single dive (generally strongest Dec–Feb).

Contact details Sepilok Nature Resort (www.sepilok.com), Borneo Divers and Sea Sports (www.jaring.my/bdivers), Pulau Sipadan Resort and Tours (www.sipadan-resort.com), Sipadan Dive Centre (www.sipadandivers.com).

Travel national and international flights to Kota Kinabalu; fly direct to Semporna (or to Tawau, then drive); 45–60-min speedboat trip to Sipadan; choice of resorts on the island.

135 BORNEO BANKS: LAYANG-LAYANG

Location 305 km/190 miles north-west of Kota Kinabalu (capital of the East Malaysia state of Sabah, in Borneo), in the South China Sea.

Main species *many trips:* scalloped hammerhead, grey reef, whitetip reef, zebra or leopard; *occasional trips:* silvertip, whale.

Viewing opportunities Layang-Layang belongs to a group of some 600 islands, reefs and shoals forming Borneo Banks, or the Spratlys as they are sometimes called. But it is one of only about 30 that are permanently above sea level. Stretched across the South China Sea from Borneo north-west to Vietnam, the vast majority of these reefs and shoals are underwater most or all of the time. Layang-Layang (or Terumba Layang-Layang, to give it its full name) actually means 'Swallows' Reef' and this probably refers to the boobies and terns, or sea swallows, that nest on the western tip of the island. It is a low-lying atoll some 7 km/4½ miles long and just over 2 km/1¼ miles across at its widest point. Basically a ring of land surrounding a 60 m/200 ft deep lagoon, it has two channels (known, imaginatively, as New Channel and Old Channel) that open into the sea on the southern side. It is best known for its scalloped hammerheads and spectacular wall diving – the walls are packed with soft corals, gorgonians and fish life and drop to incredible depths of 900–1850 m/2950–6100 ft. The hammerheads can be encountered almost anywhere around the island, although the majority of sightings seem to be off the eastern point at Dog Tooth Lair and at Gorgonian Forest off the north-east point. They are also seen quite frequently at D-Wall on the south-west coast, and there is a cleaning station, where they sometimes hang in the water while reef fish rid them of parasites, off the westernmost point at a site called the Valley. They can be found at any depth, but most sightings of the larger schools (typically 30 or 40 individuals, but sometimes several hundred) tend to be at 30–40 m/100–130 ft (although they are not infrequently seen in much shallower water and also very close to the reef). They swim together, parallel to the reef wall, moving against the prevailing current. After June, when the surface layers are warmer and the hammerheads are even deeper, it is usually inquisitive solitary individuals that appear within the range of sports divers. Silvertips are sometimes seen below 40 m/130 ft as well, and grey reef and whitetip reef sharks are always patrolling backwards and forwards. Whitetips can also be seen at a site known as Shark Cave, between D-Wall and the Valley, where as many as a dozen sometimes lie on top of one another in a deep cavern under the reef.

Bait/feed no.

Cage no.

Other wildlife hawksbill turtle, manta and eagle rays, jack, barracuda, dogtooth tuna, rainbow runner, scorpionfish, lionfish, surgeonfish, stonefish, angelfish, clownfish, pufferfish, unicornfish, grouper.

Best time of year scalloped hammerheads most common within sports-diving limits Mar–Jun, then tend to go deeper; best diving Apr–Sep.

Dive depth 20–40 m/65–130 ft plus.

Typical visibility 10–25 m/33–80 ft.

Water temperature two thermoclines on the walls make significant temperature differences as you descend: 27–29 °C/81–84 °F at surface; 26–28 °C/78–82 °F at 18–24 m/60–80 ft; 23–25 °C/74–77 °F at 27 m/90 ft.

Weather and sea notes currents mild to strong (rip tides in and near channels); normally calm seas and little wind during diving season, but conditions can change quickly; atoll normally closed Nov–Mar due to heavy seas and torrential rain.

Contact details Layang Layang Island Resort (www.layanglayang.com).

Travel international flights to Kota Kinabalu; resort flight to small airstrip on Layang-Layang; only accommodation on the island is Layang Layang Island Resort.

Note Layang-Layang is currently caught up in a dispute between no fewer than six countries: Malaysia, China, Taiwan, Vietnam, the Philippines and Brunei have all staked claims to various parts of Borneo Banks – attracted by its rich fishing grounds, its tactical position in the South China Sea and the high probability of gas and oil in the area. Layang-Layang is part of the region claimed by Malaysia, on the grounds that it is closest to its own landmass, and there has been a Royal Malaysian Naval base at the eastern end of the island since the early 1980s.

THAILAND

136–37 KOH LANTA MARINE NATIONAL PARK: HIN MUANG (PURPLE ROCK) AND HIN DAENG (RED ROCK)

Location 120 km/75 miles from Koh Phuket and 37 km/ 23 miles south-west of Koh Lanta; at the northern end of the Strait of Malacca.

Main species *most trips:* zebra or leopard; *occasional trips:* grey reef, whale.

Viewing opportunities whale shark sightings were once common in Koh Lanta Marine National Park. Although there are 15 islands altogether, two in particular stood out: Hin Muang and Hin Daeng. Just 700 m/2300 ft apart, both sites interrupt the current and cause nutrient-rich upwellings that once attracted whale sharks and a variety of other wildlife. In recent years, however, both whale sharks and grey reef sharks have become very rare. Some experts believe

that too many dive boats in the area have frightened them off, although overfishing by Thai fishermen may also have been to blame. Hin Muang consists of a series of submerged pinnacles (the shallowest rises to within 8 m/26 ft of the surface) on the edge of the deepest drop-off in Thailand (70 m/230 ft and more). It is also known as Purple Rock, after the garden of magnificent purple sea anemones that carpet the top of its largest pinnacle. For several years a young whale shark called Oscar was seen here so regularly that he was virtually adopted by local dive operators. Hin Daeng, unlike its neighbour, breaks the surface by about 3 m/10 ft (although only at low tide). Also known as Red Rock, after the red Dendronephthya soft corals covering its upper walls and slopes, it consists of a series of walls descending in steps to about 35 m/115 ft. Hin Daeng was perhaps the only place in Thailand where as many as 15 grey reef sharks could be seen together in a single school. Despite the loss of whale and grey reef sharks, there are still lots of zebra sharks (or leopard sharks, as they tend to be called in Thailand), particularly around the southern section of Hin Daeng, where they chase one another around the smallest pinnacles (especially during the mating season of Dec–Jan).

Bait/feed no.

Cage no.

Other wildlife various cetaceans, green turtle, black-banded sea snake, manta ray, stingray, barracuda, tuna, longnose hawkfish, lionfish, stonefish, pufferfish, fusilier, common reef octopus, cuttlefish.

Best time of year sharks present year-round; best diving Nov–May.

Dive depth 10–40 m/33–130 ft plus.

Typical visibility 20–40 m/65–130 ft; varies enormously with the current (best when weak).

Water temperature 26–30 °C/78–86 °F.

Weather and sea notes currents tend to be strong (though not constant) and rapidly change direction; sea conditions likely to be choppy; three main seasons: dry (Nov–Mar), hot (Apr–May) and rainy with strong winds (Jun–Oct), when diving can be difficult.

Contact details Fantasea Divers (www.fantasea.net), Koh Lanta Diving Center (www.kolantadivingcenter.com), The Dive Zone (www.thedivezone.com).

Travel accessible on live-aboards from Phuket or day boat from Saladan (Koh Lanta); international flights to Bangkok with connecting flight to Phuket; Koh Lanta can be reached by boat from Koh Phuket, Krabi Town, Koh Phi Phi Don or Baw Baw Mouang; wide choice of accommodation around Phuket and Koh Lanta.

Note in December 2001, a fishing boat, illegally using dynamite to catch fish, caused severe damage to Hin Muang and Hin Daeng.

138 PHI PHI ISLANDS: SHARK POINT

Location a rocky outcrop 8 km/5 miles south-east of Phi Phi Ley; southern end of Phang Nga Bay, midway between Phuket and Krabi; 48 km/30 miles south-east of Phuket, 42 km/26 miles south of Krabi Town, 40 km/25 miles from Ao Nang Beach.

Main species *most trips:* zebra or leopard; *many trips:* blacktip reef, tawny nurse (*Nebrius ferrugineus*); *occasional trips:* whale.

Viewing opportunities there are not many places in the world where snorkellers are virtually guaranteed close encounters with sharks – but this is one of them. Even children over 12 can have a go, if they are sufficiently confident in the water. The local operators have a 95 per cent success rate with zebra sharks (or leopard sharks, as they tend to be called in Thailand), but blacktip reef and tawny nurse sharks turn up with impressive regularity as well. The blacktips are timid, but groups of up to 12 sometimes circle snorkellers; they gain confidence at dusk and dawn, and can be quite scary for the uninitiated. There are even whale sharks passing through the area for a few months each year. The official name for the site is Hin Klai, but it is more commonly known as Phi Phi Shark Point (to avoid confusion with Shark Point off Phuket). A little rocky outcrop, rising only about 1 m/3⅓ ft above the surface at low tide, it consists of a coral reef sloping gently northwards from about 5 m/16 ft to 20 m/65 ft, where the seabed levels out with sand and scattered rocks. The leopard sharks are often sleeping around the reef or in the sand and it is very important not to disturb them: operators ask everyone to approach slowly and to avoid making too much noise or sudden movements. There is also a strict ban on touching. There are several other good places for leopard sharks in the Phi Phi Islands (which is where the Hollywood movie *The Beach* was filmed), including Garang Heng, Koh Yung and Koh Bida Nok.

Bait/feed no.

Cage no.

Other wildlife blue-spotted stingray, golden and undulated moray eels, angelfish, surgeonfish, harlequin sweetlips, blue-lined snapper, titan triggerfish, spiny lobster, cuttlefish, squid.

Best time of year zebra, blacktip reef and tawny nurse present year-round; whale sharks historically Feb–Mar, but present Dec–Apr in the past two years, with sporadic sightings year-round of at least three recognizable individuals.

Dive depth surface (snorkelling) or maximum 18 m/60 ft (diving).

Typical visibility 10–30 m/33–100 ft.

Water temperature 26–30 °C/78–86 °F.

Weather and sea notes current usually weak, but sometimes moderate; three main seasons: dry (Nov–Mar), hot (Apr–May) and rainy with strong winds (Jun–Oct).

Contact details Moskito Diving Center (www.moskitodiving.com), Barakuda Dive Center (www.barakuda.com), Island Divers (www.islanddiverspp.com), Siam UK Trading Co. (http://phi-phi.com/snorkelling/shark-watching.htm).

Travel international flights via Bangkok or direct to Phuket; ferry to Phi Phi from Phuket, Ao Nang or Krabi Town (1½–3 hours depending on boat); wide choice of accommodation.

139 PHUKET: SHARK POINT

Location 30 km/19 miles south-east of Koh Phuket.

Main species *most trips:* zebra or leopard; *occasional trips:* whale.

Viewing opportunities named after its incredibly relaxed zebra sharks (or leopard sharks, as they tend to be called in Thailand), Shark Point is Phuket's most popular day-dive. Since it is the largest island in the country and one of Thailand's main tourist destinations, Phuket's dive sites are usually quite busy – and there are nearly always lots of divers at Shark Point. But it is worth it: not just for the sharks, but for its teeming marine life. The area is considered so important for wildlife that, together with nearby Anemone Reef, it was given marine-sanctuary status in 1992. Its official name is Hin Musang, which means Shark Rock, but the more colloquial name has stuck. The site consists of a small rocky outcrop, with three submerged pinnacles lying in a line from north to south, sitting on the shallow seabed at a depth of about 18–20 m/60–65 ft. The zebra sharks are normally found resting on the sand and are incredibly approachable and easy to observe. If you do not touch or disturb them, they will often stay in one position for many minutes at a time – making them very popular with photographers. Phuket used to be a popular stopover for whale sharks (especially Feb–June), and although there are no longer as many as there used to be, there is always the possibility of a chance encounter.

Bait/feed no.

Cage no.

Other wildlife stingray, moray eel, lionfish, ghost pipefish, snapper, jack, trevally, mackerel, barracuda.

Best time of year sharks present year-round.

Dive depth 6–25 m/20–82 ft.

Typical visibility 5–30 m/16–100 ft.

Water temperature 26–30 °C/78–86 °F.

Weather and sea notes currents usually mild, but can be fairly strong (though you can drift-dive along the line of pinnacles); sea likely to be choppy; three main seasons: dry (Nov–Mar), hot (Apr–May) and rainy with strong winds (Jun–Oct), when diving can be difficult.

Contact details Fantasea Divers (www.fantasea.net), Scuba Quest (www.scuba-quest.com), South East Asia Divers (www.phuketdive.net), Andaman Divers (www.andamandivers.com).

Travel international flights via Bangkok or direct to Phuket; site is 80–90 mins by boat from Phuket; wide choice of accommodation around Phuket (connected to mainland by a bridge).

140–41 SIMILAN AND SURIN ISLANDS (INCLUDING RICHELIEU ROCK)

Location 100 km/62 miles (Similan) and 200 km/ 125 miles (Surin) north-west of Koh Phuket, in the Andaman Sea; just south of the border with Myanmar.

Main species *most trips:* zebra or leopard, whitetip reef, blacktip reef; *many trips:* whale (see main text).

Viewing opportunities these beautiful islands of soft, sandy beaches and thick forest have incredibly rich undersea gardens packed with an enormous variety of invertebrates and fish. They are also excellent for shark watching. The zebra sharks (or leopard sharks, as they tend to be called in Thailand) are particularly approachable as they rest on the sandy seabed between the reefs. It is quite an experience to lie quietly on the sand next to a shark your own size – it is important, though, to resist the temptation to touch. The Similan archipelago consists of nine different islands and, although each has its own name (except Number Five), everyone tends to refer to them simply by number. Including their surrounding waters, they cover an area of about 128 sq km/49 sq miles. They have two very different sides: in the west there are giant granite boulders (stacked on top of each other, creating caverns and swim-throughs), which are literally blanketed in brightly coloured soft corals and sea fans; in the east there are gently sloping hard coral reefs with more subtle, pastel colours. The Surin archipelago is about 100 km/62 miles away and consists of five granite islands and two rocky outcrops, covering a total area of some 135 sq km/52 sq miles (more than three-quarters of which is water). The diving here is similar to that on the east side of the Similans.

The best-known shark dive in this area takes place at Richelieu Rock, about 15 km/9 miles south-east of the Surin Islands, which has a reputation as a magnet for whale sharks. The rock is actually a five-pronged submerged pinnacle, rising from a depth of about 33 m/110 ft; one pinnacle rises above the surface and the others range from 3–10 m/10–33 ft beneath the surface. Small enough to be circumnavigated several times in a single dive, the rock is in the middle of a large expanse of open sea and produces the nutrient-rich upwellings that attract sharks, as well as a mind-boggling array of other fish and invertebrates. Whale sharks have been encountered here more often than at any other location in Thailand and often used to stay around for hours at a time. They frequently circled dive boats for 10–15 minutes at a time, and, on a good day, it was possible to see four or five individuals around this rocky outcrop. Sadly, though, they have not been seen for over a year now and it is feared that they have been taken by fishermen.

Bait/feed no.

Cage no.

Other wildlife various cetaceans, hawksbill turtle, manta, eagle and shovelnose rays, moray eel, stonefish, bearded scorpionfish, ghost pipefish, frogfish, butterflyfish, angelfish, fusilier, orange anthias, clown triggerfish, moorish idol, rainbow runner, tuna, barracuda, jack, trevally, cuttlefish, harlequin shrimp, 200 species of hard coral.

Best time of year whale sharks mainly Feb–May; other shark species present year-round; best diving Nov–May.

Dive depth surface (snorkelling with whale sharks) down to 3–40 m/10–130 ft.

Typical visibility 10–40 m/33–130 ft; generally poorer at Surins (usually 10–20 m/33–65 ft around Richelieu Rock); worst in Mar–Apr when a rise in water temperature results in plankton blooms.

Water temperature 26–30 °C/78–86 °F.

Weather and sea notes moderate to strong currents with swirls and eddies likely, but unpredictable (it is possible to shelter on the opposite side of Richelieu Rock); weakest currents tend to be on east side of Similans; surface conditions can be choppy; three main seasons: dry (Nov–Mar), hot (Apr–May) and rainy with strong winds (Jun–Oct), when diving can be difficult.

Contact details Fantasea Divers (www.fantasea.net), PIDC Divers (www.pidcdivers.com), Genesis Liveaboards (www.genesis1phuket.com), Seafarer Divers (www.seafarer-divers.com).

Travel accessible only on live-aboards from Koh Phuket (Thailand) or Kaw Thaung (Victoria Point on southern tip of Myanmar); international flights to Bangkok (or direct to Phuket) with connecting flights to Phuket or the Thai port of Ranong (then 25-min boat trip to Kaw Thaung); alternatively, 4-hour drive between Koh Phuket and Kaw Thaung.

MYANMAR (BURMA)

142 BURMA BANKS: SILVERTIP BANK

Location 240 km/150 miles north-west of Koh Phuket and 170 km/105 miles from Kaw Thaung; 160 km/100 miles off the west coast of Thailand and Myanmar, in the Andaman Sea.

Main species *most trips:* silvertip, whitetip reef, tawny nurse (*Nebrius ferrugineus*); *many trips:* grey reef, zebra or leopard; *occasional trips:* whale, bull, oceanic whitetip, scalloped hammerhead, tiger.

Viewing opportunities sharks of several different species abound in this underwater paradise of widely separated and completely submerged seamounts surrounded by deep water dropping to 400 m/1300 ft and beyond. The main site for shark watching here is Silvertip Bank, the easternmost of the four diveable banks and the one that is dived most frequently. It more than lives up to its name – there is such a thriving population of silvertips here that it is widely regarded as one of the best places in the world to see them. Some dive operators provide limited amounts of food, and this may encourage more sharks as well as making them more approachable; others do not, but the encounters are still spectacular. There are several ways to enjoy them: if a sufficiently strong current is running, it is possible to drift for 1 km/²⁄₃ mile or more over Silvertip (which is about 1 sq km/¹⁄₂ sq mile in area); alternatively, set up camp among the scattered boulders and rocks and then simply watch. The silvertips will often come in to investigate divers, frequently closer than 6 m/20 ft and sometimes within arm's length. Small groups of tawny nurse sharks, inevitably following one another around nose to tail, can be seen over the top of the bank, and almost anything can turn up in the deeper water beyond. Sharks are also frequently encountered at Roe Bank, which on a good day has huge numbers of reef and oceanic species; at Big Bank, which is excellent for tawny nurse sharks and, with a 2 sq km/³⁄₄ sq mile top, is the largest of the group; and at Rainbow Reef.

Bait/feed sometimes (depending on operator).

Cage no.

Other wildlife various cetaceans, manta and eagle rays, bird and crescent wrasse, batfish, Indian and titan triggerfish, parrotfish, angelfish, fusilier, giant surgeonfish, harlequin and oriental sweetlips.

Best time of year sharks present year-round; best diving Nov–May.

Dive depth 15–35 m/50–115 ft.

Typical visibility 10–30 m/33–100 ft (best Nov–May); better visibility (20–50 m/65–165 ft) west of 50 m/165 ft depth line).

Water temperature 26–30 °C/78–86 °F.

Weather and sea notes current variable, but often strong (especially at Silvertip Bank and all four banks in Jun–Oct) and can change direction very quickly; sea conditions can be quite rough; three main seasons: dry (Nov–Mar), hot (Apr–May) and rainy with strong winds (Jun–Oct), when diving can be difficult.

Contact details Fantasea Divers (www.fantasea.net), Genesis Liveaboards (www.genesis1phuket.com), Scuba Quest (www.scuba-quest.com).

Travel accessible only on live-aboards from Koh Phuket (Thailand) or Kaw Thaung (Victoria Point on southern tip of Myanmar); international flights to Bangkok (or direct to Phuket) with connecting flights to Phuket or the Thai port of Ranong (then 25-min boat trip to Kaw Thaung); alternatively, 4-hour drive between Koh Phuket and Kaw Thaung.

143–4 MERGUI ARCHIPELAGO: WESTERN ROCKY ISLAND AND BLACK ROCK

Location 280 km/175 miles (Western Rocky) and 400 km/250 miles (Black Rock) from Phuket; 75 km/47 miles (Western Rocky) and 165 km/103 miles (Black Rock) from Kaw Thaung; immediately north of the border with Thailand.

Main species *most trips:* whitetip reef, blacktip reef, zebra or leopard, tawny nurse (*Nebrius ferrugineus*); *many trips:* grey reef, bull; *occasional trips:* scalloped hammerhead, silvertip, shortfin mako, whale.

Viewing opportunities sharks are the main attraction at the Mergui Archipelago and there are, indeed, lots of them here (although numbers are declining with heavy pressure from shark fishing). The archipelago comprises hundreds of islands and islets, spanning an area of some 16,360 sq km/6315 sq miles and stretching from Tavoy Island in the north to Myanmar's border with Thailand in the south. The region was closed to foreigners until 1997 and, although it is now safe to explore and dive, relatively little is known about the wildlife and rugged topography below the surface. There are two sites within the archipelago with particularly good shark watching: Western Rocky Island and Black Rock. Western Rocky is the southernmost of the current dive sites and lies in the open ocean. It consists of a main island with a series of pinnacles of varying size

– the four to the east break the surface, but the ones to the south are submerged. It is best known for its resident tawny nurse sharks, which hang around a unique tunnel that runs right through the middle of the island. Divers have to be a bit careful inside because there are normally a couple of nurse sharks blocking at least one of the two exits. But there are lots of other sharks here, too, mainly to the west of the main reef, where the water gets clearer and deeper. It is often possible to see patrolling grey, blacktip and whitetip reef sharks, usually at a depth of around 26–34 m/85–112 ft, and a variety of other species turns up from time to time. Black Rock is often described as a 'high-voltage' dive because, on a good day when there is a never-ending stream of sharks, divers are constantly being buzzed. Lying roughly midway up the archipelago (but as far north as most dive boats venture), it consists of a single rocky outcrop that rises about 20 m/65 ft above the surface and measures some 50–100 m/165–330 ft across. On the south-west side there is a series of gently sloping granite plateaux that drops gradually to 40 m/130 ft and then steeply into the deep blue. The vast majority of sharks here are grey reef, but bull, whitetip reef and silvertip are among the others that make regular appearances.

Bait/feed no.

Cage no.

Other wildlife various cetaceans, white-bellied sea eagle (nest at Western Rocky), black-banded sea snake, manta, eagle, marbled and mangrove rays, stingray, moray eel, ghost pipefish, barracuda, batfish, rainbow runner, tuna, mackerel, trevally, jack, bearded scorpionfish, common reef octopus, lobster.

Best time of year sharks present year-round; best diving Nov–May.

Dive depth 6–40 m/20–130 ft.

Typical visibility 5–30 m/16–100 ft (best in dry season).

Water temperature 26–30 °C/78–86 °F.

Weather and sea notes currents can be strong; sea normally calm, but sometimes choppy at Western Rocky and often rough at Black Rock; three main seasons: dry (Nov–Mar), hot (Apr–May) and rainy with strong winds (Jun–Oct), when diving can be difficult.

Contact details Fantasea Divers (www.fantasea.net), Scuba Quest (www.scuba-quest.com), Genesis Liveaboards (www.genesis1phuket.com).

Travel accessible only on live-aboards from Koh Phuket (Thailand) or Kaw Thaung (Myanmar); international flights to Bangkok; direct flights from Bangkok to Koh Phuket, or from Bangkok to the Thai port of Ranong (4-hour drive from Koh Phuket), then 25-min boat trip to Kaw Thaung.

Note at the time of writing, Western Rocky Island is out of bounds and all dives have been suspended, pending the outcome of a dispute between Thailand and Myanmar.

INDIA

145 ANDAMAN ISLANDS

Location 450 km/280 miles north-west of Koh Phuket; 1100 km/680 miles east of the Indian mainland.

Main species *most trips:* grey reef, whitetip reef, tawny nurse (*Nebrius ferrugineus*); *many trips:* scalloped hammerhead, silvertip, blacktip reef, zebra or leopard; *occasional trips:* oceanic whitetip, whale.

Viewing opportunities after a 50-year period of almost total isolation, the Indian government has decided to allow limited, environmentally friendly tourism in the Andaman Islands. Consequently this is one of the world's newest dive destinations and relatively little is known about its underwater riches. But there do seem to be huge numbers of sharks here, and several species are already being seen with considerable regularity. Consisting of several hundred islands, islets and rocky outcrops, the archipelago stretches some 690 km/430 miles from north to south, so there are long sea journeys between many of the dive sites. Sharks can be seen almost anywhere; indeed, it would be true to say that grey reef, whitetip reef and tawny nurse can be seen virtually everywhere. However, they are particularly common at a few key sites: Narcondam Island (135 km/85 miles east of North Andaman); Barren Island (90 km/56 miles east of Middle Andaman), which is an active volcano with coral that is still recovering from an eruption in the mid-1990s; South Button Island (12 km/7½ miles off South Andaman Island); and Passage Island (in the southern sector between Little Andaman and Rutland). Oceanic whitetips and whale sharks sometimes appear out of the blue at any of the sites near steep drop-offs. Large schools of scalloped hammerheads often patrol deeper water away from the reefs, particularly off South Button, but also sometimes around Barren. Silvertips are frequently encountered around Narcondam and a site called Computer Drop, off the north-west coast of Barren, where large numbers have a habit of suddenly appearing from the depths to investigate divers. Barren is also good for blacktip reef sharks.

Bait/feed no.

Cage no.

Other wildlife various cetaceans, leatherback and hawksbill turtles, black-banded sea snake, manta, eagle and devil rays, dogtooth tuna, bluefin trevally, blue- and golden-banded fusiliers, batfish, titan triggerfish, bumphead parrotfish, Napoleon wrasse, rainbow runner, oriental, spotted and giant sweetlips, barracuda.

Best time of year sharks probably present year-round, but most trips Dec–May.

Dive depth 12–40 m/40–130 ft (depending on site).

Typical visibility 10–40 m/33–130 ft (depending on site – worse nearer to main islands).

Water temperature 23–27 °C/74–81 °F.

Weather and sea notes currents normally weak to moderate, but can be strong and irregular at some sites; three main seasons: dry (Nov–Mar), hot (Apr–May) and rainy with strong winds (Jun–Oct), when diving can be difficult.

Contact details Scuba Quest (www.scuba-quest.com), South East Asia Divers (www.phuketdive.net), Sail Asia Yacht Charters (www.sail-asia.com), Samudra – Centre for Ocean Appreciation and Awareness (www.diveandaman.com).

Travel accessible on live-aboards from Koh Phuket (Thailand) or Port Blair (Andaman Islands); international flights to Bangkok with connecting flight to Phuket (or direct flight to Phuket from some countries); flights from the Indian mainland (Madras or Calcutta) direct to the Andaman Islands; 26 of the islands are inhabited and there is limited accommodation.

Note cruises to the Andaman Islands are always dependent on Indian bureaucracy and may be cancelled at short notice. Most operators require a full boat charter, booked well in advance.

JAPAN

146 OGASAWARA ISLANDS

Location 840 km/520 miles south-west of mainland Japan.

Main species *most trips:* sand tiger, whitetip reef, sandbar (*Carcharhinus plumbeus*); *occasional trips:* scalloped hammerhead.

Viewing opportunities known by some people as the Bonin Islands, and as the Oriental Galápagos by local divers, the Ogasawara Islands are about as far removed from the hustle and bustle of Tokyo as it is possible to get. Lying roughly midway between Japan and Guam, they consist of four main island groups: the Chichijimas, the Keitas, the Hahajimas and the several smaller islands comprising the Volcanoes (best known for Iwojima, where there was fierce fighting during the Second World War). There are more than 90 recognized dive sites in the archipelago and, although many of them are Second World War wreck dives, several are outstanding for sharks. Between them, they have a sightings record approaching 100 per cent for sand tiger, whitetip reef and sandbar sharks (in season), with a 20 per cent record for scalloped hammerheads. The four main sites are: Same-ana (Shark Hole) on Kitanoshima; Sameike (Shark Pond, or Shark Inlet as it is sometimes mistranslated) on Minamijima; Shikahama on Otoutojima; and Kamenokubi on Chichijima. Sand tiger sharks are often found in the cargo holds or other dark areas inside wrecks, but one of the best places to see them is inside Shark Hole – a cave just 5 m/16 ft below the surface; the cave has a white sandy floor and participants have an opportunity during the dive to collect some of the sharks' teeth scattered in the sand. Whitetip reef sharks are best seen at Shark Pond, where as many as 30 gather in a shallow bay just 2 m/7 ft deep; they begin to leave in mid-October, when the water temperature starts to rise. Sandbar sharks and scalloped hammerheads can be seen along the sheer walls in deep-sea sites at Shikahama and Kamenokubi; the sandbar sharks are encountered in groups of up to 20 and are sometimes no deeper than about 20 m/65 ft.

Bait/feed no.

Cage no.

Other wildlife humpback whale (Dec–Mar, outside shark season, though small numbers remain until May), bottlenose dolphin, green turtle (come ashore to lay eggs Apr–May), manta ray, angelfish, jack, butterflyfish.

Best time of year sand tiger and sandbar May–Aug; whitetip reef May–Oct; scalloped hammerhead Jun–Sep.

Dive depth 2–30 m/7–100 ft.

Typical visibility 20–30 m/65–100 ft May–Jun, 30–40 m/100–130 ft Jul–Sep.

Water temperature 22–27 °C/72–81 °F May–Oct.

Weather and sea notes currents mild to strong.

Contact details Kaizin (www.kaizin.com), Charles T. Whipple (www.charlest.whipple.net), Bonin Information Service (www.bonin-islands.com).

Travel international flights to Tokyo; ferry (www.fune.co.jp/ogasawarkaiun) once a week from Takeshiba Kyakusen (Port of Tokyo) to Futami Port on Chichijima in the Ogasawara Islands (28–30 hours); there are plans to build an airport in the archipelago in the future; wide choice of accommodation.

147–151 SHARK PIT, SHARK POINT, SHARK PLACE, BELLE MARE AND WHALE ROCK

Location 855 km/530 miles off the east coast of Madagascar.

Main species *most trips:* grey reef, whitetip reef; *many trips:* bull, blacktip reef; *occasional trips:* scalloped hammerhead, tawny nurse (*Nebrius ferrugineus*).

Viewing opportunities dedicated shark dives began in Mauritius in the late 1980s and there are now several well-established sites. The best known is Shark Pit, a shallow volcanic crater (basically a depression in the seabed) at a depth of about 18 m/ 60 ft (the pit itself is 10 m/33 ft deep), where it is possible to watch as many as 25 grey reef and whitetip reef sharks resting or swimming in slow circles. Whitetip reef sharks are almost guaranteed at Shark Place, or Rempart L'Herbe, which is off the west coast; this is a deep drift dive (42–50 m/140–165 ft) on a pinnacle with steep slopes. Scalloped hammerheads are occasionally seen at Shark Place, as well as around Whale Rock off the north-west coast. Shark Point, which lies opposite Coco Beach on the north-east coast, is good for bull and blacktip reef sharks; divers have reported seeing blacktips mating here on several occasions. Bull sharks are also common around the dive sites off Belle Mare on the east coast.

Bait/feed no.

Cage no.

Other wildlife several ray species, wahoo, tuna.

Best time of year more sharks present in larger numbers in winter (Oct–Mar).

Dive depth 15–25 m/50–80 ft.

Typical visibility 10–40 m/33–130 ft.

Water temperature 20–28 °C/68–82 °F; coolest during winter (best season for sharks); east coast tends to be colder than the west.

Weather and sea notes sea can be too rough to dive off the east coast in Jul–Aug; Shark Pit only diveable in calm weather; there is often a strong surge and whirlpool effect at Pidgeon House Rock; some current likely.

Contact details Aquarius Diving (www.aquarius-diving.com), Sinbad (kuxville@intnet.mu), Cap Divers (www.wardhouses.com/ wardhouses/ diving.htm), Dive Mauritius (www.divemauritius.com).

Travel international flights to airport in south-eastern Mauritius; buses and taxis to other parts of the island; wide choice of accommodation.

The Seychelles (Map 9)

152 INNER ISLANDS: MARIE ANNE ISLAND

Location east of Praslin, in the north-east corner of the archipelago; 1600 km/990 miles east of Kenya.

Main species *most trips:* grey reef; *many trips:* tawny nurse (*Nebrius ferrugineus*), whitetip reef, blacktip reef.

Viewing opportunities close encounters with grey reef sharks are virtually guaranteed at a site called South Marianne, just off the coast of Marie Anne Island. This is one of the so-called Inner Islands of the Seychelles and is composed of granite (unlike the coral atolls of the outlying islands). The underwater granite rock formations here are dramatic – one particular section has been dubbed the Cathedral – but it is the resident population of sharks that attracts most divers. There could be as many as 100 living in the area, although it is more common to see 10–25 patrolling in a single dive. Some of them are 2 m/7 ft in length and they are often very inquisitive, coming to within an arm's length of visiting divers. Although the grey reef are by far the most common, it is not impossible to encounter three or even four different shark species on a good day.

Bait/feed no.

Cage no.

Other wildlife hawksbill turtle, eagle ray, stingray, Napoleon wrasse, bumphead parrotfish, fusilier, snapper, jack, angelfish, butterflyfish, octopus.

Best time of year sharks present year-round; best diving Sep–May.

Dive depth 6–26 m/20–85 ft.

Typical visibility 6–20 m/20–65 ft.

Water temperature 24–27 °C/75–80 °F.

Weather and sea notes no strong currents; wettest months generally Dec–Feb.

Contact details Seychelles Underwater Centre (www.diveseychelles.com.sc), Big Blue Divers (www.bigbluedivers.net), MV Indian Ocean Explorer (www.ioexplorer.com), Octopus Dive Centre (www.octopusdiving.com), La Digue Lodge Dive Centre (www.ladigue.sc)

Travel accessible by live-aboard or long day trips from Mahé, La Digue or Praslin; international flights to Mahé; flight to Praslin (40 mins by boat from site); wide choice of accommodation.

153 INNER ISLANDS: ST ANNE MARINE NATIONAL PARK

Location near Victoria (the capital of the Seychelles); 1130 km/700 miles north-east of Madagascar; 1600 km/990 miles east of Kenya.

Main species *most trips:* whale; *occasional trips:* whitetip reef.

Viewing opportunities large numbers of whale sharks gather to feed amazingly close to the capital of the Seychelles, twice every year. They can be seen almost anywhere around the 115 islands and islets in the archipelago, but historically the biggest concentration has been within 500 m/1640 ft of shore around the so-called Inner Islands. The visible tips of mountain peaks that were originally located on the giant continent of Gondwanaland, these are the most northerly islands in the Seychelles and include the capital island of Mahé as well as Praslin and La Digue. The centrepoint is St Anne Marine National Park, which encompasses six small, granite islands (St Anne, Long, Beacon, Round, Cerf and Moyenne) and seems to be a particular hotspot for the sharks. They gather here for two periods, during Jul–Aug and Nov–Dec, and form one of the densest populations of whale sharks in the world. They are here for the massive plankton blooms that occur in the park at these times of year and there can be a dozen or more in the same area at one time. Small groups of tourists are taken out to snorkel with the sharks, which range in length from 2–12 m/7–40 ft and often stop in mid-water and assume an almost vertical position when they are approached. Unlike their contemporaries at Ningaloo, they often feed on small stinging plankton (a good reason for snorkellers to wear full wetsuits in the water) and weave and turn rather than swim in straight lines. But they are easy to approach and it is not unknown to swim with several individuals during a single trip. Some operators use microlight aircraft to locate the sharks, and then direct their boats to them, and this is really the only way to be sure of finding them (although, of course, the use of microlights is severely limited by adverse weather conditions). Sometimes everyone is in the water with a shark within 15 minutes of leaving shore, but occasionally no sharks at all are found (especially when microlights are not being used). The whale sharks in the shallow waters of the park are the subject of a long-term study by the Marine Conservation Society Seychelles (incorporating the Shark Research Institute Seychelles) with support from the Seychelles Underwater Centre and the Indian Ocean Explorer. There are opportunities to join the research team for a day or a week to learn about whale shark biology and ecology and to help with their work. While the St Anne Marine National Park has an impressive population of whale sharks, there may well be large numbers in other parts of the Seychelles – it is just that there are not as many boats out looking for them. In fact, in 2001, the majority of whale-shark sightings were off the south-western tip of Mahé, around Port Launay National Park between Conception Island and Matoopa Point, but whether this is exceptional or the beginning of a new trend is uncertain.

Bait/feed no.

Cage no.

Other wildlife hawksbill turtle, schools of jacks and trevally, many remoras and cobias around the sharks.

Best time of year sharks present Jul–Aug and Nov–Dec (and a small number of individuals between these two periods); peak numbers Aug and Nov.

Dive depth surface (snorkelling).

Typical visibility 6–20 m/20–65 ft.

Water temperature 24–26 °C/75–78 °F May–Sep, 26–29 °C/78–84 °F Oct–Apr.

Weather and sea notes no significant currents; seas calmest Mar–May and Sep–Nov; strong south-easterlies in Aug prevent microlight flying; wettest months generally Dec–Feb.

Contact details Seychelles Underwater Centre (www.diveseychelles.com.sc), Island Ventures Dive Seychelles (www.islandventures.net), MV Illusions (http://mvillusions.africa.co.za), Big Blue Divers (www.bigbluedivers.net), MV Indian Ocean Explorer (www.ioexplorer.com), Marine Conservation Society Seychelles (www.mcss.sc).

Travel encounter programmes normally run from Mahé; international flights to Victoria (Mahé); wide choice of accommodation in the area.

154 ALDABRA ATOLL

Location 400 km/250 miles north-west of Madagascar; 680 km/420 miles east of Tanzania; 1150 km/715 miles south-west of Victoria (capital of the Seychelles, on the island of Mahé).

Main species *many trips:* grey reef, blacktip reef, whitetip reef; *occasional trips:* tawny nurse (*Nebrius ferrugineus*), silvertip, scalloped hammerhead, tiger, bull.

Viewing opportunities Aldabra is one of four main island clusters, far away from the main archipelago of the Seychelles: Aldabra, Assumption, Cosmoledo and

Astove. Unlike the so-called Inner Islands, which are made of granite, these outlying islands are coral atolls. Aldabra itself consists of four large coral islands enclosing an enormous shallow lagoon, with more than a dozen smaller islands inside. The entire atoll is surrounded by an outer reef. Altogether, it measures some 34 km/21 miles long and 14.5 km/9 miles wide. A World Heritage Site and home to no fewer than 150,000 giant tortoises (more than anywhere else in the world), it is one of the largest coral atolls in the world. The lagoon is Aldabra's heart and is so big (covering an area of 14,000 ha/34,580 acres) that is more like an inland sea – large enough for the whole of Manhattan to fit inside. It is tidal and twice every day is emptied and filled through four deep, narrow channels between the islands: Main (or Grand Passé), East, West and Johnny (probably a corruption of Gionnet). At high tide, seawater fills the lagoon to a depth of about 3 m/10 ft; at low tide, it is 80 per cent dry. Sediment and nutrients flowing in and out change the colour of the water from emerald green at high tide to crystal blue at low tide, and the rush of water brings sharks. Some estimates suggest that literally thousands of reef sharks of several different species enter the lagoon and, at low tide, they can be seen in water barely deep enough to cover their dorsal fins. Unfortunately, sharks are not encountered as frequently on dives here as such estimates would imply. In fact, the best way to see them is probably to wade around in the shallows through the beds of turtle grass or near the mangroves, where there are lots of small blacktip reef sharks (around 1 m/3⅓ ft in length). They will literally swim between your legs if you let them and seem too intent on hunting small reef fish to even think about nibbling human toes. Nevertheless, many divers have had good encounters with sharks while drift-diving through the channels into the lagoon. Timing is critical – too early or too late and you either have a frustratingly slow ride or end up in a dangerous current that can exceed 6 knots. The channels are steep-sided and about 18–20 m/60–65 ft deep. A dive on the steepest parts of the outer wall can sometimes result in sightings of schools of up to 20 scalloped hammerheads (although they tend to be seen more often at Astove and Cosmoledo); this is also where a variety of other species, including silvertip, tiger and bull sharks, are encountered from time to time.

Bait/feed no.

Cage no.

Other wildlife spectacular seabird colonies and endemic terrestrial birds onshore; giant tortoise, various cetaceans, dugong (occasionally), green and hawksbill turtles, manta and spotted eagle rays, stingray, potato cod, barracuda, grouper, trevally, batfish, yellow-striped snapper, surgeonfish, gold-lined sea bream, titan triggerfish, hawkfish, parrotfish, sea goldie, robber crab.

Best time of year Mar–Apr and Oct–Nov.

Dive depth 15–25 m/50–80 ft.

Typical visibility 20–50 m/65–165 ft; visibility in the channels best on the ebb tide, poorer with the flood tide.

Water temperature 24–29 °C/75–84 °F.

Weather and sea notes tidal currents in the four channels can be extremely strong (varying according to the state of the tide – best dived when about 3 knots); seas calmest Mar–Apr and Oct–Nov; wettest months generally Nov–Apr (most rain Dec–Feb).

Contact details MV Illusions (http://mvillusions.africa.co.za), Indian Ocean Explorer (www.ioexplorer.com).

Travel accessible only by live-aboard; international flights to Mahé; connecting flight to Assumption (3 hours) then boat to Aldabra (3 hours), or boat from Mahé to Aldabra (4 days); limited accommodation is planned for Aldabra and Assumption in the future.

155 FAADHIPPOLHU (LHAVIYANI) ATOLL: FUSHIFARU THILA

Location north-eastern corner of Faadhippolhu Atoll; north of Malé.

Main species *most trips:* whitetip reef, grey reef; *many trips:* scalloped hammerhead, tawny nurse; *occasional trips:* silvertip, blacktip reef, leopard, great hammerhead, guitar, tiger, whale.

Viewing opportunities there are several outstanding dive sites within a few hundred metres of Fushifaru Thila, including Fushifaru Giri, Fushifaru Corner and Fushifaru Channel. These are all good for sharks. The *thila* (an oval or round submerged reef) itself is about 150 m/490 ft long and 50 m/165 ft wide and is 10–15 m/33–50 ft below the surface. It lies in a 450 m/1480 ft wide channel within a protected marine area. The best spot for shark action is along the north-eastern edge, facing the open ocean, at the entrance to the atoll. Divers descending to a depth of about 30 m/100 ft are likely to see grey reef sharks patrolling the cliff edge and, if the current is sufficiently strong and flowing into the atoll, scalloped hammerheads. A wide variety of other shark species turns up from time to time. The sandy bottom around the *thila*, at a depth of about 20 m/65 ft, is excellent for whitetip reef sharks, and tawny nurse sharks can often be seen around the periphery. There are also a number of cleaner stations on the *thila*, which manta rays often visit (mainly May–Nov). A short distance to the north-west is Fushifaru Corner, good for grey reef sharks where the outside reef drops away sharply, and there is an exciting drift dive in the company of grey reef sharks as they hunt in the currents that sweep through Fushifaru Channel.

Bait/feed no.

Cage no.

Other wildlife long-snouted spinner dolphin, bottlenose dolphin, manta ray, eagle ray, stingray, barracuda, sea turtles, Napoleon wrasse, abundant reef fish.

Best time of year sharks present year-round (north-east monsoon slightly better).

Dive depth 15–30 m/50–100 ft.

Typical visibility 15–25 m/50–80 ft.

Water temperature 27–30 °C/81–86 °F.

Weather and sea notes year divided into two monsoon periods: north-east (Dec–Apr) and south-west (May–Nov); north-east monsoon is driest and currents generally flow east to west; south-west monsoon brings more rain, occasional strong winds and frequent moderate to rough seas, and currents generally flow west to east; best water visibility and most calm, windless days tend to be during transition month of Apr. Currents can be extremely strong. Sharks best when current flowing into the atoll, but mantas best when flowing outside.

Contact details ProDivers Maldives (www.prodivers.com), Palm Beach (www.palmbeachmaldives.com/diving/diving.htm), Kanuhuraa (www.hellomaldives.com/resorts/kanuhuraa/index_diving_subventures_kanuhura.htm), Seafari Adventures (www.seafariadventures. com).

Travel nearest resorts are Palm Beach and Kanuhuraa (25 mins from the site by dive boat), but Komandoo and Kuredu are also close (40 mins). International flights to the capital Malé (via Dubai, Colombo, Singapore and other Asian cities or by charter), then easy access to any of the four resorts in Faadhippolhu Atoll by seaplane (45 mins) or speedboat (4–5 hours).

Note ProDivers (on Kuredu and Komandoo) is reputed to be the largest dive school in Asia and offers a special shark and ray course sanctioned by PADI.

156–157 SOUTH MAALHOSMADULU (BAA) ATOLL: DHIGALI HAA/HORUBADHOO THILA AND SHARK NURSERY

Location inside Baa Atoll, towards the east; north-west of Malé.

Main species *many trips:* grey reef, tawny nurse (*Nebrius ferrugineus*); *occasional trips:* whale.

Viewing opportunities this used to be a very popular site for shark watching, until fishermen fished most of the resident grey reef sharks. In December 1999 the Maldivian government stepped in to provide official protection and, although the sharks are not as common as they once were, they are back again in good numbers. This is a classic *thila* (an underwater reef inside an atoll), rising to within 7 m/23 ft of the surface, and it lies in a wide channel far from any other *thila* or reef. It seems to act as a magnet to wildlife and is often crowded with a wide variety of schooling fish. Roughly oval in shape, and measuring some 80 × 30 m/260 × 100 ft, it is small enough to circumnavigate in a single dive. Sharks can be seen here year-round, but the best time for seeing them is during the north-east monsoon, when a strong current strikes the reef on the north-east side. The stronger the current, the better the action. There is another site a few kilometres to the north-east, called Shark Nursery, which is perhaps even more exciting. A typical dive during the north-east monsoon results in close encounters with as many as 30 predominantly juvenile (but also adult) grey reef sharks. Shark Nursery is also good for tawny nurse sharks. Whale sharks are sometimes encountered, especially in May–Nov, inside the atoll.

Bait/feed no.

Cage no.

Other wildlife long-snouted spinner dolphin, bottlenose dolphin, manta (May–Nov at Shark Nursery) and eagle rays, stingray, guitarfish, large schools of bigeye trevally, yellowfin fusiliers and batfish, dogtooth tuna, barracuda.

Best time of year sharks present year-round, but best in north-east monsoon (Dec–Apr); whale sharks mainly May–Nov.

Dive depth 7–30 m/23–100 ft.

Typical visibility 20–30 m/65–100 ft.

Water temperature 27–30 °C/81–86 °F.

Weather and sea notes year divided into two monsoon periods: north-east (Dec–Apr) and south-west (May–Nov); north-east monsoon is driest and currents generally flow east to west; south-west monsoon brings more rain, occasional strong winds and frequent moderate to rough seas, and currents generally flow west to east; best water visibility and most calm, windless days tend to be during the transition month of Apr; currents can be extremely strong (especially Dec–Feb); sea can be choppy when the wind is against the tide.

Contact details Soleni Dive Centre (www.soleni.com), Delphis Diving (www.delphisdiving.com).

Travel nearest resort is Sonevafushi, in Baa Atoll; international flights to the capital Malé (via Dubai, Colombo, Singapore and other Asian cities or by charter), then access to the resort by seaplane (30–40 mins).

158 NORTH MALÉ (KAAFU) ATOLL: MAKUNUDHU CHANNEL

Location north-west of the atoll, immediately south of Himmiya Faru; north of Malé.

Main species *most trips:* grey reef, whitetip reef; *many trips:* tawny nurse (*Nebrius ferrugineus*), zebra; *occasional trips:* silvertip.

Viewing opportunities there are several excellent shark dives in the Makunudhu Channel and, during the south-west monsoon, when the best sites are being pounded by the inflowing current, several different species are seen on almost every dive. The best place is probably Shark Point, or Kuda Thila, a finger of reef rising to within 13 m/43 ft of the surface and extending into the channel. Unlike a classic *thila* (an underwater reef formed inside an atoll), it is connected to the main reef by a sand saddle. Roughly oval in shape, and some 50 m/165 ft long, it is steeply sloping on the west and south sides. When there is a strong current, as many as 20–30 whitetip reef and grey reef sharks can be seen over the valley leading to this saddle. Most of the sharks are juveniles, but there are adults among them, too. The dive is usually conducted as a drift, but it is possible to hang on to the dead coral and watch the action from below. Silvertips occasionally turn up as well. At a depth of about 27 m/90 ft there is a large overhang, which is often frequented by tawny nurse sharks – although they are often difficult to spot in the dark interior. There is also a cleaning station nearby, where cleaner wrasse can be seen attending to grey reef and whitetip reef sharks. Several kilometres farther north, near Akirifushi, there is a sandy basin that is often used by resting zebra sharks (known, appropriately, as Sharks' Sleeping Place).

Bait/feed no.

Cage no.

Other wildlife long-snouted spinner dolphin, bottle-nose dolphin, hawksbill turtle, eagle ray, stingray.

Best time of year south-west monsoon (May–Nov).

Dive depth 13–25 m/43–80 ft.

Typical visibility 20–30 m/65–100 ft (varies enormously with the direction of the current – best with an inflowing one).

Water temperature 27–30 °C/81–86 °F.

Weather and sea notes year divided into two monsoon periods: north-east (Dec–Apr) and south-west (May–Nov); north-east monsoon is driest and currents generally flow east to west; south-west monsoon brings more rain, occasional strong winds and frequent moderate to rough seas, and currents generally flow west to east; best water visibility and most calm, windless days tend to be during the transition month of Apr; current is funnelled through the channel and becomes quite fierce at dive sites.

Contact details Eriyadu Dive Centre (www.wernerlau.com/new/eriyadu.uk/info/basis.htm), Deep Blue Dive Centre (www.hellomaldives.com/resorts/makunudhu/contents.htm), Euro Divers (www.euro-divers.com/english).

Travel nearest resorts are Makunudhu, Eriyadu, Reethi Rah and Hembadhoo, in North Malé Atoll; international flights to the capital Malé (via Dubai, Colombo, Singapore and other Asian cities or by charter), then access to the resorts by speedboat (45 mins for Reethi Rah, 50 mins for Makunudhu and Eriyadu, and 1 hour 15 mins for Hembadhoo) or *dhoni* (2 hours 15 mins for Reethi Rah).

159 NORTH MALÉ (KAAFU) ATOLL: BODU HITHI THILA

Location mid-western side of North Malé Atoll, in the middle of Hithi Channel; north-west of Malé.

Main species *most trips:* whitetip reef; *many trips:* whale, tawny nurse (*Nebrius ferrugineus*).

Viewing opportunities this is a particularly good site for watching manta rays and, in recent years, has proved to be good for whale sharks, too. Measuring some 300 m/985 ft in diameter and rising to within 12 m/40 ft of the surface, Bodu Hithi Thila is one of several large and many small *thilas* (an oval or round submerged reef) in Bodu Hithi Channel. When the current is flowing out of North Malé Atoll, in the north-east monsoon, the channel acts as a funnel and creates plankton-rich waters around the *thila*. This is where the mantas and whale sharks gather to feed (the mantas can also be seen at their cleaning stations near the centre of the *thila* – although they will only approach if divers stay to one side). There are also considerable numbers of whitetip reef sharks along the southern side of the atoll: look for them along the sandy floor at a depth of 15–20 m/50–65 ft in any one of the three bays. There is also a cave here, at a depth of about 17 m/55 ft, which is a popular hangout for tawny nurse sharks.

Bait/feed no.

Cage no.

Other wildlife long-snouted spinner dolphin, bottlenose dolphin, sea turtles, manta ray, batfish, Napoleon wrasse.

Best time of year north-east monsoon (Dec–Apr).

Dive depth 12–20 m/40–65 ft.

Typical visibility 20 m/65 ft.

Water temperature 27–30 °C/81–86 °F.

Weather and sea notes year divided into two monsoon periods: north-east (Dec–Apr) and south-west (May–Nov); north-east monsoon is driest and currents generally flow east to west; south-west monsoon brings more rain, occasional strong winds and frequent moderate to rough seas, and currents generally flow west to east; best water visibility and most calm, windless days tend to be during the transition month of Apr.

Contact details Boduhithi Coral Island (www.hellomaldives.com/resorts/boduhithi/), Taj Coral Reef Resort (www.tajhotels.com), Seafari Adventures (www.seafariadventures.com).

Travel nearest resorts are Boduhithi, Kudahithi and Hembadhoo, and the site is within easy reach of several other resorts in North Malé Atoll; international flights to the capital Malé (via Dubai, Colombo, Singapore and other Asian cities or by charter); easy access to Boduhithi and Kudahithi (60 mins) and Hembadhoo (1¼ hours) by speedboat.

160 NORTH MALÉ (KAAFU) ATOLL: RASFARI

Location mid-western side of North Malé Atoll; north-west of Malé.

Main species *most trips:* grey reef, whitetip reef, blacktip reef; *occasional trips:* silvertip, oceanic whitetip.

Viewing opportunities on the ocean side of Rasfari, just to the north of Rasfari Channel, is a protected marine area with an abundance of sharks of several different species. Deep-water pelagics are best seen a little beyond the perimeter reef: some 70 m/230 ft outside is a small circular reef, rather like a *thila* but much deeper, which sits on a gently sloping plateau and is a magnet for large fish. The top is 25–28 m/80–90 ft below the surface and makes a great viewing platform. Divers can look over the drop-off into blue water and are likely to encounter good numbers of grey reef sharks (20 or more on a good day) and may be lucky enough to see a variety of other species that turn up from time to time. The sand-filled gullies between the *thila* and main reef are good for whitetip and blacktip reef sharks, which frequently rest on the seabed here.

Bait/feed no.

Cage no.

Other wildlife long-snouted spinner dolphin, bottlenose dolphin, eagle ray, stingray, garden eel (in sand-filled gullies between circular reef and perimeter reef), big-eye trevally, great barracuda, abundant reef fish; oceanic triggerfish lay their eggs on deeper sandy slopes (usually about a week before full moon).

Best time of year south-west monsoon (May–Nov).

Dive depth 25–27 m/80–90 ft.

Typical visibility 20–30 m/65–100 ft.

Water temperature 27–30 °C/81–86 °F.

Weather and sea notes year divided into two monsoon periods: north-east (Dec–Apr) and south-west (May–Nov); north-east monsoon is driest and currents generally flow east to west; south-west monsoon brings more rain, occasional strong winds and frequent moderate to rough seas, and currents generally flow west to east; best water visibility and most calm, windless days tend to be during transition month of Apr. The small circular reef can be difficult to reach in strong currents (often strongest on the corner of Rasfari Channel) and big swells are fairly common during south-west monsoon.

Contact details Nakatcha Island Resort (www.mal-dives.com/nakatcha), Seafari Adventures (www.seafariadventures.com), Maldives Scuba Tours (www.scubascuba.com).

Travel nearest resorts are Nakatchafushi (15 mins from the site by dive boat) and Kudahithi (25 mins), but Boduhithi is also nearby (35 mins) and the site is within easy reach of several other resorts in North Malé Atoll. International flights to the capital Malé (via Dubai, Colombo, Singapore and other Asian cities or by charter), then easy access to Nakatchafushi by speedboat (50 mins) or *dhoni* (1¾ hours), and to Kudahithi and Boduhithi by speedboat (1 hour).

161 NORTH MALÉ (KAAFU) ATOLL: MANTA POINT

Location south-eastern North Malé Atoll; 12 km/7½ miles north of Malé.

Main species *most trips:* whitetip reef; *many trips:* whale shark, tawny nurse (*Nebrius ferrugineus*); *occasional trips:* blacktip reef.

Viewing opportunities as its popular name suggests, Manta Point is best known for manta rays, which gather in considerable numbers at this enormous cleaning station during the south-west monsoon (May–Nov). But this is also a good site for whale sharks, and several other shark species occur here as well. Also known as Lankanfinolhu Faru, or Lankan Reef, the top of Manta Point is 12 m/40 ft below the surface and slopes gently down to the atoll plate at about 40 m/130 ft. Whale sharks are normally encountered away from the reef, on the side facing the open ocean, while whitetip reef sharks can be found over the sandy section inside the atoll, typically at a depth of about 20 m/65 ft.

Bait/feed no.

Cage no.

Other wildlife long-snouted spinner dolphin, bottlenose dolphin, manta ray, eagle ray, moray eel, Napoleon wrasse, sea turtles, abundant reef fish.

Best time of year south-west monsoon (May–Nov).

Dive depth up to 20 m/65 ft.

Typical visibility 20–30 m/65–100 ft.

Water temperature 27–30 °C/81–86 °F.

Weather and sea notes year divided into two monsoon periods: north-east (Dec–Apr) and south-west (May–Nov); north-east monsoon is driest and currents generally flow east to west; south-west monsoon brings more rain, occasional strong winds and frequent moderate to rough seas, and currents generally flow west to east; best water visibility and most calm, windless days tend to be during transition month of Apr. Strong currents at the reef are common.

Contact details Delphis Diving (www.delphisdiving.com), T.G.I. Dive Centre (www.tgidiving.com), Euro Divers (www.euro-divers.com/english), Dive Bandos (www.bandos.com/diving.html).

Travel nearest resort is Paradise (10 mins from the site by dive boat), but Hudhuveli (20 mins) and Full Moon, Bandos, Club Med, Kurumba, Thulhagiri and others are all within easy reach (20–35 mins). All these resorts are in North Malé Atoll. International flights to the capital Malé (via Dubai, Colombo, Singapore and other Asian cities or by charter), then easy access to any of the resorts mentioned by speedboat (15–20 mins) or *dhoni* (35–55 mins).

162 NORTH MALÉ (KAAFU) ATOLL: LION'S HEAD

Location near southernmost point of North Malé Atoll; less than 10 km/6 miles west of Malé.

Main species *many trips:* whitetip reef, blacktip reef, grey reef.

Viewing opportunities in the days when grey reef sharks were fed almost daily at Lion's Head, it was probably the best-known shark dive in the Maldives. The sharks used to come up from deeper water expecting to be given free handouts. But there is virtually no shark feeding in the country now and, since the feeds at Lion's Head have stopped, grey reef sharks are seen far less frequently. Whitetip reef and blacktip reef can still be encountered here, though. Most dives take place at an overhang, shaped vaguely like a lion's head, which faces the 500 m/1640 ft deep Vaadhoo Channel between North Malé and South Malé atolls. There are plenty of sharks at the point of entry, and many divers like to sit on a nearby ledge at about 10 m/33 ft to watch them.

Bait/feed no.

Cage no.

Other wildlife long-snouted spinner dolphin, bottlenose dolphin, hawksbill turtle, abundant reef fish.

Best time of year sharks present year-round, but diving can be difficult in strong winds during south-west monsoon (May–Nov).

Dive depth 10–15 m/33–50 ft.

Typical visibility 20–30 m/65–100 ft.

Water temperature 27–30 °C/81–86 °F.

Weather and sea notes year divided into two monsoon periods: north-east (Dec–Apr) and south-west (May–Nov); north-east monsoon is driest and currents generally flow east to west; south-west monsoon brings more rain, occasional strong winds and frequent moderate to rough seas, and currents generally flow west to east; best water visibility and most calm, windless days tend to be during transition month of Apr. Strong currents are possible.

Contact details Euro Divers (www.eurodivers.com), Full Moon Beach Resort (www.unisurf.com/fullmoon/intro.htm), Club Med (clubmed@dhivehinet.net.mv), Maldives Scuba Tours (www.scubascuba.com), Seafari Adventures (www.seafariadventures.com).

Travel nearest resort is Giravaru (15 mins from the site by dive boat), but Kurumba Village, Full Moon and Club Med are also close (40–45 mins). All these resorts are in North Malé Atoll. Laguna Beach and Vaadhoo are just under 5 km/3 miles away in South Malé Atoll, on the other side of Vaadhoo Channel. International flights to the capital Malé (via Dubai, Colombo, Singapore and other Asian cities or by charter), then easy access to any of the nearby resorts by speedboat (15–20 mins) or *dhoni* (35–45 mins).

Note there is another good site for grey reef sharks, Old Shark Point, less than 5 km/3 miles away. Located on the south-east corner of Thila Fushi Channel, it is best for shark action at a depth of 20–30 m/65–100 ft when the current is flowing into the atoll. The site is exposed in south-westerly conditions and divers may experience strong, turbulent currents.

163 SOUTH MALÉ (KAAFU) ATOLL: EMBUDU CHANNEL

Location north-eastern corner of South Malé Atoll; immediately south of Malé.

Main species *most trips:* grey reef, whitetip reef.

Viewing opportunities the north-eastern corner of South Malé Atoll is well known for its sharks. There are several good dive sites, but perhaps the best known is Embudu Channel, a protected marine area. Most of the shark action takes place at Shark Point, on the southern side of the channel entrance. Where the atoll plate drops away into blue water it is possible to

wait quietly (at a depth of 27–30 m/90–100 ft) and watch the sharks and other large pelagics cruising past. Most divers watch the sharks for a while and then ascend to about 15 m/50 ft to experience a 2-km/1.2-mile drift dive through the channel – known locally as the Embudu Express. This is fast and exciting during the north-east monsoon (Dec–Apr) and it is not unusual to be accompanied by grey reef sharks at least part of the way (the stronger the current, the more sharks). The dive ends by surfacing in the shallows of the atoll reef. Whitetip reef sharks are common in the area and often encountered on this dive. Grey reef sharks can also be found on the ocean side of Embudu Thila, which lies north of Shark Point in the channel entrance.

Bait/feed no.

Cage no.

Other wildlife long-snouted spinner dolphin, bottlenose dolphin, eagle ray, stingray, Napoleon wrasse, abundant reef fish.

Best time of year sharks present year-round, but best time north-east monsoon (Dec–Apr) and Sep–Oct.

Dive depth 27–36 m/90–120 ft.

Typical visibility 25–30 m/80–100 ft.

Water temperature 27–30 °C/81–86 °F.

Weather and sea notes year divided into two monsoon periods: north-east (Dec–Apr) and south-west (May–Nov); north-east monsoon is driest and currents generally flow east to west; south-west monsoon brings more rain, and currents generally flow west to east; Embudu Express best when current flowing into the atoll (currents can be very strong).

Contact details Delphis Diving (www.delphisdiving.com), Diverland Embudu (www.diverland.de), Vadoo I. Resort Diving Paradise (www.visitmaldives.com/resorts/is_vadoo.html), Euro Divers (www.euro-divers.com/english), Seafari Adventures (www.seafariadventures.com).

Travel nearest resorts are Embudu Village and Taj Lagoon (both about 10 mins from the site by dive boat), but also accessible from Vadoo (45 mins) and Laguna Beach (55 mins). All these resorts are in South Malé Atoll. Several resorts (including Kurumba Village and Full Moon Beach) in North Malé are also within reach. International flights to the capital Malé (via Dubai, Colombo, Singapore and other Asian cities or by charter), then access to Embudu Village (35 mins by *dhoni*), Taj Lagoon (20 mins by speedboat), and Vadoo and Laguna Beach (both 20 mins by speedboat or 55 mins by *dhoni*).

Note there is an easier version of the Embudu Express, suitable for less experienced divers, which begins farther round on the outside reef.

164 SOUTH MALÉ (KAAFU) ATOLL: GURAIDHOO CHANNEL

Location south-eastern corner of the atoll; south of Malé.

Main species *most trips:* grey reef; *many trips:* whitetip reef; *occasional trips:* scalloped hammerhead, blacktip reef, whale.

Viewing opportunities there are two channels south of Guraidhoo (separated by a large reef) and the southern one has a well-deserved reputation for sharks. Some 300 m/1000 ft across, and with sheer sides, it can only be explored by drifting through in the strong current. But it is the current that attracts the sharks. They tend to gather where the channel meets the ocean drop-off and it is possible to watch them feeding from inside a large cave on the corner, at a depth of about 16 m/53 ft, before beginning the drift (looking down on the sharks, which are normally at 25–35 m/80–115 ft). Afterwards, as you glide through the channel, look out for the whitetip reef sharks that frequently hang out near the bottom at about 35 m/115 ft.

Bait/feed no.

Cage no.

Other wildlife long-snouted spinner dolphin, bottlenose dolphin, eagle ray, sailfish, grouper, Napoleon and humphead wrasse, large schools of oriental sweetlips.

Best time of year north-east monsoon (Dec–Apr).

Dive depth 15–30 m/50–100 ft.

Typical visibility 25–35 m/80–115 ft.

Water temperature 27–30 °C/81–86 °F.

Weather and sea notes year divided into two monsoon periods: north-east (Dec–Apr) and south-west (May–Nov); north-east monsoon is driest and currents generally flow east to west; south-west monsoon brings more rain, occasional strong winds and frequent moderate to rough seas, and currents generally flow west to east; best water visibility and most calm, windless days tend to be during the transition month of Apr; there is frequently a swell at this site; strong current throughout and powerful vertical currents at the big overhang.

Contact details Kandooma Diving Centre (www.kandooma.com/diving/diving.htm), Villivaru Dive Centre (www.divingworld-maldives.com), Fun Island Dive Centre (www.villahotels.com), Nautico Dive Centre (www.biyadoo.com), Aquanaut Kandooma Diving Center (www.kandooma.com/diving/diving.htm).

Travel nearest resorts are Kandooma, Villivaru, Biyadhoo and Fun Island, in South Malé Atoll; international flights to the capital Malé (via Dubai, Colombo, Singapore and other Asian cities or by charter), then access to the resorts by speedboat (35 mins for Kandooma, 45 mins for Biyadhoo and Villivaru, 50 mins for Fun Island) or *dhoni* (2½ hours for Kandooma and Fun Island).

165 FELIDHOO (VAAVU) ATOLL: MIYARU (SHARK) CHANNEL

Location channel immediately north of Alimatha Island in north-eastern corner of Felidhoo Atoll; south of Malé.

Main species *most trips:* grey reef, whitetip reef, blacktip reef; *many trips:* scalloped hammerhead.

Viewing opportunities *miyaru* means 'shark' in Dhivehi and this is, indeed, a good place to encounter sharks of several different species. The channel lies immediately north of Alimatha Island Resort. Facing the ocean on the eastern rim of Felidhoo Atoll, it is approximately 100 m/330 ft wide and 30 m/100 ft deep, and during the north-east monsoon takes the full force of the current flowing into the atoll from the ocean. Whitetip reef and blacktip reef sharks are regularly seen inside the channel. It is also a popular gathering ground for schooling grey reef sharks, which can usually be found in the channel mouth and particularly in the north corner, outside the entrance to a cave at a depth of about 33 m/110 ft. The atoll rim, where the channel mouth drops vertically into the deep oceanic waters, is also a good place for cruising scalloped hammerheads – although they are not as regular here as at some other sites. The best way to experience this dive is to enter the water at the north corner and then, following the atoll floor, cross the channel along the ridge at a depth of about 30 m/100 ft. It is an extraordinary experience, hovering in the middle of the channel out of sight of the reefs on either side, looking over the sheer drop-off into the deep blue, with nothing but sharks for company.

Bait/feed no.

Cage no.

Other wildlife long-snouted spinner dolphin, bottlenose dolphin, eagle ray, abundant reef fish.

Best time of year sharks present year-round, but best time is north-east monsoon (Dec–Apr); in the south-west monsoon (May–Nov) Miyaru loses its clear water and much of the shark action.

Dive depth 30 m/100 ft.

Typical visibility 20–30 m/65–100 ft.

Water temperature 27–30 °C/81–86 °F.

Weather and sea notes year divided into two monsoon periods: north-east (Dec–Apr) and south-west (May–Nov); north-east monsoon is driest and currents generally flow east to west; south-west monsoon brings more rain, occasional strong winds and frequent moderate to rough seas, and currents generally flow west to east; best water visibility and most calm, windless days tend to be during transition month of Apr. Currents in the channel can be very strong.

Contact details Alimatha Aquatic Resort (alidivebase@hotmail.com), Dhiggiri Tourist Resort (mmtours@dhivehinet.net.mw), Seafari Adventures (www.seafariadventures.com), Maldives Scuba Tours (www.scubascuba.com).

Travel nearest resort is Alimatha (5 mins from the site by dive boat), but Dhiggiri is also close (30 mins). Both resorts are in Felidhoo Atoll. International flights to the capital Malé (via Dubai, Colombo, Singapore and other Asian cities or by charter), then access to Alimatha or Dhiggiri by speedboat (2 hours).

166 FELIDHOO (VAAVU) ATOLL: FOTTEYO (HURAHU CHANNEL)

Location outer reef on the north coast of the eastern arm of Felidhoo Atoll; south of Malé.

Main species *most trips:* scalloped hammerhead, whitetip reef; *many trips:* grey reef; *occasional trips:* silky.

Viewing opportunities with a colourful and lively reef and a stack of overhangs and caves packed with luminescent soft corals, this is widely regarded as one of the best dives in the Maldives. The funnelling effect of the currents flowing into the Hurahu Channel results in a wonderful array of marine life. The area is superb for sharks. Hurahu Channel is about 200 m/ 660 ft wide, but is split by Fotteyo Thila into two relatively narrow passages (100 m/330 ft and 30 m/ 100 ft). There are a couple of particularly good shark sites: one on the ocean side of Fotteyo Thila and the other on the outside corner of Dhiggaru Falhu. The steep outer wall of Fotteyo Thila, which drops hundreds of metres to the seabed, should be dived at sunrise. This is the best time to encounter schooling scalloped hammerheads, which are seen on a regular basis. Close encounters with grey reef sharks are likely at any time and a variety of pelagic sharks turn up occasionally, including, on one memorable occasion, a school of more than 100 silky sharks. Alternatively, in the passage between Dhiggaru Falhu and Fotteyo Thila, it is possible to see a considerable number of whitetip reef sharks, which frequently rest on the sand in the western passage at depths of 14–22 m/45–70 ft.

Bait/feed no.

Cage no.

Other wildlife long-snouted spinner dolphin, bottlenose dolphin, eagle ray, stingray, abundant reef fish.

Best time of year hammerheads present year-round, but best time is north-east monsoon (Dec–Apr), when the current is flowing in from the ocean and visibility is at its best. Some operators recommend full moon as the best time of the month.

Dive depth 14–30 m/45–100 ft.

Typical visibility 20–30 m/65–100 ft.

Water temperature 27–30 °C/81–86 °F.

Weather and sea notes year divided into two monsoon periods: north-east (Dec–Apr) and south-west (May–Nov); north-east monsoon is driest and currents generally flow east to west; south-west monsoon brings more rain, occasional strong winds and frequent moderate to rough seas, and currents generally flow west to east; best water visibility and most calm, windless days tend to be during transition month of Apr. Currents around Fotteyo can be very strong.

Contact details Alimatha Aquatic Resort (alidivebase@hotmail.com), Dhiggiri Tourist Resort (mmtours@dhivehinet.net.mw), Seafari Adventures (www.seafariadventures.com), Maldives Scuba Tours (www.scubascuba.com).

Travel nearest resorts are Alimatha and Dhiggiri (1½ hours and 1¾ hours respectively from the site by dive boat), both in Felidhoo Atoll. International flights to the capital Malé (via Dubai, Colombo, Singapore and other Asian cities or by charter), then access to the resorts by speedboat (2 hours for both).

167 SOUTH ARI (ALIFU DHEKUNU) ATOLL: DHIGURAH ISLAND–MAAMIGILI ISLAND

Location near the southern tip of the atoll; south-west of Malé.

Main species *many trips:* whale, grey reef, whitetip reef.

Viewing opportunities South Ari is widely considered the best place in the Maldives to see whale sharks, but sightings are still largely a matter of luck. The sharks stay around for a few days or weeks, then disappear for days or weeks. They are seen on all the outside reefs in South Ari, mainly from Dhigurah Island to Maamigili Island. Dhidhdhoo Beyru Faru is one such reef on the outside of the atoll, about 1.5 km/1 mile east of Kudadhoo Beyru. It has a good enough variety of fish to make it an enjoyable dive in its own right, but the whale sharks are the real draw. Both juveniles and adults congregate here sporadically throughout the year.

Bait/feed no.

Cage no.

Other wildlife various cetaceans, including long-snouted spinner dolphin and bottlenose dolphin; manta ray. (north-east monsoon).

Best time of year sharks present year-round (whale sharks sporadically).

Dive depth surface (snorkelling for whale sharks); 5–30 m/16–100 ft for whitetip reef and grey reef.

Typical visibility 20–30 m/65–100 ft.

Water temperature 27–30 °C/81–86 °F.

Weather and sea notes year divided into two monsoon periods: north-east (Dec–Apr) and south-west (May–Nov); north-east monsoon is driest and currents generally flow east to west; south-west monsoon brings more rain, occasional strong winds and frequent moderate to rough seas, and currents generally flow west to east; best water visibility and most calm, windless days tend to be during the transition month of Apr.

Contact details Ari Beach Resort (www.aribeach.com), Holiday Island Resort (www.mal-dives.com/holidayisland), Sun Island Resort (www.mal-dives.com/sunisland), Crown Tours Maldives (www.crowntoursmaldives.com), Ocean Pro (www.oceanpro-diveteam.com), EuroDivers (www.euro-divers.com), Dive Center Little Mermaid (www.divingatthemaldives.com).

Travel nearest resort is Ari Beach, but Holiday Island and Sun Island are also close, all in South Ari Atoll; international flights to the capital Malé (via Dubai, Colombo, Singapore and other Asian cities or by charter), then access to the resorts by seaplane (30 mins for Ari Beach and 35 mins for Holiday Island and Sun Island), speedboat (2 hours for Ari Beach and 2 hours 30 mins for Holiday Island and Sun Island).

Note fishing for whale sharks was officially banned in the Maldives in 1993.

168 NORTH ARI (ALIFU ALIFU) ATOLL: HIMENDHOO DHEKUNU THILA

Location south-western corner of North Ari Atoll; west of Malé.

Main species *many trips:* whale, tawny nurse (*Nebrius ferrugineus*), leopard; *occasional trips:* grey reef, whitetip reef.

Viewing opportunities when the current is flowing

out of Himendhoo Dhekunu Channel, in the north-east monsoon, whale sharks (often juveniles as well as some adults) and large schools of manta rays frequently feed near the surface around Himendhoo Thila. Encounters are usually better when snorkelling than on scuba. The plankton-feeders come into the channel, which lies on the south side of Himendhoo Faru, when the rich current is flowing out of the atoll – and the *thila* (oval or round submerged reef) is one of the best places to meet them. The currents here can be strong and, as well as mantas and whale sharks, there is a spectacular 4 km/2½ miles of reef to drift-dive. It is quite common to see grey reef and whitetip reef sharks along the way. Emas Thila, also in Himendhoo Dhekunu Channel but officially in South Ari Atoll, is another good site for mantas and whale sharks – as is Dhonkalo Thila in Himendhoo Channel to the north.

Bait/feed no.

Cage no.

Other wildlife long-snouted spinner dolphin, bottlenose dolphin, manta ray, abundant reef fish.

Best time of year north-east monsoon (Dec–Apr).

Dive depth 15–30 m/50–100 ft.

Typical visibility 20 m/65 ft.

Water temperature 27–30 °C/81–86 °F.

Weather and sea notes year divided into two monsoon periods: north-east (Dec–Apr) and south-west (May–Nov); north-east monsoon is driest and currents generally flow east to west; south-west monsoon brings more rain, occasional strong winds and frequent moderate to rough seas, and currents generally flow west to east; best water visibility and most calm, windless days tend to be during transition month of Apr. Currents can be strong.

Contact details Moofushi (www.moofushi.com/en_sub-index.html), The Crab Dive Centre (athadmin@dhivenet.net.mv), Seafari Adventures (www.seafariadventures.com).

Travel nearest resorts are Fesdu, Moofushi and Athurugau (50–60 mins from the site by dive boat), but the site is within reach of several other resorts in North Ari Atoll. International flights to the capital Malé (via Dubai, Colombo, Singapore and other Asian cities or by charter), then easy access to all three resorts by seaplane (25 mins), and to Fesdu only by speedboat (2 hours).

169 NORTH ARI (ALIFU ALIFU) ATOLL: FISH HEAD (MUSHIMASMIGILI THILA)

Location inside the south-eastern corner of North Ari Atoll; south-west of Malé.

Main species *most trips:* grey reef; *many trips:* whitetip reef, blacktip reef.

Viewing opportunities Mushimasmigili Thila was once one of the top shark-watching sites in the Indian Ocean and has been listed among the 10 best dive sites in the world. It was particularly popular because grey reef sharks in the Indian Ocean have a reputation for being more placid than those in the Pacific (some experts consider them to be a separate sub-species). But the sharks at Fish Head have been taken by Ari Atoll fishermen for many years and, despite the area receiving official protection in 1995, have been fished relatively recently. Although the dive is not as good as it was in its heyday, a school of grey reef sharks is still resident and frequently passes within a few metres of divers. The best encounters are usually on the up-current side of the reef at a depth of about 15 m/50 ft, although there are also several cleaner stations, where it is possible to watch the sharks being cleaned by wrasse. Fish Head itself is actually a large overhang on the south-eastern corner of the *thila* (an oval or round submerged reef), although the name is normally used for the entire site. This is a typical *thila* and in a good year is packed with fish. It is nearly 100 m/330 ft long and lies 10 m/35 ft below the surface, with its sides dropping sharply down to the atoll plate at just over 40 m/130 ft.

Bait/feed no.

Cage no.

Other wildlife long-snouted spinner dolphin, bottlenose dolphin, blue-lined snapper, fusilier, yellow grunt, Napoleon wrasse.

Best time of year sharks present year-round.

Dive depth 15 m/50 ft (possible to descend to 30 m/100 ft, but the best shark watching is in relatively shallow water).

Typical visibility 20 m/65 ft.

Water temperature 27–30 °C/81–86 °F.

Weather and sea notes year divided into two monsoon periods: north-east (Dec–Apr) and south-west (May–Nov); north-east monsoon is driest and currents generally flow east to west; south-west monsoon brings more rain, occasional strong winds and frequent moderate to rough seas, and currents generally flow west to east; best water visibility and most calm, windless days tend to be during transition month of Apr. Current direction does not matter for this dive.

Contact details Sub Aqua (subaquell@dhivehi.net.mv), T.G.I. Dive Centre (www.tgidiving.com), Seafari Adventures (www.seafariadventures.com), Maldives Scuba Tours (www.scubascuba.com).

Travel nearest resort is Ellaidhoo (40 mins from the site by dive boat), but Halaveli and Fesdu are also fairly close (60 mins). All three resorts are in North Ari Atoll (some resorts in North and South Malé Atolls also run day trips). International flights to the capital Malé (via Dubai, Colombo, Singapore and other Asian cities or by charter), then easy access to Ellaidhoo by floatplane (20 mins) or speedboat (1 hour 20 mins), to Halaveli by floatplane (20 mins), speedboat (1½ hours) or *dhoni* (6 hours), and to Fesdu by floatplane (25 mins) or speedboat (2 hours).

Note although grey reef sharks used to be fed almost daily at Fish Head, this practice has now stopped. There is virtually no shark feeding anywhere in the Maldives. Despite what many dive operators tell their clients, it is not illegal, but is discouraged.

170 NORTH ARI (ALIFU ALIFU) ATOLL: MAAYA THILA

Location northern end of North Ari Atoll (3 km/2 miles north-west of Maayafushi), well inside the atoll perimeter; west of Malé.

Main species *most trips:* grey reef, whitetip reef; *many trips:* blacktip reef.

Viewing opportunities Maaya Thila has been dubbed Fish Head's little brother, although it offers an outstanding dive in its own right. A protected marine area, it is a small *thila* (oval or round submerged reef) with a series of caves, overhangs and outcrops. Some 6 m/20 ft below the surface and just 80 m/260 ft in diameter, it can be circumnavigated in a single dive. But, as with so many shark dives, it is the point where the current hits the reef that is the main focus for shark activity. In this case the best place to see the resident grey reef sharks is where the nutrient-rich current flows between the main *thila* and a large satellite rock some 20 m/65 ft to the north. It is particularly exciting to dive here at night, when the sharks are actively hunting fusiliers. The grey reef sharks, however, are merely a bonus: Maaya Thila is commonly regarded as the whitetip reef shark capital of the Maldives. On a good day divers encounter literally dozens of them. They, too, are most abundant where the current is strongest – although they can readily be found resting on the sand in the channel between the main *thila* and the satellite rock.

Bait/feed no.

Cage no.

Other wildlife long-snouted spinner dolphin, bottlenose dolphin, sea turtles, stonefish, honeycomb moray, batfish, abundant reef fish.

Best time of year sharks present year-round.

Dive depth 15–21 m/50–70 ft.

Typical visibility 20 m/65 ft.

Water temperature 27–30 °C/81–86 °F.

Weather and sea notes year divided into two monsoon periods: north-east (Dec–Apr) and south-west (May–Nov); north-east monsoon is driest and currents generally flow east to west; south-west monsoon brings more rain, occasional strong winds and frequent moderate to rough seas, and currents generally flow west to east; best water visibility and most calm, windless days tend to be during transition month of Apr. There are strong currents at the dive site.

Contact details Maayafushi (www.hellomaldives.com/resorts/maayafushi/index.htm), T.G.I. (www.tgidiving.com), Seafari Adventures (www.seafariadventures.com), Maldives Scuba Tours (www.scubascuba.com).

Travel nearest resort is Maayafushi (20 mins from the site by dive boat), but Bathala and Halaveli are also close (35–40 mins), while Ellaidhoo and Fesdu are within easy reach (50 mins). These resorts are in North Ari Atoll, but several others visit this site on day trips. International flights to the capital Malé (via Dubai, Colombo, Singapore and other Asian cities or by charter), then easy access to Maayafushi and Bathala by floatplane (25 mins), or to Halaveli by floatplane (20 mins), speedboat (1½ hours) or *dhoni* (6 hours).

171 RASDHOO ATOLL: RASDHOO-MADIVARU ISLAND (HAMMERHEAD POINT)

Location south-eastern corner of Rasdhoo Atoll (at the extreme northern end of Ari Atoll); west of Malé.

Main species *most trips:* scalloped hammerhead, whitetip reef; *many trips:* grey reef; *occasional trips:* thresher.

Viewing opportunities known internationally for its resident population of scalloped hammerheads, this is one of the best shark dives in the Indian Ocean. The sharks live in the deep blue waters beyond the outside wall of Rasdhoo-Madivaru Islands, and there may be 40 or more schooling together. Dive logs kept by local operators suggest a 90 per cent success rate. Divers jump in at the north corner of the narrow channel between Rasdhoo and Madivaru, facing the ocean, descend to 25–30 m/80–100 ft and then swim 50–100 m/165–330 ft into the blue water. The best chance for good encounters is just after dawn, when the current is running into the channel and the sharks rise from much deeper waters to depths that are accessible to recreational divers. As you swim out towards the sunrise, you begin to see the dark shapes of hammerheads in the distance; although they tend to be timid at first, it is not unusual for them to become curious enough to investigate divers quite closely. This can be a challenging dive, out of sight of the reef, and it is important to keep a check on your depth. It is also worth keeping an eye open in deep water for several other shark species, including thresher, which are seen from time to time. Whitetip reef sharks are usually encountered along the outside reef wall.

Bait/feed no.

Cage no.

Other wildlife long-snouted spinner dolphin, bottlenose dolphin, manta ray, eagle ray, tallfin batfish, garden eel, abundant reef fish.

Best time of year hammerheads present year-round, but best during north-east monsoon (Dec–Apr). Some operators believe the best encounters occur around full moon.

Dive depth 25–30 m/80–100 ft.

Typical visibility 20–30 m/65–100 ft.

Water temperature 27–30 °C/81–86 °F.

Weather and sea notes the year is divided into two monsoon periods: north-east (Dec–Apr) and south-west (May–Nov); north-east monsoon is driest and currents generally flow east to west; south-west monsoon brings more rain, occasional strong winds and frequent moderate to rough seas, and currents generally flow west to east; best water visibility and most calm, windless days tend to be during transition month of Apr.

Contact details Rasdhoo Atoll Divers (www.rasdhoodivers.com), Maldives Scuba Tours (www.scubascuba.com), Ocean Pro (www.veliganduisland.com/scubadiving.html).

Travel nearest resorts are Kuramathi and Veligandu (10 mins and 25 mins respectively from the site by dive boat), both in Rasdhoo Atoll. International flights to the capital Malé (via Dubai, Colombo, Singapore and other Asian cities or by charter), then access to the resorts by seaplane (15 mins for Kuramathi and 20 mins for Veligandu) or speedboat (1¾ hours for Kuramathi and 1 hour for Veligandu).

NEW ZEALAND

172 NORTH ISLAND: WHATUWHIWHI

Location Cape Karikari, north-east coast of North Island.

Main species *many trips:* great hammerhead, blue, shortfin mako, bronze whaler.

Viewing opportunities the healthy waters near Whatuwhiwhi (pronounced fot-ö-fê-fê) are enriched by deep ocean currents and inhabited by a huge variety of wildlife. Pelagic sharks are encountered on a regular basis at three main sites: Matai Bay, a sheltered bay some 15 m/50 ft deep; Tipps Reef, a rocky reef in 18 m/60 ft of water; and the Motoroa Islands, a cluster of small islands at the tip of Cape Karikari and on the edge of deep, blue water. There is no typical dive, since the number and species of sharks encountered vary enormously from day to day and week to week, but pelagic sharks of one kind or another are seen regularly.

Bait/feed no.

Cage no.

Other wildlife common dolphin, blue penguin, long- and short-tailed rays, eagle ray, moray and conger eels.

Best time of year Nov–Mar.

Dive depth surface to 40 m/130 ft or more.

Typical visibility 2–50 m/6½–165 ft (highly variable).

Water temperature averages 26 °C/78 °F) during main season of Nov–Mar.

Weather and sea notes strong current and swell likely in afternoons; weather usually settled Dec–Mar.

Contact details A to Z Diving (www.atozdiving.co.nz).

Travel international and national flights to Auckland; 4-hour drive north from central Auckland on State Highways 1 and 10, or 45-min flight from Auckland to nearby Kaitaia airport; choice of accommodation in Whatuwhiwhi.

173 NORTH ISLAND: TUTUKAKA

Location 30 km/19 miles north-east of Whangarei, in Northland at the top end of North Island.

Main species *most trips:* shortfin mako; *many trips:* blue; *occasional trips:* oceanic whitetip, great hammerhead.

Viewing opportunities the waters around Tutukaka are renowned for their rugged and spectacular underwater scenery and rich marine life. In fact, this is the gateway to one of New Zealand's most popular dive destinations, Poor Knights, which is just 23 km/14 miles away to the north-east. Three different sites are used for the shark dive, depending on sea conditions: Mako Reef, a rugged rocky area in some 80 m/260 ft of water and lying 13 km/8 miles south-east of Tutukaka; Lone Pin, in 60 m/200 ft of water close to a rocky outcrop between Poor Knights and the mainland; and North Reef, a spectacular pinnacle that rises from a depth of 130 m/430 ft to within 40 m/130 ft of the surface. Chum is used to attract the sharks (although they are not actually fed) and the four-person cage floats at the surface. Divers can use either scuba or snorkel, according to personal preference. Relatively few sharks are seen on a typical dive – just one shortfin mako is the norm – but close encounters are common and the animals often come right up to the cage.

Bait/feed yes.

Cage yes.

Other wildlife New Zealand fur seal, Australian gannet, barracuda, marlin.

Best time of year sharks present mainly Dec–May.

Dive depth cage suspended at the surface.

Typical visibility 20–30 m/65–100 ft.

Water temperature 19–22 °C/66–72 °F.

Weather and sea notes Dec–Jan fine and dry, Feb–Mar hot with some rain, Apr–May fine and dry; open-ocean conditions with some swell typical.

Contact details Sportsfishing Charters (www.oceanfilm.net).

Travel international flights to Auckland; national flights or coach to Whangarei; choice of accommodation in Tutukaka.

174 NORTH ISLAND: GISBORNE

Location 13–24 km/8–15 miles off the coast of Gisborne (depending on daily location); approximately equidistant between Auckland and Wellington on the east coast of the North Island.

Main species *most trips:* shortfin mako; *many trips:* blue; *occasional trips:* great white.

Viewing opportunities shark watching is relatively new to Gisborne but, since it was first introduced in 1998, it has become enormously popular. This is a trip for snorkellers and divers alike, with virtually guaranteed sightings of shortfin makos and regular sightings of blues. There are three main dive sites on the edge of the continental shelf: South Rocks, which is a long, rocky reef at a depth of about 40 m/130 ft with pinnacles rising to within some 20 m/65 ft of the surface; Ariel Reef, a 6 km/4 mile reef rising to within 10 m/33 ft of the surface; and Southern Dogleg, a deepwater site. Local fishermen radio in with shark sightings and the operator varies the location from day to day to minimize any disruption to the sharks' natural behaviour. On arrival at the site, the cage is lowered into the water and tethered to the boat. The water is chummed and, sometimes, bait is attached to the end of a rope near the cage. Sharks can arrive within minutes, although sometimes the wait may be several hours. As soon as they are around the boat, everyone enters the cage snorkellers stand on the bottom and peer down (the cage floats at the surface, so the water is effectively chest-deep) while divers are able to crouch on the bottom for a slightly better view. The number of sharks varies from one to as many as six (a mixture of males and females as well as adults and juveniles) and they frequently approach to within a metre or so of the cage.

Bait/feed yes.

Cage yes.

Other wildlife common dolphin, kingfish, trevally, barracuda.

Best time of year sharks present year-round, but best Dec–Apr.

Dive depth surface to 1.5 m/5 ft.

Typical visibility 10–20 m/33–66 ft.

Water temperature 19–21 °C/66–70 °F.

Weather and sea notes hot with afternoon sea breezes during peak period (summer); rain possible at any time of year (likely May–Sep).

Contact details Surfit Shark Cage Experience (www.sharks.co.nz).

Travel international flights to Auckland; national flights to Auckland or Wellington; boat leaves from Gisborne; choice of accommodation in Gisborne.

Note dedicated trips to observe great whites off the coast of Gisborne are currently in development.

175 NORTH ISLAND: HAWKES BAY

Location 3–13 km/2–8 miles off the coast of Napier, on the east coast of the central North Island.

Main species *most trips:* blue, shortfin mako.

Viewing opportunities better known for its award-winning wines, Hawkes Bay is also a good place for sharks. Blues and makos migrate to the region with the warm-water currents each summer. Three open-water sites are used for watching them, depending on sea conditions: near Cape Kidnappers (home of one of the largest and most accessible mainland gannet colonies in the world), some 13 km/8 miles south of Napier; and at Bare Island and Post Office Rock, which lie 6.5 km/4 miles and 3.2 km/2 miles off the coast of Waimarama Beach. They are all in water approximately 100 m/330 ft deep. On the way to the site the boat trawls for tuna, which is then prepared as bait. Chum is used to attract the sharks and bait stations are set up close to the cage (there is no handfeeding). It normally takes about half an hour for the sharks to appear. Four divers can enter the good-sized cage (3.5 m/11½ ft deep) or, if they prefer, can swim with the sharks in open water nearby. On a typical dive between 6 and 12 sharks of both sexes come to feed. They approach very closely and the blues will even brush against divers outside the cage. Each dive lasts for up to an hour and most participants manage to complete three separate dives during a single day trip.

Bait/feed yes.

Cage yes.

Other wildlife various cetaceans, Australian gannet, yellowtail kingfish, albacore, yellowfin tuna.

Best time of year Nov–Mar (best Jan–Feb).

Dive depth cage floats at the surface.

Typical visibility 10–30 m/33–100 ft.

Water temperature 19–23 °C/66–74 °F.

Weather and sea notes open-ocean conditions; summer months usually hot with sea breezes in the afternoon.

Contact details Dive HQ Napier (www.divehq.co.nz).

Travel national and international flights to Auckland or Wellington; connecting flights to Napier (1 hour and 50 mins respectively) or drive (5 hours and 3½ hours respectively); choice of accommodation in Napier.

176 MARLBOROUGH SOUNDS: OPEN OCEAN

Location 45 minutes from French Pass in Marlborough Sounds (north coast of South Island).

Main species *most trips:* blue, shortfin mako.

Viewing opportunities this is a thrilling open-sea dive conducted throughout the austral summer. The boat leaves the little village of French Pass, cruises past D'Urville Island and then heads out to the open sea. On arrival at the dive site, a three-person cage is lowered into the water. Once the chum line has been started, it can take as little as 10 minutes or as long as several hours for the sharks to appear. As soon as they are around the boat, the divers enter the cage and can observe and take photographs through a 360° gap at eye level. Bait is suspended in the water from the cage and used to entice the sharks within photographic range. A typical group consists of six divers (with a minimum of four and a maximum of ten) and the people in the cage are rotated every 15 minutes to give everyone an equal chance of seeing a range of different sharks. The action varies enormously from day to day – there can be one or two sharks or a large number; they may be all blues or all makos or a mixture of the two; and they may stay for a few minutes or for the entire trip. The sharks are frequently on, or close to, the surface and offer good views from the boat as well as the cage.

Bait/feed yes.

Cage yes.

Other wildlife dusky (most common in winter), bottlenose and common dolphins; New Zealand fur seal, little blue penguin and a wide variety of other seabirds.

Best time of year Dec–Apr.

Dive depth cage suspended at the surface.

Typical visibility 6–20 m/20–65 ft (varies daily).

Water temperature 16–20 °C/61–68 °F.

Weather and sea notes prevailing winds tend to be westerlies so, even in summer, open-ocean conditions can cause trips to be cancelled.

Contact details Sea Safaris (www.seasafaris.co.nz).

Travel international flights to Auckland; French Pass is well off the beaten track, but the nearest major centres are Wellington (southern tip of North Island – 30 mins away by plane), Nelson and Picton (French Pass is 1½ hours' drive from the main Nelson–Picton highway); self-contained cabins and backpacker accommodation in French Pass; alternative accommodation on D'Urville Island.

177 SOUTH ISLAND: KAIKOURA

Location 3–13 km/2–8 miles off the Kaikoura Peninsula; approximately halfway between Wellington and Christchurch, on the north-east coast of South Island.

Main species *most trips:* blue, shortfin mako.

Viewing opportunities few people interested in marine wildlife have not heard of Kaikoura, nestled between a chain of snow-capped mountains and the sea. From here it is possible to join trips offering close encounters with whales, dolphins, seals, pelagic seabirds . . . and sharks. It is the meeting point of two opposing currents, which fuel a highly productive food chain just offshore, where the Kaikoura Canyon plunges to depths of nearly 2000 m/6560 ft within 1.6 km/1 mile of the coast. During the summer months blue and shortfin mako sharks move towards the coast and come within easy reach of shark-watching tours. The exact dive site varies from day to day, according to sea conditions, and chum is used to attract the sharks to the boat. A rather unusual 'cage', with glass sides, is lowered into the water and floats at the surface. This dive is suitable for divers and non-divers alike (non-divers are given an introductory session in a swimming pool before the trip) and air is supplied directly from the boat. Two divers enter the cage, always in the company of a divemaster, and typically spend 10 or 15 minutes with the sharks. The divemaster feeds the sharks by hand for the duration of the dive, from inside the cage, and this brings them very close for photography. Divers are rotated regularly to ensure that all ten participants have a turn while sharks are present. If they stay around the boat, a five-hour trip is normally sufficient for everyone to have two or three dives. Sharks of all ages and both sexes are found in the area and, on a typical trip, as few as one or as many as ten blue sharks appear together with one, two or three makos.

Bait/feed yes.

Cage yes.

Other wildlife sperm whale, common, dusky and Hector's dolphins, various other cetaceans sporadically, New Zealand fur seal, wide variety of seabirds.

Best time of year sharks present Dec to late Apr/early May.

Dive depth cage floats at the surface.

Typical visibility 3–10 m/10–33 ft.

Water temperature 14–22 °C/57–72 °F.

Weather and sea notes weather usually fine during summer, but open sea conditions and strong winds can affect trips from time to time.

Contact details Shark Dive Kaikoura (www.sharkdive.co.nz).

Travel national and international flights to Christchurch; coach, train or 2-hour drive to Kaikoura; wide choice of accommodation in town.

AUSTRALIA

178 WESTERN AUSTRALIA: KALBARRI

Location 10 km/6 miles offshore from Kalbarri, at the mouth of the Murchison River; 600 km/370 miles north of Perth.

Main species *most trips:* bronze whaler, blacktip.

Viewing opportunities shark watching in Kalbarri is unique. There is nothing else quite like it in the world. Large numbers of bronze whaler and blacktip sharks are virtually guaranteed – and you do not even have to get your feet wet. The sharks habitually follow cray-fishing boats to feed on the leftover bait from their pots and, by special arrangement, a 15 m/50 ft catamaran full of shark watchers is allowed to come along to watch the spectacle. On average, 6–12 sharks (varying in length from 1.2–3 m/4–10 ft) follow each cray boat and, because they do not make a distinction, the sharks follow the catamaran as well. Suddenly appearing from nowhere, they swim within metres of the boat and will even lift their heads right out of the water to take scraps from a line. Groups of divers with their own licensed divemaster are allowed to enter the water and, in the past, have had some exciting close encounters with lots of sharks.

Bait/feed indirectly (bait from crayfishing boats).

Cage no.

Other wildlife humpback whale (May–Oct), bottlenose dolphin, various seabirds.

Best time of year sharks present Nov–Jun; best time for weather Mar–May.

Dive depth viewing from boat in 18–30 m/60–100 ft of water.

Weather and sea notes strong south-east trade winds Nov–Feb make trips unpredictable.

Contact details Kalbarri Explorer Ocean Charters (www.kalbarriexplorer.com.au).

Travel national and international flights to Perth; bus or car to Kalbarri (5 hours); airport in Kalbarri currently closed, but twice-daily flights to Geraldton (1½ hours' drive to Kalbarri); limited choice of accommodation.

179 WESTERN AUSTRALIA: NINGALOO REEF

Location 1300 km/810 miles north of Perth on the west (Coral Bay) and east (Exmouth) coasts of the North-West Cape (ranges from 100 m/330 ft to 5 km/3 miles from the shore).

Main species *most trips:* whale; *many trips:* tasselled wobbegong (*Eucrossorhinus dasypogon*); *occasional trips:* grey reef, whitetip reef, zebra or leopard, tawny nurse (*Nebrius ferrugineus*), sand tiger.

Viewing opportunities Ningaloo Reef has a legendary status as one of the best places in the world for breathtakingly close encounters with the largest fish in the sea. Whale sharks (predominantly imma-ture males) visit the waters around the reef for several months every year. Their arrival is fairly predictable and was always thought to be triggered by two mass spawnings of the corals on the reef. These occur seven to nine days after the full moons in March and April, and many other invertebrates spawn at the same time. It is the largest synchronized spawning in the world and, since it attracts a mass of other marine life, the whale sharks come to feed on the bountiful food supply. Sightings often peak approximately 21 days after the March full moon (although if the second coral spawning, towards the end of April, is as heavy as the first, large numbers of whale sharks appear in late April and early May). However, this is not always the case and some of the best sightings do not seem to be related to these mass spawnings at all. In fact, new findings suggest that some Ningaloo whale sharks feed predominantly on krill, or do not feed at all while they are here. It is therefore likely that other factors (such as water temperature in the Leuwin Current) may be just as important. The sharks typically swim 100–200 m/330–660 ft off Ningaloo, which stretches roughly parallel to the coast over a distance of some 260 km/160 miles, from Coral Bay in the south to Exmouth in the north. Historically, there were generally more sharks at the northern end of the reef, but the largest numbers occur in different places from year to year and, in recent years, there have been more in the middle of the reef around an area known locally as Black Rock. The best operators use spotter planes, which patrol up and down the reef and guide the boats below to the nearest shark. Participants are dropped ahead of the animal, then picked up again when it has moved on, ready for another drop a few minutes later. Most people find snorkelling easier than diving, because it is easier to swim fast at the surface and to get back into the boat quickly for the next run. There are strict encounter rules to protect the sharks, including a restricted approach zone of 30 m/100 ft, a limit on the number of divers allowed in the water with any one shark, and a total ban on touching or riding the sharks. The success rate for these trips is excellent. On a good day, it is possible to encounter several sharks and, sometimes, they will slow down and swim right up to people in the water.

Bait/feed no.

Cage no.

Other wildlife manta ray; sea snakes; green, loggerhead and hawksbill turtles; Indo-Pacific hump-backed dolphin, short-finned pilot whale, Bryde's whale, humpback whale (mainly Jun–Oct); night dives during the coral spawning are unforgettable.

Best time of year traditionally, Mar, Apr and early May, but in 2001 May and early Jun were best (Apr sightings were sporadic); future seasons expected to be best mid-Apr to end of May.

Dive depth surface to about 20 m/65 ft.

Typical visibility 20 m/65 ft, but may be 10–40 m/35–130 ft.

Water temperature 24–29 °C/75–84 °F.

Weather and sea notes shark watching may occasionally be interrupted early in the season (Mar) by tropical cyclones; Apr usually the best month for weather; conditions unpredictable late May–Jun, but cold fronts frequently bring blustery days and some swell; sea breezes typical in the afternoons making the sea fairly choppy (before Apr).

Contact details Exmouth Diving Centre (www.exmouthdiving.com.au), Diving Ventures (www.dventures.com.au), Diversion Dive Travel (www.diversionoz.com)

Travel numerous trips leave the small towns of Exmouth and Coral Bay, the gateways to Ningaloo Reef (about 150 km/95 miles apart). Even by Australian standards, they are remote. They are both accessible by air (the nearest airport is Learmouth, 35 km/20 miles south of Exmouth) and there is a choice of hotels, backpacker hostels and campsites in both towns. Most trips are on day boats, but there are also live-aboard options (with the advantage of being able to travel the length of Ningaloo to wherever the sharks are aggregating in greatest numbers). Plan a minimum of five days to guarantee many good encounters.

Note there are resident tasselled wobbegongs at Navy Wharf, or Navy Pier, in Exmouth. This 300-m/1000-ft pier can only be dived at high or low tides, because of strong tidal currents, but is incredibly rich and the wobbegongs are easy to find. Maximum depth is 15 m/50 ft and visibility about 5–25 m/16–80 ft.

180 WESTERN AUSTRALIA: NORTHERN ATOLL REEFS: ROWLEY SHOALS

Location 280 km/175 miles west of Broome, 2250 km/1400 miles north of Perth.

Main species *most trips*: grey reef, silvertip; *many trips*: whitetip reef; leopard; *occasional trips*: whale, great hammerhead, tiger.

Viewing opportunities Rowley Shoals consists of a chain of three coral atolls on the edge of one of the widest continental shelves in the world. Near-perfect examples of atoll geomorphology, they are all strikingly similar: pear-shaped, rising with nearly vertical sides from very deep water, approximately 14–18 km/ 9–11 miles long and 7–10 km/4–6 miles wide, and each with its own lagoon. They even have the same orientation. Their remote location and pristine condition have gained them a reputation for some of the best diving in Australia: they are home to more than 600 species of fishes, and two-thirds of Australia's tropical species are found here. Grey reef and silvertip sharks are found in good numbers at all three sites and can be very frisky during organized feeds. Tiger sharks are also seen sometimes, particularly along the outer reef walls, and are now being baited by the crew of the MV *True North* to give divers close-up views and great photo opportunities from the safety of a cage (dedicated tiger shark trips are still in the experimental stage – contact Carl Roessler (www.divexprt.com) for more information). Mermaid Reef is the most northerly and rises from about 440 m/1445 ft; it has a stunning reef wall, which plummets to the depths and is great for drift diving with grey reef sharks and silver-tips. About 30 km/19 miles to the south is Clerke Reef, which rises from 390 m/1280 ft; large numbers of grey reef sharks can be seen on the sloping edge of the reef at a depth of 20–30 m/65–100 ft. Imperieuse Reef is another 40 km/25 miles farther south and rises from 230 m/755 ft.

Bait/feed yes (some operators).

Cage yes (tiger shark feeds only).

Other wildlife turtles, giant clam, manta ray, stingray, moray eel, barracuda, very friendly potato cod and Maori wrasse (wait to be handfed and follow divers around).

Best time of year Sep–Nov.

Dive depth surface to 40 m/130 ft.

Typical visibility 20–40 m/65–130 ft.

Water temperature 24–29 °C/75–84 °F.

Weather and sea notes due to their proximity to deep oceanic waters, Rowley Shoals are among the few reefs in the world affected by a high tidal range; dramatic 5–10 m/16–33 ft tides pour massive volumes of water in and out of the coral framework and can restrict dive times; strong currents are fairly common; monsoon period Nov–Mar.

Contact details True North (www.batnet.com/seeandsea/location/rowley.html), Jodi Anne Charters (www.jodiannecharters.com/rowley.html).

Travel accessible only by live-aboard from Broome (approximately 12 hours). Daily flights from Brisbane, Sydney, Melbourne and Adelaide via Perth. Wide choice of accommodation in Broome.

181–2 QUEENSLAND: FAR NORTHERN REEFS: RAINE ISLAND AND SHARK CITY

Location 140 km/87 miles (Shark City), 160 km/100 miles (Raine Island) north-east of Lockhart River, in the Far Northern Reefs, Coral Sea.

Main species *most trips:* grey reef, whitetip reef, tawny nurse (*Nebrius ferrugineus*), zebra or leopard; *many trips:* tiger, silvertip, epaulette or carpet (*Hemiscyllium ocellatum*), tasselled wobbegong (*Eucrossorhinus dasypogon*); *occasional trips:* oceanic whitetip, great hammerhead, thresher, whale.

Viewing opportunities this remote and little-dived section of the Great Barrier Reef stretches all the way from Lizard Island in the south to Papua New Guinea in the north. With the richest and most diverse reef system in Australia, and sheer walls dropping away from just a few metres below the surface to a depth of 500 m/1640 ft or more, it has many fabulous dive sites. One particular region, around Raine Island and Shark City, is outstanding for sharks, and shark watching is an inevitable highlight of any trip here. Grey reef and, to a lesser extent, whitetip reef sharks seem to be everywhere and on some dives you can look in any direction and see them – above you, beneath you, and on all sides. Most divers visit Raine Island for its green turtles. There are believed to be more nesting here than anywhere else in the world, and each summer tens of thousands of them arrive to mate and lay their eggs. But they attract large numbers of tiger sharks, which gather around the island for a couple of months at the end of the year to feed on them. These impressive sharks patrol in search of sick or weak turtles and will even enter very shallow water along the shoreline to snatch them as they return to the sea after egg-laying. One of the best places to see tiger sharks (not only around Raine Island but anywhere in the world) is along the northern wall. They sometimes approach divers quite closely, but generally ignore them and are more intent on searching for their turtle prey. Anchoring and mooring is impossible at Raine Island, so most dives are conducted as drifts. Shark City is a short boat ride away, on the north-east side of Great Detached Reef. This is not to be confused with another site often called Shark City, which is several hundred kilometres farther south on the northern tip of Tijou Reef (where, incidentally, you can see silver-tips as well as grey reef and whitetip reef sharks). The 'real' Shark City is continuously being patrolled by the same three species, which are nearly always in view and often pass very close to divers, and is often visited by a variety of pelagic sharks. This patchy reef, some 10–27 m/33–90 ft deep, is used by a few charter boats for shark feeds and is also very good for manta rays.

Bait/feed sometimes (depends on operator).

Cage no.

Other wildlife wide variety of nesting seabirds; Bryde's whale and other cetaceans, green turtle (nesting Nov–Dec), manta (mainly Nov–Dec) and eagle rays, tuna, mackerel, trevally, Maori wrasse, potato cod, red bass, barracuda, cuttlefish, pufferfish, squirrelfish, painted cray, giant clam.

Best time of year many sharks present year-round; tiger sharks best Nov–Dec (congregate to feed on turtles); whale sharks most likely Nov–Dec; best diving Sep–Dec.

Dive depth 5–40 m/16–130 ft.

Typical visibility 18–50 m/60–165 ft (average 40 m/130 ft at Shark City, 20 m/65 ft at Raine Island).

Water temperature 24–29 °C/75–84 °F; coolest Jul–Sep.

Weather and sea notes currents possible; may be a slight swell and wind chop, but both sites protected by reef and mostly calm; some rainfall (not every day) Jan–Mar; south-east trade winds (20–25 knots) Jun–Jul; cyclones possible Dec–Apr (rare).

Contact details Undersea Explorer (www.underseaexplorer.com), Bomatu Diving Company (www.bomatu.com), Explorer Ventures (www.explorerventures.com/australia.html).

Travel national and international flights to Cairns; sites accessible by live-aboard from Cairns, Port Douglas or Thursday Island (reached by plane from Cairns); minimum 16 hours sailing time; wide choice of acommodation onshore.

183 QUEENSLAND: NORTH HORN, OSPREY REEF

Location 160 km/100 miles from shore, beyond the Great Barrier Reef (350 km/220 miles from Cairns, 310 km/190 miles from Port Douglas).

Main species *most trips:* whitetip reef, grey reef; *many trips:* silvertip, scalloped hammerhead, tawny nurse (*Nebrius ferrugineus*), epaulette or carpet (*Hemiscyllium ocellatum*); *occasional trips:* tiger, thresher, whale, leopard, tasselled wobbegong (*Eucrossorhinus dasypogon*), oceanic whitetip, great hammerhead.

Viewing opportunities with a wide variety of species and clear oceanic water, North Horn offers superb shark watching. The site itself is a reef shelf on the northern end of remote Osprey Reef, the most northerly of the Coral Sea reefs and approximately 24 km/15 miles long and 8 km/5 miles wide. North

Horn is well known for its spectacular perimeter wall, which drops more than 1000 m/3300 ft to the seabed, but it has also been a shark-feeding site for nearly 20 years. There are currently about 20 resident whitetip reef sharks (usually eight present at any one time), which inspect divers as soon as they enter the water, and 20–30 resident grey reef sharks. Silvertips are regularly seen on deeper dives descending the wall and often surprise divers by appearing suddenly from nowhere. Many other species turn up sporadically. In winter and early spring, at least 100 schooling scalloped hammerheads are encountered off the wall on a regular basis. Most dives are to and from the moored vessel but, in suitable conditions, drift dives are possible. Some of the charter boats conduct exciting shark feeds, but even without extra food the shark action here is good. Undersea Explorer conducts an extensive research programme, with onboard marine biologists, and encourages passengers to help with the work.

Bait/feed sometimes.

Cage no.

Other wildlife minke whale (Jun–Aug), Maori wrasse, manta ray, eagle ray, potato cod, schools of barracuda.

Best time of year sharks present year-round and trips run most weeks, but the monsoon period is Jan–Mar and it can be windy Jun–Aug. Scalloped hammerheads year-round, but schooling aggregations mainly Jun–Sep.

Dive depth 10–40 m/35–130 ft.

Typical visibility 30–45 m/100–150 ft.

Water temperature 24–29 °C/75–84 °F (coolest Jul–Sep).

Weather and sea notes slight currents common, may be a slight swell and wind chop, but protected by reef and mostly calm.

Contact details Undersea Explorer (www.undersea.com.au), Taka II Dive Adventures (www.taka.com.au), Tusa Dive Charters (www.tusadive.com), Explorer Ventures (www.explorerventures.com/australia.html).

Travel only possible from live-aboard boat. Charters leave Cairns and Port Douglas, where there is a wide choice of accommodation.

184 QUEENSLAND: HOLMES REEF, PREDATORS' PLAYGROUND

Location 230 km/145 miles east of Cairns, in the Coral Sea beyond the Great Barrier Reef.

Main species *most trips*: whitetip reef, grey reef, silvertip, tawny nurse (*Nebrius ferrugineus*); *many*

trips: great hammerhead; *occasional trips*: tiger, leopard, wobbegong.

Viewing opportunities Holmes Reef is a twin reef system, covering an area of 450 sq km/175 sq miles, with dozens of established dive sites. They are all pristine and visited on a regular basis by a vessel operated by Coral Sea Diving Company. Sharks can be seen almost anywhere, but the main site is Predators' Playground. No bait is used (the sharks are habituated and congregate under the boat soon after arrival), but they are fed using a bar system hanging about 4 m/13 ft below the surface. Divers wait at a depth of 9 m/30 ft, to watch whitetip reef, grey reef and silvertips come in to feed. Several other species turn up from time to time. Another shark site on Holmes Reef worth a visit is Leopards' Lair, a large pinnacle where leopard sharks can sometimes be seen resting on the sand during the day.

Bait/feed yes.

Cage no.

Other wildlife garden eel, bull and spotted lagoon rays, occasional manta ray, hundreds of small reef fishes.

Best time of year sharks present year-round. .

Dive depth up to 9 m/30 ft.

Typical visibility rarely less than 30 m/100 ft (up to 70 m/230 ft).

Water temperature average 26 °C/78 °F.

Weather and sea notes no really strong currents and the reef offers good protection in rough weather. Sep–Nov offers the best weather (relatively mild journey to the reef); Apr–Aug may have moderate to fresh winds; itineraries may be changed Jan–Feb (cyclone season).

Contact details Coral Sea Diving Company (coralseadiving@qld.cc), Tusa Dive Charters (www.tusadive.com).

Travel only possible from live-aboard boat, with regular departures from Cairns, where there is a wide choice of hotel, guesthouse and backpacker accommodation.

185–6 QUEENSLAND: FLINDERS REEF, WATANABE PINNACLE AND SCUBA ZOO

Location 230 km/145 miles north-east of Townsville, 260 km/160 miles south-east of Cairns, in the Coral Sea.

Main species *most trips:* silvertip, grey reef, whitetip reef; *many trips:* blacktip reef, zebra or leopard, epaulette or carpet (*Hemiscyllium ocellatum*), tawny nurse (*Nebrius ferrugineus*); *occasional trips:* great hammerhead, bronze whaler, tiger, oceanic whitetip.

Viewing opportunities oceanic reefs in the Coral Sea are renowned for their shark sightings – and Flinders Reef is one of the best. A dive on virtually any of the deep walls here is likely to result in close encounters with silvertip, grey reef and whitetip reef sharks, and a whole variety of other species turn up on a regular basis as well. Great hammerheads, for example, are something of a Flinders speciality and some impressive individuals in excess of 3 m/10 ft have been encountered in the area; most hammerhead sightings are of lone sharks cruising along the gorgonian-encrusted walls. Flinders is actually an atoll some 37 km/23 miles long and 28 km/17 miles wide, covering an enormous area of about 1000 sq km/ 385 sq miles, and is often dived in conjunction with nearby North and South Boomerang Reefs. Most of the diving is wall diving and the drop-offs are certainly dramatic. But the lagoon area to the north is also good for sharks, where several pinnacles form the focal point of a nursery area for juvenile grey reef sharks. The pups swim around in packs of 10–20 and, although they are quite shy if you try to approach them, are fun to watch. Zebra sharks (or leopard sharks, as they are called in Australia), epaulette and tawny nurse sharks can also be seen around the coral pinnacles within the lagoon. Watanabe Pinnacle (or Watanabe Bommie), an enormous pinnacle of rock and coral rising from the depths to within 12 m/40 ft of the surface and lying on the exposed north-west side of the Flinders complex, is literally shrouded in huge clouds of fish and can be excellent for their predators – the resident grey reef sharks. It is widely regarded as one of the best dive sites in the Coral Sea.

But perhaps the best-known dive here is a sharkfeed that takes place at Scuba Zoo, on the western side of South Boomerang Reef. This is conducted from the Mike Ball Dive Expeditions vessel *Spoilsport* and on a good day can attract as many as 30–40 sharks. The site itself is nothing special, with a flat, sandy bottom at a depth of about 15 m/50 ft, but the feed is action-packed. The dive begins by descending to an enormous 18 m/60 ft L-shaped cage on the seabed and then taking up position on top (or inside, if you prefer). The crew then bring down a 136-litre/ 30-gallon drum packed with large fish heads and tails and start banging the sides. There is a lid on top, but specially made holes let the fishy smell waft into the sea. For 20–30 minutes the drum is towed around the cage (and the divers). While you are sitting on the cage roof the sharks frequently come within arm's length – sometimes even closer. Then the crew give a signal and everyone moves inside the cage (it is compulsory to be inside during the feed itself) before the lid is removed and all the food released. The feed is remote and the bait bin is operated by a series of pulleys and ropes (at no time are the sharks handfed). This results in an intense feeding frenzy, which usually lasts for a few minutes before normality returns. Then the sharks disperse and it is safe to leave the cage to search for shark teeth in the sand before returning to the surface. On a typical dive up to 20–30 grey reef, 10–15 silvertip and one or two whitetip reef turn up for the feed, so it is a superb opportunity for observation and close-up photography. Lone great hammerheads are being seen more and more often off the deep walls near Scuba Zoo

Bait/feed yes (Scuba Zoo).

Cage yes (Scuba Zoo).

Other wildlife humpback whale (mainly May to mid-Oct), green turtle, manta (usually late summer) and eagle rays, huge schools of chevron barracuda and bigeye trevally, rainbow runner, dogtooth tuna, unicornfish, angelfish, kingfish, mullet, sweetlip, cuttlefish.

Best time of year sharks present year-round (numbers at Scuba Zoo drop during late winter/early spring: Jul–Sep); best diving Jul–Nov.

Dive depth 15–40 m/50–130 ft plus (greater depths elsewhere in the Flinders complex).

Typical visibility 30–40 m/90–130 ft (occasionally up to 60 m/200 ft); best visibility in winter.

Water temperature 22–26 °C/72–78 °F May–Oct, 27–29 °C/81–84 °F Nov–Apr.

Weather and sea notes slight currents may be experienced; Watanabe exposed and can only be dived in winds less than 15–20 knots; some rainfall (not every day) Jan–Mar; south-east trade winds (20–5 knots) Jun–Jul; cyclones possible Dec–Apr (rare).

Contact details Mike Ball Dive Expeditions (www.mikeball.com), Tusa Dive Charters (www.tusadive.com), Nimrod Explorer (www.explorerventures.com), Undersea Explorer (www.underseaexplorer.com), The Adventure Company (www.adventures.com.au), Taka II Dive Adventures (www.taka.com.au).

Travel national and international flights to Cairns, Brisbane or Sydney; sites accessible by live-aboard from Cairns or Townsville (approximately 12 hours sailing time); wide choice of acommodation onshore.

187 QUEENSLAND: LIHOU REEF, THE WALL

Location 550 km/340 miles north-east of Townsville, in the Coral Sea.

Main species *most trips:* grey reef, whitetip reef; *occasional trips:* blacktip reef, silvertip, tiger, great hammerhead.

Viewing opportunities the grey reef sharks at Lihou Reef (and, indeed, many of the other reefs in the outer Coral Sea) tend to be even bolder than the ones living closer to the mainland and can easily unsettle nervous divers. Lihou covers a huge area, some 90 km/55 miles long and 40 km/25 miles wide, and rises dramatically from the seabed approximately 1000 m/3300 ft below. There are some interesting dives around the many hundreds of pinnacles inside the lagoon, but the best shark diving undoubtedly takes place on the outer reef wall. Many divers are surrounded by grey reef and whitetip reef sharks almost as soon as they enter the water and are then followed around for the remainder of the dive. In fact, on a good day there are so many of them along the wall that, after a while, they almost (but not quite) become part of the scenery.

Bait/feed no.

Cage no.

Other wildlife humpback whale (mainly May to mid-Oct), green turtle, sea snakes, eagle ray, stingray, huge schools of chevron barracuda and bigeye trevally, rainbow runner, grouper, dogtooth tuna, unicornfish, angelfish, kingfish, mullet, sweetlip, cuttlefish.

Best time of year sharks present year-round; best diving Jul–Nov.

Dive depth 15–40 m/50–130 ft plus.

Typical visibility 30–40 m/90–130 ft (occasionally up to 60 m/200 ft); best visibility in winter.

Water temperature 22–26 °C/72–78 °F May–Oct, 27–29 °C/81–84 °F Nov–Apr.

Weather and sea notes most sites sheltered by the reef and sea normally calm; some rainfall (not every day) Jan–Mar; south-east trade winds (20–25 knots) Jun–Jul; cyclones possible Dec–Apr (rare).

Contact details Nimrod Explorer (www.explorerventures.com), Undersea Explorer (www.underseaexplorer.com), The Adventure Company (www.adventures.com.au), Taka II Dive Adventures (www.taka.com.au).

Travel national and international flights to Cairns, Brisbane or Sydney; sites accessible by live-aboard from Airlie Beach, Hervey Bay, Gladstone, Mackay or Townsville (approximately 20 hours sailing time); wide choice of acommodation onshore.

188 QUEENSLAND: MARION REEF

Location 350 km/220 miles north of Gladstone, in the Coral Sea.

Main species *most trips:* grey reef, whitetip reef; *many trips:* blacktip reef, great hammerhead, epaulette or carpet (*Hemiscyllium ocellatum*), tawny nurse (*Nebrius ferrugineus*); *occasional trips:* tiger.

Viewing opportunities Marion Reef is best known for its sea snakes, and there can be literally hundreds of them (mainly olive sea snakes) at any one time. But it is also very good for sharks. It is rather like a large coral atoll, circular in design and about 30 km/19 miles across, with a central lagoon on the inside, full of pinnacles, and some sheer walls on the outside. Grey reef and whitetip reef sharks are encountered on virtually every dive anywhere around the reef, but there are a few key sites to look for other species. Deep Lagoon Pinnacles, on the southern side, is particularly good for blacktip reef sharks, which regularly appear around the pinnacles scattered across the sandy lagoon floor. Shallow Lagoon Pinnacles, a little farther to the north-east, and Northern Gutters, right up in the north, are as good as anywhere to look for tawny nurse sharks. Finally, the outer walls can be good for great hammerheads, which are reasonably common at Action Point (where a 4.5-m/15-ft individual was recorded some years ago).

Bait/feed no.

Cage no.

Other wildlife humpback whale (mainly May to mid-Oct), green turtle, sea snakes, manta (usually late summer) and eagle rays, stingray, huge schools of chevron barracuda and bigeye trevally, rainbow runner, grouper, dogtooth tuna, unicornfish, angelfish, kingfish, mullet, sweetlip, cuttlefish.

Best time of year sharks present year-round; best diving Jul–Nov.

Dive depth 15–40 m/50–130 ft plus.

Typical visibility 30–40 m/90–130 ft (occasionally up to 60 m/200 ft); best visibility in winter.

Water temperature 22–26 °C/72–78 °F May–Oct, 27–29 °C/81–84 °F Nov–Apr.

Weather and sea notes most sites sheltered by the reef and sea normally calm; some rainfall (not every day) Jan–Mar; south-east trade winds (20–25 knots) Jun–Jul; cyclones possible Dec–Apr (rare).

Contact details Undersea Explorer (www.underseaexplorer.com), The Adventure Company (www.adventures.com.au), Taka II Dive Adventures (www.taka.com.au).

Travel national and international flights to Cairns, Brisbane or Sydney; sites accessible by live-aboard from Airlie Beach, Hervey Bay, Gladstone, Mackay or Townsville (approximately 18 hours sailing time); wide choice of acommodation onshore.

189 QUEENSLAND: LADY ELLIOT ISLAND

Location 75 km/45 miles offshore, at the southern end of the Great Barrier Reef.

Main species *most trips*: whitetip reef, blacktip reef, grey reef, leopard, tasselled wobbegong; *many trips*: bronze whaler, silvertip; *occasional trips*: tiger, tawny nurse (*Nebrius ferrugineus*).

Viewing opportunities there are more than 20 excellent dive sites around Lady Elliot Island, a small coral cay with one of the few resorts actually out on the Great Barrier Reef, and sharks can be seen at most of them. Perhaps the most exciting is Shark Pools, where dozens of whitetip, blacktip and grey reef sharks, and even bronze whalers, hunt in under 8 m/ 25 ft of water. They gather in the pools at low tide and, as soon as the tide begins to turn, race across the reef to feed on the fishes trapped in the tidal pools. The sharks tend to give scuba divers a fairly wide berth, perhaps being frightened of the bubbles, but snorkellers are frequently treated to some very close encounters. There are also tasselled wobbegongs in the nearby caves and swim-throughs. Blow Hole is another popular hangout for tasselled wobbegongs and sometimes tawny nurse sharks. A large, L-shaped cave, it is entered from above at a depth of about 15 m/ 50 ft through a large hole in the reef terrace; after a drop of 6 m/20 ft to the cave floor, there is a 20 m/65 ft swim to the exit (through a similar hole at a depth of 25 m/80 ft). Grey reef and silvertip sharks are regulars at Gropers Grovel; the silvertips investigate divers but rarely hang around for long. A towering coral head, called Anchor Bommie, which stands 7 m/25 ft tall in 20 m/65 ft of water, is good for grey reef and leopard sharks. These two species can also be seen at Lighthouse Bommies, a group of small coral heads in 15 m/50 ft of water, along with tasselled wobbegongs. Lighthouse Bommies, Anchor Bommie and Shark Pools can all be snorkelled.

Bait/feed no,

Cage no.

Other wildlife manta rays (year-round) especially at Lighthouse Bommies and Anchor Bommie; eagle, white-spotted shovelnose and black-blotched rays; green, loggerhead and hawksbill turtles (green and loggerhead lay eggs on shore Nov–Mar); huge numbers of breeding seabirds on shore; humpback whales (Jun–Oct).

Best time of year diving conditions best late winter to early summer; tropical monsoon season Jan–Mar, when cyclones can occur; most sharks present year-round, but summer best for Shark Pools and leopard sharks.

Dive depth 1–26 m/3–85 ft (depending on site).

Typical visibility 15–30 m/50–100 ft.

Water temperature 18–22 °C/65–72 °F.

Weather and sea notes slight currents are common (can be very strong at Blow Hole).

Contact details Lady Elliot Island Resort (www.ladyelliot.com.au).

Travel daily flights from Bundaberg, Hervey Bay, Maroochydore and Coolangatta. Accommodation on the island in comfortable motel-style cabins and large safari tent cabins. Easy access to all main shark sites (except Blow Hole and Groper's Grovel – access by boat) by swimming from shore.

190 NEW SOUTH WALES: LORD HOWE ISLAND

Location isolated in the Tasman Sea, 700 km/ 435 miles north-east of Sydney.

Main species *most trips*: Galápagos, grey reef (Balls Pyramid only).

Viewing opportunities Lord Howe Island is an extinct volcano that is home to the most southerly coral reef in the world. Spectacularly beautiful, wonderfully remote and often described as 'the most beautiful island on earth', it is a diver's paradise. The western side of the crescent-shaped island encloses a stunning shallow lagoon, a favourite gathering ground for young Galápagos sharks. They tend to enter the lagoon with the rising tide and then leave just before the tide begins to fall. The area around Erscott's Hole, on the south-west side of Blackburn Island, is a good place to see them. Although the sharks tend to be a little wary at first, they have a habit of rushing in to take a close look at divers: they are simply being curious and do not appear to be aggressive. When local divemasters bait the water, as many as a dozen sharks appear and will often be close enough for good photography. The lagoon and its sharks can be enjoyed by divers and snorkellers alike, and there are even daily trips in glass-bottomed boats. Galápagos sharks can also be seen patrolling the waters where the edge of the lagoon drops into 30 m/100 ft of water at Shark Reef, a few kilometres to the north of Erscott's Hole. Another excellent site is Balls Pyramid, a dramatic rocky island lying 23 km/14 miles south-east of Lord Howe Island (part of the Lord Howe Island group). It can only be dived in good conditions, but is superb for large numbers of very inquisitive grey reef and Galápagos sharks.

Bait/feed bait sometimes used in the lagoon to attract sharks closer.

Cage no.

Other wildlife giant black stingray (especially at Comet's Hole), Spanish dancer, double-headed wrasse; many endemic species, including Lord Howe Island woodhen (one of the world's rarest birds) onshore.

Best time of year Nov–May offers the most stable weather and the best visibility.

Dive depth 5–30 m/16–100 ft.

Typical visibility 20–30 m/65–100 ft.

Water temperature 20–24 °C/68–75 °F.

Weather and sea notes rain likely at any time of year (most in winter); strong winds occur unpredictably (most in winter); may be strong currents offshore (but not in the lagoon).

Contact details Howea Divers (www.lordhowe.com.au/island/diving.html), Pro Dive Travel (www.prodive.com.au).

Travel dive sites accessible from shore or by local dive boat. Lord Howe Island is reached by a 2-hour flight from Sydney or Brisbane (expensive unless purchased as part of a package deal including accommodation and diving). Choice of accommodation (but book well in advance, because no more than 400 visitors are allowed on the island at any one time).

Notes watch out for the banded scalyfin, a small fish with a nasty bite that lives in the lagoon and can be aggressive if a diver unwittingly enters its territory.

191 NEW SOUTH WALES: SOUTH WEST ROCKS: FISH ROCK,

Location 460 km/285 miles north of Sydney on the mouth of the MacLeay River.

Main species *most trips*: sand tiger, Port Jackson, spotted wobbegong, ornate wobbegong; *many trips*: bronze whaler, hammerhead.

Viewing opportunities the craggy island of Fish Rock, just 2 km/1¼ miles south-east of Smoky Cape, is one of a number of outcrops off the little town of South West Rocks. It is one of the best places in the world for close encounters with sand tiger sharks (known locally as grey nurse sharks) and offers the best ocean-cave dive in Australia. As many as 15 sand tigers cruise around in front of the cave entrance, at a depth of 24 m/80 ft, and there are normally good numbers of huge wobbegongs resting on the bottom just inside the cave and along its 125 m/410 ft length. The exit emerges at a depth of 12 m/40 ft. The south-east side of Fish Rock, where a number of gutters run for 100 m/330 ft or more in a north-west–south-east direction, is also very good for sand tigers. On the eastern side of the island, where the

rocky walls drop to 35 m/115 ft, it is quite common to see bronze whalers cruising past in the current. Many other dives in the vicinity virtually guarantee wobbegongs and sand tigers in season. A single dive in May–Jul at the twin peaks of the Pinnacle, which rise from 35 m/115 ft to within 6 m/20 ft of the surface just off the north-eastern corner of Fish Rock, can produce as many as 30 sand tigers. The saddle between the Pinnacle and Fish Rock is home to a dozen wobbegongs, and nearby Shark Alley is another outstanding spot for sand tigers. In good seas, dive boats on their way to Fish Rock frequently pass through a narrow channel between the mainland and Green Island, and some stop for a dive over a series of underwater ledges that are also outstanding for wobbegongs. In summer, with the warmer currents, hammerheads are often seen swimming at the surface around Fish Rock.

Bait/feed no.

Cage no.

Other wildlife migrating humpback whales (late May to mid-Jul and late Sep–Nov), loggerhead and green turtles (year-round), giant Australian cuttlefish, stingray, eagle ray, white-spotted shovelnose ray, moray eel.

Best time of year in recent years sand tiger sharks present year-round except Feb (greatest concentration end May–Jan); wobbegongs present year-round.

Dive depth 7–37 m/23–120 ft (depending on site).

Typical visibility 15–40 m/50–130 ft.

Water temperature 19–24°C/66–75°F; coldest Jun–Jul, warmest Dec–Jan.

Weather and sea notes occasional strong currents offshore.

Contact details South West Rocks Dive Centre (www.southwestrocksdive.com.au), Fish Rock Dive Centre (www.fishrock.com.au).

Travel Fish Rock is accessible by local dive boat. South West Rocks is about 6–7 hours' drive from Sydney (there are regular buses and trains to the nearest town of Kempsey). Choice of accommodation in South West Rocks.

192 NEW SOUTH WALES: FORSTER/ TUNCURRY

Location 300 km/185 miles north of Sydney, near the twin towns of Forster and Tuncurry.

Main species *most trips*: sand tiger, Port Jackson, spotted wobbegong, ornate wobbegong; *occasional trips*: bronze whaler, great hammerhead, shortfin mako, great white.

Viewing opportunities the spectacular underwater rock formations, large reef gutters and sea caves near the twin towns of Forster and Tuncurry are renowned for their large schools of resident sand tiger sharks (known locally as grey nurse sharks). As many as 40 can be encountered on a single dive (although groups of 5–20 are more common) and they show no fear of small groups of well-behaved divers. Despite their fearsome appearance, they are normally safe and inoffensive and offer superb opportunities for close-up photography. It is also worth searching along the gutters of the seafloor, which often contain lots of sand tiger teeth shed during mating and feeding. Sand tigers can be encountered on most reefs in the region, but there are a few recognized sites. The Pinnacles lie about 10 km/6 miles south-east of Forster/Tuncurry. These large masses of coral-covered rock protruding from the ocean floor frequently have a dozen or more sand tigers cruising between them; it is sometimes possible to lie on the seabed here and watch as they pass only a metre or so above. This is also a good area for Port Jackson sharks and wobbegongs, while a wide variety of other species (including bronze whaler, great hammerhead and mako) turn up from time to time. Nearby Latitude Rock is normally good for juvenile sand tigers. A farther 25 km/15 miles to the south are Big Seal Rock, Little Seal Rock and Edith Breakers. Big Seal Rock is a cave and sheer wall gutter, where it is possible to sit quietly and watch large numbers of sand tigers patrolling in their characteristic figure-of-eight pattern; Port Jackson sharks and wobbegongs can often be seen resting in the entrance to a small cave here at a depth of 21 m/70 ft. Sand tigers cruise through a system of steep gutters at nearby Little Seal Rock and are common around the caves, overhangs and crevices of Edith Breakers. Some 23 km/14 miles north of Forster/Tuncurry is Taurus Reef, which has a network of gutters and caves that are excellent for Port Jackson sharks and wobbegongs; the best spot for sand tigers here is the largest cave on the southern side of the reef.

Bait/feed no.

Cage no.

Other wildlife humpback whale (Aug–Dec); loggerhead and green turtles, moray eel, stingray.

Best time of year sharks present year-round but greatest numbers Sep–Feb; great whites occasionally turn up during Feb.

Dive depth 9–35 m/30–115 ft (depending on site).

Typical visibility highly variable at 1–30 m/3–100 ft (average 15 m/50 ft) depending on the site and the day.

Water temperature 19–24°C/66–75°F; coldest Jun–Jul, warmest Dec–Jan.

Weather and sea notes currents can be strong at some sites, especially offshore.

Contact details Action Divers (diving@midcoast.com.au), Blue Water Divers (www.infoweb.com.au/reef_promotions), Forster Dive Centre (forster.dive.centre@attg.lobal.net).

Travel accessible by local dive boat. Wide choice of accommodation around Forster/Tuncurry.

193 NEW SOUTH WALES: JERVIS BAY

Location 180 km/110 miles south of Sydney.

Main species *most trips*: Port Jackson, angel, spotted wobbegong, ornate wobbegong; *many trips*: tiger, oceanic whitetip, bronze whaler; *occasional trips*: sand tiger, shortfin mako, blue, great hammerhead.

Viewing opportunities with its two rugged sandstone peninsulas, protected coves and beautiful white sandy beaches, Jervis Bay is one of the best places in the world to see Port Jackson sharks. During August and September every year, thousands of them converge on this sheltered bay to breed. Single males patrol the area in search of receptive females and it is not unusual to come across large groups of females lying together. One of the best areas to see them is off Longnose Point, around the gutters, pinnacles and ledges, but they can also be seen at the Docks, Middle Ground and several other dive sites in the area. In October, although most of the adult sharks have disappeared, it is possible to see the weird, spiral-shaped egg cases and, in November and December, it is worth checking the bay's sandflats for the newly hatched youngsters. This dive site is not restricted to qualified divers – snorkellers can also enjoy the Port Jackson sharks in parts of Jervis Bay. Remember to check the sandflats for angel sharks and the huge sea caves and giant boulder reefs for spotted and ornate wobbegongs; the latter are so beautifully camouflaged they can be easy to miss. Outside Jervis Bay itself, along the continental shelf, there are many other shark species and it is possible to join organized dives, using two purpose-built cages, to see oceanic whitetips, bronze whalers and a variety of other species. Blues and shortfin makos are particularly common during winter.

Bait/feed no (inside bay), yes (outside bay).

Cage no (inside bay), yes (outside bay).

Other wildlife Australian fur seal (80–100 during winter 4 km/2½ miles south of Jervis Bay), little penguin, eastern fiddler ray, bull ray, short-tailed electric ray, weedy sea dragon, giant Australian cuttlefish, spectacular sponge gardens.

Best time of year Aug–Sep for adult Port Jackson sharks; Nov–Dec for newly hatched Port Jackson sharks; blues and shortfin makos mainly winter; oceanic whitetip, bronze whaler, sand tiger mainly summer.

Dive depth 10–40 m/35–130 ft (depending on site).

Typical visibility 15–25 m/50–82 ft.

Water temperature 14–24 °C/57–75 °F.

Weather and sea notes no distinct rainy season; may be strong currents outside the bay.

Contact details Jervis Bay Charters (www.jervisbay.com), Pro Dive Jervis Bay (www.prodivejervisbay.com.au), Jervis Bay Sea Sports (www.shoal.net.au/~jbseasports/).

Travel accessible from shore, by local dive boat or live-aboard. Jervis Bay is only 2–3 hours' drive from Sydney. Wide choice of accommodation in Huskisson, where most of the dive shops are based, and elsewhere around Jervis Bay.

194 TASMANIA: BASS STRAIT

Location 9 km/6 miles from Flinders Island, off the north-east coast of Tasmania.

Main species *most trips:* Port Jackson (*Heterodontus portusjacksoni*); *many trips:* Australian swellshark or draughtsboard (*Cephaloscyllium laticeps*); *occasional trips:* white-finned swell (*Cephaloscyllium nascione*), broadnose sevengill (*Notorynchus cepedianus*), banded wobbegong (*Orectolobus ornatus*), Tasmanian spotted catshark (*Parascyllium multimaculatum*).

Viewing opportunities nestled in Bass Strait, between Victoria and Tasmania, Flinders Island is the largest island in the Furneaux group, which comprises some 50 different islands and numerous offshore reefs. Flinders itself is a rugged island, some 64 km/40 miles long and 29 km/18 miles wide, and has many good dive sites. The granite caves of Chalky Island offer a chance to dive among sleeping Port Jackson sharks. The shallow limestone ledges of Emita Beach are home to banded wobbegongs over 2 m/7 ft long and there is an opportunity, around dusk, for divers to feed them with pieces of fish. Swellsharks are often encountered cruising through the sea grass and over the rocky reefs off Settlement Point.

Bait/feed sometimes.

Cage no.

Other wildlife bottlenose dolphin, Australian fur seal, stingray, sea dragon, yellowtail kingfish, rock lobster.

Best time of year sharks present year-round, but best conditions Oct–Apr.

Dive depth 10–30 m/33–100 ft.

Typical visibility 15–20 m/50–65 ft.

Water temperature 20–22 °C/68–72 °F in summer, 10–12 °C/50–54 °F.

Weather and sea notes calm days common; may be a slight swell and wind chop.

Contact details Flinders Island Dive (flindersdive@yahoo.com.au).

Travel international flights to Hobart or Launceston (in Tasmania) via major cities in Australia, or to Melbourne (Victoria); direct flight to Flinders Island from Victoria or Launceston; choice of accommodation on Flinders Island.

195 SOUTH AUSTRALIA: DANGEROUS REEF

Location near Port Lincoln in the middle of Spencer Gulf, Great Australian Bight.

Main species *most trips:* great white.

Viewing opportunities Dangerous Reef is perhaps the most famous place in the world for watching great white sharks, although sightings have not been as reliable in recent years as they once were. Since 1993, most dive charters have visited for a day or so (during Neptune Islands trips) just for old times' sake. But the name of the site seems to have captured the imagination of divers and film crews for many years. The sharks are attracted by the large number of Australian sea lions and New Zealand fur seals (Dangerous Reef supports the third-largest breeding population of sea lions in Australia) and are baited to the boat. At one time, as many as 200 great whites frequented this area during the course of a typical year – for periods ranging from a few days to several weeks. A very small number of trips had no sightings but, at the other extreme, many saw up to nine sharks every day. The wait could range from a few minutes to several days and, for this reason, most excursions lasted at least a week. Operators normally help divers to test the large aluminium cage, which floats at the surface, and to become familiar with entry and exit through the trapdoor in the roof before the sharks arrive. Most cages are for three or four people, but check that there are enough to accommodate all guests. Research at the reef has revealed that the sharks often swim near the bottom, looking towards the surface for fur seals and sea lions; if divers are sufficiently experienced, it may be possible to lower the cage to a depth of 27 m/90 ft to view the sharks cruising along the seabed or circling overhead.

Bait/feed yes.

Cage yes.

Other wildlife while waiting for the sharks to appear, in Oct–May dives with Australian sea lions and New Zealand fur seals are organized several kilometres away from the baited area or shore parties are organized Jun–Sep (maintaining radio contact with the main vessel in order to return quickly when the sharks appear); breeding southern right whales in the area Jun–Oct.

Best time of year May–Sep (peak Jul–Sep) is generally considered best for shark activity, but the water temperature is cooler and there can be days of poor weather; shark activity from Oct–early Jan is unreliable and there can be strong winds; Jan–Apr offers fairly reliable shark activity and the winds improve.

Dive depth surface (with an option to drop in the cage to 27 m/90 ft).

Typical visibility 5–12 m/16–40 ft.

Water temperature 17–20 °C/63–68 °F in summer, 15–16 °C/59–61 °F in winter.

Weather and sea notes weather changeable and can quickly fluctuate from calm and hot to windy and cold at any time; the sea is calmest Mar–May.

Contact details Rodney and Andrew Fox in association with Mike Ball Dive Expeditions (www.mikeball.com), Calypso Star Charter (www.calypsostarcharter.com.au).

Travel access only by live-aboard boat from Port Lincoln (Calypso Star Charter) and Adelaide (Rodney and Andrew Fox). Port Lincoln is 680 km/420 miles by road and 280 km/175 miles by air from Adelaide. There is a wide choice of accommodation in both places.

196 SOUTH AUSTRALIA: NORTH AND SOUTH NEPTUNE ISLANDS

Location entrance to Spencer Gulf, Great Australian Bight.

Main species *most trips*: great white; *occasional trips*: bronze whaler.

Viewing opportunities these remote, rocky islands are among the few places in the world where, at the right time of year, sightings of great white sharks can be virtually guaranteed. The sharks are attracted by the large number of Australian sea lions and New Zealand fur seals, which breed on the Neptune Islands, and they are baited to the boat. A very small number of trips have no sightings, but many see up to nine sharks every day. The wait can range from a few minutes to several days and, for this reason, most excursions last at least a week. Operators normally help divers to test the large aluminium cage, which

floats at the surface, and to become familiar with entry and exit through the trapdoor in the roof, before the sharks arrive. Divers can snorkel or use scuba, although some vessels have a long hose, attached to an air cylinder on deck, which helps to limit the amount of equipment inside the cage and allows many consecutive hours underwater. Most cages are for three or four people, but check that there are enough to accommodate all guests (as many as three cages are used, depending on the operator). If divers are sufficiently experienced, some operators will lower the cage to the ocean floor at a depth of 15–30 m/50–100 ft to view the sharks cruising along the seabed or circling overhead.

Bait/feed yes.

Cage yes.

Other wildlife southern right whale (breeding in area Jun–Oct); leafy sea dragon; while waiting for the sharks, dives with Australian sea lions and New Zealand fur seals are organized several kilometres away from the baited area (maintaining radio contact with the main vessel in order to return quickly when the sharks appear).

Best time of year May–Sep (peak Jul–Sep) is generally best for shark activity, but the water temperature is cooler and there can be days of poor weather; shark activity Oct–early Jan is unreliable and there may be strong winds; Jan–Apr offers fairly reliable shark activity and the winds improve.

Dive depth surface (with an option to drop in the cage to 15–30 m/50–100 ft).

Typical visibility 10–20 m/33–65 ft.

Water temperature 17–20 °C/63–68 °F (summer), 15–16 °C/59–61 °F (winter).

Weather and sea notes weather changeable and can quickly fluctuate from calm and hot to windy and cold; the sea is calmest Jun–Sep.

Contact details Rodney and Andrew Fox in association with Mike Ball Dive Expeditions (www.mikeball.com), Calypso Star Charter (www.calypsostarcharter.com.au), Diversion Dive Travel (www.diversionoz.com).

Travel access only from live-aboard boat from Port Lincoln (Calypso Star Charter) and Adelaide (Rodney and Andrew Fox), where there is a wide choice of accommodation.

PAPUA NEW GUINEA

197–9 MADANG: BARRACUDA POINT, MAGIC PASSAGE AND PLANET ROCK

Location Madang is midway along the northern coast of the Papua New Guinea mainland.

Main species *most trips*: grey reef, whitetip reef; *many trips*: scalloped hammerhead, silvertip; *occasional trips*: great hammerhead, whale, tiger.

Viewing opportunities the Madang region is considered by some as the shark capital of Papua New Guinea. Large sharks are regular visitors to several dive sites and the action can be exceptional. Barracuda Point is a reef edge, on the eastern side of Pig Island on the Madang Outer Reefs, dropping into the deep waters of the Bismarck Sea. A variety of large sharks visit the drop-off, including grey reef, silvertip and both great and scalloped hammerheads. Also on the Madang Outer Reefs, Magic Passage is a wide gap some 35 m/115 ft deep between Kranget and Lepa Islands. The entrance is the best place to look for sharks, particularly when the tidal current is flowing into the lagoon from the open sea, and almost anything can turn up. Great hammerheads and whale sharks have been seen here. Planet Rock is just 7 km/4 miles south of Madang Harbour entrance. A seamount rising from depths of 600 m/2000 ft to a small reeftop within 4 m/13 ft of the surface, it is small enough to swim around in a few minutes. There are some interesting corals and large schools of barracuda and bigeye trevally, as well as resident whitetip reef sharks, but the big draw is schooling scalloped hammerheads in season. There is believed to be a resident hammerhead, but it is rarely seen except on dives deeper than 30 m/100 ft.

Bait/feed no.

Cage no.

Other wildlife barracuda, bigeye trevally.

Best time of year sharks present year-round; scalloped hammerheads school around Planet Rock Sep–Nov.

Dive depth 4–40 m/13–130 ft (depending on site).

Typical visibility 30–40 m/100–130 ft (depending on site); visibility may drop to 15 m/50 ft in Jan–Feb; surface water at Planet Rock can have reduced visibility due to river run-off, but it is usually better a few metres down; plankton blooms possible late Nov–Dec.

Water temperature 27–29 °C/81–84 °F; coldest Jul–Aug; warmest Jan–Feb.

Weather and sea notes rain possible at any time of year, although most likely Nov–May; more wind May–Nov, but mornings usually calm with sea breezes picking up in the afternoons; currents can be strong.

Contact details Blue Sea Charters (www.blueseacharters.com), Trans Niugini Tours (www.pngtours.com).

Travel all three sites can be reached by local dive boat or live-aboard. Regular flights to the capital Port Moresby from Australia and several South-East Asian cities, and domestic flights from there to Madang. Wide choice of accommodation in Madang.

200–3 VITIAZ STRAIT: BAGABAG ISLAND, CROWN ISLAND, LONG ISLAND AND BERNIE'S WALL

Location north-east and east of Madang in the Bismarck Sea.

Main species *most trips*: grey reef; *many trips*: silvertip, whitetip reef, blacktip reef, bronze whaler, tawny nurse (*Nebrius ferrugineus*); *occasional trips*: oceanic whitetip, tiger, great hammerhead.

Viewing opportunities four widespread sites with a variety of good shark dives offering several different species. Bagabag Island lies 60 km/37 miles north-east of Madang. Grey reef sharks are common in the area, whitetip reef sharks are seen regularly, and sightings of sleeping tawny nurse sharks and very large oceanic whitetips are not uncommon. The outer barrier reefs are best for sharks and some of the passages are particularly good for close encounters. Crown Island is excellent for grey reef and silvertip sharks, which frequently occur in good numbers, especially in the south at The Saddles. Great hammerheads are occasionally seen on the other side of the island at Crown Corner. Julien's Reef, off the west coast of Long Island, is good for grey reef and silvertip sharks and, at the time of writing, the outermost reef off the north coast has a resident tiger shark. Bernie's Wall, off Saidor on the mainland, is the site of a Second World War plane wreck with beautiful drop-offs dripping with soft corals and plenty of exciting shark action. It is a great place to see bronze whalers, which can be very feisty around divers at this site; grey reef sharks are common as well.

Bait/feed no.

Cage no.

Other wildlife spinner dolphin (especially in the inner reef of Crown Island and at Western Drop-Off in western Bagabag), hawksbill turtle, giant clam, ragged pipefish, eagle ray, Napoleon wrasse, schooling barracuda and Spanish mackerel.

Best time of year year-round diving, but with distinct seasons; dry season May–Oct (but can be more windy with choppier seas); wet season Oct–May (normally with calmer seas).

Dive depth 3–50 m/10–165 ft (depending on site).

Typical visibility 20–40 m/65–130 ft.

Water temperature 27–29 °C/81–84 °F; coldest Jul–Aug; warmest Jan–Feb.

Weather and sea notes rain possible at any time of year, although most likely Nov–May; more wind May–Nov, but mornings usually calm with sea breezes picking up in the afternoons; currents can be strong.

Contact details Blue Sea Charters (www.blueseacharters.com), Jais Aben Resort (www.aquaventures-png.com), Dolphin Enterprises (www.goldendawn.com).

Travel Bagabag accessible by local dive boat or live-aboard, Crown and Long Islands only by live-aboard. Regular flights to the capital Port Moresby from Australia and several South-East Asian cities, and domestic flights from there to Madang. Wide choice of accommodation in Madang.

204–6 EASTERN FIELDS: POINT P, JAY'S REEF AND CRAIG'S ULTIMATE

Location 170 km/105 miles south-west of Port Moresby, in the Coral Sea. Local dive operators prefer to withhold the exact position of key shark sites because of shark finners.

Main species *most trips*: whitetip reef, grey reef, silvertip, tawny nurse (*Nebrius ferrugineus*), scalloped hammerhead, great hammerhead; *occasional trips*: tiger, whale, oceanic whitetip.

Viewing opportunities the Eastern Fields reef system is the most northerly of the Coral Sea reefs and is beyond the devastating impact of cyclones that sometimes damage reefs farther south. The diving is pristine, the area teeming with fish and beautiful coral formations and the water usually crystal-clear. The entire reef system is renowned for its big-fish action, but three sites are exceptional for sharks. Point P is a protected reef that regularly attracts 20 or more sharks of six different species: whitetip reef, grey reef, silvertip, tawny nurse, scalloped hammerhead, great hammerhead. Jay's Reef, on Porlock Reef, is the site of a shark feed that takes place on the outer drop-off: more than 20 silvertips and another 20 grey reef sharks come to baits placed on a coral growth that rises from the main spur. This is a particularly good site for photography because divers can easily position themselves a little below the sharks. Craig's Ultimate, on the western side of Eastern Fields, is often conducted as a drift dive. Small groups of scalloped hammerheads, and one or two great hammerheads, regularly visit this wonderfully sculptured coral reef.

Bait/feed yes (Jay's Reef only).

Cage no.

Other wildlife schooling jacks and barracuda, giant Queensland groupers, blue ribbon eel, moray eel (Jay's Reef), huge tuna (Point P).

Best time of year sharks present year-round; rainfall most months (wettest period Dec–Jan) but normally limited to a heavy afternoon downpour every few days.

Dive depth 5–50 m/16–165 ft (depending on site).

Typical visibility 40–50 m/130–165 ft; plankton blooms possible late Nov–Dec.

Water temperature 26–30 °C/78–86 °F; coldest Jul–Aug; warmest Dec–Jan.

Weather and sea notes fairly sheltered, likely to be a slight current (stronger at Craig's Ultimate).

Contact details Dolphin Enterprises (www.goldendawn.com).

Travel accessible only by live-aboard (approximately 10 hours from the capital Port Moresby). Regular flights to Port Moresby from Australia and several South-East Asian cities. Wide choice of accommodation in the city.

207 MILNE BAY

Location extreme eastern end of the Papua New Guinea mainland, midway between the Coral Sea and Solomon Sea. Local dive operators prefer to withhold the exact position of some shark sites because of shark finners.

Main species *most trips*: grey reef, silvertip; *many trips*: scalloped hammerhead, great hammerhead, tasselled wobbegong; *occasional trips*: whale, oceanic whitetip, tiger, silky.

Viewing opportunities there are many superb shark sites in and around beautiful Milne Bay. During the plankton bloom in November to December whale sharks are sometimes attracted to East Cape, at the north-eastern tip of the bay; in the same area, silky sharks frequently accompany passing cetaceans. Beyond the Cape is Boia Boia Waga Island, which is good for scalloped hammerheads in relatively shallow water near the drop-off. Banana Bommie, an incredibly rich reef with good numbers of grey reef sharks, is a little farther south-east. Well beyond the entrance to Milne Bay, off the northern side of Nuakata Island, is Peer's Reef; there are strong currents here, and it is best experienced as a drift dive, but as many as 50 schooling scalloped hammerheads can be encountered from May to November. Boirama Reef, on the western side of Boirama Island near Nuakata Island, is excellent for grey reef sharks and, at the time of writing, has a resident tasselled wobbegong. Inside the bay itself, Sullivan's Patches, just 7 km/4 miles east of the Killerton Islands, is good for grey reef sharks and is sometimes visited by scalloped hammerheads and tiger sharks. There are also two good sites along the northern coast of the peninsula, outside the bay. The first is Wahoo Reef, 11 km/7 miles west of East Cape – another reliable site for scalloped hammerheads, which often swim over divers drifting along the edge of the drop-off. The second is Bertha's Bommie, just north of Awaiama Bay, which also has scalloped hammerheads (best seen along the edge of the shallow reef close to shore) and is good for grey reef sharks. Several of the Milne Bay sites can be enjoyed by snorkellers, but considerable numbers of sharks go with the territory and snorkelling here is not for the faint-hearted.

Bait/feed sometimes at certain sites.

Cage no.

Other wildlife dugongs, minke whales, short-finned pilot whales and orcas sometimes.

Best time of year year-round diving, but with distinct seasons; May–Nov brings south-east trade winds; Dec–Apr generally calmer with short, strong winds from the north-west or south-west.

Dive depth 5–50 m/16–165 ft (depending on site).

Typical visibility 15–40 m/50–130 ft; heavy rainfall reduces surface visibility; plankton blooms possible late Nov–Dec.

Water temperature 26–30 °c/78–86 °F; coldest Jun–Jul; warmest Jan–Feb.

Weather and sea notes Milne Bay has its own mini-climate, unlike other parts of Papua New Guinea; windy weather common; rainfall varies from year to year, but wettest months tend to be May and Aug–Sep (not Jan–Mar as elsewhere in the country); currents can be strong at some sites, especially May–Nov.

Contact details Blue Sea Charters (www.blueseacharters.com), Dolphin Enterprises (www.goldendawn.com), Niugini Diving (www.niuginidiving.com), Milne Bay Charters (www.chertan.com), Mike Ball Dive Expeditions (www.mikeball.com),Bomatu Diving Company (www.bomatu.com).

Travel all the main sites are accessible by local dive boat or live-aboard and some are accessible from shore. Regular flights to the capital Port Moresby from Australia and several South-East Asian cities, and domestic flights from there to Gurney Airport, servicing the provincial capital of Alotau. Choice of accommodation in Alotau.

Note just before going to press, it was revealed that heavy fishing pressure has taken its toll on the sharks at Milne Bay and there are very few left. Sadly, encountering them is now more of a treat than a common dive occurrence.

208–10 D'ENTRECASTEAUX ISLANDS: HAMMERHEAD CORNER, SHARK ALLEY AND SILVERTIP CITY

Location north of the southern tip of mainland Papua New Guinea.

Main species *most trips:* grey reef; bronze whaler; *many trips:* silvertip; *occasional trips:* scalloped hammerhead, great hammerhead, tiger.

Viewing opportunities three widely separated dives with some wonderful shark opportunities. Hammerhead Corner in the Dart Reefs, between Goodenough Island and Cape Vogel, is very good for grey reef sharks, silvertips and, as the name suggests, hammerheads. Shark Alley, in the Star Reefs, is best known for its grey reef sharks and bronze whalers. Silvertip City, at Enif Reef, lives up to its name and offers silvertips on many dives. Tiger sharks can turn up almost anywhere in the D'Entrecasteaux Islands and are seen occasionally at these three sites.

Bait/feed no.

Cage no.

Other wildlife manta ray, eagle ray, giant clam, occasional dugong and cetaceans.

Best time of year year-round diving, but best late Oct–Dec (clear water and light winds during the doldrums, when there is a change of seasons from south-east to north-west).

Dive depth 5–50 m/16–165 ft (depending on the site).

Typical visibility 30–50 m/100–165 ft.

Water temperature 26–29 °c/78–84 °F; coldest Jun–Jul; warmest Jan–Feb.

Weather and sea notes south-easterlies blow May–Nov; north-westerlies Jan–Apr (rarely strong for more than a few hours); least rain Jun–Sep.

Contact details Niugini Diving (www.niuginidiving.com).

Travel accessible by live-aboard operating out of Lae. Regular flights to the capital Port Moresby from Australia and several South-East Asian cities, and domestic flights from there to Lae. Choice of accommodation in Lae.

211–12 HUON GULF: MCDONALD'S REEF AND SALAMAUA OFFSHORE REEFS

Location in front of Lae on the northern coast of mainland Papua New Guinea.

Main species *most trips*: grey reef, bronze whaler; *occasional trips*: whale.

Viewing opportunities the highlight of any visit to McDonald's Reef, in the Tami Islands 90 km/55 miles east of Lae, is a close encounter with the local bronze whaler sharks. They are seen on virtually every trip during the south-east season. Whale sharks are seen regularly at a number of the gulf's deep drop-offs and are present in reasonable numbers every winter. However, they can be hard to find without spotter planes and are normally encountered just by chance or when sightings are radioed in by members of the local game-fishing club. Salamaua Offshore Reefs, off the Salamaua Peninsula about 40 km/25 miles to the south of Lae, seem to be a particularly good site for them.

Bait/feed no.

Cage no.

Other wildlife lacy scorpionfish, giant barrel sponge.

Best time of year sharks present year-round; most whale shark sightings Jul–Sep; most bronze whaler sightings May–Nov.

Dive depth 2–40 m/7–130 ft (depending on site).

Typical visibility 30–40 m/100–130 ft (except at surface); surface waters often have poor visibility due to muddy freshwater flowing into the Gulf from the Markham River.

Water temperature 27–29 °C/81–84 °F; coldest Jul–Aug; warmest Jan–Feb.

Weather and sea notes sea breezes tend to develop in the afternoons, but mornings are normally calm; rainfall likely every month (most in May–Oct), but diving still good.

Contact details Blue Sea Charters (www.blueseacharters.com), Niugini Diving Charters (www.niuginidiving.com).

Travel the Salamaua Peninsula is accessible by local dive boat or live-aboard, but the Tami Islands are accessible only by live-aboard. Regular flights to the capital Port Moresby from Australia and several South-East Asian cities, and domestic flights from there to Nadzab (45 km/28 miles from Lae). Wide choice of accommodation in Lae.

213–15 KIMBE BAY: FAIRWAY REEF, INGLIS SHOAL AND KIMBE ISLAND BOMMIE

Location off the northern coast of New Britain Island between the Willaumez Peninsula and Lolobau Island.

Main species *most trips*: silvertip, grey reef, whitetip reef; *many trips*: scalloped hammerhead, blacktip reef; *occasional trips*: bronze whaler, whitetip reef.

Viewing opportunities Kimbe Bay is good for sharks and there are several dive sites with virtually guaranteed sightings. Fairway Reef lies about 20 km/12 miles offshore, near Lolobau Island, and is well known for grey reef sharks and silvertips; most of the action takes place at a small bommie (coral growth) called Kilabob's Knob off the northern end of the main reef. Some operators conduct shark feeds here. Inglis Shoal (32 km/20 miles north-north-east of Walindi) is a seamount rising from depths of 600 m/2000 ft to within 12 m/40 ft of the surface; this is a good site for scalloped hammerheads, although they are rarely seen shallower than 30 m/100 ft. Kimbe Island Bommie (45 km/28 miles north-east of Walindi) offers good numbers of grey reef sharks and silvertips and the shallow area before the reef drop-off is home to a population of blacktip reef sharks.

Bait/feed sometimes (Fairway Reef).

Cage no.

Other wildlife killer whales, spinner dolphins and other cetaceans commonly encountered in the bay; resident school of barracuda; bigeye trevally.

Best time of year sharks present year-round, but most rain falls Jan–Mar.

Dive depth 8–50 m/26–165 ft (depending on site).

Typical visibility 50 m/165 ft; plankton blooms possible late Nov–Dec.

Water temperature 28–30 °C/82–86 °F; coldest Jun–Jul; warmest Jan–Feb.

Weather and sea notes Kimbe Bay is relatively sheltered and calm May–Nov (when south-east trade winds blow), but exposed to north-westerly winds and swells (Jan–Mar).

Contact details MV FeBrina (www.febrina.com), Walindi Resort (www.walindi.com), Peter Hughes Diving (www.peterhughes.com).

Travel Inglis Shoal and Kimbe Island Bommie are accessible by local dive boat or live-aboard, Fairway Reef only by live-aboard. Regular flights to the capital Port Moresby from Australia and several South-East Asian cities, and domestic flights from there to Hoskins. Choice of accommodation at Hoskins, Kimbe and Walindi (about 40 km/25 miles away).

Location south-west coast of New Ireland, 125 km/78 miles from Kavieng, north-eastern Papua New Guinea.

Viewing opportunities this is not a shark-watching site, but is included in the directory for interest. The ancient tradition of 'shark calling' is still conducted by men from the villages between Konogogo and Kontu. Passed down from generation to generation (for a fee), 'the knowledge' is a very strict affair. The sea and weather conditions must be just right, and for a full 24 hours before the hunt the caller must avoid anything that would enable a shark to tell that he has been up to no good: he must not eat wild pig or crayfish, accept any food from the hand of a fertile woman, step on any excrement or have sex. He anoints himself, and his canoe, with secret herbs to awaken the spirit of Moro (the shark god) and paddles out alone to the reef. A couple of kilometres offshore he chants a soft, melancholy tune and shakes in the sea a rattle made out of bamboo and coconut shells, known as a *larung*. No one knows how this works (some experts believe the sharks are just curious, but others suggest that the noise of the rattle in the water mimics the sound of injured or nervous fish), but soon a shark answers the call. There are lots of different shark species in these waters, but it is specifically the shortfin mako that is called. The hunter entices the shark to the side of his canoe and kills it. The meat is shared among the local villagers.

Contact details New Ireland Tourist Bureau (www.discovernewireland.org.pg).

Location Kavieng is the provincial capital of New Ireland Province, and is situated on the northern tip of New Ireland Island. It is the gateway to a maze of islands and passages between New Ireland and New Hanover islands in the Bismarck Archipelago.

Main species *most trips*: grey reef, whitetip reef, silvertip; *occasional trips*: bull, whale, great hammerhead, blacktip reef, oceanic whitetip.

Viewing opportunities the region around northern New Ireland and New Hanover islands is widely regarded as a good place to see sharks, although the conditions at many sites are not suitable for inexperienced divers. There are relatively few species in this area, but those that do occur are here in large numbers. Grey reef sharks can be seen almost everywhere and silvertips are also common at many sites. In addition to the world-renowned Valerie's Reef (see p.267), there are seven particularly rewarding shark sites within easy reach of Kavieng. Kaplaman Reef, which is south-east of Kavieng, off Kaplaman village in northern New Ireland, has grey reef and silvertip sharks and many large pelagics. Farther south, at the southern entrance to Albatross Passage between New Ireland and Baudisson Island, Albatross Pass has a resident population of grey reef sharks (best observed on an incoming current when the visibility is better and the shark action most impressive). Helmut's Reef in Steffen Strait, off the western end of Baudisson Island, is also excellent for grey reef sharks. Planet Channel is roughly midway between New Hanover and New Ireland, between the smaller Enang and Nusalaua islands, and is another difficult dive in a fierce current; the best section of this 3-km/2-mile channel is Eagle Ray Pass, where the channel widens to meet the ocean, which is excellent for grey reef sharks. Nearby Byron Wall, at the south-west entrance to Byron Strait, is regularly visited by great hammerheads and other large sharks. Chapman's Reef is 350 m/1150 ft south off Ao Island, near Cape Matanalem on western New Hanover; it is a difficult dive with a strong current, but is rewarding, with lots of grey reef sharks and occasional whale sharks. Nearby Taun Reef, a little to the south-east, is also good for grey reef sharks.

Bait/feed no.

Cage no.

Other wildlife eagle ray, hawksbill turtle (will approach divers at Turtle Reef, 7 km/4 miles north of Bangatang Island, although this particular reef is poor for sharks).

Best time of year sharks present year-round.

Dive depth 3–50 m/10–165 ft (depending on site).

Typical visibility 40–50 m/130–165 ft.

Water temperature 28–30 °C/82–86 °F; coldest Jun–Jul; warmest Jan–Feb.

Weather and sea notes currents can be strong; Chapman's Reef often experiences a heavy swell; rainfall possible year-round, but usually in heavy afternoon or evening downpours every few days; seas calm Mar–Dec, with light south-easterly winds; rain more likely Dec–Mar with stronger north-westerly winds.

Contact details Blue Sea Charters (www.blueseacharters.com), Dolphin Enterprises (www.goldendawn.com), Archipelago Diving (www.archipelagodiving.com.au), Lissenung Island Resort (www.lissenung.com), Malagan Diving (www.meltours.com), Mike Ball Dive Expeditions (www.mikeball.com), MV FeBrina (www.febrina.com), Trans Niugini Tours (www.pngtours.com).

Travel most sites accessible by local dive boat operating out of Kavieng or by live-aboard (Chapman's Reef and Taun Reef only by live-aboard).Regular flights to the capital Port Moresby from Australia and several South-East Asian cities, and daily domestic flights from there to Kavieng. Choice of accommodation in Kavieng.

Notes just before going to press, it was revealed that heavy fishing pressure has taken its toll on the sharks of the Kavieng Region and there are very few left. Sadly, encountering them is now more of a treat than a common dive occurrence. About 125 km/80 miles from Kavieng, on the south-west coast of New Ireland, fishermen from the village of Kontu practise the ancient tradition of shark calling. A man paddles out to sea in a canoe, where he sings a soft, melancholy tune and uses a coconut-shell rattle (to imitate a school of nervous fish) to lure sharks to the boat. The sharks are then caught with a simple noose and hauled into the boat.

218 VALERIE'S REEF

Location near East Islands, on a chain of uncharted reefs off the north-east coast of New Hanover Island, Bismarck Archipelago.

Main species *most trips:* silvertip; *occasional trips:* bull, blacktip.

Viewing opportunities Valerie's Reef, or Silvertip Reef as it is sometimes known, was once the most famous site in the world for guaranteed close encounters with silvertip sharks. Named in honour of the renowned shark authority and underwater film maker Valerie Taylor, it is one of hundreds of coral reefs in the Bismarck Archipelago. Until recently it was the permanent home of between 9 and 12 large, female silvertips, but it has just been targeted by shark finners and several of the animals have been killed. One particularly large individual, dubbed Queen Emma and well known to local divers, was among the sharks taken. The New Ireland Fisheries Authorities have since banned shark finning in the province, but it may be a while before other silvertips take up residence and Valerie's Reef regains its reputation as one of the best places to photograph this species at close range and in crystal-clear water. Some live-aboard operators are baiting the reef on a regular basis in the hope of speeding up the process (visiting divers began to feed

the sharks in 1989, and sporadic feeding continued until recently, but was stopped when the sharks took up permanent residence) and the numbers are increasing once again. Just before going to press, two of the original individuals reappeared. In the past the silvertips turned up even before the anchor had been dropped. They investigated divers as soon as they hit the water and then accompanied them on their swim to the reef. Although they frequently came disconcertingly close to divers, they were surprisingly well behaved and not aggressive. Hopefully the newcomers will react in exactly the same way. This is one of the few dive sites in the area where the more excitable grey reef sharks do not occur.

Bait/feed fed in the past, but practice now stopped.

Cage no.

Other wildlife large schools of barracuda and trevally, eagle rays, Queensland groupers.

Best time of year sharks present year-round.

Dive depth 12–40 m/40–130 ft.

Typical visibility 45 m/150 ft; plankton blooms possible late Nov–Dec.

Water temperature 29–30 °C/84–86 °F year-round.

Weather and sea notes the dive is best with a slight current from the south-east and light winds; swells are common. Rainfall most months (wettest period Dec–Feb), but normally limited to a heavy afternoon downpour every few days.

Contact details Blue Sea Charters (www.blueseacharters.com), Dolphin Enterprises (www.goldendawn.com), Divex Indonesia-Archipelago Diving (www.divex-indonesia.de), Lissenung Island Resort (www.lissenung.com), Malagan Diving (www.meltours.com), Mike Ball Dive Expeditions (www.mikeball.com), Trans Niugini Tours (www.pngtours.com), Bomatu Diving Company (www.bomatu.com).

Travel accessible by local dive boat or live-aboard operating out of Kavieng. Regular flights to the capital Port Moresby from Australia and several South-East Asian cities, and domestic flights from there to Kavieng. Choice of accommodation in Kavieng.

Note Valerie's Reef silvertips do not normally harass divers, but this species can be dangerous if over-stimulated. It is advisable to swim beneath the surface to avoid too much splashing, always to wear dark gloves and to keep your hands close to your body to avoid them being mistaken for food.

MELANESIA

219 SOLOMON ISLANDS: NEW GEORGIA ISLANDS

Location north-western side of the Solomon Islands; 2400 km/1500 miles north-west of Fiji, 2000 km/ 1250 miles north-east of Australia, in the Solomon Sea.

Main species *most trips:* blacktip reef, whitetip reef, grey reef; *many trips:* silvertip, scalloped hammerhead.

Viewing opportunities the New Georgia Islands offer some of the best diving in the Solomon Islands and are the permanent or seasonal home of several shark species. There are two outstanding sites in the west near Gizo (the second-largest town in the archipelago): Grand Central Station and Hot Spot. Grand Central Station is off the north-western tip of Ghizo Island (different spelling from the town, but pronounced the same) and lies at the meeting point of two ocean currents. This is a stunning dive on a wall that drops straight down to 50 m/165 ft and is such a good place for sharks that it has been compared to Palau's legendary Blue Corner. It normally begins as a drift along the wall, at a depth of about 30 m/100 ft, before everyone settles down on a ledge blanketed with beautiful soft corals. This makes an excellent vantage point from which to watch the sharks hanging in the current. Hot Spot is a relatively new dive off Ghizo, first identified in 1995. Consisting of a small pinnacle rising to within 5 m/16 ft of the surface, it is surrounded by water dropping to more than 300 m/ 1000 ft in the ocean depths. Effectively, it is an open-ocean dive. Nearby Secret Spot is a much deeper dive, where divers descend down a wall to around 45 m/150 ft, in the hope of encountering silvertips that gather in considerable numbers here. There are two good shark dives near the village of Munda (on the south-western tip of New Georgia Island): Top Shelf and Shark Point, both of which are good for grey reef and whitetip reef sharks. Shark Point is on the edge of an incredible drop-off, falling straight into the ocean depths at several thousand metres, while Top Shelf has a gentle current, which makes for an easy dive and yet is just enough to attract good numbers of sharks. There are also some great sites in and around Marovo Lagoon, in the east, which is the largest saltwater lagoon in the world and a proposed World Heritage Site. Sharks can be seen almost anywhere here but the island of Uepi, on the northern edge of the lagoon, is particularly good. The best place is The Elbow, on the north coast, which is a steep drop-off with sheer walls falling to over 600 m/1970 ft. There are two projections from the wall (which give the site its name) covered with colourful hard and soft corals, but the main attraction is the school of 10 or more scalloped hammerheads that sometimes gather in the area. Kokoana Passage is also very good for scalloped hammerheads, especially on an incoming tide. Inside Point, a steeply sloping wall at the Marovo end of Charapoana Passage, has a resident population of grey reef sharks which frequently patrol the point when the incoming tide is running.

Bait/feed no.

Cage no.

Other wildlife sea turtles, manta and eagle rays, king trevally, batfish, barracuda, Spanish mackerel, unicornfish, surgeonfish, dogtooth tuna.

Best time of year many sharks present year-round; hammerheads at Uepi most common Jun–Nov.

Dive depth 20–45 m/65–150 ft.

Typical visibility 18–30 m/60–100 ft (highly variable in Marovo Lagoon, according to tide conditions); best Oct–Nov.

Water temperature 26–30 °C/78–86 °F.

Weather and sea notes significant currents at Ghizo Island, but normally mild at Uepi and Munda; no defined seasons (average 25cm/10 in of rainfall per month year-round), but slightly wetter Nov–Mar; can be strong south-east trade winds in Apr–Oct.

Contact details Dive Gizo (www.divegizo.com), Uepi Island Resort (www.uepi.com), Solomon Sea Divers (www.pacificislandtravel.com/solomon_islands/diving/solomonseadivers.html), Bilikiki Cruises (www.bilikiki.com).

Travel all sites accessible by live-aboard or individual sites by day boat; international flights via Fiji, Papua New Guinea or Australia to the capital Honiara; live-aboards depart from Honiara or Gizo; flights from Honiara to Seghe, then 12 km/7½ miles by motorized canoe to Uepi, or direct to Gizo; choice of accommodation.

Note some operators have postponed dive trips to the Solomon Islands temporarily, due to the political unrest.

220 SOLOMON ISLANDS: RUSSELL ISLANDS

Location south-western side of the Solomon Islands; 2400 km/1500 miles north-west of Fiji, 2000 km/ 1250 miles north-east of Australia, in the Solomon Sea.

Main species *most trips:* grey reef, whitetip reef, blacktip reef, tawny nurse (*Nebrius ferrugineus*); *occasional trips:* silvertip, tiger.

Viewing opportunities many divers visit the Solomon Islands to see the remnants of the fierce fighting that took place here during the Second World War. Tankers, battleships, troop carriers, bombers and fighters can be found scattered among the shallow reefs and deep harbours. But the archipelago is rapidly gaining a reputation for shark diving and the Russell Islands, in particular, offer some excellent close encounters. Grey reef, whitetip reef and blacktip reef sharks can be seen almost anywhere, but two sites are particularly good: Fonagho, a finger of reef gradually sloping from 5 m/16 ft to about 30 m/100 ft, and a very similar point at Karumolun. Perhaps the most unusual (and unpleasant-sounding) dive takes place on Mbanika Island: the site is called Shark Point, but the dive actually takes place in the waters opposite an abattoir. Several times a week large numbers of sharks gather over a sandy shelf close to shore to feed on offal thrown out by the slaughterhouse. Divers enter the water a day or two after the sharks have finished eating, and are often rewarded with close encounters with grey reef, blacktip reef, whitetip reef and tawny nurse sharks; tiger sharks turn up from time to time, as well. The sandy shelf drops to about 30 m/100 ft, but the dive usually takes place at a depth of 10–15 m/33–50 ft. Mary Island, which lies to the west and slightly north of the Russell Islands, is a good place to see resting whitetip reef sharks (on the outer reef slope) and some divers are lucky enough to encounter silvertips in the blue water beyond.

Bait/feed no (but indirectly with offal from Mbanika abattoir).

Cage no.

Other wildlife various cetaceans, manta and eagle rays, yellowtail and red-bellied fusiliers, chevron barracuda, dogtooth tuna, oceanic triggerfish, giant clam.

Best time of year sharks present year-round.

Dive depth 20–35 m/65–115 ft.

Typical visibility 18–30 m/60–100 ft; best Oct–Nov.

Water temperature 26–30 °C/78–86 °F.

Weather and sea notes no defined seasons (average 25 cm/10 in of rainfall per month year-round), but slightly wetter Nov–Mar; can be strong south-east trade winds in Apr–Oct.

Contact details Bilikiki Cruises (www.bilikiki.com), Dive Adventures (www.diveadventures.com).

Travel accessible by live-aboard or day boat; international flights via Fiji, Papua New Guinea or Australia to the capital Honiara; direct flights to the Russell Islands from Honiara (25 mins); limited choice of accommodation.

Note some operators have postponed dive trips to the Solomon Islands temporarily, due to the political unrest.

221–22 FLORIDA ISLANDS: TWIN TUNNELS AND PASSAGE ROCK

Location between Guadalcanal, Malaita and Isabel; 2400 km/1500 miles north-west of Fiji, 2000 km/1250 miles north-east of Australia.

Main species *most trips:* grey reef, blacktip reef, tawny or Indo-Pacific nurse (*Nebrius ferrugineus*); *many trips:* whitetip reef.

Viewing opportunities these are two very different dive sites, but both are good for shark watching. Twin Tunnels consists of two ancient lava chutes or chimneys (each about 4 m/13 ft in diameter), which run vertically down from a patch reef at about 14 m/45 ft to a depth of some 34 m/110 ft. After about 30 m/100 ft the two parallel tunnels then meet and open up into one long horizontal tunnel. The dive exits through a hole in the main tunnel, at around 37 m/120 ft, which brings you out at the reef wall. When the current is flowing into Twin Tunnels, they are teeming with fish and blacktip reef sharks frequently explore inside; they often approach divers very closely before disappearing. Grey reef sharks regularly patrol the deep-blue water around the exit. The vertical wall here is full of black and soft corals and gorgonians, but it can be a bit of an anticlimax after such an exciting dive. Passage Rock is a long vertical drop-off, where the currents are strong and the wall falls into the ocean depths. The swirling water here attracts grey reef sharks, which are best observed from a secure point below the worst of the current. Unfortunately, they tend to be quite nervous of divers, especially if too many bubbles are carried to them by the current. The top of the reef at Passage Rock can also be good for tawny nurse sharks.

Bait/feed no.

Cage no.

Other wildlife green turtle, giant trevally, dogtooth tuna, barracuda, kingfish, lionfish, schools of fusiliers, painted crayfish (in a small cave at the bottom of the western tunnel).

Best time of year sharks present year-round.

Dive depth 18–40 m/60–130 ft.

Typical visibility 18–30 m/60–100 ft; best Apr–Jun and Sep–late Nov.

Water temperature 27–30 °C/81–86 °F.

Weather and sea notes strong currents likely

around Passage Rock; no defined seasons (average 25 cm/10 in rainfall per month year-round), but slightly wetter late Dec–Mar; can be strong south-east trade winds Jun–Jul.

Contact details Bilikiki Cruises (http://bilikiki.com).

Travel international flights via Fiji, Papua New Guinea or Australia; live-aboards depart from Honiara (the capital).

Note some operators have postponed dive trips to the Solomon Islands temporarily, due to the political unrest.

223–4 SOLOMON ISLANDS: LAULASI AND BUSU ISLANDS

Location 16 km/10 miles from Auki on the north-west coast of Malaita, south-eastern Solomon Islands (100 km/62 miles from Honiara); 2400 km/1500 miles north-west of Fiji, 2000 km/1250 miles north-east of Australia.

Viewing opportunities this is not a shark-watching site, but is included in the directory for interest. Sharks are worshipped and revered in many parts of the Solomon Islands and a few of the people of Laulasi and Busu Islands, in particular, still believe that their ancestors live on as sharks. This is where the ancient tradition of 'shark calling' takes place. In the old days, until the 1970s, the elders or shamans would bang rocks together underwater to attract sharks into the shallows close to shore. Then a small boy from the village would handfeed them pieces of pork, starting with the smallest shark, before apparently climbing on to the back of the biggest for a ride around the lagoon. Although the handfeeding itself has officially stopped, a simpler form of the ritual still takes place and it really does seem to work. No one in the shark-calling communities wears red or black, which are taboo colours, because the red represents blood and the black represents the black pigs that provide the pork.

Contact details Solomon Islands Ministry of Commerce, Employment and Tourism (www.commerce.gov.sb).

Note some operators have postponed dive trips to the Solomon Islands temporarily, due to the political unrest.

225–6 VANUATU: ESPIRITU SANTO AND REEF ISLANDS

Location 1800 km/1100 miles east of Australia, 800 km/500 miles west of Fiji.

Main species *most trips:* grey reef, whitetip reef; *many trips:* blacktip reef, bronze whaler, silvertip; *occasional trips:* scalloped hammerhead.

Viewing opportunities sharks are seen on many dives around the 80 or so islands and islets of Vanuatu. The outer islands are particularly good and it is almost impossible to dive them without seeing at least one shark. Stretching across more than 725 km/450 miles of ocean and surrounded by very deep water, the dive sites are both widespread and varied. The most common species are whitetip and grey reef sharks, but blacktip reef, bronze whalers and silvertips are by no means uncommon and a variety of other species turns up from time to time. Espiritu Santo is the island that inspired James A. Michener to write his classic *South Pacific* and is the most popular destination for divers in the republic. One of the biggest draws is SS *President Coolidge*, the largest wreck dive in the world; launched as a luxury passenger liner in 1931, she was converted into a troop carrier at the beginning of the Second World War and was sunk by an American mine in 1942; she now lies on her side in Santo Harbour. The *Coolidge* is home to a rich variety of reef fish as well as a resident grouper, called Boris, who has been handfed by divers since 1970 and now weighs 200 kg/440 lb. The wreck is not particularly good for sharks, but grey reef, blacktip reef and whitetip reef can be seen in the vicinity.

In the past (1988–2000) shark-feeding dives have been conducted in 21 m/70 ft of water off Bokissa Island and as many as 30 reef sharks attended almost daily. It was widely regarded as one of the best action-packed shark feeds in the Pacific, but shark numbers have declined dramatically in the past year and the feeds have been suspended until the population recovers or returns. In the meantime, one of the best places to see all three reef shark species in Espiritu Santo is Submarine Reef. Another is a very steep wall that lies on the north-east side of the small island of Sakao, off the north-eastern tip of Espiritu Santo. Known as Sakao Wall, it starts just below the surface and faces the open sea, so a variety of reef and oceanic species can be seen here. Sharks are encountered all the time at the Reef Islands, in the northern part of the archipelago, and are particularly common at a site known as the Ammunition Dump; on a good day, several dozen can be seen patrolling near the coral head on the edge of the reef. Nearby Bronzie's Wall, to the west of Ammunition Dump and also in the Reef Islands, is very impressive as it drops from just below the surface to depths of more than 300 m/ 1000 ft; as its name suggests, it can be a good place to see bronze whalers, which are often very curious and may approach divers closely.

Bait/feed no (feeds have taken place in the past and may resume in the future).

Cage no.

Other wildlife eagle ray, grouper (Boris is around the *Coolidge* only Feb–Aug), dogtooth tuna, trevally, lionfish, butterflyfish, anemonefish, damselfish, angel-fish, sweetlips, squirrelfish, ghost pipefish, trumpet fish, goby (living harmoniously with dozer shrimps).

Best time of year sharks present year-round, but best diving May–Oct.

Dive depth 20–60 m/65–200 ft (some dives on the *Coolidge* are very deep and well beyond the scope of most recreational divers).

Typical visibility 10–30 m/33–100 ft (best around offshore islands).

Water temperature 26–32 °C/78–90 °F; drops to 23° C/74 °F in Aug–Sep.

Weather and sea notes currents generally mild, but can be moderate to strong at Sakao Wall and Bronzie's Wall; rain likely Nov–Apr (mainly Dec–Feb); trade winds blow (consistent 15–20-knot wind) Jun–Sep.

Contact details Nautilus Scuba (www.nautilus-scuba.com), Aquamarine Diving (www.aquamarine-santo.com), Allan Power Dive Tours (www.allan-power-santo.com), Jackpot Charters (www.jackpot.com.vu).

Travel international flights via Fiji, Papua New Guinea, Australia or New Zealand to the capital Port Vila; daily flight to Santo (45 mins); choice of accommodation on Espiritu Santo; Reef Islands best dived from a live-aboard.

Note the island of Malekula (especially on the west or lee side where there are steep walls and canyons) is also excellent for shark watching – particularly when the current is strong.

227 VANUATU: NEW CALEDONIA

Location 1500 km/930 miles off the north-east coast of Australia, 1700 km/1050 miles north-west of New Zealand.

Main species *most trips:* whitetip reef, grey reef; *many trips:* tawny nurse (*Nebrius ferrugineus*); *occasional trips:* zebra or leopard, silvertip, blacktip, bull, sandbar (*Carcharhinus plumbeus*), sicklefin lemon (*Negaprion acutidens*), silky, great hammerhead, oceanic whitetip, tiger, whale.

Viewing opportunities this is one of those places where it can feel as if anything is possible. As many as five different shark species have been encountered on a single dive here, several are seen on a regular basis, and an incredible variety of others turn up from time to time. The territory of New Caledonia consists of a main island (known simply as Mainland, or Grande Terre, and one of the largest islands in the South Pacific), the Isle of Pines off the southern tip, the Loyalty Islands to the east (including Maré, Lifou, Tiga

and Ouvéa), the Belep Archipelago in the north-west, and numerous other islands and islets. It encircles an incredible 24,000 sq km/9300 sq miles of emerald-green lagoon and has a 1600 km/1000 mile long barrier reef. There are many good sites for sharks and some species – both whitetip and grey reef sharks – can be seen almost anywhere. One of the best places is Kasmira Reef, which consists of four coral heads on the sand and is best dived at low tide. Local operators estimate that zebra sharks are seen on 90 per cent of dives (both males and females live here and are so curious that they frequently investigate divers very closely), while whitetip reef and tawny nurse sharks often put in an appearance as well. Boulari Passage is particularly good for grey reef sharks (and manta rays) and there are huge numbers of both grey reef and silvertip north of Ouvéa at the Pleiade. Some of the other more popular shark dives take place at Vallée des Gorgones, Passe de Gié, Banc de Sable and Faille de Noupoa.

Bait/feed only Noumea Diving at Boulari Passage.

Cage no.

Other wildlife humpback whale (Sep–Dec), minke whale (occasional Oct–Dec), sperm whale (occasional late Oct–Nov), dugong, loggerhead and green turtles, sea snakes, manta (best Apr–Jun) and eagle rays, moray eel, lionfish, butterflyfish, Spanish mackerel, giant grouper, trevally, much endemic wildlife onshore.

Best time of year most sharks present year-round, but best Apr–Jun; diving year-round.

Dive depth 5–26 m/16–85 ft.

Typical visibility 10–30 m/33–100 ft.

Water temperature 20–27 °C/68–81 °F; coldest in Aug, warmest in Jan.

Weather and sea notes currents typically mild to moderate (strong in the passages early in the year); warm season with wind and occasional short rains Jan–Mar.

Contact details Kunie Scuba Center (kuniescuba@canl.nc), Koulnoué Dive Centre (tel: 687-42-8359 / fax: 687-42-8175), Nouméa Diving (www.noumea-diving.nc).

Travel international flights to Tontouta International Airport (New Caledonia); inter-island transportation by air or sea; wide choice of accommodation.

228 FIJI: MANA ISLAND: SUPERMARKET

Location off the north-west coast of Mana Island, in the Mamanuca Islands, 20 km/12 miles north-west of Viti Levu.

Main species *most trips:* grey reef, whitetip reef, blacktip reef; *occasional trips:* tiger, bull.

Viewing opportunities Supermarket is perhaps Fiji's best-known dive site. Until his untimely death in September 2000, the star of the show was legendary 'Sharkman' Apisai Bati. Api, as he was known to his friends, was a member of the Tavua Island Shark Clan and was raised to carry on the traditional role as a guardian of the sharks. Over the years he gained the confidence of local sharks, many of which he came to know as individuals (Suzy and Smillie are two of the regular grey reef sharks), and was able to handfeed them without the benefit of protective clothing. Feeding still takes place at Supermarket twice a week, and about 10 sharks of various species typically attend (as few as five or as many as 30). Most of them are whitetip reef sharks, but some grey reef and blacktip reef usually turn up as well. Supermarket is a small reef located inside the Malolo Barrier Reef, which protects the Mamanuca Islands. Divers descend to a depth of 9–12 m/30–40 ft and position themselves on a shallow plateau of rock and rubble on the seabed. The feeder is about 5 m/16 ft away, in a natural amphi-theatre of sand, and produces fish one by one from a bag. There may be as many as 44 divers (divided between several different operators) per feeding session. Once all the food has gone (usually after about 10 minutes) there is an opportunity to explore the site further. There is an excellent wall dive nearby, dropping sharply into the deep blue, which may be conducted as a drift dive, but can also be done from permanent moorings. There are nearly always sharks present along the wall, whether or not food has been provided at the start of the dive.

Bait/feed yes.

Cage no.

Other wildlife green and hawksbill turtles, manta ray (summer), potato cod, moorish angelfish, puffer-fish, magnificent goby, longfin spadefish, clownfish, grouper, humphead and Napoleon wrasse, yellow-margined moray eel.

Best time of year sharks present year-round.

Dive depth 9–12 m/30–40 ft.

Typical visibility 15–35 m/50–115 ft.

Water temperature 26–30 °C/78–86 °F, depending on season.

Weather and sea notes site can experience some surge and current may be strong, but nearly always accessible; higher water and air temperatures, more rainfall (occasional afternoon storms) and calmer seas Nov–Apr; choppier conditions in winter; from mid-morning to evening cooling trade wind blows from east and south-east for most of the year; cyclones possible Jan–Mar.

Contact details Aqua-Trek Mana (www.aquatrek.com), Subsurface Fiji (www.fijidiving.com), Castaway Diving (www.castawayfiji.com).

Travel international flights to Nadi Airport (Viti Levu); wide choice of accommodation in the Mamanucas; nearest island is Mana; most resorts accessible by a short boat ride or scenic flight from Nadi.

Note operators have a code of conduct for shark diving at Supermarket, which includes a restriction on the number of divers and safety rules for the vessels.

229 FIJI: VATU-I-RA CHANNEL: E6 AND HI8

Location southern end of Vanua Levu Barrier Reef, between the two main islands of Vanua Levu and Viti Levu; 2100 km/1300 miles north of New Zealand, 3200 km/1990 miles north-east of Australia.

Main species *most trips:* whitetip reef; *many trips:* scalloped hammerhead, grey reef, blacktip reef; *occasional trips:* silvertip, zebra or leopard.

Viewing opportunities E6 and Hi8 are both seamounts in the Vatu-i-ra Channel, with steep sides covered in soft corals and sea fans, rising from a depth of more than 1000 m/3300 ft. Their tops just break the surface at low tide and can be snorkelled at high tide. The larger of the two is a world-famous dive site in its own right and was dubbed E6 by Rob Barrel, captain of the live-aboard *Nai'a*, because divers here tend to take huge quantities of film (E6 is the process used to develop many slide films). Also known as Mount Mutiny, and lying about 9 km/6 miles to the west, Hi8 is similarly named for all the underwater video footage it inspires. The two seamounts intercept the nutrient-rich current flowing just outside the narrowest part of Bligh Water, between the two main Fijian islands of Viti Levu and Vanua Levu, and can be great places to see pelagics. Scalloped hammerheads, grey reef sharks and occasional silvertips are usually encoun-tered on the two sides facing the current, cruising around the drop-off looking for food. Whitetip and blacktip reef sharks can be seen at the Cathedral, a spectacular horseshoe-shaped grotto lit from above and lined with a riot of colourful gorgonias and soft corals. There is a resident whitetip reef shark here, normally encountered at about 23 m/75 ft, and there are usually some other whitetips resting on the canyon floor.

Bait/feed no.

Cage no.

Other wildlife eagle and manta rays, schooling barracuda, trevally, surgeonfish, many reef fishes.

Best time of year sharks present year-round.

Dive depth 10–37 m/33–120 ft.

Typical visibility 10–30 m/33–100 ft; best Jul–Sep, worst during plankton blooms (Nov–Apr).

Water temperature 27–29 °C/81–84 °F Nov–Apr; 24–27 °C/75–81 °F May–Oct.

Weather and sea notes currents usually mild; strong surge common at the surface; Dec–Apr tends to be hot and wet, May–Oct generally dry; choppy seas common Jul–Sep; strong winds or cyclones possible Jan–Mar.

Contact details Nai'a Cruises (www.naia.com.fj), MV Princess II (www.princessii.com), Fiji Aggressor (www.aggressor.com), Mollie Dean Cruises – Sere-ni-Wai (www.sere. com.fj), Crystal Divers (www.crystaldivers.com).

Travel the site can only be dived from live-aboards; international flights direct to Fiji or via Hawaii; some live-aboards pick up at Nadi International Airport.

230 FIJI: KORO ISLAND: SHARK FIN POINT

Location off the north-east point of Koro Island, in the Lomaiviti group; 2100 km/1300 miles north of New Zealand, 3200 km/1990 miles north-east of Australia.

Main species *most trips:* grey reef, whitetip reef.

Viewing opportunities shaped rather like a shark's tooth, Koro Island is the sixth-largest of the 300 or so islands in Fiji. It is rarely visited by live-aboard dive boats, but does have an action-packed drift dive at Shark Fin Point (only possible when the tide is running) with lots of grey reef and whitetip reef sharks, as well as eagle rays and an impressive school of about 500 barracudas.

Bait/feed no.

Cage no.

Other wildlife barracuda, eagle ray.

Best time of year sharks present year-round.

Dive depth 12–40 m/40–130 ft.

Typical visibility 15–37 m/50–120 ft; best Jul–Sep, worst during rains and plankton blooms (Nov–Apr).

Water temperature 27–29 °C/81–84 °F Nov–Apr; 24–27 °C/75–81 °F May–Oct.

Weather and sea notes strong current when tide is running; Dec–Apr tends to be hot and wet, May–Oct generally dry; choppy seas common Jul–Sep; strong winds or cyclones possible Jan–Mar.

Contact details Fiji Aggressor (www.aggressor.com).

Travel accessible by live-aboard or from Koro Island; international flights direct to Fiji or via Hawaii; regular flights via Suva to Koro or direct by seaplane; choice of accommodation on the island.

231 FIJI: WAKAYA ISLAND: WAKAYA PASSAGE

Location the southernmost point of the barrier reef around Wakaya in the north-eastern Lomaiviti group, to the east of Viti Levu; 2100 km/ 1300 miles north of New Zealand, 3200 km/1990 miles north-east of Australia.

Main species *most trips:* scalloped hammerhead, grey reef, whitetip reef; *occasional trips:* bronze whaler, great hammerhead, thresher, blacktip, silver-tip, tawny or Indo-Pacific nurse (*Nebrius ferrugineus*), zebra or leopard.

Viewing opportunities Wakaya Passage is best known for its scalloped and great hammerheads, but is actually a good place to see several different shark species. The passage begins at a depth of about 11 m/35 ft, where there is a sandy bottom, and then slopes gradually to 27 m/90 ft before dropping away over a beautiful wall cloaked with staghorn coral, sea fans and soft corals. There is a school of resident hammerheads here, ranging in length from about 2.5–4m/8–13 ft, and they often cruise in to investigate divers. They are normally found near the passage floor at a depth of around 27 m/90 ft and several can be seen together; on one memorable occasion, no fewer than 17 were encountered. Grey reef and whitetip reef sharks are also fairly common. Bronze whalers are another draw, although they tend to stay below 30 m/100 ft and are not seen that often. A little farther north, at Blue Ridge on the outer edge of the barrier reef, a lone hammerhead has been resident for many years. Blue Ridge is also good for manta rays (some of which have shark bites on the leading edges of their wings) and bright-blue ribbon eels.

Bait/feed sometimes.

Cage no.

Other wildlife various cetaceans, hawksbill turtle, manta (less frequent Jan–Mar), marble and eagle rays, barracuda, snapper, Napoleon wrasse, blue ribbon eel, dartfish, jewfish, lionfish, blue fusilier.

Best time of year sharks present year-round.

Dive depth 12–40 m/40–130 ft.

Typical visibility 15–37 m/50–120 ft; best Jul–Sep; highly variable and changes with the tides.

Water temperature 27–29 °C/81–84 °F Nov–Apr; 24–27 °C/75–81 °F May–Oct.

Weather and sea notes currents usually negligible, but can be moderate; Dec–Apr tends to be hot and wet, May–Oct generally dry; choppy seas common Jul–Sep; strong winds or cyclones possible Jan–Mar.

Contact details Fiji Aggressor (www.aggressor.com), Nai'a Cruises (www.naia.com.fj), MV Princess II (www.princessii.com), Sere-Ni-Wai (www.sere.com.fj), Ovalau Watersports Fiji (www.owlfiji.com).

Travel international flights direct to Fiji or via Hawaii; accessible via live-aboard or from the private resort island of Wakaya (www.fiji-islands.com/wakaya.html).

232 FIJI: GAU ISLAND: NIGALI PASS/SHARK ALLEY

Location the largest island of the Lomaiviti group, to the east of Viti Levu; 2100 km/1300 miles north of New Zealand, 3200 km/1990 miles north-east of Australia.

Main species *most trips:* grey reef; *many trips:* whitetip reef; *occasional trips:* scalloped hammerhead, silvertip, blacktip reef.

Viewing opportunities shark feeds began at Nigali Pass in 1994 and the aim has always been to provide enough food to pique the curiosity of the local grey reef sharks, but not enough to let them become dependent. Consequently there is no handfeeding here. This narrow cut through the main barrier reef around Gau Island (also known as Nigali Passage or Shark Alley) naturally concentrates a considerable number of energetic grey reef sharks. Most of them are resident females and, on a typical dive, anything from 8 to 25 turn up. The dive is normally conducted as a drift: divers are dropped well up-current and, having drifted through the channel, are picked up just under 1 km/½ mile away. The quality of the dive depends very much on the tide and it is best dived on the ebb about 1½ hours before low tide, when clear seawater flows through the 100 m/330 ft opening while most of the lagoon is emptying through the northern passes. If it is conducted at the wrong time, the visibility tends to be poor and the current can exceed 4 knots. It is a thrilling experience and, towards the lagoon side of the pass, everyone is funnelled past the large, inquisitive sharks – which far outnumber the divers. Scalloped hammerheads and silvertips are also sometimes seen in the pass. Halfway into the channel there is a Y-junction where, at a place dubbed 'the bleachers' at a depth of about 20 m/65 ft, it is possible to position yourself behind some boulders and watch the sharks swim past. Then take the right-hand fork and finish the dive in the shallows among lettuce corals teeming with juvenile fish.

Bait/feed yes.

Cage no.

Other wildlife hawksbill turtle, sea snakes, manta and eagle rays, huge schools of trevally, barracuda and bigeye jack, marbled grouper, Napoleon wrasse.

Best time of year sharks present year-round.

Dive depth 18–30 m/60–100 ft.

Typical visibility 15–37 m/50–120 ft; best Jul–Sep, worst during plankton blooms (Nov–Apr).

Water temperature 27–29 °C/81–84 °F Nov–Apr; 24–27 °C/75–81 °F May–Oct.

Weather and sea notes four-hour window of opportunity for diving each day (when currents and tides are right); current can be strong (3–4 knots); Dec–Apr tends to be hot and wet, May–Oct generally dry; choppy seas common Jul–Sep; strong winds or cyclones possible Jan–Mar.

Contact details Nai'a Cruises (www.naia.com.fj), Fiji Aggressor (www.aggressor.com), MV Princess II (www.princessii.com), Sere-ni-Wai (www.sere.com.fi).

Travel international flights direct to Fiji or via Hawaii; some live-aboards offer direct transfer between Nadi International Airport and vessel; luxury resort (www.bayofangels.com) currently being built on Gau.

233 FIJI: VITI LEVU: BEQA LAGOON

Location off the southern coast of Viti Levu; 2100 km/1300 miles north of New Zealand, 3200 km/1990 miles north-east of Australia.

Main species *most trips:* blacktip reef, grey reef, whitetip reef, bull; *many trips:* silvertip, tawny nurse (*Nebrius ferrugineus*); *occasional trips:* oceanic whitetip, tiger.

Viewing opportunities some of the best dive sites around Viti Levu (Fiji's largest and most populated island) lie within Beqa Lagoon, an area of about 360 sq km/140 sq miles just to the south. Fiji is often described as the 'soft coral capital of the world' and Beqa (pronounced Beng-gah) is a riot of colour with its proliferation of soft corals. The lagoon is formed by the rim of an ancient volcano, making a circular chain of islets and a long barrier reef. Several different shark species can be seen on most dives, but the regular feeds at Sharkfin Reef (or Sharkfin Passage as it is sometimes called) offer the most intense encounter in the region. Sharkfin is situated on the mainland side of Beqa Passage, away from the lagoon. The operators empty huge quantities of fish (discarded by the local fish factory) into the ocean while divers watch from a safe distance on the reef at a depth of about 30 m/100 ft. The sharks arrive very quickly and there are usually eight resident bull sharks (up to 3 m/10 ft long) among them, along with grey reef, blacktip reef and whitetip reef. Silvertip and Pacific nurse sharks often turn up as well, and the chance for a free feed sometimes even attracts oceanic whitetip and tiger sharks.

The feed usually takes about 20 minutes and there is a 10-minute safety stop. A particularly good site for whitetip reef sharks is nearby Shark's Reef, which is inside the lagoon where several bommies (the Australian name for underwater pinnacles) sit in a circle on the sandy seabed at a depth of about 15 m/50 ft.

Bait/feed yes.

Cage no.

Other wildlife spotted eagle ray, giant trevally, grouper, Napoleon wrasse, barracuda, titan triggerfish.

Best time of year sharks present year-round.

Dive depth 30 m/100 ft.

Typical visibility 15–37 m/50–120 ft; best Jul–Sep, worst during rains and plankton blooms Nov–Apr.

Water temperature 27–29 °C/81–84 °F Nov–Apr, 24–27 °C/75–81 °F May–Oct.

Weather and sea notes mild or no current; Dec–Apr tends to be hot and wet, May–Oct generally dry; choppy seas common Jul–Sep; strong winds or cyclones possible Jan–Mar.

Contact details Crystal Divers (www.crystaldivers.com), Marlin Bay Resort (**www.marlinbay.com**), Lalati Resort (**www.lalati-fiji.com**), Beqa Divers (**www.beqadivers.com**).

Travel international flights direct to Nadi on Viti Levu (or via Pacific island hubs); resorts on Beqa Island or day trips from Viti Levu; choice of accommodation on Beqa and Viti Levu.

Note grey reef sharks in Beqa Lagoon are sometimes misidentified locally as bronze whalers. There is some disagreement about shark feeding around Beqa Lagoon and a few operators prefer to introduce divers to sharks under more natural conditions.

FRENCH POLYNESIA

234–6 MARQUESAS ARCHIPELAGO: HAMMERHEAD SENTRY POINT, EIAO AND HATUTU

Location off the southern coast of the main island of Nuku Hiva, just outside Taiohae Bay (in the eastern corner); 1400 km/870 miles north-east of Tahiti, 500 km/310 miles from the closest point of the Tuamotus.

Main species *most trips:* scalloped hammerhead, silvertip, whitetip reef; *occasional trips:* great hammerhead.

Viewing opportunities diving in the Marquesas Archipelago is a real adventure. The most northerly

archipelago in French Polynesia, and farther from a continental landfall than any other group of islands on earth, this is about as remote as it gets. There are 15 islands and islets here (just six of which are inhabited) and relatively few established dive sites. The Hammerhead Sentry Point (sometimes known as the Hammerhead Sentinel or La Sentinelle aux Marteaux) is one of the best places in the Pacific for scalloped hammerheads. It is conveniently close to the village of Taiohae (on the main island of Nuku Hiva) and, although the visibility is not brilliant, sightings are virtually guaranteed. According to the local dive operator's records, they are seen on 75 per cent of dives (in season). Divers enter the water immediately below some steep basalt cliffs, which plunge below the surface to a sandy bottom at about 50 m/165 ft, and then swim along the wall. The depth of the dive varies according to the sharks – sometimes they are within 15 m/50 ft of the surface but, at other times, they may be as deep as 40 m/130 ft. It is simply a matter of luck. They do not seem to be as nervous as the hammerheads in many parts of the world and are often so curious that they approach divers quite closely. No one seems to know why they gather in this particular area, although the females are believed to give birth near the wharf inside Taiohae Bay.

Scalloped hammerheads can also be seen at Motumano Point, off the south-western corner of Nuku Hiva, and at Matateteiko, which is a little farther north but still on the west coast. Matateteiko is interesting, because the hammerheads often patrol over a shallow rocky platform that continues (perpendicular to the island cliffs) for about 100 m/330 ft towards the open sea. Whitetip reef sharks can be seen at both Motumano and Matateteiko, and are particularly common on the opposite side of the island at a site some 400 m/1300 ft south of Tikapo Point.

Two other islands in the Marquesas group are known to be excellent for sharks: Eiao and Hatutu. Both uninhabited, they lie close to one another to the north-west of Nuku Hiva. Their main attraction is a resident population of large and inquisitive silvertips, which approach divers closely on virtually every trip. Eiao is particularly good, because the sharks patrol backwards and forwards with relentless regularity underneath a major seabird cliff. As if that is not enough, both these outlying islands are good for schooling scalloped hammerheads and some divers have had lucky close encounters with solitary great hammerheads some 3–4 m/10–13 ft long.

Bait/feed no.

Cage no.

Other wildlife melon-headed whale (one of best places in the world to see this species – the site off the east coast of Nuku Hiva has a concentration of as many as 400 every morning and, if sea conditions permit, it is possible to dive or snorkel with them), manta, eagle and leopard rays, stingray, moray eels (including the endemic dragon moray), snapper, trevally, barracuda, tuna, pufferfish, parrotfish, triggerfish, butterflyfish, octopus, lobster.

Best time of year sharks present year-round.

Dive depth 10–30 m/33–100 ft.

Typical visibility 5–20 m/16–65 ft (poor because sea is rich in plankton and alluvium); typically about 15 m/50 ft at Hammerhead Sentry Point and can drop to 5 m/16 ft at low tide.

Water temperature 28–30 °C/82–86 °F year-round.

Weather and sea notes very exposed (no reefs or lagoons to provide shelter), so swell often high and winds can be strong; currents generally mild at Hammerhead Sentry Point, but likely to be strong at Motumano Point and Matateteiko; surge likely at Motumano Point; rainy season Nov–Dec; mild trade winds common, with cooler winds Jul–Aug.

Contact details Centre Plongée Marquises (www.marquises.pf/pagestour/page108.htm).

Travel accessible by live-aboard or day boat from Taiohae; international flights to Tahiti; connecting flight to Nuku Hiva (3½ hours); limited choice of accommodation on Nuku Hiva.

237–9 MANIHI: THE DROP-OFF, THE BREAK AND TAIRAPA PASS

Location 530 km/330 miles north-east of Tahiti, 177 km/110 miles north-east of Rangiroa, in the Tuamotu Archipelago.

Main species *most trips:* blacktip reef, grey reef, whitetip reef, tawny nurse (*Nebrius ferrugineus*); *occasional trips:* great hammerhead, silvertip, oceanic whitetip, Pacific lemon (*Negaprion acutidens*), whale.

Viewing opportunities best known as a major centre for black pearls and as the home of many large pearl farms, Manihi now has a growing reputation for shark diving. The main dive sites are in the south-west corner of the atoll, where the only major pass enters the lagoon (which measures 27 × 8 km/17 × 5 miles). Sharks abound in this area and grey reef, blacktip reef and whitetip reef are seen in great numbers on virtually every dive. It is common, for example, to see gatherings of 25 or more small (1 m/3⅓ ft) whitetip reef sharks. There are three main shark dives. Tairapa Pass is the 100 m/330 ft wide entrance to the lagoon and is normally experienced as a drift dive. The best time for sharks is when the current is flowing into the lagoon. The dive starts on the ocean side, where the

depth is about 25 m/80 ft, continues over a shallow coral shelf at about 5 m/16 ft and ends where the slope drops down again inside the lagoon. The current draws divers through enormous shoals of fish with lots of tawny nurse sharks in attendance, good numbers of whitetip reef sharks in the undercuts along the northern side, and several blacktip reef and grey reef sharks swimming around. Silvertips can occasionally be seen here, as well. The grand finale is a wild encounter with hundreds of angry titan triggerfish, protecting their nests inside the lagoon, as well as their attending resident blacktip reef sharks. The middle and southern sides of the pass had been spoiled by large quantities of rubbish dumped by people living in the nearby village of Turipaoa, but a determined clean-up has now returned this area to its original condition. The Drop-Off is on the ocean side of the atoll, just outside Tairapa Pass, where the wall plummets from 3 m/10 ft to an incredible 1370 m/4500 ft. Schools of yellowtail snapper, paddle snapper, pyramid butterflyfish and other fish are so dense here that they actually block out the light, but the real excitement comes from the abundant resident blacktip reef sharks. A few grey reef sharks are commonly seen here and, occasionally, silvertips and oceanic whitetips meander through the enormous schools of fish. The Break is also on the ocean side, where a large cut in the reef forms a kind of coral amphitheatre. This is where a high-energy shark feed takes place. As the boat approaches, blacktip reef, grey reef and whitetip reef are already gathering for the feast; great hammerheads, oceanic whitetips and Pacific lemon sharks occasionally make an appearance as well. By the time everyone is ready, there are often so many sharks that it can be difficult not to land on one when you roll backwards into the water.

Bait/feed yes (The Break).

Cage no.

Other wildlife various cetaceans (including humpbacks Jul–Oct), manta ray (Sep–Oct), spotted eagle ray, marbled grouper (thousands breeding in the south-west corner late Jun to early Jul), titan triggerfish, Napoleon wrasse, barracuda, marlin, sailfish.

Best time of year most sharks present year-round; great hammerheads Jan–Feb; diving year-round.

Dive depth 9–24 m/30–80 ft (depending on site).

Typical visibility 30–60 m/100–200 ft; poorer during the rainy season.

Water temperature 26–29 °C/78–84 °F with little seasonal variation.

Weather and sea notes Tairapa Pass conducted as a drift dive; no strong currents outside the pass; rainy season Nov–Dec; mild trade winds common with cooler winds Jul–Aug.

Contact details Manihi Blue Nui Dive Center (www.bluenui.com).

Travel international flights to Tahiti; national flights from Tahiti to Manihi; Manihi Pearl Beach Resort (www.pearlresorts.com) is the main hotel on the atoll; limited choice of alternative accommodation.

240–1 RANGIROA ATOLL: AVATORU PASS AND TIPUTA PASS

Location north coast of Rangiroa, next to Avatoru and Tiputa villages; 330 km/205 miles north-east of Tahiti in the Tuamotu archipelago.

Main species *most trips:* grey reef, whitetip reef, blacktip reef, silvertip; *many trips:* great hammerhead, lemon, tawny or Indo-Pacific nurse (*Nebrius ferrugineus*), tiger (see **Notes**); *occasional trips:* blacktip, silky.

Viewing opportunities dubbed by many as the Shark Capital of the Pacific, Rangiroa more than lives up to its reputation. Sharks seem to be everywhere throughout the Tuamotu archipelago, but few places can be more 'sharky' than here and few shark dives more exhilarating than Tiputa and Avatoru Passes. Rangiroa, or 'Rangi' as the locals call it, is a huge coral atoll measuring 75 km/47 miles from east to west and 25 km/16 miles from north to south. It is the second-largest atoll in the world. The inner lagoon, which looks more like an inland sea, opens to the Pacific through Tiputa and Avatoru. Named after a couple of nearby villages, they lie on either end of the same *motu* as the airport, with Avatoru to the west and Tiputa to the east. Fast-flowing tidal currents rush through these narrow openings in the reef – at full tidal flood they can exceed 5 knots – and they are home to bewildering numbers of sharks: grey reef, whitetip reef and blacktip reef sharks are virtually guaranteed. Always conducted on an incoming tide (an outgoing tide would literally suck you out to sea), these drift dives are not for the faint-hearted. Indeed, the experience was once described as flying out of control with a gang of accommodating Hell's Angels.

Tiputa Pass is deeper and longer than Avatoru and, since the current is stronger, there are more sharks. The dive normally begins at Shark Cave, in the external reef wall on the left side of the pass, which is a gathering ground for grey reef sharks. The greatest numbers are near the bottom (at 65 m/215 ft) but, on a good day, huge numbers fill the sea all the way to the surface. Most of them are juveniles averaging 1–1.5 m/ 3⅓–5 ft in length and readily approach divers. The cave (which is actually an overhanging rock) is at a depth of 26–35 m/ 85–115 ft and everyone watches the action here for a while before moving on. There are normally a few whitetip reef sharks in some of the neighbouring caves, some of which also harbour a few tawny nurse sharks. Then you move into the current with yet more sharks (several dozen is the norm – but many divers report encountering several hundred) and get propelled through the pass safely into the calm waters of the lagoon. It is common to be carried right through the middle of huge schools of sharks. In May and June, huge numbers of grey reef sharks gather around the canyons of Tiputa Pass to mate – an unforgettable sight with an average depth of about 30 m/100 ft. Great hammerheads can readily be seen for a few months each winter at the Valley, a dive site nearby, where they cruise in deep water (45 m/150 ft) in search of eagle rays; their arrival here is timed to coincide with the eagle ray mating season. Hammerhead dives are normally conducted as 10-minute drifts from the Grotte aux Requins.

Avatoru Pass is a similar dive, with just as many different shark species, but fewer sharks. However, a site outside the pass (not a drift dive) is exceptionally good for silvertips. In the Indo-Pacific, silvertips are nearly always associated with deep-water drop-offs, where they patrol at depth, but they will come to the surface to investigate any unusual activity. At Avatoru, almost as soon as divers hit the water, four or five massive silvertips appear from nowhere to find out what is going on. They can be seen without using bait, but some dive operators may place fish scraps on a gently sloping part of the reef, at a depth of about 20 m/65 ft, to encourage even closer encounters. Silky sharks can occasionally be seen in blue water beyond the pass.

Bait/feed occasionally (for photographers or film crews working with silvertips).

Cage no.

Other wildlife bottlenose dolphin, hawksbill and green turtles, manta ray (best Jul–Oct), spotted eagle ray, barracuda, grouper, Napoleon wrasse, dogtooth and yellowfin tuna, marlin, sailfish, wahoo.

Best time of year most sharks present year-round; mating grey reef May–Jun; great hammerhead Dec–Mar (mainly Jan–Feb; best diving conditions Sep–early Nov.

Dive depth 15–45 m/50–150 ft (extreme depth of 45 m/150 ft necessary for great hammerheads at the Valley).

Typical visibility 24–30 m/80–100 ft (occasionally reaches 60 m/200 ft).

Water temperature 26–29 °C/78–84 °F; warmest in summer.

Weather and sea notes moderate swell and strong tidal current in and around the passes; usually windy Jul–Aug; rainy season Nov–Mar, dry season Apr–Oct.

Contact details Raie Manta Club
(www.raiemantaclub.free.fr), The Six Passengers
Diving Center (www.the6passengers.com/anglais),
Dream Dive (www.dreamdive.pf), Rangiroa
Paradive (www.chez.com/paradive), Manihi Blue
Nui Dive Center (www.bluenui.com).

Travel international flights to Tahiti; connecting
flights to Rangiroa; choice of accommodation on
Rangiroa.

Notes several other dive sites in Rangiroa are good
for sharks, including Les Failles (grey reef and silvertip), Manta Point (silvertip), Mahuta (nursery for grey
reef and good for whitetip reef and blacktip reef),
Shark Point (grey reef and great hammerhead) and
Big Blue (silvertip and silky). 7–10-day tiger shark
expeditions to other parts of the Tuamotu archipelago
are sometimes organised from Rangiroa and involve
hanging a bait cage filled with fish scraps from the
boat; on average, they have a 70 per cent success
rate. Tigers measuring up to 5 m/16 ft are sometimes
seen but, since no protective cage is used, dives are
usually conducted with smaller individuals.
Neighbouring Tikehau, to the west of Rangiroa, is
famous for its Shark Hole, where divers can regularly
encounter huge numbers of grey reef sharks and
blacktip reef sharks along a vertical wall.

242–3 FAKARAVA: GARUAE PASS AND TUMAKOHUA PASS

Location 350 km/220 miles north-east of Tahiti, in
the northern sector of the Tuamotu archipelago.

Main species *most trips:* grey reef, whitetip reef,
blacktip reef; *many trips:* bignose (*Carcharhinus
altimus*), scalloped hammerhead, tawny nurse
(*Nebrius ferrugineus*); *occasional trips:* tiger, silky,
great hammerhead, silvertip.

Viewing opportunities this is wild, action-packed
shark diving with a large concentration of sharks of
several different species (including rarely seen
bignose sharks). The second-largest atoll in the
Tuamotus, after Rangiroa, Fakarava is roughly rectangular in shape and measures an impressive 60 km/
37 miles in length and 25 km/16 miles across. Much
wilder and off the beaten track than Rangiroa, it has
two prime shark dives at opposite ends of the atoll:
Garuae, or North Pass, and Tumakohua, or South Pass.
Garuae, in particular, offers great encounters with
both reef and pelagic sharks. Grey reef are the most
common and are generally the most approachable,
but there are also lots of whitetip reef and blacktip
reef sharks and encounters with silvertips, scalloped
hammerheads and tawny nurse sharks are by no

means unusual. Most dives here are conducted as
drifts, usually starting in the open ocean and floating
with the current through the passes into the lagoon,
on the incoming tide. When the tide is going out,
the current around Garuae, in particular, can be
dangerous with lots of turbulence – but there are
dives along the outer reef away from the worst of
the turmoil. These incoming and outgoing tides have
been described as 'shark rush hours' because so many
sharks turn up, like clockwork, at the same times each
day. Garuae is the largest pass in the Tuamotus and
nearly 1 km/²/₃ mile wide, although it has an average
depth of just 15 m/50 ft. It is an absolutely thrilling
dive among wonderful coral and in the company of
massive shoals of fish and often dozens of different
sharks. Tumakohua is much smaller, although twice
as deep, and is a slower, less challenging drift. There
are sometimes large numbers of grey reef sharks
here (just before entering the lagoon there is a cave
at about 27 m/90 ft where it is possible to wait just
to watch the sharks patrolling) and there are often
whitetips resting on the sand between the coral. But
the real jewel in the crown of Tumakohua is a population of bignose sharks, which often congregate with
the grey reef.

Bait/feed no.

Cage no.

Other wildlife manta ray, tuna, marbled grouper
(breed here in Jul), barracuda, Napoleon wrasse,
trevally, unicornfish, Moorish idol, angelfish,
triggerfish.

Best time of year sharks present year-round.

Dive depth 15–40 m/50–130 ft.

Typical visibility 24–30 m/80–100 ft (often reaches
60 m/200 ft).

Water temperature 26–29 °C/78–84 °F; warmest in
summer.

Weather and sea notes moderate swell and strong
tidal current in and around the passes (especially
Garuae: drift dives can be extremely dangerous when
the tide is going out and operators avoid this time);
usually windy Jul–Sep; rain possible Apr–Oct.

Contact details Aqua Polynesie
(www.aquapolynesie.com), Archipels Croisieres
(www.archipels.com/scuba_diving_cruises.htm),
Te Ava Nui Plongee
(http://tuamotu.plongee.free.fr/teavanui.htm).

Travel international flights to Tahiti; connecting
flights to Fakarava; accessible by live-aboard or very
limited accommodation on Fakarava.

244–5 BORA BORA: TAPU AND MURI MURI

Location 240 km/150 miles north-west of Tahiti in the Leeward Islands (north-western end of the Society Islands).

Main species *most trips:* blacktip reef, grey reef, whitetip reef, tawny nurse (*Nebrius ferrugineus*), Pacific lemon (*Negaprion acutidens*); *occasional trips:* great hammerhead, oceanic whitetip, whale.

Viewing opportunities sharks are frequently encountered both inside and outside the picture-postcard lagoon of Bora Bora, but the two main dive sites are on the ocean side. Boats leave the lagoon via Teava Nui Pass, which is the only pass and a good place in itself to see blacktip reef, whitetip reef and Pacific lemon sharks. The nearest site is Tapu, just south of the pass outside Motu Tapu, on the western side of Bora Bora. Even without feeding, it is possible to see as many as 25 blacktip reef sharks and nine resident lemon sharks in a single dive here. The blacktips are remarkably fearless and often approach very closely – and quickly – almost as soon as divers hit the water. The resident lemon sharks are big (several around 2.7 m/9 ft, with some up to 4 m/13 ft), but tend to keep their distance and swim around slowly near the seabed. Divers drop to about 10 m/33 ft, then slowly descend down the reef slope to a maximum of 40 m/130 ft and are surrounded by blacktips most of the way. If the current is strong enough, this dive can also be conducted as a drift. The other site is Muri Muri, also known as the White Valley (because it consists of a spectacular white curved sandbar running for about 300 m/985 ft through rocky and coral terrain) or Shark Point, which is off the northern tip of Bora Bora near the airport. It is home to many grey reef sharks, which tend to follow divers around, and there are some blacktip reef sharks too. Some divers have even been lucky enough to see great hammerhead and whale sharks in the area. Schools of grey reef sharks tend to hang around at 21–40 m/70–130 ft, but when they are fed they rise nearer to the surface. The food is literally tossed overboard, but the sharks seem to recognize the sound of the boat's engine and begin to gather long before divers enter the water. They usually stay around for the duration of the dive. There is a third site, called Turiroa, which is not frequently dived but worth a mention. With a kidney-shaped sandy bottom, at the south-west point, it is a great place to see whitetip reef and tawny nurse sharks, which lie on the sand at about 30 m/100 ft.

There are also snorkelling trips inside the lagoon to watch blacktip reef sharks (sometimes misidentified here as grey reef sharks) being handfed. A local guide jumps into 1–1.5 m/3–5 ft of water with a bucket of bait and ties a rope between two coral heads. The snorkellers then jump in and line up behind the rope – partly to keep everyone a few metres away from the feeding sharks and partly to avoid drifting in the strong current. Several dozen sharks, mostly in the 1.2–1.5 m/4–5 ft range, turn up on a typical day. Be careful not to confuse this encounter with a similar one advertised in the Bora Bora Lagoonarium, which is an outdoor aquarium with captive sharks.

Bait/feed sometimes.

Cage no.

Other wildlife various cetaceans (including humpbacks Jul–Oct), manta ray (Fafa Piti), eagle ray, leopard ray, bat ray, stingray, barracuda (large schools at Muri Muri), Napoleon wrasse, grouper, moray eel (very tame at Tapu and frequently peer in divers' masks).

Best time of year sharks present year-round.

Dive depth 1.5–40 m/5–130 ft.

Typical visibility 30–46 m/100–150 ft; best visibility outside the reef.

Water temperature 25–29 °C/77–84 °F; coolest Jul–Aug, warmest Dec–Mar.

Weather and sea notes waves can be rough and currents strong at Muri Muri; no current at Tapu; strong currents may be experienced on the snorkel shark-feed; winds in Jul can make diving difficult outside the lagoon; wet and humid season Nov–Apr, dry season May–Oct.

Contact details Bora Diving Center (www.boradive.com), Bora Bora Blue Nui Dive Center (www.bluenui.com), Nemo World (www.nemodivebora.com), Top Dive Bora Bora (www.topdive.com).

Travel international flights to Tahiti; national flights from Tahiti to Bora Bora (45 mins); free ferry across lagoon to the main island; wide choice of accommodation.

246–9 MOOREA: TIKI POINT, SHARKS VALLEY, OPUNOHU CANYONS AND THE ROSE GARDEN

Location 18 km/11 miles north-west of Tahiti in the Windward Islands (south-eastern end of the Society Islands).

Main species *most trips:* blacktip reef, grey reef; *many trips:* whitetip reef, Pacific lemon (*Negaprion acutidens*); *occasional trips:* tawny nurse (*Nebrius ferrugineus*), oceanic whitetip, tiger.

Viewing opportunities shark dives in Moorea virtually guarantee encounters with several different species and, not surprisingly, with the added benefit of superb visibility, this strikingly beautiful island is rapidly earning a reputation as the shark-diving capital of the South Pacific. Shark feeds are particularly popular and have been conducted here since Philippe Molle of M.U.S.T Dive began to encourage sharks to take food in 1985. Nowadays some operators even offer training courses for budding feeders. The divemasters normally wear chainmail gloves and carry large fish carcasses, wrapped up in sacks, to the feeding sites. The fish are cut up underwater and the smaller pieces are literally handed to the sharks in what is described as a 'controlled feeding frenzy'. A variety of sharks dart in and, with a shake of the head, tear off bits of fish. The most common species on these dives are blacktip reef, grey reef and lemon sharks. The blacktips are the smallest (typical lengths 1–1.5 m/3 1/3–5 ft) and the lemon sharks the largest (2.7–3.7 m/9–12 ft). They all tend to stay around the divers even after the food has gone. Shark dives take place at several key sites – mostly outside the lagoon, but there is also a shark feed inside it, specifically designed for snorkellers.

Tiki Point, or the Tiki as it is sometimes called, is a very popular dive just beyond the outer reef in northwest Moorea, off the little island of Motu Fareone. This is a superb dive, with 20–35 blacktip reef, 10–25 grey reef and a handful of breathtakingly large Pacific lemon sharks (best Nov–Jul) pretty much guaranteed. With whitetip reef sharks in the area, and sometimes a nurse shark or two, no fewer than five different species can be seen on a good dive. Tiki is particularly popular with shark photographers because the visibility is reliably excellent. The site consists of a long coral wall, falling away from the outer reef edge. The boat moors in 10–12 m/33–39 ft of water and divers assemble on the bottom before swimming together down the slope to the feeding site at a depth of around 20 m/65 ft. Sharks Valley is also just beyond the outer reef, a few minutes away from Tiki Point. Introduced as a commercial dive for the first time in 2001, it is fairly similar, with the same three main species, but since the reef break is a bit deeper than at Tiki the current can be slightly stronger. The Opunohu Canyons dive takes place outside the reef, off the north coast and virtually opposite the village of Papetoai. It consists of a series of canyons radiating out from the outer reef at a depth of 10–22 m/33–72 ft. Sharks are common here, even without feeding, and blacktip reef in particular are an integral part of any normal dive in the area (10–30 is the norm). Divers kneeling on the bottom of one of the small canyons to watch the organized feeds are often rewarded with an encounter with a resident lemon shark known as Léone – claimed to be the biggest on record. The nearby Rose Garden, or the Roses, is a deeper dive (minimum 40 m/130 ft) beyond the outer reef between Opunohu Bay and Cook's Bay. No feeding takes place in this incredible, otherworldly setting (the name comes from the spec-

tacular *Montipora* coral formations that blanket the seabed), but it can be quite breathtaking when blacktip reef, grey reef and lemon sharks cruise by or come in for a closer look. Tiger sharks are occasionally seen, but their appearances are unpredictable, so encounters are purely a matter of chance. Oceanic whitetips are rarely seen by chance, but have been successfully baited here, by chumming in deeper water.

Bait/feed yes.

Cage no.

Other wildlife humpback whale (Jul–Oct), various other cetaceans, sea turtle, barracuda, moray eel, stingray, eagle ray.

Best time of year most sharks present year-round; lemon less common Aug–Oct; best diving conditions during dry season, but good year-round.

Dive depth 20–41 m/65–130 ft (depending on site).

Typical visibility 18–61 m/60–200 ft; visibility can be reduced during rainy season.

Water temperature 26–29 °C/78–84 °F year-round.

Weather and sea notes most dives with mild current and few waves; strong currents possible at Sharks Valley; Tiki Point can be inaccessible in strong winds Jan–Feb; swell and surge at Opunohu Canyons and on all north-coast dives Dec–Apr due to northerly winds; dry season May–Oct, rainy season Nov–Apr (most rain Feb–Mar).

Contact details Bathy's Club Moorea (bathys@mail.pf), Moorea Underwater Scuba-Diving Tahiti – M.U.S.T Dive (www.mooreaisland.com/mustdive/index.html), Moorea Fun Dive (www.fundive.pf), Scubapiti (www.meer.net/~jguionne/scubapiti/homepage. htm).

Travel international flights to Papeete (Tahiti); air taxi (7 mins) or ferry (30 mins) to Moorea; wide choice of accommodation on the island.

MICRONESIA

250 PALAU: PELELIU CORNER

Location southernmost tip of Peleliu Island at the southern end of Palau; 960 km/600 miles east of the Philippines.

Main species *most trips:* grey reef, whitetip reef, blacktip reef; *many trips:* leopard (*Triakis semifasciata*); *occasional trips:* great hammerhead, oceanic whitetip, tiger, bronze whaler.

Viewing opportunities exposed to strong currents much of the time, Peleliu Corner is a challenging but rewarding high-voltage dive. The site takes its name from the inside corner of a vertical wall just off Peleliu Island, starting at around 6 m/20 ft and dropping to over 300 m/1000 ft. Drift diving with a reef hook (a hook and a brass clip on either end of a 1 m/3⅓ ft rope – one end is attached to a rock or piece of dead coral and the other end to the diver) is the only option, since currents from both sides of Palau converge at this wild corner of the South Pacific. Most dives actually begin away from the Corner and then drift towards it, before hooking on to watch groups of grey reef, whitetip reef and blacktip reef sharks and other big fish. Sharks are plentiful as long as the current is running and close encounters are common, although not as reliable as at Blue Corner. Since this is an oceanic site, Peleliu Corner has the added advantage of occasional sightings of pelagic species such as great hammerhead (Jan–Feb) and oceanic whitetip. Tiger sharks are sometimes encountered, too, especially by divers hooked on to the reef. The reef gets much deeper beyond Peleliu Corner and advanced divers can enjoy an action-packed ride in blue water, known as the Peleliu Express. This is an incredibly exciting dive in its own right, and sometimes rewards divers with close-up views of oceanic whitetips, bronze whalers and grey reef sharks, as well as occasional pods of short-finned pilot whales.

Bait/feed no.

Cage no.

Other wildlife short-finned pilot whale, long-snouted spinner dolphin, hawksbill and green turtles, various sea snakes, marlin, giant clam, barrel sponge, bumphead parrotfish, dogtooth tuna.

Best time of year sharks present year-round; great hammerhead Jan–Feb; diving year-round, but best conditions Nov–May.

Dive depth 6–40 m/20–130 ft.

Typical visibility 15–46 m/50–150 ft (varies according to current); poorer visibility Jun–Nov (due to run-off during rains); best visibility at flood tides on outer walls.

Water temperature 27–29 °C/81–84 °F year-round.

Weather and sea notes site has strong currents year-round (especially at full moon) with severe side-ways and vertical water movement; seas can be rough at any time of year, but especially during south-west monsoon (traditionally Sep–Nov, but sometimes Jun–Nov); used to have dry and wet seasons (until 8–10 years ago), but now this no longer applies and the weather is less predictable.

Contact details Fish 'n Fins (www.fishnfins.com), Sam's Dive Tours (www.samstours.com), Ocean Hunter (www.oceanhunter.com), Big Blue Explorer (www.palauscuba.com), Palau Aggressor (www.aggressor.com).

Travel international flights via Manila (Philippines), Taiwan or Guam; connecting flights to Palau, then flight or ferry to Peleliu; choice of accommodation.

Notes each diver must carry a surface signal device (safety sausage) for this dive. Dive site names have been changing at Peleliu recently; what used to be called Peleliu Corner is now being called Peleliu Cut (referring to a cut in the reef on one side of the peninsula), while the term Peleliu Corner has become the name for the end of the peninsula. Peleliu Express is on the opposite side from the Cut and stretches the entire length of the reef.

251 PALAU: BLUE CORNER

Location south-west corner of Palau on the seaward side of Ngemelis Wall; 960 km/600 miles east of the Philippines.

Main species *most trips:* grey reef, whitetip reef; *many trips:* blacktip reef; *occasional trips:* tiger.

Viewing opportunities the legendary Blue Corner is probably the best-known dive site in Palau and, in international diver surveys, is frequently ranked as the best dive site in the world. It is often said that it was named for its sharply pointed corner in deep blue water; in fact, when it was first discovered by the original owner of Fish 'n Fins, he gave the location as 'the corner by the Blue Holes' and this was simply shortened over time. It consists of a triangular coral shelf with vertical walls on both sides, projecting a couple of hundred metres out of the main wall into the ocean. With a strong upwelling, caused by the meeting of tidal and ocean currents, it is home to huge numbers of fish and schooling grey reef sharks. The currents here are usually strong (sometimes strong enough to rip the mask off a diver's face) and this is quite a tricky dive. But the stronger the current, the more sharks you are likely to see. It tends to flow north–south during the outgoing tide and south–north during the incoming tide (south–north is the best time to dive) and this dictates which side of the wall the dive begins. Sometimes this involves dropping down from the coral shelf or plateau, or it is possible to drift from the nearby Blue Holes. There are designated areas on the wall (at an average depth of 15 m/50 ft) where divers secure themselves using a reef hook. This consists of two hooks on either end of a 1 m/3⅓ ft rope – one end is attached to a rock or piece of dead coral and the other end to the diver. The current keeps the line taught and leaves both hands free, which is ideal for photographers and videographers. It also prevents damage to the living reef, caused by divers trying to hold a steady position with their hands. Just before the corner there is a particularly strong upwelling, known as the elevator, which must be avoided or it is easy to miss the hook-in and get swept upwards in the current. There are huge numbers of reef sharks here – on an average dive 10–20 are cruising along the edge of the reef facing the current – and as many as 70 have been encountered at one time. They are curious and, although not aggressive, will approach divers quite closely. During the mating season (May–Jun), when many of the females have nasty-looking bite marks, extra care should be taken. At this time of year schools of moorish idols swim along the wall and it is sometimes possible to watch the sharks herding them against the surface. Whitetip reef sharks are also common and can usually be seen resting on the reef flat (9–18 m/30–60 ft) and, with care, can be approached quite closely. In recent years, a lone tiger shark has been seen quite regularly at Blue Corner. It can be a busy site with many divers and boats – early in the morning or late in the evening, depending on the tide, are usually the best times.

Bait/feed no.

Cage no.

Other wildlife various cetaceans, hawksbill turtle, blue marlin, sailfish, yellowfin tuna, dogtooth tuna, barracuda (huge schools), titan triggerfish, Napoleon wrasse, bumphead parrotfish, manta ray, eagle ray, grouper.

Best time of year sharks present year-round; diving year-round, but best conditions Nov–May.

Dive depth 9–24 m/30–80 ft.

Typical visibility 15–46 m/50–150 ft (varies according to current); poorer visibility Jun–Nov (due to run-off during rains); best visibility at flood tides on the outer walls.

Water temperature 27–29 °C/81–84 °F year-round.

Weather and sea notes strong currents typical; seas can be rough at any time of year, but especially during south-west monsoon (traditionally Sep–Nov, but sometimes Jun–Nov); used to have dry and wet seasons (until 8–10 years ago), but now this no longer applies and the weather is less predictable.

Contact details Fish 'n Fins (www.fishnfins.com), Sam's Dive Tours (www.samstours.com), Ocean Hunter (www.oceanhunter.com), Big Blue Explorer (www.palauscuba.com), Palau Aggressor (www.aggressor.com), Peter Hughes Sun Dancer II (www.peterhughes.com).

Travel international flights via Manila (Philippines), Taiwan or Guam; connecting flights to Palau; choice of accommodation.

Notes zebra sharks, which are sometimes referred to locally as spotted leopard nurse sharks, are frequently found at nearby Blue Holes, where they rest on the sandy bottom at about 40 m/130 ft. They are a mixture of adults (with spots) and juveniles (with zebra-like stripes) and can be approached quite closely. Whitetip reef sharks rest here as well.

252 PALAU: SHARK CITY

Location 12 km/7 ½ miles west of Ulong Island, in south-west Palau; 960 km/600 miles east of the Philippines.

Main species *most trips:* grey reef; *many trips:* whitetip reef; *occasional trips:* scalloped hammerhead.

Viewing opportunities Shark City is a deep, V-shaped crevice in a vertical reef wall and has a good reputation for wild drift dives, as well as for sharks. Jutting far out into the currents of the Philippine Sea, on the western barrier reef to the west of Ulong Island, it was originally named for its abundance of grey reef sharks – and still produces the goods. The timing of this dive is critical (it is best when the tide is moving), but it can result in some excellent close encounters. Both grey reef and whitetip reef sharks are common around several nearby dive sites, such as the mouth of Ngerumekaol Pass, and whitetips often rest inside the massive cave at Siaes Tunnel (if you move slowly and do not blow too many bubbles, you can approach them quite closely).

Bait/feed no.

Cage no.

Other wildlife hawksbill turtle, manta ray, moray eel, wahoo, yellowfin tuna, blue marlin, barracuda, jack, bumphead wrasse.

Best time of year sharks present year-round.

Dive depth 6–35 m/20–115 ft.

Typical visibility 15–46 m/50–150 ft (varies according to the current); best visibility at flood tides on the outer walls.

Water temperature 27–29 °C/81–84 °F year-round.

Weather and sea notes strong currents likely; seas can be rough at any time of year, but especially during south-west monsoon (traditionally Sep–Nov, but sometimes Jun–Nov); used to have dry and wet seasons (until 8–10 years ago), but this no longer applies and weather now less predictable.

Contact details Sam's Tours (www.samstours.com), Ocean Hunter (www.oceanhunter.com), Palau Aggressor II (www.aggressor.com), Fish 'n Fins Dive Shop (www.fishnfins.com).

Travel international flights via Manila (Philippines), Taiwan or Guam; connecting flights to Palau; choice of accommodation.

253–5 PALAU: NEW DROP-OFF, BIG DROP-OFF AND TURTLE WALL

Location south-west corner of Palau, around Barnam's Wall, on the seaward side of Ngemelis Wall; 960 km/600 miles east of the Philippines.

Main species *most trips:* whitetip reef, grey reef; *many trips:* blacktip reef; *occasional trips:* whale.

Viewing opportunities Jacques Cousteau once described Big Drop-Off as the best wall dive in the world. Its sheer beauty, with hard and soft corals, sea fans and abundant reef fish, attracts divers from all over the world. It is also good for whitetip reef sharks, which can sometimes be seen herding huge schools of snapper. The dive begins in extremely shallow water (knee-deep at low tide) and yet this section of Ngemelis Wall drops steeply to over 185 m/600 ft. The best way to experience it is to make the most of the gentle current and allow yourself to drift gently along. Nearby Turtle Wall (between Big Drop-Off and New Drop-Off, and known as Fern's Wall by some locals) was named for the hawksbill and green turtles that gather here, but is also very good for whitetip reef and grey reef sharks. It is usually conducted as a drift dive, running either east or west depending on the direction of the currents. There is a much stronger current at New Drop-Off, which makes the shark watching even better, and on a good day the site can be alive with shark action. The stronger the current, the more grey reef sharks there are around – just a few if it is weak, but as many as 10–30 if it is strong. Whitetip reef sharks are also seen here on most dives and can usually be found resting in the sand gullies at around 12 m/39 m. Sometimes known as West Ngemelis Wall, New Drop-Off is similar to Blue Corner in that it consists of a shallow shelf jutting into the ocean. The diving style is similar, too, beginning at 4.6–9 m/15–30 ft (depending on where divers jump in), then descending the top section of the wall and hooking on to the reef at designated areas. The sharks often come in very close, especially when divers are hooked on and watching quietly. Whale sharks and a variety of pelagics are occasionally spotted from Big Drop-Off, Turtle Wall and New Drop-Off, so it is always worth keeping an eye on the blue water off the wall.

Bait/feed no.

Cage no.

Other wildlife various cetaceans, hawksbill and green turtles (especially Turtle Wall), blue marlin, wahoo, sailfish, yellowfin tuna, barracuda (huge schools), titan triggerfish, Napoleon wrasse, bump-head parrotfish, manta ray, eagle ray, grouper, various sea fans, barrel sponge.

Best time of year sharks present year-round; diving year-round, but best conditions Nov–May.

Dive depth 1–40 m/3⅓–130 ft.

Typical visibility 15–46 m/50–150 ft (varies according to current); poorer visibility Jun–Nov (due to run-off during rains); best visibility at flood tides on outer walls.

Water temperature 27–29 °C/81–84 °F year-round.

Weather and sea notes current at Big Drop-Off usually mild, but changeable with back eddies; current at New Drop-Off stronger and can push divers sideways or up and down; seas can be rough at any time of year, but especially during south-west monsoon (traditionally Sep–Nov, but sometimes Jun–Nov); used to have dry and wet seasons (until 8–10 years ago), but now this no longer applies and the weather is less predictable.

Contact details Fish 'n Fins (www.fishnfins.com), Sam's Dive Tours (www.samstours.com), Ocean Hunter (www.oceanhunter.com), Big Blue Explorer (www.palauscuba.com), Palau Aggressor (www.aggressor.com), Peter Hughes Sun Dancer II (www.peterhughes.com).

Travel international flights via Manila (Philippines), Taiwan or Guam; connecting flights to Palau; choice of accommodation.

256 PALAU: SILVERTIP CITY

Location north end of Velasco Reef, 32 km/20 miles north of Kayangel Atoll (which is 16 km/10 miles off the northern tip of Babeldaob); 960 km/600 miles east of the Philippines.

Main species *most trips:* silvertip, grey reef; *many trips:* bronze whaler, tawny nurse (*Nebrius ferrugineus*); *occasional trips:* oceanic whitetip, tiger, scalloped hammerhead.

Viewing opportunities this is one of relatively few places around the world where silvertip sharks could actually be described as common. A long way from anywhere, in the middle of the open ocean, Velasco Reef is a spectacular sheer wall starting at 18–24 m/60–80 ft and dropping into the ocean depths. Silvertips can be seen almost anywhere along its current-swept length and tend to congregate along the most impressive drop-offs. The largest individuals (as big as 3 m/10 ft) are usually at 40 m/130 ft or deeper, but smaller ones (as little as 0.6 m/2 ft) often come much closer to the surface. If you are at all nervous around sharks, do not get separated from your buddy here, because it can get quite unnerving if a group of silvertips decides to take an active interest in you. Fast-swimming and inquisitive, they will approach divers quickly, directly and closely. They are particularly abundant at the aptly named Silvertip City, towards the northern end of Velasco Reef, where they suddenly appear out of the blue on a regular basis. Other pelagic sharks turn up at Silvertip City from time to time, and there are small groups of tawny nurse sharks here, too. Just south of this site is Shark Central, where anything from oceanic whitetips and tigers to scalloped hammerheads have been recorded on a few lucky dives.

Bait/feed no.

Cage no.

Other wildlife blue marlin, sailfish, sapphire triggerfish, rainbow runner, bumphead parrotfish, bluestripe and yellowtail fusiliers, wahoo, king mackerel.

Best time of year sharks present year-round.

Dive depth 18–40 m/60–130 ft.

Typical visibility 15–46 m/50–150 ft (varies according to the current); best visibility at flood tides on the outer walls.

Water temperature 27–29 °C/81–84°F year-round.

Weather and sea notes strong currents likely; seas can be rough at any time of year, but especially during south-west monsoon (traditionally Sep–Nov, but sometimes Jun–Nov); used to have dry and wet seasons (until 8–10 years ago), but this no longer applies and weather now less predictable.

Contact details Sam's Tours (www.samstours.com), Sun Dancer II (www.peterhughes.com), Dive Asia Pacific (www.dive-asiapacific.com).

Travel international flights via Manila (Philippines), Taiwan or Guam; connecting flights to Palau; choice of accommodation onshore, but best dived from a live-aboard.

257–9 CHUUK: NORTHEAST PASS, NORTHWEST PASS AND NORTH PASS

Location 1030 km/640 miles south-east of Guam; 5440 km/3380 miles south-west of Hawaii.

Main species *most trips:* grey reef, whitetip reef; *many trips:* silvertip; *occasional trips:* blacktip reef, oceanic whitetip, lemon, nurse, whale, great hammerhead.

Viewing opportunities formerly known as Truk Lagoon, Chuuk consists of a cluster of 12 tiny volcanic islands and many lesser islets in an enormous lagoon surrounded by 225 km/140 miles of coral reef. Roughly 50 km/31 miles wide, and sometimes described as a lake in the middle of the ocean, it is best known as the graveyard for several hundred Second World War ships, submarines and planes.

Indeed, it is the undisputed wreck-diving capital of the world. Although these wrecks are the main draw, there are lots of sharks in Chuuk and shark diving in and around the lagoon has become immensely popular. Shark Reef, for example, which is inside the lagoon (a little south-east of centre, near Eten) has half a dozen resident grey reef sharks, while Shark Pass is often used by live-aboards for shark feeding. There are three passes in the northern half, with strong currents and a great reputation for grey reef sharks. Since they link the lagoon with open water, they can also be good for pelagic species such as oceanic whitetip, which can sometimes be seen in the blue beyond the reef. All three passes are normally conducted as drift dives, timed to go with the flow from the open sea into the lagoon. Northeast Pass is next to three idyllic islands (Fannuk, Moch and Eten) complete with swaying coconut palms. Here, the reef has formed into a system of hills, deep valleys and drop-offs with spectacular coral gardens and a huge tree of endangered black coral. Grey reef sharks are normally seen deeper down where the greatest abundance of coral, where the currents are strongest and the food supply richest. Northwest Pass, on the other side of the lagoon, is best dived around Canon Island drop-off, where the reef is on a steeply sloping wall and then drops straight down into the ocean depths. This is a particularly exciting dive because the local grey reef sharks are rather territorial and have a habit of stealing food from the local fishermen, so they can be quite provocative and often come right up to divers. Silvertips and whitetip reefs are also seen here quite often, although they are far less gregarious than the grey reefs. The North Pass dive begins as a swim, heading west along the outer reef wall, until you hit the current and get washed into the lagoon. The dive is fairly relaxed until the current, where large numbers of grey reef sharks gather to feed.

Bait/feed sometimes (one feed a week by the crew of Truk Aggressor II – mainly grey reef).

Cage no.

Other wildlife long-snouted spinner dolphin, hawksbill turtle, manta ray, tuna, humphead wrasse, grouper, sea fan.

Best time of year sharks present year-round.

Dive depth 6–30 m/20–100 ft.

Typical visibility 15–45 m/50–150 ft; up to 30 m/100 ft inside the lagoon and 45 m/150 ft outside the walls and slopes; poorest May–Dec.

Water temperature 27–29 °C/81–84 °F.

Weather and sea notes strong currents in the passes; consistently warm and humid (typically over 70 per cent); frequently windy Dec–Apr; brief rain showers year-round, but slightly more May–Dec.

Contact details Truk Aggressor II
(www.aggressor.com), Truk Odyssey
(www.trukodyssey.com),
SS Thorfinn (www.thorfinn.net).

Travel international flights from Honolulu, Tokyo,
Taipei, Hong Kong, Manila and Cairns to Guam;
connecting flights to Weno; choice of accommodation.

260–3 POHNPEI: AHND ATOLL, DAWAHK PASS, PEHLANG PASS AND PALIKIR PASS

Location eastern Caroline Islands; 1690 km/1050
miles south-east of Guam, 5215 km/3240 miles
south-west of Honolulu.

Main species *most trips:* grey reef, whitetip reef;
many trips: blacktip reef; *occasional trips:* oceanic
whitetip, great hammerhead.

Viewing opportunities the largest and highest
island in Micronesia, measuring some 22 km/14 miles
across and with a 798 m/2620 ft peak, the island of
Pohnpei is largely unknown as a dive destination. But
the diving here is spectacular. Sharks can be seen at
most of the established dive sites, although there
are four main hotspots: Palikir Pass (or Shark City);
Dawahk Pass (or Tauak Pass, as it is often called);
Pehlang Pass (sometimes spelt Poahlong, Pehleng or
Palang), otherwise known as Shark Corner; and Ahnd
(or Ant) Atoll.

Palikir Pass lies on the north-west side of the island
and is a good place for grey reef and whitetip reef
sharks. Blacktip reef sharks are occasionally seen in
shallower water here, too, and sometimes cruise the
breakwater on the reef. The grey reefs are resident
and the local school can number 30–100 animals,
depending on the strength of the current (the
stronger, the better). The site is also known for its
cleaning station, where the sharks queue up to be
cleaned by small wrasse. Palikir is a great drift dive,
beginning in the open ocean (where the seabed is
just over 100 m/330 ft deep and there is a chance of
seeing oceanic whitetip sharks), travelling through
the pass (where the bottom rises to 45 m/150 ft) for nearly
1 km/½ mile and ending up in the lagoon. The current
here is often strong, but the visibility can be outstanding. Great hammerheads are occasionally seen
at nearby Dawahk Pass, which lies a little farther
south. Best dived at high tide, when the visibility is
particularly good, Dawahk is also good for grey reef
sharks, which gather to feed in the strong current (up
to 5 knots in the pass itself). It is also worth checking
the blue water beyond the barrier reef for pelagics.
Pehlang Pass, which has been likened in both appearance and quality to the much more famous Blue
Corner in Palau, is yet farther south but also on the

west coast. It is another drift dive and the current here
is strong but manageable. This is a good place to see
grey reef and whitetip reef sharks, with occasional
blacktip reefs, and the visibility is best on an incoming
tide. The dive usually begins from anchor, outside the
breakers on the left side of the pass, and divers make
their way down to about 24 m/80 ft at the entrance
corner to watch the large numbers of grey reef sharks
that gather here. If the current is still pushing into
the lagoon near the end of the dive everyone drifts
through the pass.

Finally, Ahnd Atoll is in a little world of its own
some 35 km/22 miles south-west of the capital
Kolonia. A bumpy 1½-hour boat trip, but spectacular
with its low white sandy beaches and turquoise
lagoon, this is the best place to see pelagics such as
oceanic whitetips. It has superb visibility (perhaps
because there is less run-off here as it is offshore) and
even offers a wild drift dive in the company of grey
reef sharks in the Toawoanioai Passage.

Bait/feed no.

Cage no.

Other wildlife long-snouted spinner dolphin, sea
turtle, manta ray, eagle ray, Napoleon wrasse,
barracuda, triggerfish, parrotfish.

Best time of year sharks present year-round.

Dive depth 24–30 m/80–100 ft.

Typical visibility 30–46 m/100–150 ft; varies
enormously with tide position; worse during rainy
season.

Water temperature 27–28 °C/81–82 °F.

Weather and sea notes west side of island
sheltered from most wind and current; strong
currents on outer walls of Ahnd and in the passes;
on really windy days (especially late Nov to early May)
a swell can make the crossing to Ahnd Atoll quite
uncomfortable.

Contact details Village Tour and Dive Service
(www.eguam.com/97/11/village.html), Aqua World
Pohnpei (aquaworld@mail.fm), Blue Oyster Tours
and Dive Shop (tel: 320-5117, fax: 320-5227),
Ehu Tours (tel: 320-2959, fax: 320-2958).

Travel international flights to Manila, Guam or
Honolulu; connecting flights to Pohnpei; limited
choice of accommodation in capital village of Kolonia.

264–6 MARSHALL ISLANDS: MAJURO, ARNO AND MILI ATOLLS

Location 4200 km/2600 miles south-west of Hawaii.

Main species *most trips:* grey reef, whitetip reef;
many trips: silvertip, blacktip reef; *occasional trips:*

Galápagos, Pacific or sicklefin lemon, tawny nurse (*Nebrius ferrugineus*), silky, oceanic whitetip, whale.

Viewing opportunities the Marshall Islands consist of no fewer than 1240 islands, atolls and reefs, but cover a total land area of just 180 sq km/70 sq miles. They stretch across an astonishing 1500 km/930 miles of ocean and run in two parallel chains: Ratak or Sunrise Chain in the east, and Ralik or Sunset Chain in the west. Grey reef and whitetip reef are almost like shadows – they seem to be around on every dive – but you have to search actively for some of the others. Blacktip reef sharks, for example, are quite common, but tend to be very shy and normally stay in such shallow water that divers rarely see them unless they specifically go and look (except at a brand-new site called Iroij Point, about 1.6 km/1 mile from the better-known Aquarium, where they are very bold indeed). Other than Bikini Atoll (see pp. 286–87), there are three main atolls of interest to shark watchers: Majuro, Arno and Mili. They are all in the Ratak Chain and, with nearly 645 km/400 miles of outer reef between them, as well as numerous passes and huge pristine atolls, they are packed with sharks of many different species. Sharks can readily be seen in many other parts of the archipelago, of course, but these three atolls are tried and tested.

Majuro is the capital of the Marshall Islands, and sharks of one species or another are seen on virtually every dive here. It is famous for its abundance of whitetip reefs, which are particularly common in the channels and passes, as well as grey reef sharks in groups of 20–40 or more. But a variety of other species can be seen on the ocean side of the reef – most notably Galápagos, but occasionally silky, oceanic whitetip and even whale. There are several particular sites which, as well as producing whitetip reef and grey reef on virtually every dive, sometimes have a few surprises in store: Mile 14 (one of Majuro's most famous shore dives) has occasional blacktip reef, silvertip and Pacific lemon; Delap Point has a few blacktip reef and silvertip; and Northshore has some Pacific lemon. The Aquarium is often littered with sleeping whitetip reefs on its sandy seabed, while all three reef-shark species can be seen above, darting in and out of schools of literally thousands of pelagic fish. Finally, Shark Street is worth a mention for its whitetip reefs – as many as 25 can be seen on a single dive on this north-easterly section of the outer reef. Arno Atoll is just a 16-km/10-mile boat ride from Majuro and, although there are generally fewer whitetip reefs here, there are probably more grey reef sharks. This is also one of the best atolls for blacktip reef sharks, which can be found in the shallow reef waters facing the ocean and very close to shore around the islands inside the lagoon; Illian Point is particularly good for blacktip reef sharks (and some-

times has silvertip and Pacific nurse sharks as well). Shark Central, Northwest Point and South Point are all good for whitetip reef and grey reef, with occasional blacktip reef and silvertip. In recent months some very large silvertips (including a 3-m/10-ft female at a depth of just 20 m/65 ft) have been seen quite frequently at both Majuro and Arno. Mili is the southernmost atoll in the Ratak Chain (a 20-minute flight from Majuro) and has a similar variety of species. Arguably, though, there are even more reef sharks here than in either of the other two atolls. Grey reef literally appear to be everywhere and more blacktip reef are seen around Mili than most places. Reihers Passage is particularly good, and Northwest Passage is renowned for its Galápagos sharks. But the truth is that, if the conditions are right, almost any dive in the Marshall Islands can turn into a memorable shark encounter.

Bait/feed no.

Cage no.

Other wildlife various cetaceans (including humpback, sperm and short-finned pilot whales), sea turtles, manta and spotted eagle rays, stingray, three-banded anemone fish (endemic), large schools of jack, barracuda, snapper and unicornfish, dogtooth tuna, rainbow runner, Napoleon wrasse.

Best time of year sharks present year-round; best diving May–Sep (rainy but less wind).

Dive depth 10–40 m/33–130 ft.

Typical visibility 25–50 m/80–165 ft (sometimes more).

Water temperature 28–29 °C/82–84 °F year-round.

Weather and sea notes strong currents at some sites; less wind and calm seas May–Sep; wet season May–Nov; islands just border the typhoon belt (typhoons uncommon, but storms possible during spring and autumn).

Contact details Marshalls Dive Adventures (www.rreinc.com/mda.html), Bako Divers (www.bakodivers.com).

Travel international flights to Guam or Honolulu; connecting flights to Majuro and from there to other atolls by boat or plane; choice of accommodation on Majuro.

267 MARSHALL ISLANDS: BIKINI ATOLL

Location 965 km/600 miles north-west of Majuro (capital of the Marshall Islands) in the central Pacific.

Main species *most trips:* grey reef, whitetip reef; *many trips:* blacktip reef, silvertip; *occasional trips:* Pacific nurse, lemon, tiger.